D0897557

ASYLUM AND EXTRACTION IN THE REPUBLIC OF NAURU

ASYLUM AND EXTRACTION IN THE REPUBLIC OF NAURU

Julia Caroline Morris

CORNELL UNIVERSITY PRESS ITHACA AND LONDON

First published 2023 by Cornell University Press

Library of Congress Cataloging-in-Publication Data

Names: Morris, Julia, 1984– author.
Title: Asylum and extraction in the Republic of Nauru / Julia Caroline Morris.
Description: Ithaca [New York] : Cornell University Press, 2023. | Includes bibliographical references and index.
Identifiers: LCCN 2022012764 (print) | LCCN 2022012765 (ebook) | ISBN 9781501765841 (hardcover) | ISBN 9781501765858 (pdf) | ISBN 9781501765865 (epub)
Subjects: LCSH: Nauru—Economic conditions. | Nauru—Foreign economic relations. | Nauru—Emigration and immigration—Economic aspects. | Noncitizen detention centers—Economic aspects—Nauru. | Noncitizen detention centers—Political aspects—Nauru. | Asylum, Right of—Economic aspects—Nauru. | Refugees—Nauru. | Noncitizen detention centers— Government policy—Australia. | Phosphate mines and mining—Economic aspects—Nauru. | Phosphate mines and mining—Political aspects—Nauru. | Australia—Emigration and immigration—Government policy.
Classification: LCC HC682.25 .M67 2023 (print) | LCC HC682.25 (ebook) | DDC 337.9685—dc23/eng/20220829
LC record available at https://lccn.loc.gov/2022012764
LC ebook record available at https://lccn.loc.gov/2022012765

For the people of, and the people sent to, Nauru.

Contents

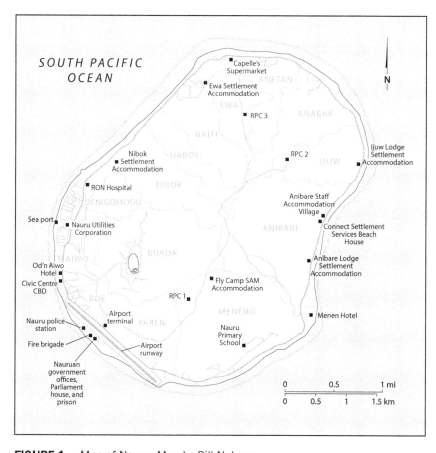

FIGURE 1. Map of Nauru. Map by Bill Nelson.

ASYLUM AND EXTRACTION IN THE REPUBLIC OF NAURU

.

INTRODUCTION

A small island indeed, only about 3½ miles long and 2½ miles wide, a place where primitive native life and stirring enterprise are almost side by side in striking fashion.

—Sir Albert Ellis, Discoverer of Nauru Phosphate (1946)

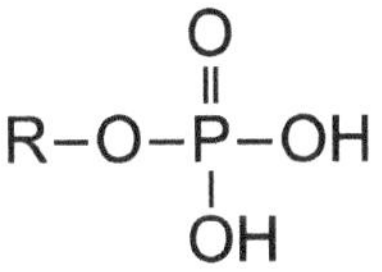

$$R-O-\overset{\overset{\displaystyle O}{\|}}{\underset{\underset{\displaystyle OH}{|}}{P}}-OH$$

FIGURE 2. Phosphate.

$Ca_3(PO_4)_2$ *(phosphate rock)* $+ 2H_2SO_4$ *(sulfuric acid)* $=$
$Ca(H_2PO_4)_2$ *(single superphosphate)* $+ 2CaSO_4$
(waste calcium sulfate/gypsum):

The treatment of phosphate rock with sulfuric acid liquefies and isolates the phosphorous usable by plants. This produces "superphosphate," a fertilizer used to intensify crop productivity and restore soil nutrients. Waste calcium sulphate is discharged for disposal.

The Refugee: *"Someone who is unable or unwilling to return to their country of origin owing to a well-founded fear of being persecuted for reasons of race, religion, nationality, membership of a particular social group, or political opinion."*

Refugee Status Determination or RSD is the process by which government or UN-HCR workforces screen out the "genuine" refugee from the migrant. The idea of "the refugee" holds firm political economic appeal as a symbol of liberal democratic statehood or explicator of state inequalities. Those who receive negative asylum claims are subject to safe and timely expulsion to their country of origin or a selected alternative.

FIGURE 3. The Republic of Nauru. Photo by Julia Morris.

When I arrived in Nauru to conduct my fieldwork after ten months spent crisscrossing Europe and Australia, piecing together the global refugee industry, I experienced a jolting shock. I stepped out of the aircraft into a heady wave of equatorial heat and immersed myself in a refugee company town in miniature. Barely perceptible imprints in the sand still evoked the long-abandoned phosphate trains of the British Phosphate Commission's (BPC) colonial extraction years, when Nauru's coral atoll was mined in earnest for the lucrative fertilizer compound. Rows of white colonial company town architecture set out in a gridded geometry, formerly occupied by Australian phosphate workers, lay faded. Pools of sewage and potholed dirt tracks led to once bougainvillea-covered bungalows for colonial executive administrators. Phosphate loading bays rusted into yellowed copper decay, testifying to the country's past industry in extracting phosphate as fertilizer for global consumptive demands.

But in these imperial ruins rose new infrastructural convergences, vital to Nauru's refashioning as a contemporary company town around a mineral and then a migrant commodity. After a brief post-independence heyday when Nauruans took over their colonial phosphate enterprise in 1968, earning the world's second highest GDP per capita after Saudi Arabia, the small sovereign state's economy crashed dramatically in the 1990s. On an on-again, off-again basis, following 2001 and 2012 agreements between Nauru and Australia, anyone who made their way by boat and claimed to be a refugee in Australian territorial, now excised, waters was offshored by the Australian government to Nauru or Papua New Guinea's (PNG) Manus Island for refugee processing and resettlement. Histrionic debates about national security, coupled with a deep history of selective nation building, constitute some of the political currency of offshoring asylum for Australia.[1]

While Nauru's phosphate cantilevers went unrepaired, three refugee processing centers crowned the country, gleaming from in-between dilapidated phosphate extraction fields. In a new refugee appeals courthouse, a form titled "Nauru Refugee Status Determination Assessment Quality Control Checklist: Based on the United Nations High Commissioner for Refugees (UNHCR) Quality Assurance" lay on a side table. Housing for refugees and for refugee service personnel speckled the coral limestone atoll's urban fringe. Around the country's ring road, identikit white vans performed refugee and phosphate workers' collection rounds in close succession, distinguished only by RPC or RonPhos logos imprinted on auto bodies, indicating Regional Processing Centre or Republic of Nauru Phosphate Corporation. In 2015 alone, the Nauruan government received over AU$50 million from the Australian government to process and then resettle asylum seekers classified as "unauthorized maritime arrivals" (UMAs). The numbers of people sent to Nauru were small (1,355 asylum seekers between 2013 and 2016). However, in comparison to Nauru's wider population of 10,500 people, these influxes were significant for the country. The island population was buoyed by a new human commodity, replacing the previous marine sediment and phosphate exports.

Tremendous windfall profits combined with vast infrastructural development projects in Nauru: from a new hospital and courthouse to the reinvigoration of bygone government departments and local training in refugee legislation and determination. At the time of my fieldwork, 31 percent of the local population was employed in refugee industry labor forces, rising swiftly from 7 percent in 2013, and easily overtaking the country's beleaguered phosphate industry, which declined from employing 15.1 percent of the island's population in 2013 to 9.6 percent in 2015.[2] New populations wandered the streets, easily discernable in tariqas, burqas, and some skin-tight jeans. There were signs for Farsi cuisine and Rohingyan takeaway, testament to the new commodity world growing in the shadow of rusted phosphate turrets. But outside a refugee resettlement house by the fish-and-chips shop, weatherworn banners flapped in the sea breeze, hinting at some of the country's resource politics:

"We're refugees not criminals!"
"No Cambodian inside! Cambodia never ever."
"Nauru GULAG"
"Australian people open your hearts."

"Urgh, you seen this one?" Jackie, a Nauruan phosphate worker turned refugee industry worker, and one of my closest friends and informants in the field, leaned over, as we sat together in her backyard. She passed over her iPad, gesturing for me to read the headlines. I only needed a glance to spot the latest Australian media newsflash accusing Nauruans of violence against refugees. She sighed. "I try to stop reading this stuff, just makes me mad now. I felt so sorry for them, used to be so kind to them, but the lies the refugees tell. If they're fleeing persecution, why are they so picky?"[3]

Nauru operates prominently on the global scene, as Jackie's iPad reading suggests. Across the summer of 2016, the small sovereign state found itself at the center of another global media frenzy with the Nauru Files Leaks by the *Guardian* Australia. With a catalogue of over two thousand filed incident reports, Nauru's offshore refugee operations were characterized as an exceptionality, "a dark, wretched Truman Show without the cameras," a "gulag archipelago" (Baird 2016), rife with "horrible mistreatment," "squalor," "trauma and self-harm" (Farrell, Evershed, and Davidson 2016). Media outlets and spokespeople around the world took up this narrative, stressing the brutal conditions for refugees through narratives of suffering, persecution, and vulnerability. Others leveled anti-civilizational accusations on Nauruans as savages, claiming that the country was outside the rule of law and international oversight, with Nauruans chasing refugees with machetes through the streets. "Regular—we're not talking several incidents. Regular, systematic attacks from local population. People are hacked with machetes," said Amnesty's Anna Neistat in interview on National Public Radio on August 11, 2016, after flying to Nauru on a three-day "refugee mission." "Every single woman I spoke to told me that they cannot go out because now they're absolutely at the mercy of the locals." Headlines such as "Nauru, Refugees and Australia's 'Torture Complex'" (Kampmark 2016) and "Nauru Rule of Law 'Nonexistent'" (ABC 2015) are commonplace.

This book provides a unique glimpse into the remote and difficult-to-access site of the Republic of Nauru. Next to no ethnographic research has actually been conducted in Nauru on the country's everyday refugee processing and resettlement operations. My work lends a new perspective to life in Nauru, reframing the offshore asylum system as part of a global industry that shares deep parallels and continuities with the island's colonial industry in phosphate extraction. I utilize a theoretical frame centered on resource extraction to argue that the figure of the refugee has become entangled in extractive capitalism. This entails a literal form of extracting value from migrants (as resources for carceral, humanitarian, and knowledge industries) but also encompasses sociolegal technologies of extraction. People are required to recount intimate experiences and narratives of trauma in order to move elsewhere. Value is generated from the extraction of people's vital energies, lived time, material resources, and physical features, while generating profit for a vast industry of corporate, nongovernmental, governmental, and other actors. By focusing on the political and moral economies that operate in Nauru, the book shows the continuities between a history of resource extraction on the island and the extractive logics applied to refugees. It also illustrates the connections forged between Nauru and distant regions, detailing the consumptive politics (around phosphate and later refugees) that has, for decades, shaped the island's landscape and peoples.

This historically contextualized ethnographic inquiry informs a second line of argument: that colonial forms of extraction create the conditions of possibility for offshore refugee processing on Nauru. What I seek to do is simultaneously unpack local legacies of Australian colonialism and extraction in the region to consider the role Nauru's latest extractive project occupies. Across the centuries, Nauru has been subject to capitalist rearrangements in order to give power to Australia's economy. A continuum exists between historical forms of resource extraction and the current extraction of value, where colonial relations have created the conditions in which this is possible. The inquiry as a whole results in a better understanding not only of the financial and moral value extracted from refugees but also of the human costs of their submission to an extraction model. Offshoring migrants to a small Pacific island is a horrific practice, as this book makes clear. By bringing Nauru's phosphate and refugee industries into conversation, my research shores up the environmental and social devastations entailed in both industry sectors.

These dynamics are important to consider as many governments have looked to the Australian-style practice of turning back boats and offshoring asylum and resettlement operations. Recent years have seen government and organizational investment in ever more containment regimes and militarized border technologies that zigzag Global North to Global South, including the expansion of off-shored and outsourced sites. Entire global arrangements are configured to satiate Western publics from lingering racialized colonial insecurities of what Ghassan Hage (2002) describes as being "under siege." This tendency signifies a new form of extractive capitalism that taps into forms of neocolonial domination and asymmetric relations of dependency. By delving into these local particularities, I look to unearth the foundation that allows Australia—and other countries including the United Kingdom with Rwanda, the European Union with Turkey, and the United States across Central America—to carry out these kinds of outsourced asylum arrangements.

The connections I make between Nauru's phosphate and refugee industry sectors are not metaphorical. I take my lead from scholars looking at the toxic interrelationship between industry sectors and the racialized geographies where they take place (Agard-Jones 2013; Fortun 2001; Schept 2020). The locations where toxic industries are positioned are no accident. They are distributed in radically unequal patterns, where histories of coloniality, racialization, and inequality critically determine who is subject to a politics of exposure. Yet, activist representations of "vulnerable refugees" versus "savage Nauruans" undermine these shared histories of exploitation. This points to the sociocultural power of the figure of the refugee, leveraged by nations, NGOs, corporations, activists, and individuals, as I found in my research through a methodology of "following value."

Following Value

My research came about not by following a commodity from the point of extraction or by targeting Nauru's specific operations, but by following value through fifteen months of ethnographic fieldwork between Geneva, Australia, Fiji, and Nauru. I began with a focus on capitalist value generation relating to the institutions that find profit from immigration securitization. I approach value as a malleable category more akin to valuation, not stable to a particular object, but rather constituted in process (Grüneisl 2020). An emphasis on valuation helped me understand the emergence (and often performance) of newness in processes of evaluation and valorization (Antal, Hutter, and Stark 2015). This broadened my understanding of whose bodies, what spatial practices (detention, camps, transfers, deportation), and which boomtown sites attract overwhelming value for stakeholders: governments, corporations, NGOs, activists, migrants, and publics alike. The sociolegal status of migrants is central to the circuits of value produced by migration governance practices (Coddington, Conlon, and Martin 2020), illustrating how valuation varies over time and space, and is situated in particular sociocultural contexts (Appadurai 1986). Time, place, and context, for example, all strongly influence who is determined to be a refugee, often relating to the geopolitical zeitgeist.[4]

Despite not having a focus on asylum seekers or refugees per se but rather on the broader governance regime that people are subject to, my preliminary discussions with UN agencies and humanitarian divisions invariably magnetized around the figure of the refugee. My research soon became enveloped in this discursive field of study, taking on something of an improvisational character, as I was towed into and became a part of the social world of meaning, whereby "not only new products, styles and practices come to be selected and positioned as valuable in communities, organizations, and markets" (Hutter and Stark 2020, 1) but so too do people's bodies. This starting point led me to a methodology focused on "following value," in particular, the moral and political economic values that come to play around refugees as commodities.

The production of people as refugees cannot be easily traced to a "bounded locus of production" but arises "from a dispersed intersubjective realm of circulation and exchange" (Kajri Jain cited in Grüneisl 2020). Yet the framing of people's movement in refugee terms has long related to the industrialization of refugee production and the rise of refugee legal frameworks, institutions, and cultural production during the early twentieth century (Morris 2021a). These circulations generate linkages and interdependencies that tie sites of valuation to the system of knowledge production emanating from Geneva, and specifically UNHCR. From a budget of US$300,000 and 34 staff members in 1950, UNHCR is now a bureaucratic leviathan of more than 9,300 staff, operating in some 132 countries around the world, with an annual budget of over US$7 billion. Refugee studies centers, programs, and policy institutes proliferate from Oxford to Toronto, Bangalore to Cairo, Sydney to Dar es Salaam, and beyond. Global #RefugeesWelcome movements lobby around a morally irrefutable imaginary of "first-world" magnanimity. Recognizing UNHCR's exponential power as a global industry supermajor, with important implications for how people move across borders, led me to concentrate my initial research in Geneva.

Geneva was—in retrospect—a logical place to "study up, down, and sideways" (Nader 1972) how a brand-new commodity market tied to refugees is brought into the world, and functions once in existence. In Geneva, I conducted in-depth interviews and spent time with personnel from most major UN institutions, international NGOs, intergovernmental organizations (INGOs), academic institutions, commercial firms, and many state government bureaus whose work intersects with refugees. I signed up to listservs, attended nonprofit and academic conferences, and collated a wealth of documentary material. I attended UNHCR's NGO consultations in 2014, along with other regional industry networking meetings in Bangkok and Washington, DC. Government representatives often participated in these meetings, many of whom were passionate about refugees, and not in simplistic opposition, as is often depicted. One government representative, sporting a nose piercing and dreadlocks, stressed how they always made sure refugees were "on the table" at roundtable discussions. A former Australian immigration minister led me through their photo album, filled to bursting with refugee-camp visits, genuinely expressing passion and concern for refugees. On the other hand, the CEO of a prominent NGO laughingly advised me on the best government MPs to lobby for increases in funding and refugee import quotas.

A focus on value initially led me to follow the international refugee operations through to Australia. No better example of refugee industry politics exists than on the former Pacific colony. Since the 1920s, Australia has operated an industry-accredited operation of refugee determination and resettlement, in tandem with strict immigration entry requirements and controversial offshore asylum policies. The Australian government helped establish UNHCR and was one of the Geneva Convention's first signatories. Like the majority of Australia's once–public-led services, most of which were privatized under the Hawke and Keating Labour governments in the 1990s, the efficiency of markets at finding low-cost solutions are the main rubric of Australian refugee processing and resettlement. The Australian government has contracted out its refugee operations amongst a complex network of private sector refugee "service providers" comprised of NGOs, ecumenical professionals, commercial firms, academic institutions, and state bureaucratic organizations.[5] Alongside this, a vocal pro-refugee movement calls for "welcoming refugees to Australia." Tireless lobbying across agencies and within government seeks to up refugee resettlement quotas. Since 2009, levels were set at 13,750 refugees annually, 20 percent of which were made available to migrants claiming asylum outside regulated entry processes (onshore protection grants). In 2015, the government increased their existing intake, publicly announcing that they would take an additional 12,000 refugees from Syrian conflict zones, precertified by affiliated agencies. Because of the operational success of the spectacle of offshore processing in "stopping the boats," in tandem with a dramatic increase in maritime policing and boat turnbacks, they also increased their resettlements quotas to 18,750 refugees from 2018 to 2019.[6]

I traveled around Australia as a doctoral research student, meeting with most of the major commercial firms and NGO service providers operating in this space, along with Immigration Department and government representatives, policy advisors, academics, media personnel, activist campaigners, members of the general public, and migrants making or having received asylum claims. Many of them occupied blurred roles across these categories.[7] I attended rule-making workshops and built up extensive contacts through my Geneva and prior research, and through sheer snowballing persistence. Without following value, I never would have come to Nauru. Material production is irrelevant to the accumulation of capital insofar as Nauru has always been about the spectacle rather than the reality of actual numbers. The numbers of migrants sent to Nauru are minute on a wider scale, 1,233 asylum seekers in August 2014 at the peak of operations, but the moral intensity and contractual dollars are huge.[8]

While Australia certainly has a well-instituted refugee industry sector (refugee determination case officers, refugee tribunal judges, refugee social workers, refugee legal prosecution and defense firms, refugee clinicians, and more) that could easily put Nauru's new project into action, the apparent ease with which Australia's industrial architecture extrapolates to Nauru masks a contentious operational context. Contracts on Nauru are lucrative, more than triple what they would be on Australia's mainland. Figures like AU$1.5 billion for refugee management, AU$450 million for refugee health, and AU$354 million for refugee infrastructure flow easily around this space.[9] However, fieldwork made immediately apparent schisms that have erupted across the global and Australian refugee sector around the offshore refugee industry.

I was repeatedly told about the controversial nature of working on Nauru and how offshore refugee work is "different" to performing the same function in Australia's mainland refugee sector. Many organizations that conduct similar work in Australia were also quick to make the distinction. They emphasized that offshore work does not sit with their values and principles. I was in Canberra when "Close Nauru" was spelt out in smoke in the sky. Government bureaucrats shielded their eyes against the sun, and many smiled in support as the unidentified biplane whizzed by. Seemingly everyone had an opinion on Nauru and was at pains to discuss offshore processing with me. Many believed that the operations should close in favor of similar Australian mainland procedures. Many were also in favor of the offshore operations, believing that the government should close the spaces for "queue jumpers" entering into Australia in unregulated ways. Nauru was, for them, an important node in the deterrence spectacle that dissuaded unregulated boat arrivals. I also spoke with Australian publics: angry, fearful, or fed up with the idea of refugees in an age of industry and media scares, political scapegoating, and sheer compassion fatigue.

Like a latter-day Albert Ellis, Nauru's first British Phosphate Commission prospector, I followed financial and moral values to their epicenter: the boomtown of Nauru's extractive sites. It took arriving in Nauru for me to fully realize the extent of the entire institutionalized cycle and commercial industry operating around asylum: the jolting shock I encountered when first landing on the island. As later chapters make clear, many of the toxic hazards and harms of this industry sector relate to the refugee laws and regulations that bring Nauru into being. The professionalization of refugee law across a transnational class of refugee industry experts and enterprises is part of what Hannah Appel (2012) calls in the oil and gas industry a "modular capitalist project," all of which makes its transferability possible.[10] As Roger Olien and Diana Davids Hinton (1982) find in relation to oil booms, boomtown situations create a transient and mobile workforce that easily moves to new areas of discovery as market opportunities emerge. The institutionalization of the refugee industry enables the reconstitution of a routine industrial fabric from place to place in response to the expansion of industry activity.[11] During my fieldwork, the majority of industry contracts in Nauru were professionalized contracts around refugee processing, closely followed by resettlement practices that attempted to integrate refugees into the Nauruan community post-determination.

I knew that the Nauruan government was anxious about allowing researchers' access, fearful of pro-refugee activism that might hamper their source of livelihood. Campaigns to end offshore operations do have something of a history in Nauru. Staff from major industry firms like Amnesty and Human Rights Watch, as well as snuck-in activist organizers, have all done exposés on Nauru's operations. It has become difficult to obtain a visa for Nauru because the majority of visitors come with the goal of toppling the country's primary industrial enterprise, like proverbial offshore oil rig campaigners. In reality, as I later detail, extreme practices of risk regulation in Nauru looked to stopper international legal challenges and sustain the government's economic dependency on refugees. The representation of Nauru as a "black site" outside of international oversight also interested a spectrum of international organizations and industry personnel in the country's regulation. Some of the same industry players that critiqued Nauru assisted in the island's industrial developments behind the scenes. Insofar as their work entailed educating a non-Western population in conduct appropriate for a liberal democratic polity, this was—I found—a civilizational project also replete with moral values of helping refugees.

I first went to Fiji as a visiting research student at the main University of the South Pacific (USP) campus. There, I delved into Nauru's historical archives, most of which are kept in Fiji or Canberra, though some are in the British National Archives in Kew, owing to colonial Phosphate Commission legacies. I learnt a great deal about Pacific colonial pasts and the intersecting networks of missionaries, capitalist enterprises, governments, and locals that make extractive projects happen. Suva is the headquarters of NGOs, INGOs, interagency forums, and media outlets focused on the Pacific. I was brought into direct encounter with Pacific media circulation about Nauru, most of which adopts the same civilizational critique and politics of vulnerability around refugees. Many of Nauru's government administrators, lawyers, medical staff, and teachers also come from Fiji, while lower-rung positions are often staffed by Kiribati workers. Living in Fiji dispelled any simplistic assumptions for me of "oppressor" versus "oppressed," and of the challenges of a postcolonial framework in illuminating the complexities of extractive operations.

I then applied for a research permit through Nauru's small USP satellite campus on the basis of my research focus honed in Fiji, exploring Nauru's post-developmental continuities through the phosphate and the refugee industries. My interest was not in refugee activism; I was not interested in "studying refugees" or in replicating humanitarian-geared assumptions. I was keen, like many anthropologists, on helping the communities in which I embed myself. This I made clear in my research communication, all of which came with ethical clearance. This is something I also hope I have accomplished: bringing to light the impactful realities of Nauru's refugee industry on *all* populations, set within a history of extractive pasts and presents.

In Nauru I became as much a part of the many slices of everyday life as I could. I lived with locals and foreign personnel, learning about and coming into contact with people's many different experiences. Many locals were grateful for my presence, keen to dispel savagery claims, as much as some asylum seekers and refugees were keen to detail the suffering they had experienced, and others, their disassociation from activist campaigns. I was at first under suspicion from Australian refugee industry workers and Australian Immigration Department personnel on the island. However, my continued presence in Nauru under the protective auspices of USP, and my involvement with people in all walks of life, made suspicions largely unsustainable, or at least not pursuable to some degree. My identity as a white British female doctoral student undoubtedly helped. I was not treated with the same level of suspicion that I would have been as an Australian, enveloped in highly polarized end/support offshore debates, and possibly direct activist practice. Conversely, I was often adopted, invited to many events in sympathetic concern of the lone young woman in the field. As an anthropologist, I was also seen as somewhat benign—in government interviews, officials would veer off on excitable asides, referencing TV series like *Bones* or charting their kinship ancestries, even when I made clear the discipline extended beyond these archetypal signifiers.

In Nauru, I fully embedded myself in company town life. I helped with everything from the Rotary Club to the Globe Theatre's touring Globe-to-Globe *Hamlet* production. I learnt how to catch noddy birds, husk coconuts, and spear fish. I drank kava and sang liturgical hymns with government bureaucrats, as much as I spent time with phosphate lorry drivers, waitresses, and dinner ladies, played bingo and gossiped with ministers' wives, and ate pancakes with Australian law enforcement agents and bureaucrats. I often hitchhiked, striking up deep conversations with all manner of residents, from refugee industry employees to presidential advisors, from Australian government contractors to Fijian security details, from certified refugees to uncertified asylum seekers. I went to Thursday Ladies' Night at the Joules Bar, I ran in (and won!) the women's division of the country's annual Coca-Cola Cup, I hung out at the boat harbor, I went to NGO aerobics and film nights, I attended every festival on offer, and regularly attended Sunday church. I helped out with school speech days, taught Year Six classes, and manned USP stalls at government service days. I learnt a great deal about phosphate mining, taking tours around factory floors and extraction sites and spending hours with chemists conducting test samples for exportation. In short, I participated, observed, and learnt from people living in Nauru.

Following refugee industry workers to Nauru's offshore sites was essential in understanding the money, knowledge, and expertise through which new industrial worlds are made, not to mention the immense moral values around this space. Without having conducted the prior research in Geneva and Australia, I never would have received the same abrupt shock when stepping out of the aircraft into the company town world of Nauru. Living in Nauru also enabled me to see the sets of daily practices and networks through which media narratives are constituted (Ginsburg, Abu-Lughod, and Larkin 2002). The media has shaped everyone's lives in Nauru, stirring the country's waters externally on an everyday basis. Activists in Nauru and in Australia are part of the construction of this representational universe, as are incensed publics on a global scale. Migrants and Nauruans more than anyone feel the repercussions of these realities—as racialized objects of rescue and/or less worthy and disposable.

In Nauru, I was free to do what I liked, provided I did not go into the RPCs without administrative clearance. During my fieldwork period, I went into Nauru's refugee resettlement housing, but I did not even attempt to enter its processing centers. This will certainly provoke criticism of my research. With persistence, I probably could have arranged entry. My decision against pursuing processing center access was largely because I found that, like with phosphate, the material processing infrastructure was almost superfluous to the productive life of the refugee industry, the economic arrangements of which, as my opening vignette illustrates, enveloped the entire country's fabric. Like the Chicago trading market Caitlin Zaloom describes, in Nauru, "city and market rose together" (2006, 181). Being in Nauru reinforced the reality of how industrial procedures shape the landscape of one high-value site. It is significant that the entire country of Nauru is labeled as an "offshore" "regional processing country," a company town in its starkest form. I could freely speak and engage with everyone from asylum seekers and refugees to industry workers outside the facilities, all of whom can come and go openly or at designated times. Access would also have been treated with a great deal of suspicion, as the dominant perception was that my research would come with an activist agenda once I made clear that I was not a contracted industry worker. It was already the immediate assumption from migrants, workers, and residents alike that I supported resettling refugees in Australia. It is also important to my other argument that much of

Nauru's industrial operations are assembled and cyclically feed into resource economies and politics on the Australian mainland and globally.[12]

I am certainly conscious of my role within processes of extraction, also deriving capital from following zones of continual extractivism. In this regard, my methodological approach takes its inspiration from social scientists focused on addressing carceral logics (Davies et al. 2021). Drawing on the pioneering work of abolitionist activist-scholars like Angela Davis and Ruth Wilson Gilmore, this approach focuses on advancing transformative changes by meaningfully engaging with the unequal distribution of power, rather than centering practices such as mass incarceration, policing, and borders as societal givens.

Nauru's refugee processing operations have been through a number of changes since my ethnographic research period, many of which I will later describe. I am now reliant on the workings of some of the media imaginaries that I critique. But having lived in Nauru, where the media interact so heavily with people's quotidian lives, I am all the more attuned to how Nauru is shaped by and shapes the global imaginary.

Zones of Extraction

Nauru does not fit the usual mold of a refugee resettlement country, which is normally characterized as one with a substantial domestic economy and home market, developed infrastructure and welfare system, or geographical proximity to sites of displacement. The United States, Canada, and Australia, flanked by Nordic countries, resettle the most refugees. Turkey, Pakistan, Lebanon, and Jordan host the most refugees, pushed to move from conflict-ridden sites just across their borders. Owing to its sheer geographical isolation, Nauru had no history of refugee processing or resettlement. The country was not a signatory to the Geneva Refugee Convention, nor did it have its own state asylum procedures. Among many in government and the public, there was little understanding of what a refugee was. But under the 2001 and the 2012 agreements, the cash-strapped sovereign state, bankrupt in the 1990s after ostentatious spending of phosphate wealth, resurged on the back of refugee wealth.

Across the course of the first phase, from 2001 to 2008, the Australian government sent 1,465 asylum seekers to Nauru.[13] Then, between 2013 and 2016, 1,355 asylum seekers were sent to Nauru; again, these were slim numbers but significant in relation to the local population, and they were given widespread statistical inflation in Australia. The majority of Nauru's new "resources" were individuals from Iran, Iraq, Pakistan, Afghanistan, Sri Lanka, Somalia, and Bangladesh. They put forward asylum claims to Australia through the international legal requirements of the 1951 Geneva Convention, which categorizes a refugee as a person who can prove "a well-founded fear of being persecuted for reasons of race, religion, nationality, membership of a particular social group, or political opinion." If certified as refugees by seconded Australian Immigration Department personnel, migrants were given a refugee visa for indefinite stay in Nauru. Behind the scenes, the Australian government then funded small business start-ups to encourage their integration in the small island nation.

The number of asylum seekers sent to Nauru is minute. However, the political economic value of the offshoring spectacle remains colossal for the Australian government. Catch slogans like "Stop the boats" hold populist appeal across political party lines. This treatment of migrant boat arrivals in Australia stems from a selective history of nation building operationalized across the country's brutal settler state foundations (Dauvergne 2016). The figure of Australia as the island continent remains embedded in unresolved anxieties of a still-colonial nation founded on the usurpation of indigenous land and sovereignty (Perera 2009). The boom in disproportionately managing the mobility and labor of poor people of color also sits on the legacy of slavery and the indentured labor trade (Perera and Pugliese 2018). The current iteration of what Catherine Besteman (2020) calls "militarized global apartheid" is built on a history of racialized segregation, white supremacy, and resource extraction. Enormous logistical, insurance, banking, and financial industries buoyed the system of global slavery that linger long after emancipation and independence movements. The management of trade routes, movement of labor, and racialization and categorization of populations shapes and is part of the environment we currently inhabit. To bring insights into the African diaspora to bear, such "protracted colonial logics of the plantation" characterize global configurations of race and whiteness, which define many aspects of life in different parts of the world today (McKittrick 2013, 3). Across the Pacific region, many islanders experienced wholescale forced displacement and indentured labor to support colonial powers' economies.[14] This plantation history instituted a racialized economy and mobility hierarchies of who can and cannot move elsewhere, all of which serve as a palimpsest for projects of human commodification.[15]

Within extractive regimes, there also remain enduring legacies of exploitation and empire building. Countries with postcolonial ties around forms of extraction all too frequently find themselves tied into patterns of imperial dependency, becoming financially induced into new border-enforcement industries. Dependency, scholars from Wallerstein to Rodney have long argued, is intrinsic to colonial economies. Colonial institutions reorganized local political and economic structures to better facilitate processes of extraction, producing "new exposures and enduring damage" to which people "remain vividly and imperceptibly bound" (Stoler 2008, 195, 193). This is certainly the case in the Pacific, where trade patterns are characterized by narrow export sectors, limited regional trade, and a high dependence on imports (Teaiwa et al. 2002). Development and structural adjustment programs promoted by former colonial powers, now replaced by aid and development partners, especially undermine local governance systems and place islanders in unequal and disadvantaging trade relations. Such policies preclude the articulation or promotion of alternative systems of society or political economy. Nauru's refugee project reconfigured practices of dependency and sociolegal affiliations, refashioning the country as a company town in line with new forms of human production—all at immense human costs. Rooting the history of Nauru firmly in these colonial pathways, this book broadens the purview of Nauru's industrial history outside its regional boundaries.

Once, the global economy benefited tremendously from Nauru's high-grade phosphate, utilized to increase agricultural yields and food production, largely in the Global North. Nauruans—like other surrounding phosphate islanders (K. M. Teaiwa 2015)—saw little of these profits, receiving a fraction of the overall price obtained on the global market. Now, the spectacle of migrant "illegality" (de Genova 2002) generates a multitude of images and discursive formations that fuel anti-immigrant sentiments for Australian political and organizational profit. Migrants are racialized as "illegal"—"as invasive violators of the law, incorrigible 'foreigners' subverting the integrity of 'the nation' and its sovereignty" (de Genova 2013, 161). The imaginary of a bordered nation then not only allows for the fantasy of controlling incoming numbers of black and brown Others but also reassures the centrality of white Australians to the destiny of the nation (Hage 2000). Australians who have never left their homes can imagine their nation's imperial reach. This goes for right-leaning and left-leaning representations alike. Racialized configurations of black and brown refugees saved by white Australians through resettlement programs simultaneously reinforce a civilizational superiority. Such humanitarian representations feed into the unifying sense of Australianness that is part of the potent political force of borders.

Practices of border making are also, Mezzadra and Neilson (2013) show, essential to providing low-wage labor power, and thus indispensable to capitalism at large. Borders demarcate the inclusion and exclusion of citizens and noncitizens. Borders also differentially include some noncitizens as subordinated labor power through graduating legal categories (such as "illegal" or "temporary"). Keeping people in precarious labor categories, as legally vulnerable undocumented workforces, is now a key method through which global political economies have taken shape. The ties that bind Nauru to other places are also premised on the circuits of consumption crucial to the formation of world systems of trade and production. Nauru in particular provides the theatrical staging of the "illegal migrant," especially as it revolves around so-called boat people. Yet, underneath the spectacle of enforcement, undocumented and temporary migrant labor is indispensable to Australian agriculture and other major industries, and receives little attention (Verma 2019).[16] Combined with a militarized spectacle of apprehensions, detentions, and deportations, Nauru instead heightens the visibility of a racialized migrant illegality. Nauru thus remains within the global orbit of promoting capitalist growth, holding far-reaching impacts on the landscapes and peoples beyond its island fringe. Nauru once again incentivizes the growth of Australian and other economies, but, as is so often the case with toxic industries, at the expense of people's lives.

Considering these trends, this book demonstrates how liberal representations are simultaneously connected to a consumptive politics. Inasmuch as we are all directly implicated in phosphate consumption—as Katerina Teaiwa (2015) eloquently shows in her ethnographic work in Banaba—there are also continuities in the contemporary linkages of Nauru's refugee industry to global consumer societies. With Nauru's refugee industry, far-off publics are again connected to the island's newest resource extractive project, now through the consumption of distant suffering. The immediate global reach of media technologies form part of what media studies scholars show to be a networked sociality (Chouliaraki 2012). The image of the refugee as victim, as voiceless, or as a threat shapes the public imagination, placed next to humanitarian appeals for financial support (Johnson 2011). Under a market logic, distant publics can extract political, economic, and moral value in the process of consuming media pertaining to asylum offshoring. Meanwhile, depictions of the at risk/risky refugee body affirm the fantasy of Australia as a bounded white nation with migrants as exotic objects for salvation or exclusion. This is part of the politics of consumption of this industry sector. There is an insatiable public demand for refugees across the political spectrum: despite the realities that only a fraction (7–8 percent) of the global migrant population are classified as refugees. Tracing these linkages between people in Nauru and consumer societies elsewhere helps us recognize how we are all again enmeshed in the politics of consumption.

Asylum and Extractivism

Environmentalists have long recognized the impact of resource extraction on world ecosystems (Nash 1993; Sawyer 2004; Taussig 1980)—though to date the impact of human economies has not featured prominently in these discussions. Building on Marx's analysis, scholars have done much to illuminate the social processes that make objects into valuable exchange items and commodities. Such diverse ranges of commodities as food (West 2012), the environment (Smith 2007), and oil (Appel, Mason, and Watts 2015) have all been subject to analysis. When it comes to humans, research has examined prisoners, slaves, and people who are trafficked as commodities (Agustín 2007; Davis 2003; Koptyoff 1986; Sharp 2000). But missing here is an empirical understanding of new forms of human commodities and especially, in the current era, the figure of the refugee as a commodity.[17]

In recent years, social scientists have gravitated toward the concept of extractivism as a way of studying the exploitation of people and the environment in the global rush for resources. Moving beyond extraction, extractivism is an ideological construct, an analytical and political concept, connected to deep logics of exploitation and subjectification (Arboleda 2020). Extractivism is the form of accumulation, associated with colonialism and imperialism, whereby territories, populations, and animal and plant life were rendered into commodities for the taking so as to enrich world economic centers (Jacka 2018). It is also an ideological mindset (Jalbert et al. 2017) of removing resources under the guise of "development," ultimately benefitting wealthy countries at the expense of poorer ones. What is new about extractivism today is the expansion of corporations and nongovernmental organizations into ever-growing resource frontiers globally (Mezzadra and Neilson 2017). My ethnographic research makes visible the expanding reach of capital into domains of human resources that depend on prior civilization projects of discovery and plunder (Gómez-Barris 2017). The expansion of systems of capitalist extraction has simultaneously made many localities in the Global South unsustainable. Living standards and life expectancy are bitterly stratified, all of which provokes out-migration (Sassen 2014). This cyclically forces people to confront the extractive demands for their labor, along with the fortified borders of the Global North.

Within critical migration studies, researchers have started to consider more carefully the institutional assemblage that governs people's mobility. Nicholas de Genova (2013) looks at the dynamics of illegalization through the organizational inscription of migrants' deportability. The legal production of migrant "illegality," de Genova argues, is accomplished through scholarship and an organizational reliance on analytic categories. Drawing on this framework, Ruben Andersson details the dramatic industry that revolves around the production of illegality in "the business of bordering Europe" (2014). Worldwide, governments' obsessions with illegal migration are underscored by a multibillion-dollar business, amidst trends of privatization and transnational cooperation. This scholarship is valuable, but it overlooks the industry around the production of legality (Coutin 2003), in particular the international legal system that produces people as refugees. It assumes that asylum constitutes a worthy exception, rather than a similarly damaging industry terrain, which in fact bolsters the established order. The depoliticizing representation of asylum has troubling consequences in that it helps governments solidify systems of border control. Migrants are placed under greater control and management to prove their worth through a politics of deservingness (Ticktin 2011). Individuals must represent themselves through a discourse of suffering or fortitude in order to move elsewhere, struggling to render themselves valuable to capitalist regimes (Rajaram 2018). In the process, people's vital energies, lived time, material resources, and physical features are extracted, profiting a vast industry of corporate, non-governmental, government, and other actors. By sieving deserving from undeserving, refugee organizational practices constitute forms of governance over people's lives through a rational-legal authority framed around protection.[18]

The Kurdish-Iranian writer Behrouz Boochani (2018) makes a powerful intervention in disrupting the epistemic conditions that allow for offshoring and other such damaging postcolonial arrangements to take place. Boochani, who was held in Manus Island for over six years, and his longtime collaborator Omid Tofighian, intentionally refer to all migrants held in detention as refugees and/or prisoners. By arguing instead that all migrants are refugees, Boochani looks to reclaim who decides refugeehood and trouble hierarchies of deservingness. Using the concept of Manus Prison theory, Boochani and Tofighian also draw attention to pressing intersections beyond migrant struggles, such as connections between detention, incarceration, and racialized policing (Tofighian 2020). They articulate the web of intersecting oppressions (colonialism, race, class, disability, sexuality, and militarism) that maintain society's dominant hierarchies. In seeking to reclaim refugeeness, however, Boochani comes up against the global dominance of commonplace tropes of refugees as risky or at-risk bodies. Boochani's reconstructive biopolitics also looms close to reinforcing a nativist/migrant dialectic defined by, respectively, a temporal and spatial static-ness or, alternatively, a hyper mobility. Yet, Boochani's approach—challenging what he and Tofighian call a *system-e hākem* or "kyriarchal system" (following the work of the radical feminist scholar Elisabeth Schüssler Fiorenza)—paves an opening to more meaningful solidarities that protest state territorial power from within. Boochani also contests the victim-savior binary, including patronizing depictions of "refugees in romantic ways" and, on the other side, associations with "criminals, rapists, terrorists and other dangerous people" (Boochani and Tofighian 2020, 20). Instead, Boochani and Tofighian push back against these dehumanizing tropes, demanding that refugees be recognized as "humans with different backgrounds, different cultures, different personalities and characters" (Boochani and Tofighian 2020, 20).

As Liisa Malkki also argues in relation to "refugees," the term supplies "a broad legal or descriptive rubric" that eclipses a tremendous amount of heterogeneity (1995, 496). There is a thematic tendency for much sociological work to reinforce the methodological nationalism of representing "refugees" as a given. Refugee status is constituted as a recognizable, generalizable, psychological condition. This position disregards how "refugeeness" is socially constructed and managed by powerful forces of discourse and consequent policy. In reality, a resource has to be assembled or "made up" (Hacking 1985), much like a social or legal categorization. Part of the challenge in developing and disseminating better understandings of the problems at stake, and advancing more effective strategies, is the emotional and political economic investments in the asylum system. The subject of refugees has strong popular humanitarian appeal involving innocent victims fleeing violence and persecution.

Another key challenge in unpacking the production of refugees as a resource is the self-representational labor of this industry. The refugee industry presents conditions unusual in other toxic industries in that migrants claiming asylum are also central laborers in this hazardous working context. My analysis in this book is based on an understanding of asylum as a form of unfree labor. Anthropologists have used this framework to examine the extraction of unpaid labor, generally under threat of coercive force (Calvão 2016). Within this, the exploitable labor of migrant workers has been the subject of much ethnographic investigation (Holmes 2013; Rajaram 2018; Xiang 2006), as has the burgeoning trafficking industry (Agustín 2007; Howard 2017; O'Connell Davidson 2015), with which the refugee industry at times intersects, and often presents many parallels. However, the notion of unfree labor has yet to be used in reconceptualizing asylum *itself* as a form of dehumanizing labor "that is at once exploitative and generative of new forms of belonging" (Calvão 2016, 456). I find that this concept allows for a more detailed understanding of the labor-intensive and risk-laden project of claiming asylum. It also brings to the fore the imbalanced structural conditions and forms of dispossession that precipitate—and disallow—people's movements across nation-state borders, except through a narrative of suffering.

Freedom of movement is easy for some and not others (Loyd, Mitchelson, and Burridge 2013). Populations are differentially treated because of ethnoracial differences and their relevance to global capital (Ong 1999).[19] Certainly, the problem of mobility is immensely more critical when the ability to live and reside is contingent on the legally recognized category of refugee status. But as later chapters show, constant dehumanization, fear, and risk are a feature of the asylum process. Meanwhile, this system of "biological citizenship" (Ticktin 2011) generates immense value for industry personnel—financial, geopolitical, and moral in nature—while reproducing the continuities between movement and inequality.

Yet, what is striking in much of the refugee and migration studies scholarship is the invisibility of the global refugee industry and the forms of capitalism that migrants' extraction engenders. In reality, the refugee categorization is buttressed by a dramatic organizational landscape, where workforces are reliant on refugee representations for their livelihoods. In fact, recent years have seen legal tribunals and consultants, healthcare professionals, social workers, humanitarian institutes, research centers, and academics specifically coalescing around refugee issues (Cabot 2019; Morris 2019, 2021a; Ramsay 2019; Sukarieh and Tannock 2019). Some determine if individuals are refugees or help present them as such; others contractually care for asylum seekers and refugees; some elicit research projects with, for, or around asylum seekers and refugees; still more return rejected asylum claimants to their point of origin from camps, processing or detention centers, prisons, and other localities around the globe. Migrants also have to define themselves through state categories as survival strategies (Fiddian-Qasmiyeh 2014; Harrell-Bond 1986). These subjectification relations are implicated in the continuity of existing industry power structures with its "fetishistic qualities" (Watts 2004, 61).

Scholars such as Bridget Anderson, Heath Cabot, Nicholas de Genova, Liisa Malkki, Georgina Ramsay, Miriam Ticktin, and William Walters are all critical of the ways in which scholarship can reproduce state categories of migration. Their research provides valuable critiques of the very categories of "refugee" and "migrant," as well as some of the institutions wedded to these categories. My work builds on these approaches, looking at the global value (moral, political, and economic) extracted from migrants in the process. Commercial and performance-based concerns play an important part of UNHCR and its development terrain, as does a concentrated effort to push the refugee as a legal category and the paternalistic structures of refugee protection agendas (Johnson 2011; Morris 2021a). The framework of resource extraction enables us to clearly see not only the financial value but also the moral value that is obtained from migrants' bodies by a spectrum of industry actors.

#RefugeesWelcome

Nauru is an important context from which to unpick the workings of the transnational refugee industry and some of the rationalities its apolitical, and at times antipolitical, figurations obscure. The country's industrial assemblage rests on the foundations of global displacement and market formations in Australia and worldwide. However, an opposing narrative obscures Nauru's industry operation. Photographs and videos of refugee self-harm pair with headlines like "Australia's

Offshore Cruelty" and "Refugees Attacked 'on a Daily Basis' on Nauru," overtaking the global media sphere. Academic publishing is replete with such titles as *Repeating Despair on Nauru: The Impacts of Offshore Processing on Asylum Seekers* (2012) and *Offshore: Behind Manus and Nauru* (2016). Documentaries like *Chasing Asylum: The Film the Australian Government Doesn't Want You to See* (2016) and *Freedom or Death* (2011) and books such as *The Undesirables: Inside Nauru* (2012) and *Yearning to Breathe Free: Seeking Asylum in Australia* (2007) all create quite a different impression. Headlines like "Nauru Outside the Rule of Law," "Refugees Released from Nauru Detention Protest Slave-Like Conditions," and "Australia Asylum: Dutton Says Nauru Is 'Safe' for Refugees" operate prominently on the global scene.

Although I agree with many of their conclusions, these scholars, journalists, and activists separate Nauru's history from its social and political economic context. The perspectives of locals about the operations of the industry in their country remain invisible and anonymous, including local legacies of Australian colonialism.[20] Given the lack of research conducted in Nauru or from those not associated with activist campaigns, it is unsurprising that most scholarship comes from this perspective. Mainstream work that has been conducted from time spent in Nauru is often designed to fulfil a particular objective: as apologist for involvement in the industry and/or polemic to end offshore processing. This is sometimes done by framing Nauruans and Australian contractors as violent barbarians based on fleeting time spent in the country (see, for example, Human Rights Watch and Amnesty International 2016). Ironically, it is this argumentative tendency that has dissuaded the Nauruan government from granting exorbitantly priced visas to journalists and researchers, aside from those sympathetic to the country's operations (see Kenny 2015, 2016).

Madeline Gleeson (2016), for example, drew her work from secondary sources, arguing that refugees in Nauru are "free, but not safe," assaulted, stoned, kicked and beaten, or threatened with death by locals. Mark Isaacs (2014), a former contracted Australian Salvation Army worker in Nauru, also paints the picture of a "wretched life" in Nauru that obscures locals' perspectives, while idealizing refugees as victims. The focus of much dominant scholarship about Nauru is all too often on continuously recreating humanitarian fantasies of "black sites" of despair. In these representations, refugees are abused and targeted by thuggish Nauruans or Australian contractors, and white Australian humanitarians sweep in as saviors. Such a perspective can objectify people through a human rights piety, while extracting moral (and at times economic) value in the process.

These representational discourses also stem from the external narratives of the primitive and underdeveloped that informed Nauru's colonial political and ecological exploitation. Differential sovereignty has always defined Nauru and

Australia's relations. This involves notions of primitivity and debasement common in colonial discourse, which casts the West in the role of savior (Stoler 2002). So too, humanitarian frameworks that target Nauruans as a barbarous people in violation of legal values run the risk of mirroring "the Eurocentric scale of 'civilization' attendant to colonialism" (Mahmud 2010, 12). In the process, little is revealed of Australia's historical relationship of extractive imperialism and exploitation of its Pacific neighbors.

Over the years, Australia has developed a powerful refugee advocacy movement. Activists (made up of full-time activists, incensed citizenry, industry personnel, and migrants) ally to bring refugees in Nauru and Manus Island to Australia, many through prominent #RefugeesWelcome-style campaigns. The work of some activists concentrates on organizing in Nauru with migrants held offshore, enabled by social media and cellular networking technologies. The focus of organizing efforts is diverse, and importantly makes publicly visible the violence of the Australian government's offshoring policy. Yet, at times, activist discourses connect to problematic colonial tropes of violent Nauruan savages against innocent refugee victims. Narratives recall nineteenth-century imperial popular culture models of old. Stories of missionaries killed by indigenous people were conveyed in a heroic mode and became an important means whereby imperial publics learned about empire (Obeyesekere 1992). These sorts of representations persist into the present under widespread media publicity. Certainly, many asylum seekers and refugees in Nauru do critique the offshoring policy in powerful ways. However, there are profound civilizing undertones in media framings that clearly mimic colonial discourse: that of white Australian salvationism to lift up helpless refugees, combined with Nauruan underdevelopment.

Such concern for the bodies of suffering strangers, as exhibited in activist discourses around Nauru, has roots in the advancement of colonial enterprises. In the eighteenth and nineteenth centuries, philanthropic abolitionists took up a civilizing mission around laboring subjects of color. The "protection" of slaves was a core element of the salvational rhetoric of abolitionists (Heartfield 2011). Drawing on a civilizational vocabulary, abolitionists advanced a system of indentured labor and infrastructural practices to manage trade routes and the movement of people (Elbourne 2016). #RefugeesWelcome campaigning extends from these histories of colonial migration governance. By upholding practices of asylum, activists run the risk of limiting the movement of poor people of color from the Global South beyond submitting an asylum claim. Meanwhile, such solidarities center on a form of coloniality that re-privileges the racialized white liberal individual as the actor of hospitality (Picozza 2021).[21]

Contemporary models of racialized management also directly connect to the colonization of mobile Pacific worlds (Banivanua-Mar 2007). Denigrations of

Nauruans as savages legitimize the exploitation of domestic publics in the Global South as labor forces within outsourced border arrangements. Such stubborn rhetorical tropes, like colonial representations of "exotic people inhabiting the edge of empire" (Behlmer 2018, 21), advance the industry developments that bring Nauruans and migrants together in the offshored/outsourced borders of the Global North.

Perhaps more so than other projects of border making, examined by scholars of Europe's racialized migration regime (Cabot 2014; Dzenovska 2018; Follis 2012), Nauru's refugee industry brings moral values overwhelmingly to bear in a civilizational project entangled in the raced histories of colonialism, empire, and white supremacy. It is certainly expected that there is an overwhelming reaction to the system of offshoring asylum from Australia, which is replete with toxic harms. Rather, my contention is that the importance of making these harms visible must include an understanding of migrants', local, and workforce perspectives beyond vulnerability and anticivilizational frames. In this industry sector, the toxic effects are threefold: negatively impacting migrants, Nauruans, and contracted personnel in a brutally dehumanizing environment. The majority of local islanders, as later chapters detail, are actually incredibly critical of the refugee industry in their country. However, most Nauruans were not consulted in the decision about the housing of the toxic phosphate industry and later the refugee industry, a tendency that scholars of resource extraction so often find. To put it in the words of Traci Brynne Voyles, who examined the history of the uranium industry on Navajo land in the US Southwest, Nauru's indigenous inhabitants have also been "placed under erasure to be 'always disappearing' in the face of settler colonialism's advance" (2015, 8).

Dominant activist frames obscure the shared experiences of Nauruans and migrants as subjects of racial inequalities. Instead, race is redefined through a moral compass. Humanitarians make decisions on whose lives are more valuable as paternal objects of rescue, and whose are less worthy: a hierarchy in which Nauruans firmly rank low. Migrants are represented as exotic outsiders in need of salvation, where paternalistic intervention is required from superior Westerners to save non-Western victims from the animalistic savagery of Pacific Islanders. By centering their claims making on a moral vernacular of vulnerability, civilization, and savagery, activist representations reiterate a racialized objectification reminiscent of colonial times. How people are cast is an important part of the process of accumulation and dispossession (West 2016). Racist ideologies around migrants and Nauruans set up barriers against shared systems of recognition. Ultimately, such representations intensify segregations that obscure human relationality and hold little emancipatory potential, exasperating capitalist investment in the process.

A major caveat to make from the outset is that I do not focus extensively on the individual experiences of asylum seekers and refugees. However, I do draw on deep conversations and time spent with migrants at all points of the asylum process in Nauru. Many people, as I detail, have been through incredibly difficult circumstances, and for a variety of reasons sought to move elsewhere. I refrain from a deep biographical approach for several reasons. This angle has already been well covered as it relates to Nauru, where refugee experiences have been given exponential visibility (see Green et al. 2017; Metcalfe 2010; Refugee Action Committee 2017). Refugee stories have also become a big business—bought, sold, and traded as part of the demands of refugee self-presentation. Uncertainties around whom or what to believe are paramount in this context.[22] It is this uncertainty that has led to the bodily and psychologically scrutinizing practices of RSD—the inequalities of which, as I describe in chapter 2, are part of the self-representational labor of this industry sector. These uncertainties are all the more extreme in Nauru's operations, where many migrants, in sheer desperation, look to circulate any narrative that might help them escape a deeply dehumanizing environment.

At the same time, an overemphasis on stories of suffering has galvanized a vast body of disinterested and impassioned Australian publics, with Australians keen to send asylum seekers offshore, and Nauruans morally and/or financially driven to carry out the refugee work entailed, all resulting in the industry's cyclical perpetuation. I prefer not to be part of similar operations by also extracting stories from migrants under immense scrutinization.[23] Nor do I want in any way to identify those awaiting or having received refugee status determinations—all too easy in Nauru's small island context. Instead, I balance my analysis by illuminating the inequalities of the overall operations.

A very real danger is that, as I try to tackle the offshore asylum system in this way, my research can be utilized to emphasize ending all refugee resettlement operations. It might be stressed that my research gives evidence to the falsities of migrants' claims to asylum or the enormous operational expenditures spent on supporting asylum seekers and refugees in Nauru. I am certainly cognizant of this eventuality, but believe it important to display the limitations of humanitarian approaches, from which new offshored/outsourced setups are cropping up all the time. I see it as important also to pull analyses back to how and why people are made into refugees, the vast expenditures on border enforcement and militarization, and the global gains from enabling the mobility of people, whether as refugees or no. Pro-refugee campaigns and normative critiques often gain little traction. Instead, they actively rile the dynamics that bring destructive company town worlds like Nauru into existence. These worlds, my research shows, are easily transferable with their attendant hazards and harms.

A Note on Terminologies

Throughout this book, I use the categories I critique, often with purposeful objectification, in an attempt to "get with the fetish" of the figure of the refugee, to "hijack," and "re-contextualise" it (Cook, Crang, and Thorpe, 2004, 174), all of which require some definition. Although the terms "refugee" and "asylum seeker" are relatively new inventions (Gatrell 2013; Shacknove 1985), both have acquired an incredible amount of baggage over the years, drawing to mind advertisements of economic scrounging and/or third-world suffering. As a rhetorical device, the word "refugee" has become fixated with a discourse of populist fear. Refugees are often represented as terrorists or the disingenuous motives of so-called low-skilled economic migrants. At the same time, the figure of the refugee has become an evocative technique for advocates lobbying for an expansion to refugee resettlement quotas and industry funding ad nauseam. Discourses of persecution and protection are key to this construction. All too frequently, refugees are heavily conflated with asylum seekers, automatically pinned to anyone making their way across borders outside of state visa channels, sometimes regardless of their actual legal status. Many people do not self-identify as refugees or use the term as a marker of distinction. Others do and find that the refugee identity holds a great deal of meaning to their lives. I do not dispute the legitimacy of people's legal claims to asylum nor question the nightmarish experiences many have been through. However, part of what I illuminate is how the paradigm can artificially divide and segregate people, maintaining essentialized distinctiveness through negative or paternalizing associations. I also seek to bring to the fore the forms of extractivism and global inequalities that push people to seek refuge in the first place.

I often use the term "migrants" to refer more broadly to asylum seekers and refugees in Nauru, taking care to distinguish them from the island's longstanding migrant population.[24] In Nauru, all asylum seekers and refugees are migrants in some way.[25] Asylum seekers are migrants awaiting refugee claims, subjected to intense examinations before certification. Refugees are also migrants, ones who have been certified as displaying a "well-founded fear of persecution" and permitted access to the country's associated social welfare provisions. At large, the legal procedures surrounding "refugee status determination" (or RSD) and facilities and provisions provided throughout the processing and resettlement phases are dependent on the geographical location and mode of transport from which a migrant makes an asylum claim or receives a successful determination. However, the entire operations hinge on Article 1A of the 1951 Geneva Convention. This has shapeshifted somewhat into the current working definition delineated by its 1967 Protocol. The Protocol removed temporal and geographic restrictions and made the category open and targeted to all.[26]

Article 1A of the 1951 Convention:

> A. For the purposes of the present Convention, the term 'refugee' shall apply to any person who:
>
> (2) As a result of events occurring before 1 January 1951 and owing to well-founded fear of being persecuted for reasons of race, religion, nationality, membership of a particular social group or political opinion, is outside the country of his nationality and is unable or, owing to such fear, is unwilling to avail himself of the protection of that country; or who, not having a nationality and being outside the country of his former habitual residence as a result of such events, is unable or, owing to such fear, is unwilling to return to it.

The 1967 Protocol:

> 2. For the purpose of the present Protocol, the term 'refugee' shall, as regards the application of paragraph 3 of this article, mean any person within the definition of article 1 of the Convention as if the words 'As a result of events occurring before 1 January 1951 and . . .' and the words '. . . as a result of such events', in article 1A(2) were omitted.
>
> 3. The present Protocol shall be applied by the States Parties hereto without any geographic limitation, save that existing declarations made by States already Parties to the Convention in accordance with article 1B(1)(*a*) of the Convention, shall, unless extended under article 1B(2) thereof, apply also under the present Protocol.

Since this time, a number of additional terminologies have been added to the industry jargon, some of which are descriptive or normative labels, while others have solidified into legal categories. Most of them find relevance to the Nauruan context, and all of them have deep social implications. These will become clear over the course of my narrative.

Like phosphate before it, Nauru's refugee industry is a temporary one and tied into the political whims of the Australian zeitgeist. I greatly respect many of the people I met on Nauru. I was bestowed with an incredible amount of warmth, kindness, and generosity. Nauru's isolation is only relative; many people are well traveled, and all are globally interconnected. I met some who could tell me the best spots for afternoon tea in Melbourne, and others who directed me toward—or were themselves—a wealth of historical archives. Still others jokingly collected first editions of Nauru's unashamedly racist Australian-written histories or engaged in debates far beyond me around post-developmental critique. This book does not ridicule or deride Nauru and the country's many multifarious peoples. Nor does it mean to belittle the work of migrants and activists in Nauru, Australia, and beyond who have devoted a great deal of their resources to ending an unjust system. Rather, it is an attempt to bring to the fore what the Australian government and activist campaigners obscure under divergent yet convergent frames. It is a genuine concern with what will be left in Nauru in the wake of another failed, and ultimately destructive, industrial enterprise. The utopian rationalism at work is clearly deeply imbalanced, characterized, unlike phosphate, by ever-plentiful reserves of people on the move. It is only through an active effort to qualitatively rethink and refute the international refugee system that more equality will be achievable. Otherwise, the seemingly universal tendency toward human commodification and mobility governance remains relentless.

BUILDING THE WORKINGMAN'S DREAM

The Treasury Department would like to advise the general public that it will be paying out land rentals for the Refugee Processing Centre (RPC), Statesite and Rontel this week. It is further advised that beneficiaries with Bendigo Bank accounts will receive their rent payments in their account on Wednesday 22nd July 2015.

The rest will receive their cheques on Friday 24th July between 2 P.M.–5 P.M. at the Post Office and cashing of cheques at the Nauru Revenue Office from 2 P.M.–5 P.M.

—Treasury Department Noticeboard, Government Buildings, the Republic of Nauru

Nauru Post Office, Civic Centre, Aiwo District. July 24, 2015. It's a sunny day. People jostle to get inside the post office. The small dusty building, sandwiched between Nauru's phosphate headquarters and Bendigo Bank, the latest addition on the country's scene, is abuzz. The Civic Centre has become noticeably livelier over the past few weeks with the resurrection of international banking. Over a decade with no bank is enough to provoke a bit of excitement. But as we maneuver our way inside, it becomes apparent that this is not another promotional event.

"Oh, just the refugee processing royalties," casually remarks Georgia, a Nauruan friend and a phosphate worker. I spend a lot of my time with Georgia during my stay in Nauru, often accompanying her on errands around the island or chatting in her office about the latest local gossip. This time, a trip to help her with groceries takes a different turn. She notices my quizzical looks as she steers me into Nauru's post office, adding, "Every two months we collect them. You know, my family has many lands. If it's phosphate, we go down the road. It's just the same for refugees and rocks. This really isn't bad. Sometimes you can wait all night to get in. Come back later, you'll see. It might be going around the building."

Several landowners bide their time playing poker on smartphones. Children crawl on the floor. A middle-aged man slumps past, still groggy from the night before. Another leans against the wall, wearing a khaki shirt marked with the logo for Transfield, the Sydney refugee managerial contractor; his friend beside him sports a shirt reading Wilson Security, their Melbourne-based security sub-contractor. Others from the Nauru Rehabilitation Corporation, the ironically named national phosphate mining firm, also mill about, but in dwindling numbers, testament to the fading industry of Nauru's yesteryear. Homegrown security firms are also now a ubiquitous presence, many earning high-paying subcontracts for guarding the refugee housing and worker industry complexes that have sprung up in recent years.

Curious, I ask Georgia, "Which RPCs are on your family's land?"

"I think 1, 3, and 4, and maybe one of the resettlement sites."

"I thought there were just three centers?"

"Hmm . . . 1, 2, 3," she counts on her fingers. "I can't remember. Let me look at my statement, then I'll tell you."

There's confusion over which queue to go in.

"This is such a stupid system, it's so stupid," she sighs. "You queue to collect then you queue again to sign. That's what takes the time."

We stand patiently in the first line. Forty-five minutes later, we reach the front. The clerk flicks through several pages, trying to locate Georgia's surname. After a painstaking search, her surname is ticked off. An envelope labeled with her name is removed from a folder and alphabetized into a pile at the front of the second line.

We wait in the second line.

Her surname is again located, the envelope is reproduced and her signature is taken. This time the envelope is hers to keep. Inside: a rental payment statement. Royalty recipients compare their tallies.

We go next door to the revenue office, which now also serves as the Bendigo premises. A signboard is propped up at the side, a few leaflets scattered about: "Savings account? Now's the time." But we keep to the orderly queue at the other side, where her statement is again exchanged, this time for cash. Grand total: AU$159.90. Those with more finite partitions of land are not so fortunate. We pick up her cousin's land owings: it comes to just AU$12.69.

"Why's his so low?" I ask.

"Well, you see here, his share is between 5,760 family members. Me, I'm lucky, I have a 480th share in our land. Like I said, my family are big landowners. But you know, for those others, well, at least it gives them something for the weekend."

The idea of the refugee as a commodity is very natural and explicit in Nauru. Stumbling across Royalties Day was by no means the first time I came into close encounter with the circulation of refugees through Nauru's financial streams, albeit it was one of the more extreme. Frequently, my conversations with people in Nauru would weave interchangeably between phosphate and refugees. Nor did I

FIGURE 4A. The phosphate royalties office in Nauru. Photo by Julia Morris.

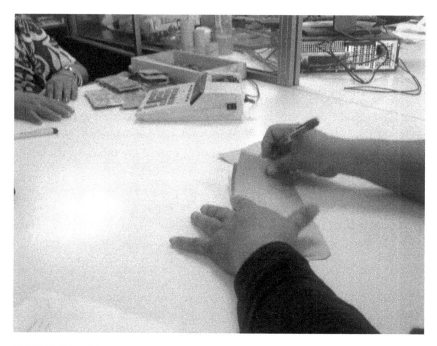

FIGURE 4B. A local landowner collecting payments for refugee industry land leasing. Photo by Julia Morris.

have to read shrewd parallels between Nauru's two industries, even if I initially wrapped my questions with woolly tact. I worried that I might offend local islanders by insinuating that their entire country rode on a refugee economy or upset migrants whose bodies held such value for an entire Equatorial country. In fact, people in and out of government, asylum seekers and refugees alike, were open that refugees had overtaken phosphate as Nauru's main resource sector.

In one of my first government meetings, Eva, a local bureaucrat, nonchalantly said, "The refugees, it's just like phosphate, but hopefully we've learnt a bit from the last time. The big thing we need to think about is planning for when we no longer have refugees." Casual references like this were all too frequent in conversation, giving a sense of how refugees formed a normalized part of Nauru's capitalist economy. Yet, as the latter part of Eva's statement makes clear, Nauru's new industry sector was also temporally positioned within the politics of memory that linked two eras of massive infrastructural, bureaucratic, and social developments around one major commodity. The deep-seated anxieties about Nauru's resurged wealth and the anticipation of its decline structured the modes of reasoning through which Nauruans inhabited the country's latest industry transformations. This was reminiscent of "the dreamtime" of Oman's oil boom described by Mandana Limbert (2010). Here, too, local understandings were inflected by a remembered past and likely future poverty, on which the discovery of refugees sat as a miraculous interlude.

Visually, the refugee industry brought with it many of the same features observable in other commercial arrangements transformed by newfound extractive wealth. As our discussion continued, and I pressed Eva to elaborate on these similarities, she pointed out key aspects of Nauru's resurged industry life since refugees. "I mean there's the traffic for one. You know, when the refugees weren't here, we never had rush hour. Now all these cars, it's crazy." She gestured to Nauru's fly-in-fly-out offshore refugee industry and the dramatic increase in local and foreign worker employment required to carry out the labor-intensive project of the arrangement. Over a short space of time, just out the window of her office in Nauru's main government building, I lost count of the Australian-driven 4WDs, RPC-bound passenger-transportation vans, local vehicles, and motorbikes driving by. Music blared in through the open window, carried by the salty sea breeze.

I asked Eva about the contrast between Nauru's bankruptcy years and the refugee industry heyday the country was experiencing. Eva continued the conversation with a sigh. "I mean it's a good thing that we're back on our feet, but things definitely have changed. For one, we have boom boxes on full blast night and day. Parties all the time. It's almost like the phosphate days. You should have seen it then." She paused, looking almost wistful. I recalled the sepia photos I had seen of that era—the lavish banquet spreads at the now faded Menen Hotel, everyone dressed to the nines—wondering if that was what Eva also pictured. She continued before I could ask, "You know, I often say, when the refugees came, Nauru again turned green." When I looked at her quizzically, she added, "Green with money, I mean." It was a widely acknowledged fact that Nauru was remade through and by refugees.

This chapter takes a step back in time, historicizing Nauru's resurgence as a refugee company town within the country's first boomtown operations of copra and then phosphate. Compared to mining and oil towns, the offshore refugee company town is a new industrial setup: a timing that reflects the current political climate around asylum seekers and refugees as threats, as problems, or as objects of rescue. Yet, in many ways, Nauru's refugee industrial arrangement is due to a spatial and temporal environment already in existence. The political project around refugees depended upon and was conjured into being by specific modalities of power brought during the colonial regime. What this chapter seeks to do is show how the organization and materialization of one industry can shape another. This includes the ways in which not only the industrial landscape and settlement formed but also the country's governance systems were shaped in line with the particular methods of industrial production. In fact, a central part of this book's overall argument is that the refugee industry was so easily facilitated in Nauru because of the dramatic structural changes initiated by phosphate extraction. Ethnographic attention to these deep historicities shows that the continuous transformations of extractive landscapes is eased by past systems of colonial upheaval, what Ann Stoler (2008) calls attention to in terms of the physical marks left on places and in people's memories over time. Historical continuities between the refugee and phosphate industries in Nauru are evidenced through reappropriations of the built environment and memories of the many colonial phenomena that have affected the region. But these industries are also tightly linked through close sociolegal arrangements, land-use regulations, and constituted economic dependencies, along with racist positionings that have sought to legitimize successive industry booms.

As scholars show, regions with past histories of quarantine, incarceration, and militarization are particularly convenient for warehousing and isolating migrants (Loyd, Mitchell-Eaton, and Mountz 2016; Mitropoulos 2015).[1] By isolating migrants in remote sites—often once grounds for military testing, mining industry, and past carceral regimes—governments can strategically attempt to dislocate them from connections with activists and advocates. The strategic isolation of migrants simultaneously functions as a spectacle of enforcement and deterrence.[2] Meanwhile, for Pacific Islanders, militarization is a continuous structuring force that connects imperial histories in the region (Shigematsu and Camacho 2010). Islands have long been seen as expendable spaces for nuclear testing (T. K. Teaiwa

1994).[3] These placements involved an organizing logic that naturalized racial difference and a racist paternalism toward colonies and territories, all of which shape the environment Nauruans inhabit. I examine these industrial overlaps to signal how past configurations of extraction provide continuities to long-standing and contemporary practices of managing and extracting value from migrants' bodies. Within this, I look to foreground the specificities of islanders' experiences of colonialism, while also recognizing more generalizable neocolonial pathways that emerge. With the push toward outsourcing border regimes, and the persistent use of former colonies and dependencies for such extractive sites, it is imperative to understand the relationship between imperialisms and the iterability of the global refugee industry. These interconnected extractive landscapes are the focus of this chapter.

A Company Town in Nation

The industries stand unparalleled in the tropical world for the care, attention to, and comfort of the employees . . . The health and comfort of all are assured by well-planned systems of sewerage, fresh and salt water in unstinted abundance, electric light, fresh food supplies refrigerators and telephones connecting every office, workshop, and house. Every nook and corner of the settlement is lit up at night, giving the impression, when viewed from a few miles out at sea, of an approach to a great town.

—British Phosphate Commission (1929)

Michael Powles: In some ways Nauru was run a bit like what the Americans would call a company town?
Ludwig Keke: Yes it is. That's my personal view.

—Ludwig Keke, former Speaker of Parliament
and ambassador to Taiwan (2011)

A company town is traditionally defined as a community shaped around a dominant business enterprise and is a form of "enclaving" found throughout the world's mineral frontiers (Appel 2019; Vitalis 2007). Company towns were established in places where extractive industries such as coal, metal mining, lumber, and oil held a monopoly franchise.[4] Generally speaking, the company town differs from the factory or farm, which are the principal workplaces for employees (Crawford 1995; Porteous 1970). Instead, characteristic of the company town is how the industrial landscape and settlement forms are shaped in line with the particular technical and social necessities of the method of industrial production. Essen in Germany, Cadbury's Bournville in England, Pullman's in Illinois, and Moomba gas town and Jabiru uranium town in Australia are some of the more famous company town models. Nauru is no different, governed around a succession of major industries across the course of the nineteenth to twenty-first centuries. Once termed "a company town" by former Speaker of Parliament Ludwig Keke, Nauru's latest incarnation extends from a colonial history rooted in international commercial trade.

The Coconut Boom

The chances of migrants arriving and claiming asylum were slim on the coral atoll. Nauru's size and distance from other archipelagos—595 kilometers east of its nearest neighbor, Kiribati—the fringing coral reef and easterly trade winds coupled with strong Equatorial currents kept the island off international trading scenes later than most. Unlike other islands in the vicinity, Nauru had "none of the tropical fruits, which are generally very prolific in these islands" (Fearne 1798). It lacked the sandalwood, tortoise shell, or bêche-de-mer of the lush verdant lands of Fiji, Samoa, and Tonga. But Nauru, Anaoeoro, or "Pleasant Island," as Captain John Fearne first recorded, slowly found itself within global trading currents.

Traders arrived from the 1830s on Nauru, setting up stations with tobacco, alcohol, hardware, guns, ammunition, hard biscuits, and tinned food around the whaling season. European business was conducted largely around imported goods, while Nauruans traded in coconut products and handicrafts (Simpson 1843). As coconut oil became a primary commodity on the European trading scene, large-scale commercial interests turned to Nauru in the mid-eighteenth century. German companies dominated the western Pacific trade. The Hamburg firm of J. C. Godeffroy & Sohn was the pioneer firm, establishing a trading base in Samoa in 1857. Once the German firms identified the profitability of Nauru's rich coconut supplies, business was expanded over to Nauru from the Jaluit regional offices in the Marshall Islands (Fabricius 1895). The firms recruited resident traders to purchase copra from the islanders. Agents and independent traders bought their copra from the chiefs in return for retail goods (Moss 1889). Those who cut and dried the copra then received a share of the goods as the chiefs saw fit. By 1888, ten traders were on the island, some acting as agents for Robertson & Hernsheim and the Deutsche Handels—und Planttagen-Gesellschaft der Siidsee-Inseln zu Hamburg of Samoa (DHPG), along with the British New Zealand firms Tiernan Venture and Henderson & McFarlane. Chiefs with title to large tracts of land became very wealthy through their control of the copra profits.

Trading companies and commercial interests largely drove the expansion of colonial empires. Trading companies were often given official recognition by the Reich and empowered to perform acts on the government's behalf (Firth 1973).

These so-called charter company colonies saved the Reich the expense of a regular bureaucratic organization in the colonies, administering the territory through their own officials and bearing costs, in exchange for trading rights and concessions. With the rapid development of German trade in the Pacific, commercial rivalries became more acute as British, Australian, and New Zealand companies sought control over high-value resource sites. Although traders preferred to keep government involvement to a minimum, they sought consular protection to consolidate their activity and ward off increased competition.

In Nauru, traders and beachcombers had provoked enough local antagonism to require imperial protection. To popularize their trade locally, traders issued free samples of tobacco and alcohol, along with rifle demonstrations. With the takeoff of fermented sour toddy on Nauru, introduced by shipwrecked Kingsmill Islanders in the 1870s, alcohol and firearms soon grew out of control. In 1878, a drunken dispute erupted during a marriage feast. A chief from one of Nauru's perpetually warring district clans tampered with a bottle of coconut oil brought as a present for the bride. A pistol went off, and the young chief of a rival high family was shot. Stoked by traders keen to offload their cargo, the argument soon led to a ten-year civil war. Fatalities amongst Nauruans and traders were plentiful. Importantly for traders and Nauruans alike, the island's unsettled conditions made commerce difficult.

Chancellor Otto von Bismarck was initially disinterested in joining the scramble for colonial possessions. He viewed distant colonies as a drain on state resources and a distraction from European politics (Hezel 2000). But with Franco-British rivalry at a peak in the 1880s and increasingly vocal demands at home, Bismarck began to see the value of establishing protectorates in East and West Africa and in the Pacific (Fabricius 1895). On June 24, 1884, Chancellor Bismarck informed the Reichstag that he would extend official protection to German traders wherever they had established a commercial predominance. Germany's growing commercial presence was also seen as a threat by the nearby Australian Queensland and New Zealand governments (Viviani 1970). Still part of the British imperial empire until 1901, and unable to claim territories themselves, the Queensland government agitated London's Colonial Office for annexation of New Guinea and the need to ensure their strategic stronghold. On April 6–8, 1886, Germany and the United Kingdom came together at the Anglo-German Convention to demarcate their respective areas of imperial influence. As part of the land divvy, Germany, urged on by its regional trading firms, established its Marshallese Protectorate to cover "the small but fertile island called Pleasant Island" (Fabricius 1895, 171).[5]

On April 17, 1888, Jaluit officials and the imperial commissioner arrived into Nauru on the gunboat SMS *Eber*. Nauru's chiefs were imprisoned overnight in a copra shed until all arms were surrendered, then tasked with helping German administration instate order. Over eight hundred firearms and more than a thousand rounds of ammunition were handed over. A compilation in the style of the Domesday Book was produced; it was called the *Grundbuch*, and it detailed all individual landholdings of Nauruans, the eight trading stations, and transactions relating to land claims and boundaries (MacSporran 1995). The traditional boundaries drawn up for the *Grundbuch* then served as the delineation for tax districts. Bismarck's policy required that the expansion of German protectorates must as far as possible avoid involving the Reich in any direct expenditure. In order to pay for Nauru's administration, Jaluit levied annual copra taxes. Jaluit operated through indigenous collaboration, holding chiefs responsible for local enforcement. The chiefs were tasked with collecting the copra tax of their districts. In return for exerting their influence in the company's interests, chiefs received special concessions, including one-third of the collected tax in German marks, and alleged rides in the German warship (Firth 1973).

But the promise of a flourishing coconut trade failed to translate into a sufficiently viable pioneer vision. Prolonged droughts reduced the crop yields in the 1890s, with traders petitioning for reductions in taxes from the Marshallese administration (Viviani 1970). Nauruans refused to make more copra than was needed to pay their taxes. In one particular slump, no ship landed on Nauru for eight months. The German administration generally left Nauruans undisturbed except for tax collection. The nature and viability of the copra industry was such that little moved beyond the small-town trading stations already established. However, the demarcations of land of the *Grundbuch* served as a medium through which land became equated with commercial value.

Tania Murray Li (2014) articulates this phenomenon well in her work on the inscription of value onto land. Land does not have an intrinsic quality of "resourceness"; rather, land is rendered investible through an assemblage of devices including laws, taxation, title deeds, fences, landmarks, and zoning, as well as the practices through which experts, villagers, and other actors are enrolled. The way that land is circumscribed is important, as it serves to intimately regulate people's experiences with their surrounding environments, along with sustaining social, economic, and racial divisions. During Nauru's colonial period, a critical part of the island's conceptual restructuring and integration into the industrial capital world lay in the commodification of nature. Land, always in short supply, occupies an important place for the majority of Nauruan families. Writings of anthropologists and missionaries (Delaporte 1920; Hambruch 1915), as well as my conversations with older generations of Nauruans, show that all land on Nauru was "owned" in some way: whether loosely demarcated by individual tribal domains or families. This extended to ownership of wells, the coral

reef, fishing rights, and lagoons (MacSporran 1995). But the assigning of exchange value and use value to things and people as part of the global trade (coconuts, later phosphate, and then refugees) involved a different kind of
abstraction. Land served as the basis for seeing value, bringing, as Anna Tsing
puts it when describing the messiness of capitalism in the Indonesian rainfor-
est, "capitalist universals into action" (2005, 4). In Nauru, the demarcations of
land provided a medium through which land became space, and equated with
commercial value. Statistical picturing devices, such as that of the *Grundbuch*,
made large-scale investments in land thinkable. Once represented in this manner, the meaning of land changed as agriculture became more commercialized,
and the political power of chiefs and Nauruan elite expanded.

At the same time, assembling resources for global investment requires something to be defined, delimited, and imagined as a commodity. Coconuts certainly had value to Nauruans as food, while the leaves of the tree would be used to
make clothing, housing, and everyday utensils. But buying and selling a coconut
was antithetical to Nauruan practice. Under the early traders and then German
administration, physical items like coconuts were measured and sold, becoming
commodities for exchange. Meanwhile, the trade in coconuts was increased to
meet world demand for cosmetics and cooking as part of a modernization narrative of economic progress. Discourses of economic development were established
in Nauru, as the island was wholly reorganized through projects such as the
property-titling programs of the *Grundbuch*. Thus, the flow of goods, ideas,
money, and people became a ubiquitous part of Nauruans' daily lives.

The colonizing forces of missionaries also profoundly informed the uneven
power dynamics brought about by phosphate and later by refugees. At Jaluit's
request, Nauru's first long-term missionary, the German Protestant Reverend
Delaporte and his wife were brought to the island in 1899, gradually setting up
a European-style church, school, and moral codes for Nauruans, supported by
the copra administrators.[6] Missionaries were instrumental in advancing public
works projects, including European-style churches and schools, and in exerting
power over routine activities and modes of perception and practice. Protestant
and later Catholic missionaries put forward moral codes for Nauruans, practices
such as immoral dances and the worshipping of erected stones were banned, and
European-style clothing was firmly encouraged. Nauruans were positioned as
poor and backward, and pushed to seek ways to improve their situation. Indeed,
the reports and correspondence of missionaries reflect the low regard that visitors had for local islanders, who were typically pathologized as "dirty, unkempt,
almost nacked [*sic*] natives"; once "raw heathen" before "the miracles of modern missions" (Delaporte et al. 1909, 1, 3).[7] Nauruans were racialized as inferior
and excluded from white circles of influence and power. These relations extended

outward, from the future of the community to an encouraged support for colonial and national policies and distant markets.

In 1902, the first resident Roman Catholic missionary, Father Grundl, came to Nauru from Germany. He was followed in 1903 by Father Kayser, who opened a Catholic mission in 1907 in Arubo and another in 1920 in Yaren District, along with a Catholic school that is still in operation to this day. Infrastructural developments took hold across Nauru, including Western-style wooden framed homes and community meeting spaces, a main road, transportation such as bicycles, a medical dispensary, and more schools, which were represented locally and abroad in terms of modernization and improvement. In this way, emotional and affective relationships were forged with the development of the built environment, which signified that Nauruans were becoming advanced and modern. But it was the discovery of phosphate in Nauru that soon transformed the island into the distinctive company-town form, a timing that reflected changing commercial interests.

The Global Phosphate Boom

In 1798, the British economist Thomas Malthus famously made the doomsday prediction that the human population would soon outgrow its ability to feed itself, raising alarm bells and spurring the humanitarian and business-savvy impulses of scientific experimentation. Bone meal and manure, long used by agriculturalists worldwide, had only a limited and frugal future. However, with world populations on the rise, agricultural productivity needed to be increased faster than demand (Bogaard et al. 2013). The expansion of farming and pastoral activity in the Americas, Australasia, and Japan also called for methodologies that would free farmers from relying on animals to produce fertilizer, and heighten their crop yields.

Chemists went hard to work developing solutions to the population conundrum. The German chemist Justus von Liebeg, the "father of the fertiliser industry," emphasized the importance of nitrogen, phosphorous, and potassium in plant nutrition (Brock 1997). Popularizing the "law of the minimum," Liebeg advocated the need to extract and increase the scarcest mineral nutrient to improve plant growth, not the minerals already in abundance in the plant. The British agricultural scientist Sir John Lawes built on Liebeg's efforts, and those of James Murray. Lawes discovered that mineral phosphates could be treated with sulfuric acid to make superphosphate, which rapidly released phosphate into the soil for use by plants. Lawes's "artificial manure" came on the market in 1843, and he set up his first factory in London's Deptford in 1844. After these experimental days, the phosphate industry took off. By 1855, 600,000 tons of phosphate fertilizers were being applied in England alone, most of the product coming from

Lawes. The technology spread like wildfire. Prospectors began searching for deposits of the valuable rock that would meet the needs of Western agriculturalists and consumers. The discovery of large deposits of rock and alluvial phosphate in America, along with Morocco and Tunisia, fomented the beginnings of a global fertilizer industry.

The Pacific Islands Company grew out of John T. Arundel and Company, a London-based firm that worked the Pacific trade in copra before later moving into the phosphate business. The late 1800s were a depressing time for the Pacific Islands Company, "the day of small things" (Ellis 1936, 51), which boded poorly for "the financial barometer." By 1890, all known phosphate deposits in the Central Pacific had been worked out. Anything and everything called for phosphate analysis. Australian farmers were clamoring for higher grades of phosphate, and the company had resorted to scraping residual guano around the Queensland coast. But Henry Denson, the office manager of the Pacific Islands Company, had an unusual-looking doorstop. It was given little regard, except when brought out as a curiosity from his passing visit to Nauru (Williams 1971). In July 1899, Albert Ellis, a Sydney-based officer with the Pacific Islands Company, took an interest in the peculiar rock, so remarkably like the Baker Island deposits he had been sampling. Ellis put the specimen through his routine chemical tests. Lo and behold, the results were far better than Ellis had hoped: 78 percent phosphate of lime, superphosphate, ore of the richest quality! "There never was a 'gusher' more welcome or more opportune," Ellis reflected on these times (Williams 1971, 58). "A gleam of sunshine has come in a discovery which I think will prove extremely valuable to the P I Coy," Denson quickly wrote to Arundel, the company director. "The whole island I firmly believe to be one huge mass of Rock Guano. How this is to be worked, I cannot suggest, as you are aware the island is under German jurisdiction and under German laws" (Williams and Macdonald 1985, 11).

"A Fine Democratic Example"

Industrial and governmental secrecy engulfed transactions between the German and British governments, the soon renamed Pacific Phosphate Company (PPC), and the Jaluit-Gesellschaft, resulting in a joint venture in 1906 that sanctioned phosphate mining on Nauru. As part of the agreement, Jaluit retained the monopoly of trade on Nauru, receiving £2,000 and royalties of one shilling per ton of phosphate (equivalent to roughly £259,000 today and royalties of 5 pence per ton). Meanwhile, overall phosphate profits were divided in the ratio of two-thirds for the PPC and one-third for Jaluit. In return for the mining rights, the PPC took up the administrative payments originally paid to Germany by Jaluit. Shares in the PPC were also given to Jaluit and German administrators. Before mining began, the chiefs representing the tribes of Nauru were called together for a meeting with German officials and Pacific Phosphate Company representatives. It was agreed that documented landowners would be paid for the lease of their land and the loss of any trees. Payment for the phosphate mined was calculated at a half-penny for each ton of rock exported, most of which concentrated on mining the central plateau Topside. The *Grundbuch* register of land holdings, set up by the German administration for copra extraction, ensured the administrative and legal frame for phosphate extraction, making it easier for phosphate companies to plan their investment.

As soon as the terms were established, the PPC began the planning and building of the settlement. An important aspect of company town development is that it depends on a precedent. The PPC were already active in mining projects in the region, particularly on nearby Ocean Island (K. M. Teaiwa 2015). They brought the home-building campaigns from their other industry pursuits to re-create Nauru as "the jewel" of their phosphate towns. The PPC hired a German manager for the island operation and a mix of British and German employees, including experienced phosphate workers from Ocean Island. The phosphate administrators were initially eager to have Nauruans employed in the labor force in low-rung manual positions. Racialized hierarchies unevenly organized the positions that Nauruans could access. Few Nauruans were interested in the backbreaking phosphate work. In 1906, one hundred Nauruans were contracted for a year to mine for phosphate but, "fed up with digging" (Viviani 1970, 35), no one renewed their contracts. Instead, colonial labor for the phosphate fields and the building of the company town infrastructure came from workers recruited in China and the Caroline Islands, as purported skill level mapped onto racial and national categories, and schedules and salaries.

Meanwhile, Nauruans became erroneously characterized through tropes of lazy, passive, and savage islanders. Take this description written by D. L. Oliver, an American visitor of phosphate executives to Nauru, who describes Nauruans as "favoured wards [who] became increasingly parasitic upon the mandate administration and the phosphate industry" (Viviani 1970, 59). Oliver's account resonates with aspects of Syed Hussein Alatas's Orientalizing framework around the "myth of the lazy native." Alatas describes how peninsular Malays were depicted by British colonialists as "the indolent, dull, backward and treacherous native . . . requiring assistance to climb the ladder of progress" (1977, 8). This racist depiction sought to place Malays in positions of dependency, wherein colonial rule connected to an ideology of progress. So too in Nauru, the phosphate commissioners soon thought it strategic not to recruit Nauruans into the industry. By projecting a vision of corporate paternalism, they could fend off critics of the operations and advance the phosphate industry locally.

After German rule folded with World War I, intense political grappling divvied the island between a tripartite British, Australian, and New Zealand administration as a League of Nations–mandated territory. Nauru was technically awarded to Great Britain, but Australia and New Zealand argued for a shared division. Their farmers had become reliant on the low prices they gave themselves, which enabled them to become leaders in the global food market. "Its phosphate deposit marks it of considerable value, not only as a purely commercial proposition but because the future productivity of our continent absolutely depends on such a fertilizer," cabled W. A. Watt, the Australian treasurer, to Prime Minister Hughes in May 1919, encouraging him to do what he could to secure the phosphate island (Viviani 1970, 42). Under the Nauru Island Agreement (1919), the Australian government purchased 42 percent of the company, Great Britain 42 percent, and New Zealand 16 percent. A commissioner from each country was appointed to the board of the newly inaugurated British Phosphate Commission (BPC), along with an administrator to "make ordinances for the peace, order and good government of the island." Under the BPC, the phosphate town expanded rapidly into "not only a business success, but . . . an enviable respectability" (Williams 1971, 42).

The Phosphate Town

Company towns, for Crawford (1995), are generally characterized by a two-part style. On the one hand lies the industrial landscape, shaped around the system of manufacture. On the other hand lies the model town, designed to create an attractive way of company life. The phosphate town of Nauru was no exception. Urban growth was controlled around phosphate processing. Deep-sea moorings went up with rapid speed. A wooden jetty with a north and south arm was built for exporting the phosphate onto specialist phosphate ships. The first phosphate digs and eventually a crushing plant and a storage bin were all in line with the jetty. Puffing railway engines ferried the rock from the extraction fields along a light rail system to the shining new crushing and drying plant. A second jetty and unit were soon added, this one built of steel, much safer for the phosphate loading process. The railroad tracks extended to the end of the jetty straight to the new phosphate ships ready to be loaded with tonnage for farmers and global consumers. The mining was extraordinarily successful, with over eleven thousand tons of phosphate shipped to Australia in the first year alone (Williams 1971).

Well-laid-out settlements provided housing for the pioneering offshore phosphate workers. Ordered housing quadrants, churches, social clubs, and sports and tennis grounds remade the landscape so that a little bit of the suburbs transferred out to the field. The single large residences of the high-rung administrators

FIGURE 5A. Former British Phosphate Commission–era company town housing. Photo by Julia Morris.

FIGURE 5B. Contemporary refugee industry company town housing. Photo by Julia Morris.

were built high on the hill, fringed with bougainvillea, and open to the cool sea breeze. If married, officials lived in commodious furnished bungalows, while the bachelors had two-room houses built of concrete topped with corrugated iron roofs.[8] Electric light was made universal, and a complete telephone system installed. Every one of the "stag" bungalows was named after the native town of its present or previous occupant, such as "London," "Leeds," "Liverpool," "Belfast," "Londonderry," and "Aberdeen." Upon request, Nauruans' traditional thatched homes were replaced with shining new concrete structures. Each house had a tank for collecting rainwater, a shower, and a saltwater flushing toilet. There were free daily distributions of ice, weekly deliveries of household goods such as soap and cordials, and free public laundries and dryers. Nauruan children were educated in the mission schools under the London Missionary Society (LMS) and the Catholic Sacred Heart Mission, who also trained Nauruan teachers.

The phosphate trading executives were practicing Congregationalists and astute businessmen with long-standing ties to the LMS. They viewed having missionaries in Nauru as a useful means of exerting social control over islanders and instilling them with Christian values. In turn, the industrialization of Nauru received great support from Nauru's European missionaries, who reaped financial and material benefits from the arrangement. The mission's presence in Nauru was strongly reliant on the political and material resources from the mining industry, as well as the increased numbers of foreign workers attendant in their services. In one report, Delaporte lauded the phosphate industry's accomplishments, pointing to the amount of phosphate they had exported, and writing that Nauru's "commercial importance has brought to it the blessings of civilization" (American Board of Missionaries 1913, 115). "We are thankful," Reverend Delaporte wrote in another report, "that our phosphate deposits are to be worked by a company whose leading officials are Christian gentlemen" (cited in Garrett 1996, 275). Delaporte went on to applaud "the sympathetic cooperation of the Phosphate Company and its officers," in the form of "free transportation of supplies, teachers, missionaries etc., and in many other ways." The support was very much needed; since 1902, the LMS had reported heavy debts to the American Board of Commissioners for Foreign Missions as a result of its extensive international work.

Over the next decades, phosphate transformed Nauru, creating a booming economy that had profound effects across the island. Across the burgeoning company town district, a nine-hole golf course added to the luxury world. There was also an outdoor picture theater installed for Europeans, which showed films twice a week, where "chairs were set out under the stars" (Goodey 2014, 123). A separate "natives" outdoor picture theater was established, in addition to a Chinese theater, as part of the racial differentiation foundational to the country's development. Other forms of landscaping looked to secure the settlement's long-term prosperity and erase the dispossession of islanders from their land. A system of sewerage drained the phosphate town's new ring road, constructed of coral crushed together with phosphate rock. Curvaceous streetlights fringed the new sidewalks that glimmered at night, making the new phosphate town "perhaps unequalled in any industry in the British Empire" (BPC 1929, 19). Free hospitals were established that later included operating theaters, a dental clinic, and eventually, pathology and radiography departments.

Other Pacific Islanders were recruited as indentured labor forces to keep the streets sanitized and clean for the company town to flourish. Visitors admired the gardens and pretty hedges that beautified the homes, the walks, and the streets of the community, and "the finest plant in the Pacific" (Williams 1971). Employees and their families played billiards in the clubhouse and "two sets of tennis before tea." They frequented the local cricket grounds and organized evening entertainment, designed to counterbalance the exacting demands of their jobs. Company town newspapers provided local export statistics and sought to give a sense of company unity. Nauru also boasted a well-equipped refrigerating plant. "Fresh meat was issued three or four times a week, the cattle and sheep being brought alive from Sydney, and slaughtered on the island," wrote Clifford Collinson (1923, 249) on his Nauru visit in *Life and Laughter 'Midst the Cannibals*, adding, "They even have ice-cream every Tuesday!" "There is an air of comfort and cleanliness that is delightful, making the surroundings seem ideal. A fine democratic example. The industries stand unparalleled in the tropical world . . . to the lasting credit of British enterprise" (BPC 1929).

Royalty payments were certainly exploitative in that Nauruans received little of the overall price obtained on the global market. Between 1908 and 1913, approximately 630,000 tons of phosphate rock was shipped from Nauru. Nauruan landowners received £1,320 of the commodity value of £945,000 of this tonnage (Viviani 1970, 35). However, locally, many Nauruans also became monetarily wealthy through their backyard extractions, even as they had little say in the dramatic and deeply segregating upheavals that took shape around them. "The bank balances of some of these brown-skinned Nauruan plutocrats are by no means to be despised. The old dame who nursed me could write her cheque any time for more than three hundred pounds!" Collinson (1923, 248) goes on to write in the starkly racializing terms that characterized the booming phosphate town.[9]

In Nauru, zoning and laws accomplished practices of segregation. When the British Phosphate Commission arrived, they instituted the Movement of Natives Ordinance 1921, which demanded strict curfews that forbade Nauruans, Pacific Islanders, and Chinese to be in European settlements between sunset and sunrise. Norms of separate and unequal rights and privileges governed life in the phosphate company town. Schools, hospitals, and shops were firmly segregated into "native," "European," and "Chinese." Some of the forms of paternal segregation were advanced by the support of local leaders keen to institute law and order among a populace that had once feuded for ten years. Nauruan chiefs petitioned the local administrator for the creation of new laws such as the Arms, Liquor and Opium Prohibition Ordinance 1936. The Ordinance prohibited the consumption or possession of liquor by Nauruans and the manufacture of alcoholic liquor in the island. However, these regulations were encouraged, and usually suggested, by the BPC administration, who sought to quell any signs of a labor uprising or coup d'état for phosphate control. In order to seek support for their extended presence across the island, the phosphate company administration later opened a branch of the Commonwealth Savings Bank in Nauru in 1922. Nauruans were astute. Within one year, local islanders had deposited over £2,000, later earning the nickname "the Scots of the Pacific" (Viviani 1970, 52). Over the next few decades, after continued agitation, Nauruans' royalties increased.

The vision of profitable philanthropy and backyard consumerism fell apart with the advent of World War II. A brutal Japanese occupation during World War II halted the project (Garrett 1996). Geographically, the island was an ideal base for launching air offensives and occupying North American and Australian sea routes. For many years, the Japanese had also been seeking better access to Nauru's phosphate. Before the war, Japan had purchased roughly half of the island's phosphate, but not at the cut prices afforded Australian farmers (Viviani 1970). The Japanese had enviously witnessed a revolution in the productivity of Australia's agriculture from the use of Nauru's high-quality phosphate. The Germans were also keen to regain control of Nauru's phosphate lands. In December 1940, they sank three of the BPC's four phosphate tankers en route from Nauru, before later bombing the oil tanks and the phosphate pier. The BPC officials evacuated all European women and children in July 1941. Then, on December 22 and 23, 1941, the Japanese launched their offensive, bombing the wireless station by aircraft. The following year, they bombarded the island with planes and cruisers, resulting in the phosphate administrator's surrender.

In the interim, the phosphate commissioners all but abandoned the island, repatriating the majority of Chinese and Pacific Islander mining workers, and removing vital parts of machinery from the phosphate infrastructure to Melbourne. Only a few of the phosphate administrators stayed, including the administrator at the time, Lieutenant-Colonel Chalmers, Doctor Bernard Quinn, and the Catholic priests Kayser and Clivaz. Ellis (1936) wrote, "With their genial natures and friendly manners [they will] not suffer at the hands of the Japanese." Ellis was optimistic. Under the Japanese occupation, many Nauruans were forced to work constructing airfields and military fortifications or deported to the Japanese naval headquarters at the Truk Islands, over a thousand miles north (now the Chuuk State within the Federated States of Micronesia). Backbreaking labor, starvation, and humiliation characterized the Japanese period.[10] Nauruans were not as harshly treated as the Chinese and Gilbertese, some of whom were executed. Nauruans were instead favored to the extent that they were seen as useful for Japan's envisaged phosphate control. They were taught Japanese in school, and some continued in former employment, but punishments were severe, and food was scarce. All forty-nine of the island's leprosy patients were sent adrift in a leaky boat, and they all drowned. Several Nauruan girls were molested, and some forced to serve as attendants in the Japanese officers' club. Some women gave up their children for adoption so that they might not die of starvation (Deireragea 1995). Many were forced to watch public executions; several committed suicide; many died of starvation or from punishment wounds; others were forced to eat rats for survival. By the time Japan surrendered to the Australian occupation force in August 1945, only half of the population had survived. Of the 1,200 Nauruans evacuated to Truk Atoll, only 737 returned to Nauru, repatriated by Australian troops on the *Triona* phosphate ship—crudely underscoring the market-based calculations that structured Australian concern. The Australian British phosphate commissioners positioned themselves as liberators of Nauruans from Japanese wartime colonialism, rescuers of "smiling brown people" (Ellis 1946, 5) who "have suffered grievously at the hands of the ruthless Japanese" (71), "restoring [Nauru] to its usual sanitary and healthy atmosphere" (83). This "imperial myth of liberation" (Shigematsu and Camacho 2010, xxi) attempted to occlude violent histories of phosphate extraction on the island, and legitimize mining in the future through the representation of paternal benevolence.

Upon his return, carefully stowed phosphate cogs in hand, Ellis, by then the British phosphate commissioner for New Zealand, was quick to turn to the "dire effect" to the industrial workings (1946, 16). He noted the easterly breeze, good for phosphate shipping operations, and admired the rendition of "You'll Come A-waltzing Matilda with Me" performed by a small group of returning Nauruans. But, "tragic and harrowing," Ellis wrote, the company town was "quite destroyed" (1946, 52). He was "shocked by the devastation." The moorings were gone, the cantilever and conveyor belts were unusable, the loading bin was destroyed, and the staff houses, stores, workshops, and laborers' quarters had been leveled to the ground. To cap it all, "Our worst fears were realised . . . the boat harbour . . . was completely wrecked." Although the BPC had accumulated stocks of phosphate in Australian and New Zealand ports, from 1942 they had to buy more than three hundred thousand tons of phosphate per year from

Florida, Makatea, and Morocco for Australian consumption (Viviani 1970). This cost over AU$400,000, and panic had set in about future agricultural productivity. In 1939, 40 percent of the phosphate shipped to Australia and New Zealand came from the BPC's fleet on Nauru and Ocean Island, delivered to twenty-nine fertilizer works at eighteen ports (Williams 1971, 43).

Immediately, BPC employees were brought back in, and the tasks of laying moorings, constructing storage tanks, and repairing the cantilever were begun. The speed with which the phosphate company town was remade was astounding. "To the sound of the music of hammer on nail, sawing timber and the churning of concrete mixers, the buildings went steadily up" (Goodey 2014, 110). Suburban villas met with new trade stores, an aircraft runway, motorcars, post office, basketball and volleyball courts, and a cricket clubhouse. In 1947, Nauru officially became a UN Civilizational Trust Territory, and the island's administration returned to the same three powers. The BPC again controlled the island's resources, with Australian farmers paying only a third of the world price for Nauru phosphate, and only 2 percent of profits to Nauruans (Hughes 2004).

Following World War II, many of Nauru's leaders began to protest their paternalistic treatment. They had been largely abandoned by the phosphateers who returned with eyes gleaming toward the operational reparations of Nauru's extractive frontier. Their island had been fought over, bombarded, and blasted purely for its mineral resource, with little consideration for local welfare. Even during Nauru's company town reconstruction, priority was given to the restoration of the industry and housing for phosphate employees, all of which was achieved by 1948 (Viviani 1970). But it was not until 1949 that local housing was even given attention, with Nauruans still living in huts constructed from salvaged scrap materials from the war (Pollock 2014). Even by 1951, only 319 total houses had been completed. The houses were insufficient in size and number for the expanding population, and cost AU$850 each. The majority of expenses were also borne by Nauruans through the Nauru Royalty Trust Fund, set up by the phosphate administration in the 1920s, in addition to a Landowners Royalty Trust Fund paid directly Nauruan landowners. Several of the overseas teachers and missionaries also came with civilizational complexes, treating Nauruans with racist discriminations. Few Nauruans were content to return to the former company town dependency, in which their revenue was far at odds with Australian profits. In the nineteen years in which the commissioners had worked the phosphate, up to World War II, Nauruan royalties had risen from 0.5 pennies (d) a ton in 1920 to only 8 d a ton in 1939 (Viviani 1970). Of the 8 d (equivalent to roughly £3.65 today), half was cash payment, one-quarter went on works and education for the Nauruan community, and one-quarter was held in a trust for the Nauruan landowners. After the war, the BPC increased local housing, water, transport, and medical and educational facilities, absorbing the costs. However, many Nauruans were keen to extricate themselves from the cycle of paternalistic mendicancy.

The chief at the time, Timothy Detudamo, had spent time in the United States through the American Board of Missionaries. There, and in Australia, he observed systems of agricultural manufacture. Across the fifties and sixties, many Nauruans also went abroad on phosphate freighters. Others trained as teachers, doctors, policemen, and in the ministry in Australia, Fiji, and nearby Pacific islands. New groups like the Nauru Scouts had affiliations with Melbourne's Geelong Rovers, traveling to Australia for jamborees.[11] Detudamo and others well knew the value that their phosphate accorded on the global agricultural market, some of the foods of which were imported back through their local cooperative and BPC-run stores. They were keen for Nauruans to take on more of a role in the business and control their own economic destiny. "Education, they were always telling us education," one older Nauruan told me when looking back on this time. "That's how we could be the ones running the show."

After World War II, the local governing body, the Council of Chiefs, asked for royalty increases, but had to settle on what the BPC agreed, which was far different from market value. Although royalties dramatically increased across the 1950s and 1960s after UN and Australian Congress of Trade Unions pressure, negotiations were often hostile. Thomas Cude, the chief of police under the BPC in the 1940s, refers to "the troublesome Geelong boys," writing in his diary, "I don't blame them so much as Mr. Hurst who was responsible for their training and education in Australia" (Cude 1945–1947). Post-war, several Nauruans also sought phosphate employment, initially in minor administrative positions, but with the view to future promotion. The BPC officials would only employ Nauruans in lower-run clerical positions or in the phosphate fields, blocking them from advancement in the fear that they might take over the lucrative operations.

Like elsewhere, decolonization efforts were well underway in the Pacific in the late 1960s and 1970s. With the economic viability of Nauru's commercial phosphate industry, Nauru's educated elite, the "Geelong boys," tirelessly lobbied for their independence. They had the support of many in the United Nations, the Trusteeship Council, Australian liberal lobbyists, academics, and others who also argued for a greater degree of Nauruan self-government through phosphate revenue. It was not until 1951 that elections were first permitted for the Nauru Local Government Council. Detudamo was first elected as head chief, followed by Raymond Dadabu in 1953. Then, upon Dadabu's death in 1955, Hammer DeRoburt was elected: a young local school teacher educated at Geelong Technical College in Victoria. The phosphate commissioners envisaged that Nauruans would agree to be resettled on Curtis Island or in Australia. This was the case with Banabans from the BPC's other worked phosphate island, who agreed to move to Rabi in 1945. As part of the proposed move, Nauruans would be expected to renounce their sovereignty in favor of Australian citizenship. However, Nauruans refused the deal. Instead, in 1967, Nauruans, with DeRoburt at the helm, purchased the assets of the British Phosphate Commissioners for AU$20 million over three years. The production plants were passed into the control of the newly set up and locally owned Nauru Phosphate Corporation. In 1968, after fervent agitation, Nauru became an independent sovereign state through their territorial resource.

The Miracle of the Boom

The result was that in the 1970s Nauru earned the world's second highest per capita GDP (at the time, over AU$50,000 per person per year), second only to Saudi Arabia, taking on the colonially instated phosphate industry to a heady level. The new government increased extraction to over two million tons annually, catapulting their profits into the hundreds of millions. By the mid-1970s, phosphate sale prices also increased fivefold, with profits considerably more, because Nauruans sold the ore at global market price, rather than the discount the BPC gave to Australian and New Zealand farmers.

Nauru's newly independent government let loose with full abandon. They splurged on a fleet of seven Air Nauru Boeings and a state Nauru Pacific shipping line. They exported over two million tons of phosphate per year, with peak export earnings of almost AU$382 million in 1974 (Hughes 2004). Shopping sprees to Dubai resulted in ostentatious displays of wealth. Prime international real estate, a public treated to free international medical care and education—often abroad in Australian boarding schools—heavily subsidized utilities, and absolutely no taxes made Nauru the envy of many neighboring islands. They purchased an AU$7 million office building, topped by a revolving restaurant on the island of Saipan in the Northern Marianas chain, an AU$3 million hotel development, and an AU$400,000 floating cocktail lounge on Majuro in the Marshall Islands. Regionally, Nauruans also became known as the "Little Angels" of the South Pacific for these efforts to support unsteady regional Pacific Island economies.

New chemical treatments of the phosphate ore raised purity levels to a staggering 91 percent, paving the way for alternative industrial uses. Markets were expanded from Australia and New Zealand to Japan, South Korea, Taiwan, Indonesia, and the Philippines. Many Nauruans chose not to work, while workers were brought in from the nearby island states of Kiribati and Tuvalu, Hong Kong, and the Philippines. Managers, supervisors, technicians, schoolteachers, and top government administrators were recruited from Australia, New Zealand, and Britain: the three countries that formerly ruled Nauru jointly.

But mismanagement and poor investment—AU$4 million lost in the unsuccessful London musical *Leonardo: A Portrait of Love* and another AU$24 million to investment scams—combined with dwindling phosphate resources and a skyrocketing diabetic population keen on imported canned goods, fast food, and beer. School truancy was high, and politics was of little interest to the majority of Nauruans, who zipped around the world in resplendent style on the back of spectacular phosphate wealth. They imported Ferraris and Land Rovers to the newly independent state, and filled swimming pools with live terrapins. Often, government MPs would commandeer the state Boeing 737s at 10 percent capacity, taking families and friends on trips to Hong Kong or Tokyo, leaving passengers and their luggage on the tarmac. It was alleged that, on a whim, the president would frequently send jets to pick up extravagant food for lavish dinners held in the marble ballrooms of the Menen Hotel.

In 1998, the Bank of Nauru crashed. Eight Americans were convicted in New York of larceny and fraud of US$37.5 million from the government's investment arm, the Nauru Phosphate Royalties Trust. An Australian businessman and accountant were convicted of attempted trust money fraud. Air Nauru had run an annual loss of up to AU$40 million. By 1996, the fleet was down to a single 737. Nauru, under President Rene Harris, borrowed loans to pay off existing loans, including AU$236 million from the United States–based GE Capital Corporation. When Nauru defaulted on GE loan payments, receivers moved in and took over Nauru's prized central Melbourne skyscraper, Nauru House, and the remaining 737. The government was forced to sell the Grand Pacific Hotel in Suva—with its ornate fountains, sauna baths, boutiques, and salons—and later their hotels in Waikiki. Upon my arrival in 2015, their remaining major property, an office building rented to a NASA engineering contractor in Houston, was up for grabs.[12]

By 2000, the country had external public debts of AU$280 million and internal debts of AU$265 million (Maclellan 2013). This quickly rose as the government took on debt to repay Bank of Nauru customers. The AU$1.3 billion in reserve in the Nauru Phosphate Royalties Trust in 1990 had declined by 77 percent to an estimated AU$300 million in 2004, due mostly to extravagant spending, mismanagement, and misappropriation. In 2004, the government was stopped and ration cards were handed out. With the shortage of power, all phosphate mining ceased. Unable to pay the satellite phone bills, the entire country lost global contact for several months.

Although these years were characterized by immense hardship, many locals I spoke with did look back on them fondly. Statements like "It was a better time"; "We shared what we had"; "Went fishing"; "Got into walking instead of driving"; "Told stories by candlelight" colored nostalgic anecdotes I often heard. But, ultimately, as the country was keen not to renounce their sovereignty by ceding to Australia, the economic prerogatives were more pressing. Any and every resurgence scheme was tried. "I did some weird and wonderful things, I had to," Nauru's former finance minister recalled to me of that time. "Bugger protocols, the country was running dry. You know the sign of poverty when you see the white upturned rocks on the reef. That's desperation of people looking for food. They broke coral to get eels out of holes, they were so desperate."

The government attempted to sell passports and expand into offshore banking.[13] They skipped between Taiwanese and Chinese for any financial dregs of consular recognition or rebuttal.[14] The whole country ran on a shoestring staff, who had little incentive to turn up to work with salaries paid by IOU checks. The local Capelle's Supermarket largely spotted the entire island. Most Nauruans lived on ration cards; many supplemented their diets with reef fish, coconuts, and breadfruit. Supplies of water and electricity were sporadic; thoughts of law and governance were tentative at best. Then in 2001 came *Tampa*. Like the phosphate days, secrecy once again engulfed Nauru. As George Pittman (1959, 9) once wrote of Nauru's mineral modernization, this was again "a discovery which would change Nauru from a little island living by itself in the middle of the ocean to a place which ships and aeroplanes would visit and which would play a part in the modern world."

From Phosphate to Refugees

> Its . . . deposit marks it as of considerable value, not only as a purely commercial proposition but because the future productivity of our continent absolutely depends on such a fertilizer.
>
> —W. A. Watt, British treasurer, May 1919

The refugee company town is a new industrial formation growing in popularity, shaped by the political potency of border spectacles, and, in Australia, the figure of "the boat people." From its violent settler state foundations and subsequent federation in 1901, Australia continues to harbor geographical anxieties surrounding alleged imminent invasions (Perera 2009). The country was founded on the colonial displacement of indigenous populations and a heavy reliance on explicitly white European immigration. One of the first pieces of legislation that was passed when Australia became a nation was the Immigration Restriction Act, which formalized mechanisms for adhering to a "white Australia." Against this background, boats occupy a particular place in the Australian psyche, because they represent uncontrolled, unplanned entry (Higgins 2017). As an anxiety-ridden settler colony, fearful of its outpost position from the mother country, Australia continues to articulate a national identity (even after the initial nation-building project) and assert dominant status (Hage 2000). This found its apotheosis in Prime Minister John Howard's legendary 2001 statement, "We will decide who comes to this country and the circumstances in which they come."

A political crisis was sparked when the Norwegian merchant vessel *Tampa* was refused entry to Australian waters, with 433 migrants seeking asylum (predominately Hazaras from Afghanistan) brought aboard from an Indonesian fishing boat (Marr and Wilkinson 2003). At the time of the *Tampa*'s arrival, the Howard coalition was faced with a looming election. In 1999, 3,721 asylum seekers arrived to Australia's shores, followed by 2,939 asylum seekers in 2000: small numbers compared with elsewhere, but inflated by the Labour opposition. Howard needed to maintain electoral support in the Australian hinterlands, where the notion of "boat people" had gained scapegoating appeal under Pauline Hanson's One Nation Party. The Howard coalition enflamed Australian popular opinion around the need to contain "the boat people," preying on deep-rooted fears around "boat people," "queue jumpers," and "illegals," and sensationalizing the numbers of attempted arrivals. But refugees present conditions unusual in other forms of resource extraction and human carceral industries because there is a widespread activist movement in support of the moral values of asylum. At the time of the *Tampa*, a vocal activist lobby argued that the Australian government needed to bring the asylum seekers to Australia, heightening immigration policy, refugees, and asylum seekers into a politically charged issue.

When the *Tampa* arrived, the Australia government was at an impasse with where to send people. Although the boat's captain was widely lauded as a hero, "a maritime Good Samaritan" (Crock 2003, 49) who undertook "a dangerous rescue mission in heavy seas, hauling asylum seekers to safety" (Lusher and Haslam 2007, 52), he was, involved senior Australian bureaucrats informed me, under the duress of his boat passengers, who insisted he take them to Australia. This intensified the stalemate. Not keen to appear devoid of compassion or a soft touch, the Australian Immigration Department did not want to accept the attempted arrivals, but had difficulty with where to send them. The Indonesian government were fed up with the Australian policy of pushing back boats into their territorial waters, and refused to take the Australian phone calls. Alexander Downer, the Australian foreign minister, later recalled, "Howard said to me, 'Go and find someone who'll take them.' So, I went back up to my office and got my staff together there and said, 'Well now, we are literally going to have to think up a country to send these people to that'll take them.' One of my staff, she said 'Well, look, you had that call from Rene Harris, the president of Nauru, a week or so ago pleading for AU$200,000 or AU$300,000 so he could pay for some oil, so what about ringing him?' That was a good idea I thought. So, I rang Rene Harris and he said, 'Yeah, that would be fine.'"[15]

As soon as the new site was found, the Australian government put through a series of migration amendment acts that excised islands and ports from Australia's migration zone.[16] Anyone claiming asylum at an excised place or in Australian waters by boat without a valid visa would be transferred to Nauru or Papua New Guinea for "offshore refugee processing." In the first era, next to no effort was made to develop a long-term refugee processing or resettlement site. All migrants certified as refugees were ultimately resettled outside of Nauru; those whose claims were denied were returned to their countries of origin or an alternative destination. Nor was there any effort to indigenize the refugee operations to Nauru and develop a body of laws and principles for the small country around refugee status determination and resettlement. The emphasis was on "offshore," not "regional" processing.

The Nauruan government and public wanted little to do with the operations, some fearful of their new arrivals: 1,465 asylum seekers across the course of the first phase, 2001–2008. Few locals wanted the operations to go on for longer than required to secure the much-needed resurgency cash: an AU$20 million down payment, AU$100 million in foreign aid, and an emergency grant of AU$12 million in 2003 to pay public servants' Christmas wages (Appi 2012). The operations took place at a processing site enclaved deep in Nauru's phosphate extraction fields, Topside, and later in the former state house buildings, contractually managed by the International Organization for Migration (IOM). First UNHCR and then Australian Immigration Department personnel assessed each asylum seeker under Australian law, with the intermittent assistance of Australian mainland refugee defense lawyers. Nauruan residents held menial jobs in facility management, cleaning, and security: a thousand locals at the peak of the operations. In 2007, the newly elected Rudd Labour government halted the offshore arrangement, under accumulated activist pressure. Instead, they moved toward a system of Australian mainland and Christmas Island processing. Nauru's last asylum seekers were processed and then resettled in Australia by the following year.

A Depressing Time for the Financial Barometer

But by 2012, waves of change were again brewing far beyond Nauru. The Labour government—headed by Rudd and then Gillard—was still in power. However, with a looming election, fears of the "boat people" had resurged in the Australian public, fueled by the opposition Liberal coalition, now under Tony Abbott. The Labour government's policies had resulted in a steady increase in migrant boat arrivals, latched onto by the Abbott government as evidence of Labour's weakness. The Abbott coalition found popular currency with their political line of "turning back the boats," presented in security but also humanitarian terms through a reversed angle of "protecting lives at sea."[17] The refugee crisis scares, the War on Terror residues of 9/11, and reports of spiraling numbers also generated more paranoia and popular revulsion around boat people and the places they came from.

Not to be outdone, the Labour government quickly followed suit, taking a stronger stand on undocumented boat arrivals outside of Australia's regulated system of refugee resettlement or outside of asylum claims by nonmaritime means. Initially, Labour did not move toward offshore processing in Nauru. Due to some of Nauru's past controversies, made prominent by activist campaigners, the government explored other maritime border enforcement strategies to display to voters. The government was also keen to create more permanent third-country resettlement operations within a regional cooperation framework (RCF). This would send asylum seekers to one long-term site far beyond Australia for processing and resettlement.

Like the chemists of Nauru's phosphate yesteryear, lawyers and a new class of refugee industry professionals had been hard at work developing solutions to the human-movement conundrum. In particular, in a climate of public disinterest, UNHCR, the international refugee agency, has become ever more concerned with their own global relevance and institutional capital, brokering refugee resettlement relations between countries. UNHCR's new Pacific regional policy of the RCF came out of the Bali Process, a network forum set up in 2002, shortly after the *Tampa* arrival. The Bali Process was designed for regional governments to broker deals around migrants outside of national asylum systems. Through Bali process involvement, UNHCR and IOM—the network's overall convener—broker and invent mechanisms of refugee resettlement cooperation, like those adapted to Nauru, while protecting their capitalist and strategic interests.[18]

Before Nauru's resurrection as a long-term processing site, the Australian and Malaysian governments looked to create a third-country system of resettlement. But the plan met with high-profile action from Australia's major refugee rights players. A high court ruling led by Melbourne refugee defense lawyer David Manne removed the possibility of Malaysia as a seat of third-country resettlement, despite UNHCR agreeing to the industry contract for refugee processing. In a challenge spearheaded by Australian refugee lawyers, and an unlikely alliance between the Green and Liberal coalition parties, the judgment stipulated that Malaysia was not legally bound by international law and so could not provide appropriate refugee protection.[19] Australia's Migration Act incorporates the Refugee Convention into state law. The high court decried that refugee resettlement alliances could only be made with countries that had signed the Refugee

Convention.[20] In response to the popular propaganda to end offshore operations (Amnesty and Australian activists widely circulated depictions of Malaysians as refugee beaters), and given a lack of UN support, the East Timorese government opted against the offer. Other Pacific Island governments had already expressed reservations in the past about "the unknown risks" of the "emerging refugees market," which would have "adverse impacts on our communal life as Pacific communities" (Australian Government 2002). Nauru, meanwhile, still reeling from the 2008 closure, having just recognized the republics of Abkhazia and South Ossetia in financial desperation, flew a government minister out to Geneva to accede to the Refugee Convention, the Convention against Torture (CAT), and its Optional Protocol (OPCAT).[21] They also became Bali Process members, opening their island wholeheartedly to refugee processing.

But the Labour government was still reticent to reopen Nauru's offshore processing sites. In June 2012, Gillard and the minister for immigration and citizenship, Chris Bowen, set up the Expert Panel on Asylum Seekers. This brought together Air Chief Marshal Angus Houston (a retired senior officer of the Royal Australian Air Force), Professor Michael L'Estrange (former head of the Australian National University's National Security College, Howard advisor, and Department of Foreign Affairs and Trade [DFAT] chief), and Paris Aristotle (one of Australia's leading refugee advocates, government resettlement advisor, and CEO of the Victorian Foundation for Survivors of Torture, which was contracted to provide refugee counseling services across Australia). Drawing on consultations and written submissions across sectors, the panel controversially backed reinstating Nauru and Manus as "a circuit breaker" to "reduce the attractiveness of Australia as a destination point for irregular migration" (Expert Panel on Asylum Seekers 2012, 12), along with upping Australian refugee resettlement quotas and those for asylum seekers by any means other than maritime arrival.

This was a blow for the Gillard government. They failed to enact their meticulously planned Malaysia deal, which had taken months of careful brokerage. They were now faced with having to use the opposition's bill of reinstating Nauru and Manus. With the recommendation to establish offshore processing legislation, the Gillard government obtained UNHCR's begrudging blessing from the Geneva headquarters. In 2012, Gillard and Nauru's then president, Sprent Dabwido, signed a memorandum of understanding, and the Nauruan refugee business was reinstated. Meanwhile, in September 2013, the Abbott coalition won a landslide victory against the Rudd Labour government, pointing toward the offshore closure "bungles" (P. Kelly 2014).[22] They gave assurances of "stopping the boats" through the grand spectacle of offshore deterrence, which solidified into primary bipartisan policy.

The Jewel in the Crown

> There had to be absolute guarantees against non-refoulement and then there
> were all the other issues in the crock around education for children, training
> for adults, adequate healthcare, and all of the appropriate oversight and mon-
> itoring mechanisms and all of those things that form part of the architecture
> for managing how you process asylum seekers anywhere in the world.
>
> —Offshore refugee advisor, Canberra, personal interview, 2015

Like in the phosphate years previously, refugee legal and social workers got to
work quickly to make the new offshore refugee town, "perhaps unequalled in
any industry in the British Empire" (BPC 1929, 19). Because of the operation's
controversial nature and significant number of Australian contractors involved,
the operations had to be in line with Australian occupational standards. Having decided to push ahead with the scheme, neither the Australian nor Nauruan
governments wanted the political or economic devastation of a high court challenge that saw the project's reversal. Central to the Expert Panel's recommendations was that the operations must be subject to clear guiding principles. In
their report, they advised that mechanisms would need to be in place to process
people effectively as per international standards, such as those disseminated by
UNHCR in guidebooks like *Handbook and Guidelines on Procedures and Criteria for Determining Refugee Status* (2011) and *Refugee Resettlement: An International Handbook to Guide Reception and Integration* (2002). These handbooks
served as forms of technocratic governance for designing the operations. These
guidelines, and other standards, were later referenced by affiliated government
and agencies in arguing that the operations met best practice.[23]

As Australia was the project's financier, site of industrial expertise, and overall supplier of human resources, the task fell principally on the Australian government to build Nauru's refugee operations. As per the Expert Panel report and
stipulations of UNHCR bureaucrats, international and state agencies would need
authorization to quality-control and risk-assure the offshore manufacturing
sites. Stalwart businesses and bureaucracies like UNHCR, the Red Cross, and
the Committee for the Prevention of Torture (CPT), and state statutory organizations like the Commonwealth Ombudsman and Comcare Health and Safety
would go with a fine-tooth comb over Nauru's processing sites with heightened
concern. They would check the country's compliance against standard operating procedures, and stopper the risks attached to the offshoring of refugee processing operations. The system needed to be legally watertight from these
pragmatic standpoints, but many government bureaucrats on both shores also

held a deep belief in the morality of asylum. For government staff, offshore processing might be a vote-winning imperative, but many wanted the operations conducted as benevolently as possible, as long as they lay under the enforcement spectacle of maritime deterrence.

There were several more pressing reasons to ensure that the reality of Nauru met international protocols. International law is only binding in Australia if cited in national legislation. Section 198a of the Migration Act (1958) binds the Australian government into Geneva Convention obligations. Together, Australia and Nauru as refugee processing partners cannot:

> (i) *refoule* a person to "another country where his or her life or freedom would be threatened on account of his or her race, religion, nationality, membership of a particular social group or political opinion"; and must
>
> (ii) make an assessment, or permit an assessment to be made, of whether or not a person taken to the country under that section is covered by the definition of refugee in Article 1A of the Refugees Convention as amended by the Refugees Protocol.

Because parliamentary legislation codifies the Geneva Convention, the Australian High Court takes seriously attempts to break international, and by default, state law. Eagle-eyed activists are always on the lookout for legal flout, as with the Malaysia RCF loophole. Importantly, this time round, the Australian government looked to emphasize the shift from *offshore* to *regional* processing. The project was not about extrapolating industry operations from Australia, but *training* Nauruans to carry out refugee determination and resettlement procedures. Regional cooperation required distributing roles between countries. If Australian workers took on too much obvious responsibility, it might present loopholes for Australia's legal teams working to end offshore operations. As one of Nauru's planners, an Australian Immigration Department official, explained to me in interview, "There was a real question around how do you second an Australian officer to make a decision about an international obligation to an individual on behalf of another country. Who has an obligation to provide protection to that person? There's a chance that we'd invoke some sort of a protection obligation." Creating national refugee operations for Nauru aligned with the Australian government's line that sending asylum seekers to Nauru transferred their international obligations. It also aligned with the Nauruan government's goal of extracting more revenue through increased local employment. In order to cement this position, the two governments openly changed Nauru's designation from an "offshore processing country" to a "regional processing country."

A Refugee Terra Nullius

In 2012, at the dawn of round two of processing asylum seekers, Nauru had none of the labor or industrial expertise to run an asylum and resettlement operation in "the mainland style." Previously, Nauruan residents had held menial jobs in facility management, cleaning, and security. No one in Nauru was trained in conducting refugee status determination, in refugee social work, or medical care. Most of Nauru's past infrastructure had fallen into disrepair, requisitioned as phosphate corporation premises, or ransacked by locals for useful spare parts. The tropical climate had taken its toll on the Menen Hotel—the logical port of call for accommodating the large fly-in-fly-out workforce required for the operations. Little in the way of Australian health and safety standards were being met. Electrics at the Menen were unsafe and bound to fail Australian occupational health and safety requirements. Materials, tradesmen, and laborers would need to be brought in from the Australian mainland, given the shortage of skilled labor and materials on Nauru. All these extensive works would have to be geared around the three-month monsoon season, which extended from November to February. As one Australian government official succinctly put it to me, "When I arrived on Nauru, all I could say was 'bugger.'"

But like in the pioneering phosphate days, persistency persevered. As the refugee processing and resettlement industry is such a well-honed sector in Australia, tendering processes tempted many organizations to expand their readymade fabric to the small country. Specializations in remote environments are also easy to come by, owing to Australian outback and offshore mining work throughout the Pacific region. However, the necessity of involving such a number of Australian contractors meant further obligations for financial investment. Not only would there be on-the-ground regulation but, as chapter 3 details, the Immigration Department could not evade Australian occupational health and safety requirements. Extensive refurbishments would be required to bring the infrastructure to Australian certifiable standards. In the Australian Immigration Department's first financial year of Nauru's reopening (2012–2013), a total of AU$344 million was spent on the project, from operating and capital expenditure to departmental costs. In the following 2013–2014 financial year, this rose to AU$1.3 billion as the country was packed full of the refugee expertise, enterprise, and institutional practice at work in Australia and worldwide. "Because of the 'stop the boat' thing, money has not been an issue when it comes to Nauru," an offshore planner in Sydney remarked to me.

As elsewhere, a mix of NGOs, INGOs, and commercial businesses found industry contracts as "refugee service providers" on Nauru in what was often described as a "mundane" tendering process. They brought in, in the words of one offshore policy advisor I spoke with in Canberra, "all of those things that form part of the architecture for managing how you process asylum seekers anywhere in the world." From refugee legal claims and medical services to operational security and child welfare, numerous organizations buoyed Nauru's refugee developmental practice. Canstruct Pty Ltd construction solutions, Craddock Murray Neuman Lawyers, International Health and Medical Services, Overseas Survivors of Torture and Trauma, Royal Flying Doctors, Save the Children Australia, Translating and Interpreting Service National, Transfield Services, and Wilson Security are but some of the major firms that found success in the tendering process. Nauru once again became something of a charter company colony, but now to the neoliberal outsourced (and locally advantageous) extreme. I came into daily contact with many refugee industry personnel, most of who performed the same work in Australia and worldwide. Many had long-standing CV credentials in forced migration and refugee studies from industry disciplinary institutions. As they all piled into Nauru, I recognized many as central industry workers from Australia and elsewhere, having spent the previous nine months interviewing CEOs and staff in Australian boardrooms and coffee shops and seen them at refugee studies conferences including in Bristol to Bangkok.

Some, like Transfield Services and Wilson Security, hold experience in offshore mineral mining sectors, entering the refugee industry as new corporate players. Others, such as Brisbane Catholic Education Services, have troubling histories of colonial-era assimilationist indigenous education in Australia. These dynamics reveal the postcolonial continuities of the contemporary raced markets that thrive on governing new populations.[24] On more than one occasion, I also met offshore refugee workers who had relatives who had once worked in Nauru's phosphate industry, as the overlapping imperial histories of extraction found their apotheosis in Nauru. These kinds of connections are not merely happenstance but actually commonplace. They point to the political economic entanglements of Australia's and Nauru's industrial environments, which are based on a history of close labor connections and socioeconomic dependency in the region. It also brings into sharp focus the guiding forces of global patterns of extractivism, whereby Nauru occupies the front lines of toxic industry environments.

As anthropologists have all too often found in hazardous industrial contexts (Murphy 2016; Petryna 2002), refugee expertise was also crucial to the building of Nauru's new industry world. Under the terms of the Nauru memorandum of understanding, the Australian government established a Joint Advisory Committee for Regional Processing Arrangements (JAC). JAC was divided into two subcommittees: (1) the Refugee Status Determination (RSD) and Claims Assistance Subcommittee and (2) the Physical and Mental Health Subcommittee. The Physical and Mental Health Subcommittee focused on enhancing medical provisions in the processing centers and the local hospital, whereas the RSD Sub-committee advised on matters relating to refugee processing operations. The subcommittees consisted largely of Australian representatives from mainland advisory bodies and prominent refugee legal and medical industry profession-als. The Nauruan government were keen to uphold excellence in their refugee operations, but had little idea of what refugee determination entailed. While con-cern for human welfare and the rule of law was for many their raison d'être, none had devoted their work to specializing in refugees. A few Nauruan gov-ernment representatives held positions in JAC, but this was largely a token ges-ture. While labeled as a joint endeavor, the committees consisted almost entirely of Australian representatives, in which UNHCR staff maintained observational status, giving advice around operational improvements.

The other notable challenge was the need to train Nauruans in conducting refugee status determination—a commonplace industry practice explored in chapter 2. To qualify an Australian public servant takes a minimum of six months. The training is intense: the determination trainee observes others mak-ing credibility assessments, they are then observed and quality-controlled over a long period. Refugee assessors also have access to information-sharing provi-sions with other countries such as the United States in places like Iraq and Af-ghanistan, which can be used to inform the decision making of an individual's credibility of fear. While the Australian government is closely allied with the American government, one of only four countries in the "Five Eyes" arrange-ment, the Nauruan government has a colorful history of US diplomatic relations. They have a legacy of offshore banking with Russia in the late nineties, launder-ing AU$70 billion of funds (Hughes 2004), and selling passports across the Middle East (a thousand passports by 2003 for AU$1,500 each).[25] The small yet entrepreneurial country has also had instantaneous alliances with China over Taiwan depending on the financial offer of the day, including close relations with Cuba.[26] They then had the history of Operation Weasel in 2003: a failed deal with the CIA in which they were set to lodge North Korean scientists in their shop-front Beijing embassy in exchange for cash payments.[27]

With this past, Nauru was unlikely to ever be given access to the allied information-sharing provisions required for RSD assessment in the "mainland style." As an Australian Immigration Department official tasked with setting up the operations explained to me, "Without the intel data access, even the most qualified Nauruan officer will still not be able to make as a strong a decision as an Australian officer and that's in the best case scenario across the board. That's not what we've got on Nauru." Nor were any Nauruans I spoke with interested in or felt legally capable of being part of the legal determination operations. In a country that has relied on extrajudicial authority since colonial rule, lawyers are a handful in number. This was another part of the colonial legacies that enabled Nauru's refugee industry, underscored by deep civilizational and developmental hierarchies of Nauru as an uncivilized backwater. Although many Nauruans held the international asylum system in great esteem, they felt unable to engage in some of the intricacies of its operations that were aligned globally with far-away white Western liberal democracies. And so, while outwardly stressing that "Australia's role extends to assistance and support only . . . departmental staff are not decision makers" (Australian Government 2013), "Nauru is responsible for the RSD process . . . it is the case that Nauru manages and controls the RSD process" (Mackinnon 2014), labor for the RPCs—like Nauru's phosphate era before it—also came through an influx of Australian workers into Nauruan government positions. Instead, in this new industrial era, Nauruans took on superficial high-ranking and menial positions. The Nauruan secretary for justice gave his final shop-front signature to refugee determinations, behind which operated a back office manned by Australian-seconded "Nauruan government" employees.

The demand for labor was so overwhelming that other Pacific Islanders were once again attracted by Nauru's new boomtown possibilities. Islanders from Samoa, the Marshall Islands, and Fiji flocked to Nauru in search of lucrative job opportunities in the refugee industry and the island's resurging development terrain: as security personnel, teachers, doctors, lawyers, government workers, shopkeepers, and more. The small island's population mushroomed from 10,279 in 2012 to 13,049 by 2016.

A Refugee Company Town

> Here was material in scores of millions of tons which would "make the desert bloom like the rose" . . . One could visualise a great industry springing up on this lonely spot, quite dwarfing all of our previous efforts.
> —Albert Ellis describing his first impression of the phosphate deposits on Nauru, May 28, 1900 (Williams 1971)

When I arrived in 2015, the extent to which the Australian government had gone to build the country in the "mainland style" was astounding. Nauru revolved around industrial manufacture like the days of yesteryear, remade as a refugee company town. Processing sites had gone up with rapid speed: RPC 1, RPC 2, and RPC 3 in the country's old phosphate heartlands. Nauru's phosphate-financed airline, Nauru Airlines, was reinvigorated as Our Airlines, now importing asylum seekers to Nauru. "Pursuing the fastest growth in the company's 18—year history," they added three aircrafts to their fleet during 2014 alone. In

FIGURE 6A. The Republic of Nauru Phosphate Corporation company bus driving on the main road conducting workers' collection rounds. Photo by Julia Morris.

FIGURE 6B. The Transfield Services refugee company town bus driving on the main road conducting workers' collection rounds. Photo by Julia Morris.

this reinvigorated company town era, asylum seekers were processed in Nauru's shining new RPCs. Those who were successful were then given Nauruan refugee visas: first for five years, then ten years, extended on an ad hoc rolling cycle. The Nauruan government took AU$1,000 per person per month in visa fees, their second largest source of revenue, at some AU$9 million per year. As more asylum seekers were certified as refugees, resettlement housing was soon added, air conditioned and built of steel, complete with separate Australian-run generators. When certified, refugees were assigned resettlement housing around Nauru by Australian contracted caseworkers. Now, electric light and Wi-Fi emanated from the refugee-processing, resettlement, and worker residential sites, all of which glimmered at night, "giving the impression, when viewed from a few miles out at sea, of an approach to a great town" (BPC 1929, 58).

Like "the occupational hierarchy of the plant . . . imposed upon the town" in the company town arrangements described by J. D. Porteous (1970, 411), segregated zoning was also a part of the refugee industry environment. Asylum seekers and refugees were contained in separate securitized housing compounds. These industry enclaves corresponded with race, nationality, gender, and the inequalities of the global state system that disallowed their movement elsewhere. When some asylum seekers began receiving unsuccessful refugee status determinations, asylum appeals courts extended the operations. Charter jets then forcibly deported denied asylum seekers from Nauru—just one of the many violent effects of this human extractive industry, discussed in chapter 2.

Meanwhile, the high-rung Australian offshore project administrators, on fly-in-fly-out cycles from Australia, occupied former phosphate administrators' large residences up on the hill. These commodious abodes were still fringed with bougainvillea from the phosphate industry years, and open to the cool sea breeze. Every one of the "stag" bungalows for lower-rung industry workers (shared with two, sometimes three to a room) was made from gleaming white aluminum and steel, now named things like "Den's Place," "Pak's Corner," and "Lad's Corner." Brand-new white trucks and shipped-over Land Rovers were parked outside, all with attached safety hazard lights for heading up to the phosphate-turned-refugee extraction fields.[28] The ordered quadrants of BPC blue-collar housing were now occupied by Nauruan landowners, the BPC phosphate leases since expired. Most company town residences had sunk into abandon without the BPC corporate sheen. Long gone were the nine-hole golf course and cricket pavilion of the phosphate company town days. Now, refugee industry workers set up an outdoor picture theater comprised of an inflatable screen on special occasions. Workers watched Aussie rules football games from chairs set out under the stars.

Australian refugee industry workers frequently took to walking the country through the Nauru Hash House Harriers: a colonial-style walking group first set up during the industry's arrival in 2001. These events starkly extended Nauru's racializing segregations from the phosphate years, as only Australian political and industrial elites or Taiwanese diplomats ever attended. Company-organized events also flourished, but as chapters 4 and 5 detail, not to such widespread success. However, company football thrived as major contractors encouraged local teams by sponsoring football jerseys. Company town newspapers

FIGURE 7A. Phosphate corporate diversions: golf in British Phosphate Commission–era Nauru. Photo courtesy of the British Archives at Kew.

FIGURE 7B. Refugee corporate diversions: the Nauru Hash House Harriers. Photo by Julia Morris.

provided statistics on the numbers of asylum seekers and refugees in the country, as well as pictures of the blessing ceremonies of the new RPC buildings that cropped up with rapid speed. Visiting dignitaries would often be toured around Nauru's refugee processing centers alongside phosphate industrial operations.

In *The Magical State*, Fernando Coronil (1997, 5) looks at the processes by which Venezuela, a once poor agrarian country, became the site of rapid wealth accumulation with the expansion of the oil industry. Coronil discusses the Venezuelan dream that came along with the rise and fall of the Venezuelan petrostate, referring to the "oil illusions" produced by state leaders of a Venezuela flush with rampant progress and modernity. At the time of Venezuela's oil boom, the state leaders glorified themselves as "agents of progress" and "modernity," proclaiming Venezuela's "second independence": "manufacturing dazzling development projects that engender collective fantasies of progress, [petro-magic] casts its spell over audiences and performer alike. As a 'magnanimous sorcerer,' the state seizes its subjects by inducing a condition or state of being receptive to its illusions—a magical state." Like the mythic land of oil fantasy described by Coronil (1997, 2), the Nauruan government presented themselves as "magnanimous sorcerers" through "exalted self-representations," "fashioning political life into a dazzling spectacle of national progress."

In the past, political instability has characterized Nauru's ever-rotating government chambers. In the forty-two years since independence in 1968, there have been thirty-six changes in government, on average a new government after every 1.16 years (Ratuva 2011). But while Nauru's parliamentary system has seen a cycle of presidents, President Baron Waqa remained in office for six years, from June 2013 to August 2019, including for the vast majority of the offshore refugee industry's second instantiation, and throughout the entirety of my fieldwork. Waqa was charismatic, well educated, and generally well liked by the public, and under him, the political system remained stable.[29] David Adeang, his second-in-command at the time, and who remains a high-profile figure in the Nauruan government to this day, does not have the same charm but undoubtedly has the business acumen. Ascending the ranks through different ministerial portfolios, Adeang has been indispensable in keeping Nauru on an even keel. This stability is grounded on the contribution of refugee industry wealth toward the country's sustainability, including the amount of interest in regulating the operations. Now that Nauru again has a resource sector for economic resurgence, the IMF, the World Bank, the Asian Development Bank, and UN development agencies, among others, all agreed to help Nauru achieve long-term sustainable development goals, as much as Nauruans are keen to elicit their assistance.[30]

"Ladies and gentlemen, in my government's effort to improve the livelihoods of Nauruans, we have honored our pledges of giving back what belongs to the people," declared Baron Waqa in his 2015 Independence Day speech. "We have honored and paid all pending salaries . . . we have also paid backpay salaries to all government employees. In addition, we are up to date on all land lease payments for properties in use by Government and state-owned enterprise. This is unprecedented in our history and my Government will be fair and continue to honor what is owed to the people." With the economic boom once again on the rise—six hundred asylum seekers were sent to Nauru to start (for the Australian government at that time, an industry of AU$859,363 per person per day)—the government began repaying backdated phosphate mining. In 2014, they liquidated the Nauru Phosphate Royalties Trust with holdings of over AU$90 million, distributed to local landowners. Mobile phones, Wi-Fi services, and Bendigo Bank all came to the country. The Nauruan government reopened the state supermarket, refurbished and crowned with the country's first automatic teller machine. The newly invigorated Air Nauru, now renamed Our Airlines, purchased a third aircraft to cater to the increase in offshore worker and local demand. Locals once again holidayed in Brisbane, flush with land-leasing and RPC employment wealth, not to mention a host of other entrepreneurial schemes.

As in the phosphate years, the vision of local profitability was brought into resurgence. Shares in firms like Transfield Services were now given to local administrators and bought by a number of Australian industry personnel I spoke with, working for NGOs, government agencies, and commercial firms alike. As my opening vignette with Georgia described, landowners earned money from leasing the land for the refugee processing and resettlement housing. The system of land holdings that developed out of the *Grundbuch* formed the administrative frame for refugee land leasing. Now, land acquired new forms of value tied into refugees, which added to copra and phosphate value from the past company town days.

Refugees, like phosphate and copra in centuries past, appeared as a mass commodity that was represented as Nauru's savior. A number of entrepreneurial local schemes took over, including stocking supermarkets with halal cuisine: catering to the new company town demographics created by a human import commodity (largely Iranians, Afghanis, Pakistanis, and Sri Lankans). But underneath this fabulous fiction, the extractive operations were plagued with toxic tolls. Alongside the magical displays of the effects of refugee wealth in the local papers—"New home owners awarded housing loan from the Nauru government's housing scheme" (Republic of Nauru 2012a) and "Civil servants and private sector learn innovative new business ideas" (Republic of Nauru 2012b)—other company town hazards became commonplace. "A group of transferees at the processing centre are engaging in a peaceful protest. They have also indicated they have stopped eating meals" (Republic of Nauru 2012b); "Ten asylum seekers to stand trial in April over rioting charges" (Republic of Nauru 2013)—such stories hinted at some of the country's violent extractive consequences. While the numbers of asylum seekers sent to Nauru are small, in comparison to Nauru's wider population, these influxes are significant for the country and the global border spectacle at large. In fact, Nauru's newest extractive industry has dramatically shaped a new "company town" world, whereby a landscape of human extraction has been superimposed over the landscapes of earlier commodities, each with their own modes of toxic violence.

Nor did the glittering performance of resource magic sufficiently dazzle and divert the Nauruan public. The culture of the refugee industry is similar to other extractive industries but has its own characteristics. The realities of forcibly processing and resettling humans—and particularly the moral toxicity around the figure of the asylum seeker and refugee—in the country provoked far more hazards that the state's modes of magical capture could counterbalance. While a storyline of invasion and deterrence is used to garner Australian public support for Nauru, a politics of fear and compassion fatigue also converged around the idea of "refugees" in Nauru. These fears all came to interact in and shape Nauruans' fears of their new imported resource. Activism in Australia against offshoring asylum seekers and refugees also made Nauru subject to an unprecedented level of social conflicts and global derision. The country has been the target of a tremendous activist scene, with discourses leveled of savagery and underdevelopment. In the meantime, organizers in Australia frequently portray the offshore arrangement as an exception that operates against (not in fact through) the refugee legal system. However, as I argue in chapter 2, refugee legal systems are also implicated as forms of border enforcement, looking to distil the "deserving" from "undeserving" migrant, but under the banner of humanitarianism. These discourses further benefit organizations that often have teams of trained individuals at their disposal to carry out the work required in other boomtown regions, thus ensuring the iterability of this extractive arrangement.

MINERAL MEETS MIGRANT METALLURGIES

Phosphate—key to life. A miracle of nature harnessed by man's ingenuity for the benefit of all. An island shrouded by repetitive routine behind which lies a prolonged continuity of persistent endeavor and technical awareness.

—Nauru Philatelic Bureau, 1983

I cling to the back of Tony's motorbike as we rattle up the dusty track, making our way to Nauru's Topside phosphate extraction fields. The air is thick with clouds of rock and dust that billow about the potmarked landscape. The vast majority of soil and vegetation has been stripped away—80 percent of the country's surface area subject to strip-mining—leaving a barren wasteland of limestone and coral. In some places, up to forty feet of earth has been gorged out in the hunt for $Ca_3(PO_4)_2$. The sunbaked pinnacles ward off the possibility of rainfall quenching the landscape and reigniting growth or restoring the pandanus and coconut groves that once covered the country's upper atoll. The occasional warble of a black noddy bird (*Anous minutus*) is just perceptible from its nesting tree tucked deep in the pinnacles. A cultural symbol of Nauru and ceremonial food source, noddies are threatened by the loss of trees and light pollution from phosphate mining in the Topside district. It is the stark fluorescent lights that emanate from the refugee processing centers, local hunters show me on multiple occasions, that now contribute to dwindling hunting yields. Histories of extraction and hunting pressures have burdened the island's fragile ecosystems, pushing noddy birds to migrate elsewhere.[1]

After asking around about an exploratory trip of Nauru's phosphate mining fields, I was introduced to Tony. Many people said that Tony would be the best guide to the country's industrial sites, and they were right. A local islander in his late fifties, who spoke impeccable English from time spent at boarding school in Melbourne, like so many others in his phosphate boomer generation, Tony is no stranger to the industry. One eye missing, voice caked in dust—the legacy of a

FIGURE 8.   Sifting the contaminate from dry limestone rock. Photo by Julia Morris.

lifetime growing up and then working in the industry—he is well versed in phosphate hazards.

Nauru is a country where the phosphate industry and its attendant pollutancies—toxic waste, respiratory and diet-related diseases, and dependency—are palpable. The effects of phosphate extraction are not felt just by those directly employed in extraction fields and processing factories, like Tony, but extend far beyond the labor-intensive point of production. From 1906, Nauru's phosphate ore has been mined and exported in earnest to global agriculturalists. Ironically, this has left little viable ecosystem for Nauru's agricultural development. Phosphate wealth might have industrialized Nauru, but it has left a cycle of dependency on imported fast foods (McLennan 2017). Nauru's healthcare system is wracked with the consequences of colonial interventionism (McLennan and Ulijaszek 2014). The last published Nauruan Ministry of Health report (2011) found 77.8 percent of Nauru's population to be overweight and 45.6 percent obese. In 1975, the prevalence of diabetes in Nauru was 34.4 percent. This ranked Nauruans second in the world for the highest ever recorded rate of diabetes, as they simultaneously placed second in the world for per capita GDP, after Saudi Arabia. Now, with the government spending approximately 20 percent of its annual health care expenditure on diabetes, the numbers have fallen slightly (Thu Win Tin et al. 2015). But at 30 percent, Nauru still has one of the highest diabetic rates in the world. These rates are coupled with a spectrum of diet-related noncommunicable diseases, including cardiovascular disease, stroke, and heart attacks. Preventable cancers, including gastrointestinal, cervical, and lung cancer are significant across the local population (Palafox et al. 2004). A life expectancy of fifty-five years is one of the byproducts of colonial-era lifestyle change, and the human costs of an extraction-based economy.

Nauru remains on the frontlines of toxic chemical exposure. In a number of respects, the country's latest industry in processing asylum seekers comes with tremendous pollutant effects, like the state's industrial enterprise of phosphate extraction. In the phosphate industry, dry rock circulates on conveyer belt extraction rounds. Dust and toxins are released into the atmosphere from an unnatural metallurgical process, all with immense social and ecological repercussions. In Nauru's refugee industry, human bodies were fed through a dangerous legal manufacturing cycle of untold human and economic costs. What this chapter seeks to do is bring Nauru's two major industries into conversation to detail the harms that are a part of both extractive sectors. In the refugee industry, the particular forms of ecological damage are human in nature. People are compelled to present themselves through legal narratives of trauma and enter into the exploitative realm of this labor market for their survival: what I show to be a form of "intimate extraction," based on my understanding of asylum as a form of unfree labor. Like other dehumanizing labor regimes, self-harm, anger, fear, and frustration were everyday realities in Nauru. Here, I draw on conversations with migrants as to their experiences in undergoing asylum adjudication. Recalling phosphate's extractive consequences, I emphasize the violent effects of this metallurgical process, in which objectification and ideological differentiation are central.

I have repeatedly drawn the analogy between phosphate and refugees, but it is no coincidence that these extractive operations converge on the lives of minority populations. Asylum seekers and Nauruans have to endure the kind of heavy pollution and degrading treatment that Steve Lerner (2010) describes as "a sacrifice zone." Across extractive sectors, scholars have found that environmental racism plays a crucial part in where toxic industries are located: all too often in minority and low-income communities (Auyero and Swistun 2009; Bullard 1990; Lerner 2010). These uneven placements have important resonances with the geographies of containment that are taking shape across the Global South, and the people—largely black and brown—whose lives they impact (Besteman 2020). From industrial pollutants in the body to the psychological suffering of asylum, the lives of poor people of color are entangled in the forces of capital and disproportionately subject to toxic materials, experiences, and discourses. Toxicologists and scholars looking at toxic industries describe this as the "body burden," to account for the accumulated presence of harmful substances in the body (Agard-Jones 2013; Murphy 2016). In my view, the disproportionate exposures of hypercriminalization, violence, and precarity that black and brown migrants are subject to, as part of a differential access to mobility, are also a form of environmental racism that is being enacted on migrants' bodies globally. The health of migrants is sacrificed and not protected to the same degree as the health of the affluent and majority white, whose movement is readily allowed elsewhere. Instead, poor migrants of color disproportionately absorb the burden of the spectacle of Global North protectionism on their bodies, as do Nauruans. In the meantime, these exposures amplify Global North consumption. Western publics unceasingly consume the material and conceptual "border zones" between citizen and alien, home and colony, first and third world (Sheller 2003). Nauruans and poor migrants of color thus both work the underbelly of capitalism, where cheap labor is relied on for hyper profits.

For scholars attentive to the effects of toxic pollution, the story of Tony and the toxic substances that have wreaked havoc on his body is depressingly familiar. Yet, while the hazards of phosphate mining are now well documented (Emsley 2000; K. M. Teaiwa 2015), less understood are the toxic effects of asylum on people's lives. The majority of scholarship critical of asylum systems skews industrial risks in terms of the geographical or built environment in which RSD is conducted, such as immigration detention centers or offshored arrangements. Others pinpoint these harms to processes of border frontiering and shrinking spaces of asylum. The demanding asylum process that migrants go through is obscured under a kind of "commodity determinism" (Watts 2004), and little is said about the exploitative labor practices of acquiring refugee status. How these representations are angled matters. Framing extractive harms in relation to the built environment or incumbent politics elides the asylum operations that exasperate human harms. To use the extractive analogy again, this is much the same as arguing that it is the built environment of the factory, not the extractive operations themselves, that accounts for elevated rates of psychiatric disorders, self-harm, and suicide. Positivist rhetoric on asylum can conceal, and idolatrize, that people must recount intimate experiences and narratives of trauma in order to move elsewhere. Such depoliticizing frames spread the dominant ideology of the benevolence of asylum and can enforce similar industry setups elsewhere. Victimizing representations ironically give more moral value to the mobile global industry tasked to carry out the operations in places like Nauru on an everyday basis. Abuses are thus able to reoccur because it has become socially, culturally, and legally acceptable to put certain groups of people at risk and in demeaning power relations.

Part of the reason asylum appears to have gained so much authority is the power of industry supermajors in this field in relating the story of RSD and its effects to the security apparatuses of state power. This is connected to the "politics of invisibility" that Olga Kuchinskaya (2014) describes when looking at the health effects of radiation from Chernobyl in Belarus. The production and propagation of invisibility around radiation exposure involved efforts from experts and lay practices that redefine the scope of inquiry. Just as reframing radiological contamination requires infrastructural efforts, the harms of asylum are also concealed behind humanitarianism, labor, laws, and expertise that position asylum systems as benevolent. And yet, the concealment of the risks related to making an asylum claim is hardly a simple case of cold state or industry strategies. Rather, moral values and colonial histories of white salvationalism play as much a part as strategic geopolitical or financial value, whereby committed practitioners and publics feel as if they are bettering people's lives. The subjectification relations engendered among migrants are also directly implicated in rendering invisible the health effects of claiming asylum. Migrants have to redefine themselves to fit into certain categorizations: staking claims on their bodies in order to obtain resources for survival, and thus ensuring the continuity of the refugee industry.

This chapter examines the extractive practices that operate in Nauru whereby the country's mineral and migrant resources are assessed from raw materials into commodities. I start with a focus on phosphate processing, which sieves valuable mineral from dry rock. I then move to a detailed look at Nauru's latest enterprise in refugee processing, in which an asylum seeker's veracity is determined under the assessment of refugee status determination or RSD. By bringing phosphate and refugee assessment into dialogue, I aim to shed critical light on the toxic interrelationships between phosphate and refugee processing, and the laborers at their core. I also trace the specific historical continuities that led Nauru from one colonial extractive enterprise into another. Decades of uneven growth in Nauru meant that the country was more susceptible to another hazardous industry project than other sovereign territories in the vicinity. Nauru's histories of contamination simultaneously produce a "toxic layering" that acclimates residents to "the banality of toxicity" (Ahmann 2018). Islanders' multiple exposures are folded into particular dispositions surrounding the refugee industry. Yet, the crucial ties of Australia to Nauru are rarely made visible in ways that make clear how the organization and materialization of one industry shapes another. I think through these industrial overlaps and continuities in terms of Nauru's legal practice, as it has transitioned from phosphate to refugees. This means exploring the labor-intensive project of transnational refugee expertise that helped make Nauru's processing system a possibility and allows similar setups to modulate to other regions. Countering dominant representations that mythologize refugee legal institutions as emancipatory, I continue to ask how we can move toward a place where proving suffering and worth need not be a condition for people's mobility.

Phosphate Extractions

During my fieldwork, deforestation was advancing at a steady pace around Nauru. Not only were Nauru's once-untouched areas of agricultural fertility the targets of extraction, but mining was going deeper into the earth as the surface area available dwindled. When the BPC first began mining in Nauru, phosphate deposits were found close to the surface, about thirty to forty feet below ground. Large digging machines could easily remove the sandy topsoil to obtain the sand, clay, and rock mixture—the matrix—from which phosphate rock is extracted. As mining expanded at a heady rate across the twentieth century and post-Nauruan independence, primary reserves of phosphate were eventually exhausted in 2006. To continue to fulfil economic quotas, mining of secondary phosphate began the following year. The elongated grab buckets of the rehab-emblazoned extractor trucks that ply up and down the atoll are part of the secondary mining process. They signal the resource depletion panic as the government struggles to maintain political hold, and landowners clamor for the ease of phosphate dollars.

Most residents I spoke with gave a depressing sigh when discussing the expansion of excavation down from the island's phosphate plateau. But in longer conversations, they had contradictory responses to the continued—albeit haphazard—presence of mining on the island. Theirs is a story that diverges from those common to other mined territories, a story of desperate need in a region where work and resources have been disappearing (Auyero and Swistun 2009). For Nauruans, phosphate holds a significance that is much more than a commercial concern. Phosphate is a cultural identity, representative of independence and self-governance and embedded in the memories and imaginations of generations of Nauruans. The vision of nationhood and progress animated by the exuberance of the phosphate boom still saturates the country. Photos, posters, and ornaments of phosphate adorn hotel lobbies, government buildings, domestic and community spaces, signaling just how integral phosphate is to the Nauruan cultural imagination, and to contemporary global life. Growing up amid these postcolonial performances of cultural power, as Andrew Apter (2005) describes in oil-boom Nigeria, and the ecosystem of a company town designed to propagate these ideals, has given many Nauruans a complicated stance on the phosphate industry. Even in the face of environmental disaster and toxic danger, many islanders still retain a deep sense of pride in their history of phosphate independence. Phosphate holds meanings of self-determination and decolonization, and of Nauruans as powerbrokers in the region. On more than one occasion, islanders pointed out to me that, unlike nearby Banabans, bought out by the Phosphate Commission and relocated to Rabi Island in Fiji, Nauruans still lived on their land. Phosphate wealth and the retainment of their land in the face of dispossession contribute to the uneasy relationship that Nauruans have with the toxicity that surrounds them, in a country defined by the dictum "Tomorrow will take care of itself."

Tony, like other islanders, has a complex relationship with the phosphate industry. He is at once appalled by the bulldozing of forests and proud of the industry he has so long worked in, which catapulted Nauru onto the international stage and helped satisfy global consumptive demands. His concern about Nauru's hazardous production practices and toxic wastes seesaws against the undeniable importance of phosphate to Nauru's political economy and a pride in the global landscapes that Nauru helped to flourish. Pressing economic requirements also compete for Tony's attention to his endless health problems. He juggles an assortment of jobs to make ends meet, along with reef fishing for his family. Tony has resolved in earnest that I must see the phosphate industry's latest environmental incursions to get a fuller picture of the ecological damages brought about by mining. We pass through expanses that ten years ago would have been covered in tangled vegetation. Now, owing to sheer land depletion, many new areas have found themselves as sites of extraction. The talk at the moment is on Buada Lagoon. The sign that proclaims Buada as "the jewel of Nauru" as you enter the landlocked district is no exaggeration. Fringed by papaya and coconut trees, Buada is a far cry from the dust moonscape encountered elsewhere around the island. It is an area that Nauruans never fail to reference as an Edenic echo of a land that time forgot, from when the island was not so contaminated.

For me, Buada held joyous surprises. I spent the first weeks of my fieldwork worrying about vitamin deficiency. I consumed Birds Eye frozen peas and stockpiled apples on the days when flown-in shipments arrived from Australia to Nauru's government-owned supermarkets: part of the contradictory logics of the fertilizer nation. Nauru's phosphate is still exported to heighten the agricultural landscapes of countries like Australia, New Zealand, and Japan. But while the farmlands of the Global North reap the benefits of Nauruan phosphate, local islanders face minimal crop yields, flown-back wilted Australian produce, a stagnating life expectancy, and some of the highest diabetes and obesity rates worldwide. However, one month into my fieldwork, I learned that in Buada district's one hundred fertile hectares I could find wild cherimoya fruits and a local variety of swamp cabbage. The salt-soaked circumference of Nauru's lower

fringe and the land decimation of the country's upper one make this rich produce unique to Buada. In Buada's brackish lagoon, locals breed milkfish and ti-
lapia, following a tradition that harks back hundreds of years. A Taiwanese
community farm flourishes. Chinese cucumbers, bright red tomatoes, and crisp
cucumbers all grow at unprecedented rates. My visits to the vegetable gardens
resulted in takeaway bags of greens, unobtainable in Nauru's Spam-heavy supermarkets, unless at exorbitant import prices. I watched local school groups
pay visits to the fertile beds for classes on gardening and cooking techniques. I
also spoke with eager Taiwanese agricultural practitioners, deployed on long
stints to the island, carrying out research to identify the best species for the Nauruan climate in the hopes of encouraging agricultural development.[2]

The rehabilitation of Nauru's decimated lands has a checkered history. The local joke of "Rehab? Rehab do the mining" is no exaggeration. In 1999, the Nauruan government instated the Nauru Rehabilitation Corporation (NRC) as a
statutory corporation tied into the state mining firm, which up until 2005 was still
named the Nauru Phosphate Corporation. Unlike the Nauru Phosphate Corporation, NRC's original purpose was to rehabilitate the mined land so that a sustainable ecosystem could flourish. The move toward environmental reconstruction
has a legal precedent. In 1989, the Nauruan government filed proceedings against
Australia at the International Court of Justice, demanding reparations for the rehabilitation of phosphate lands mined under Australian administration. A highly
publicized case ensued that focused on the Phosphate commissioners' inattentive-
ness to land rehabilitation. The Nauruan government, with the support of the Sri
Lankan Melbourne-based lawyer Christopher Weeramantry, successfully argued
that they were victims of environmental degradation.

In 1993, the two parties reached an agreement outside of court. One provision of the agreement required that Australia award AU$107 million to Nauru
as compensation for the environmental damage. Nauru waived the right to make
any further claim to issues arising from either the administration of the island
during the mandate and trusteeship era or phosphate mining itself. The Australian Keating government paid Nauru AU$57 million in partial settlement of
the claim. They also established the Nauru Rehabilitation Trust Fund for the remaining AU$50 million, earmarked and administered through AusAid (now
DFAT) for Nauru's rehabilitation.[3] Annual installments of AU$2.5 million were
paid into the trust fund. The British and New Zealand governments contributed
AU$12 million each in recognition of the lower than global price paid to Nau-
ruan farmers in the colonial years.

NRC originally had the target of rehabilitating twenty hectares of land a
year. Tony takes me to a small plot of land with a few sage bushes that marks the
fruits of NRC's rehabilitation goal. He chuckles as I gaze dumbfounded at the

one-hectare demonstration site, explaining that most of the money found its way elsewhere. Instead, in 2008, the Nauru Rehabilitation Corporation became the state phosphate mining company, subcontracted to RONPhos. New diggers were flown over or requisitioned from RONPhos's use. RONPhos took over the processing and marketing of phosphate rock.

This control of phosphate mining by the Nauru Rehabilitation Corporation captures the contradictory reality that Nauruans inhabit. Even today, there is little governmental will to burst the bubble of Nauru's once stunning success by being publicly clear about phosphate's toxic dangers. The connections between phosphate and health are rarely made visible and are spoken of largely behind closed doors. As with the refugee industry, the government frowns on studies that go too deep into the extractive consequences of their phosphate industry sector, unless these are geared toward condemning the colonial mining era. Nevertheless, many of Nauru's older generations talk fondly of the BPC years as a time of cleanliness, economic prosperity, and order. This company town paternalism and attempts to invisibilize toxic pollution still contribute to an amnesia for some when it comes to being overt about phosphate dangers.

The intersections of political sovereignty, cultural identity, and indigenous resource development are similar to the story that Andrew Needham (2014) tells in the Navajo Nation. The Navajo reservation, which encompasses northeastern Arizona, southeastern Utah, and northwestern New Mexico, became packed with coal-burning power plants and two of the largest strip mines in the world, which generate electricity for export and metropolitan growth in Phoenix, Los Angeles, and other cities. Navajo nationalism arose in connection with the metropolitan demand for resources: both as a response to the subordination of Navajos within the American Southwest's political economy and as metropolitan growth gave new value to Navajo resources. The importance of energy development to Navajo nationalism that Needham describes is eerily similar to the deep nationalist pride that Nauruans retain from controlling extraction on their terms. This, along with a lack of economic opportunities and recognition that global agricultural growth depended on the resources on their land, contribute to a habituation—and, for some, even apathy or blindness—to contamination. Yet, the toxic dangers of phosphate are very much real and ever present. The following sections turn to the phosphate extractive process and devastating effects of toxic contamination on people's bodies, as also entangled with and buoyant to the refugee industry's operations.

Metallurgical Processes

From the point of extraction to later repercussions, the social and environmental impact of phosphate mining on Nauru has clearly been immense. Tony takes me to the loading bridge, where we speak with Jeremiah, a coral picker and occasional truck driver, who walks me through the process. Jeremiah knows all too well the immediate pollutancies of the phosphate industry, wheezing to catch his breath as we walk through the phosphate fields: chronic bronchitis. As he traces the movement of limestone rock along the conveyer belt, I notice a finger missing on his left hand. "Ah," he says, catching my gaze. "I lost it rightttt there." I look a bit closer, following his line of sight to the top of a rickety structure—the screening and crushing station—where limestone rocks shoot helter-skelter across tracks. Against the midday sun, I can just make out the shadowy outlines of two figures perched atop the wood-and-steel edifice.

We ride over to the station, and he takes me up a steel staircase running through the structure's core. We dodge limestone rocks that hurtle down from the belts. Perched on railings next to the conveyer belt are two younger Nauruan men—flip-flops, shorts, long steel rods raised at the ready. They smile momentarily to greet us, but keep their eyes glued to the earthen sod that circulates beneath them, often leaning in to brush away twigs, leaves, coral, sometimes a large clump of dirt that does not meet their screening. Here, Jeremiah tells me, leaning in too closely to determine phosphate from coral, is where he lost his finger. "Is this sort of thing common?" I ask, thinking to Tony and his missing eye. I need not ask; looking at the two phosphate pickers in their flip-flops, legs splayed over the rocks that hurtle across the circulation belt, I can anticipate his response.

This element of the phosphate certification process is just one of several assessments rounds that screens valuable rock from crude contaminant. Once the contaminated phosphate is mined or "raised" from the ground, it is brought here, to the crushing and screening plant by dump trucks from the working faces. The phosphate rock is first crushed into sizes of 50 mm, then circulated on a conveyer belt that snakes through the plant. Here, it is subject to three sorting rounds, of which manual assessment is the second. Like other practices of commodity assessment, the purpose of the sorting is to screen out contaminate (dirt, coral, leaves, and so forth) from the high-value phosphate sent down to the main plant. Watching the amount of extracted land that slowly builds into two sand dunes—one side high-grade phosphate, one side contaminate swept off the conveyer belt by a steel rod—I cannot help but think of the devastating ecological loss to Nauru. Further down the road sit the relocated piles of ground phosphate rock marked with signs like #0931, #160. Each pyramid designates a different landowner's revenue, ready to be weighed before the final stages of calcination and transportation. I am shown Nibok and Anibare districts, two dusty peaks visible on the left-hand side. Buada district, #186.

Nor are the drastic amounts of non-phosphate contaminate reunited with the gaping holes around Nauru's districts. Initially, under the BPC, non-phosphate contaminate was separately crushed and used for Nauru's company town industrialization. The elaborate roads and buildings of Nauru's past phosphate heyday are constructed from coral and limestone phosphate rock. Under RONPhos and following local desires, the repackaging of land has intensified through new entrepreneurial schemes. Even coral limestone pinnacles have found themselves subject to new resource projects: as decorative stone or aggregate for road and port construction or sent to surrounding Pacific island states in sizes of 50 mm, 20 mm, and 5 mm for an ever-growing catalogue of purposes. Climate-change construction in particular has spurred this growth sector. As I ponder the ecological loss to Nauru, contaminate piles find currency in increasing the land mass of surrounding Pacific island countries. Regular shipments are sent out to the Marshallese and Tuvaluan governments, who are fearful of land loss due to encroaching seas, as Nauru continues to underwrite the development of other regions.

Phosphate has also provided the material residues for a new extractive industry sector to emerge, giving further afterlife to rubble (Gordillo 2014) in the configurations of the industrial present. During my fieldwork, the Australian construction firm Canstruct would purchase the residual limestone rock from phosphate mining for building company town development projects: such as refugee housing foundations and a new courthouse and school, all of which were sprouting up at an extraordinary rate. With the amount of phosphate raw material required for refugee industry construction, Canstruct workers sometimes sped up the process by crushing their brokered phosphate aggregate at the side of the RPCs in their own screening and crushing site. These convergences underscore the ways that processes of destruction can become part of the configurations of the present, as well as a material manifestation of historical overlaps of violence and dislocation. This is necessary for thinking about how the organization and materialization of one industry shapes another. The refugee industry not only sits on the rubble of the latter's debris but is also made through the phosphate industry's debris to create ongoing forms of destruction. In Nauru's company town context, "phosphate and refugees," one phosphate executive remarked to me, "operate in deep symbiosis."[4]

Phosphate Pollutancies

I have first-hand experience of the most direct byproducts of processing rock for phosphate. My rental accommodation sits in Aiwo District, just down from the main phosphate factories, which house the drying kilns and calcination reactor. When it is first mined, phosphate ore contains a number of gangue minerals, including carbon, bone phosphate lime, and a high level of moisture otherwise indiscernible to the naked eye. At Aiwo's main factory complex, the wet phosphate rock undergoes several processes of beneficiation. This breaks down the ore by removing the contaminants, which results in a higher-grade product (concentrate) and a waste stream (tailings). Nauru's phosphate rock is widely certified as premium grade, requiring a lesser process of beneficiation than its counterpart in other regions. However, it also contains a high level of naturally occurring carcinogenic cadmium, averaging about 80–120 mg Cd/kg P, well above global averages (Feary 2011; Gale 2016; IWP-Nauru and Leney 2004). In one particular study in the early 1990s, local residents and a number of sites were tested for evidence of cadmium contamination. The researchers concluded that a "high potential for human exposure to cadmium by both ingestion and inhalation on Nauru is clearly indicated" (Blake 1992, 67). As Nauru is surrounded by the Pacific Ocean, there is salt content within rainwater, which has led to increased Cd mobility in the soil (Morrison and Manner 2005).

Cadmium is released into the air through the industrial heating process, but also in the water and soil that dust particles and cadmium-containing solubles come into contact with. Even in low doses, cadmium is highly toxic (Czeczot and Skrzycki 2010). People who work in or live near waste sites and factories are particularly vulnerable to cadmium exposure. Cadmium also circulates through the food commodity chain, eventually absorbed by plants from the soil onto which the fertilizer product is applied. Acute exposure to cadmium can produce a spectrum of severe health disorders: respiratory damage, kidney and liver damage, osteomalacia (softening of the bones), osteoporosis (loss of bone mass and weakness), and even the so-called cadmium blues. Increasing evidence of cadmium's toxicity during the 1940s and 1950s has led many states to place limits on cadmium exposure for workers in manufacturing sites. Limits are also leveled on public consumption in imported fertilizers and food commodities at large. As the next chapter details, in Nauru these guidelines were predominately enforced by the BPC, which is accountable to the United Nations. As became the case decades later with the refugee industry, the BPC were often called to task by Australian and international campaigners to defend company town administration. When the mining went into Nauruan hands, in-house guidelines over phosphate pollutants fell into abandon. However, for manufacturing exports, quality control guidelines over phosphate purity only became more intense.

After it was recognized that Nauru's phosphate rock contained high levels of cadmium and given the likelihood that toxic chemicals had been distributed into majority-white bodies outside Nauru, agriculturalists took notice (Mann and Ritchie 1994). This delayed attention is just one of many environmental injustices that Nauruans have lived through, which highlights whose bodies are seen as expendable for toxic industries. Immense attentivity goes locally into global export: concerns that were often relayed to me during my visits to the phosphate laboratories. These form part of the contemporary preoccupation with purity attached to agro-food anxieties that impose a neocolonial hygienic mission in supply countries (Freidberg 2003). Phosphate buyers now demand regular product testing before any shipment is exported, to give added quality assurances. Contracts with buyers stipulate strict contaminate levels for optimum product, and RONPhos obtain penalty charges of AU$20,000 per level exceeded. Nauru's onsite phosphate laboratory collects hourly samples from products during drying, analyzing cadmium content in addition to bone phosphate lime and moisture levels. RONPhos chemists also send samples to Australian laboratories for quality control every two weeks to give added assurances. Buying companies then test phosphate samples when in dock at the port.

Alongside striving to meet global protocols and buyers' demands, the Nauruan government presents contradictory points of view around the actual impacts of mining locally. Yet, Nauru is clearly a landscape saturated with the pollutant aftereffects of the phosphate industry. A century after Nauru's company town heyday, Nauruans are surrounded by contaminated grounds and waters. I only had to step out of my door or take a walk past the plants to experience the geochemical signatures of phosphate. Leach water was noticeably a problem across Aiwo's congested residential areas. In heavy rains, a polluted lake with toxic waste collected outside the state hospital, and my neighbors traversed it daily. The underground drainage pipelines that zigzagged down from the plants, rusty from years of neglect, bubbled through into the pool. Uncontrolled landfill practices, including an unmonitored landfill atop the atoll, fed into the toxic sludge visible around the island. Although the desalination plant serviced the country with potable water, I was advised by several of my Nauruan neighbors, and all of my Australian refugee industry workers and migrant informants (the former of whom lived to their occupational health and safety guidelines), never to drink from the tap, especially in Aiwo. Workers and migrants in the refugee industry enjoyed easy access to imported bottled water and shipments of fresh produce that was difficult to source locally. Yet, Nauruans still have some of the highest rates of diarrhea and other water-borne diseases in the Pacific region.[5]

Numerous reports done over the years have found the island's soil and water streams to be highly polluted with metals (lead and zinc) from blasting and mining, with asbestos from centuries of poor building materials, and with leachate from uncontrolled landfill practices (Republic of Nauru 2013; Thoma and Tstitsi 2009). Cadmium sludge from over a century of phosphate mining also threatens the quality of Nauru's soil and groundwater resources. The island's size and limited land for landfills—coupled with the high cost of waste treatment in the country—place a toll on the disposal of liquid, chemical, and hazardous wastes. Fecal coliform bacteria and E. coli overflow from septic tanks on the island, while soakage pits are woefully mismanaged, allowing untreated wastewater to soak into the ground and infiltrate the surrounding soil. This combines with a laissez-faire attitude surrounding the disposal of chemicals from Nauru's power station and the storage and disposal of fuels—partially explained by a history of paternal colonial governance then abandonment, which continues to affect everyday ways of life in Nauru.[6]

Phosphate pollutants and other forms of contamination have clearly had a devastating impact on Nauru, but during my fieldwork, the clogging dust everyone spoke of was initially not so discernable to me. I knew that in Nauru the leading cause for hospital admissions after pregnancy was respiratory diseases, in particular acute bronchitis, from conversations with medical staff, from unpublished local hospital reports, and from my everyday observations. Although the Nauruan government frowned on medical staff drawing these connections, I also knew that lung cancer figured high among Nauruans: I had even attended the funeral of one close islander whose wife had died from it during my fieldwork. However, during my time in Nauru, phosphate processing had stopped. The dust spouts at the batching plants that overlook Aiwo lay dormant. No phosphate shipments were taking place, nor had they for months prior to my arrival. Meanwhile, panic had descended at RONPhos, in government hallways, and local gossiping circles. Nauru's mooring system lay broken. Four of the floating buoys used to anchor ships had been disconnected by high winds, one floating off the Denig district shoreline. Phosphate was stockpiling in the storage bins, which were heaving over capacity.

During my many visits to the RONPhos offices, I often found anxious management on the phone to Australian and Japanese buyers, trying to explain that loading ships could not possibly land into port. Alternatively, managerial administrators were preoccupied with warding off landowners and government ministers, all questioning when phosphate shipments would restart. My trips to the plant and living in a nonprocessing Nauru illuminated what must have been the lived experiences of the country's past monoeconomy, where panic resulted when the spouts did not flume. However, they were uninformative about life in the industry I had heard so much about. Only the dust that covered each surface gave me a picture of what Nauru might be like when operations were up and running. My neighbors described how backyard water tanks in Aiwo District soon filled with dust and debris. They recounted weekends spent scrubbing the tank interiors, attempting to rid their tap water of phosphate dust, which threatened their clean water supply. In the meantime, as phosphate flumes lay dormant, daily riots enveloped the RPCs; migrants whose asylum appeals were denied were deported on a regular basis. The extractive consequences of phosphate seemed benign in comparison to the nightmarish experiences felt by those across Nauru's refugee industry.

Then suddenly, a few days before I left, wondering whether I would witness a shipment, I woke up and stepped out onto my Aiwo doorstep into thickened fog, at odds with blue-skied equatorial climes, into an air that was heavy and bronchial. Plumes of smoke rose from the plant behind me, which had resurged into life. Phosphate rock chugged along the raised conveyer belts that crossed the main road. Workers excitedly swarmed around the port, yelling directions to a tugboat driver working as a makeshift mooring. He attempted to maintain direction in the dangerous riptides, with a phosphate loading ship anchored off his starboard. Phosphate dust poured into the ship's belly from a funnel spout at the end of the second cantilever. Billows of smoke enveloped the westward side of the country, curling in and around oblivious children climbing on a jungle gym in the school playground by the loading site. I choked and strained to catch my breath. After months of panic from locals and government alike, during which time the Nauruan government had not met their annual phosphate production and export figures, RONPhos workers had put together a ramshackle mooring system. Ropes and a small lifeboat enabled phosphate buyers to dock near the rusty but workable second phosphate cantilever. It was then that I experienced the full extent of living in a mineral extraction district.

Human Extractions

In many ways, Nauru's latest industry of processing asylum seekers also holds an extremity of toxic dangers. In the phosphate industry, dust and toxins billow across Nauru's company town district from an unnatural metallurgical process to affect people's homes and bodies. Poisoned soils, polluted waters, and contaminated air all contribute to the suffering that many residents experience from living in a contaminated place. In Nauru's refugee industry, migrants were also subject to a hugely extractive operation. They were made to relive violent pasts to prove their worthiness for residency, undergoing invasive legal and medical evaluations. People lived each day with fears about the outcomes of their cases, uncertainties regarding relocation efforts, and the violence that stemmed from confining a multitude of individuals from differing—and at times conflicting—ethnic groups in a carceral context. These operations took place in Nauru's contaminated phosphate world, where all residents are exposed to disproportionately elevated levels of hazardous chemicals. In the confluence of these ravaging industries, a lethal pattern of racial discrimination persists that sacrifices majority-black and -brown populations on the altar of agricultural and capitalist fecundity. Both systems of consumption, whereby migrants and Nauruans are denied the right to flourish, are linked to material dispossession and accumulation: land and movement are commoditized as capital circulates both through nature and human bodies.

Extractive Metallurgy

Extractive metallurgy is the process whereby valuable raw metals are removed from an ore and refined into purer form. Nauru's phosphate goes through many processes of beneficiation that break down the ore by removing the contaminants. As with other practices of commodity assessment, ensuring certifiable refugeeness is essential to the global refugee industry (Harper, Kelly, and Khanna 2015). Asylum seekers are treated with suspicion, whereas, in contrast, citizens or migrants from Euro-American countries or wealthy socioeconomic backgrounds are seen as safe and reliable. Nauru's phosphate rock is subject to extreme levels of product testing because of mainland pollution scares. Similarly, the forms of assessment in place in Nauru's refugee processing system became all the more elaborate where the Australian government saw the origin of asylum claimants arriving by boat as hazy and unreliable. Migrants lodging asylum claims underwent extensive "rituals of purification" (Douglas 1966) that ensured the problematic distinction between the categories of deservingness of refugee versus economic migrant. They were also subject to extreme levels of assessment because of Australian and Nauruan government fears of violating the principle of non-refoulement. Many screening and quality assurance procedures looked to ensure that Australian mainland legal challenges could not end the offshore operations, which might be used against the reigning Australian political party by their opposition.

In this section, I start my narrative at the point from where migrants are picked up in the Indian Ocean.[7] I do not focus on people's backstories before they are sent to Nauru, because these are often immaterial with regards to whether or not individuals find themselves moved to the island. Instead, I begin from where migrants are transported to Nauru, from many provenances and backgrounds, and circulated through new industry-trading routes to the Equatorial Pacific. These processing operations are incredibly labor-intensive. In order to dissuade people from advancing asylum claims, so-called voluntary returns are available throughout the entirety of the processing operations run by IOM. In recent years, in contexts where "refugee status has been increasingly determined by the politics of immigration, not by the circumstances of the individual seeking asylum" (Ticktin 2006, 95), western governments have clamped down on supporting the asylum claims of migrants outside of institutionalized state resettlement systems. Although the Australian government obtained a great deal of political economic capital from the offshore deterrence spectacle, neither the Australian nor Nauruan governments wanted those who received refugee status to live on the island long-term. IOM first started their controversial Assisted Voluntary Return and Reintegration (AVRR) program in 1979, and it has since exploded in popularity, particularly in Europe.[8] Now contracted in over seventy countries, IOM representatives, who were active in Nauru's offshore industry throughout my fieldwork, persuade migrants claiming asylum to return to their country of origin, offering them return transport, sometimes business setups, and financial incentives. This is not an appealing prospect for many, when their countries of origin might be marred in conflict and returning could hold personal dangers or limited possibilities. As a result, many people prefer to go ahead with pursuing their asylum claims. Regardless of the legal structures, many enter into a political ball game where they end up having a case for asylum because their countries of origin disallow their return—as was often the case in Nauru.

As a biopolitical tool, legal infrastructure made migrants legible in particular ways, engineered as economic subjects for the refugee industry. I turn now to look at the on-the-ground realities of this legal system in order to capture the consequences of these forms of human extraction, and the transnational industry that makes these toxic effects possible. The majority of migrants I spoke with in Nauru were placed in positions where making asylum representations was their only means of moving across state borders. This is not to deny that most people have been through traumatic experiences and should be legitimately legally recognized as refugees. Instead, it is indicative of the sort of injustices that the asylum system can generate, where certain populations must represent themselves through narratives of suffering to move across nation-state borders.

Offshore Circulations

During my fieldwork, all migrants intercepted by the Australian coastguard in the Timor Sea or Indian Ocean and lodging asylum claims were sent to Christmas Island. Christmas Island, another phosphate-turned-refugee isle, became the main industry hub for deciding whether to send people to Manus Island or Nauru. All migrants underwent a preliminary post-transfer assessment (PTA) by Australian Immigration Department RSD officers and contracted International Health and Medical Services (IHMS) clinicians at the processing center on Christmas Island's own Phosphate Hill. Everyone was logged by boat ID under the operational term "suspected irregular entry vessel" (SIEV), and they were commonly referred to as "client" or "transferee" or by their boat ID by medical, social worker, refugee determination, and other workforces. This was, several asylum seekers in Nauru told me, a hugely objectifying process; as one individual put it, he "felt like cattle being inspected." In the extraction of phosphate, roasting and crushing are done to remove impurities in the form of gangue minerals. Here, the equivalent of routine chemical tests include a PTA interview, a health induction assessment, and bio-data collection to determine refugee-status probability and "fitness to travel" to Pacific processing sites. During these assessments, vulnerabilities, family links to Australia, and a synopsis of each individual's backstory were noted into electronic medical and RSD registry databases that traveled with the migrants to the offshore processing sites.[9]

To clear asylum seekers for the processing stages, the initial Christmas Island health assessments included a public health screen, nursing general assessment, and general practitioner evaluation. All asylum seekers underwent physical examinations, chest X-rays, and blood and urine tests for particular diseases, such as hepatitis B and C, HIV, and syphilis. Clinicians' evaluations of each individual's mental health were also conducted, including the prevalence of torture and trauma (T&T), post-traumatic stress disorder (PTSD), or other psychiatric diagnoses relevant to refugee status determination.[10] These many technical procedures reveal how migrants' bodies are pathologized as unclean and categorized within differentiating discourses of "cultural competences, sexual proclivities, psychological dispositions, and cultivated habits" (Stoler 1995, 141). Alison Bashford (2004) discusses how healthcare regimes have become one means of ensuring the boundaries of citizenship. For Bashford, writing on what she calls "imperial hygiene," the colonial management of race in the eighteenth and nineteenth centuries joined with public health policies to constitute the new boundaries of a "racialized cordon sanitaire." Clearly, there are deeply racist policies made manifest through these border-control policies. People from particular countries—largely in the Global South—are represented as posing an imminent danger through the language of quarantine and containment. Miriam Ticktin (2011) observes similarities in the healthcare system for asylum seekers in France. Regimes of care enacted by nurses, doctors, social workers, and immigrants play a crucial role in governing immigration. The process of selecting immigrants on the basis of illness and experiences of violence inscribes ideas of what Ticktin calls "the morally legitimate suffering body." Yet, this measurement of an alleged universal suffering through medical and scientific procedures maintains people as far less than human.

From the Christmas Island assessments, all migrants lodging asylum claims were marked for suitability of transfer by IHMS medical inspectors. Doctors, nurses, and social workers became key gatekeepers, making crucial decisions as to who was sent to the offshore processing sites. Receiving a red screen meant that an individual had complex medical requirements that were expected to require medical attention unavailable offshore. A green categorization indicated an asylum seeker's suitability for offshore processing, identifying them as having no significant physical or mental health issues. An amber designation operated somewhere in-between, with further assessment required. In order to manage red alerts, the Australian government put incremental funding into the medical setups at Christmas Island and Nauru's regional processing sites. Not only did they want to prevent possible bad press that might force the operation's closure, but they also sought to ensure fewer medical evacuations (medevacs) to the mainland.[11] Medevacs are expensive operations manned by organizations like the Royal Flying Doctors of Australia. But importantly, physically sending an asylum seeker or refugee to the Australian mainland often led to high-profile activist campaigns, which the Australian Immigration Department sought to avoid.[12] It also reduced the political potency of the narrative that no asylum seeker arriving by boat will *ever* be resettled in Australia. Because of the Nauruan government's compliance with the Australian government's directives, Nauru swiftly became Australia's main offshore processing site. This included the processing of the asylum claims of children, all of whom were processed in Nauru from 2013 to 2019 in an extensive operation contractually managed by Save the Children and mainland advisory teams.[13]

Extractive Enclaves

> A stretch of trackless prairie sometimes becomes, almost overnight, a community numbering thousands of people who establish themselves in temporary buildings, tents, dugouts, lean-to-shelters, or even within four topless walls of burlap, or in the open. These mushroom communities have been aptly termed "rag towns."
> —*Oil Booms: Social Change in Five Texas Towns* (1982)

Company town models are not static but are constantly being reworked to cater to the particularities of new modes of extraction. Ken Maclean (2008) uses the term "extractive enclaves" to describe temporary encampments that are constructed around natural resource ventures in Burma. Resource extractors seek to consolidate control over commodities and populations, creating spaces that make "intensive forms of commodity extraction possible" (Maclean 2008, 140). Maclean's descriptions pair starkly with the global refugee industry's settlement patterns and those experienced by migrants in Nauru. As the refugee industry has taken off as a growth sector, the business of enclaving and pushing migrants through a panoply of assessment procedures has created real estate booms similar to patterns recognizable in other industries, where resources are present in commercial quantities. For-profit immigration detention centers, camps, and community detention arrangements have become commonplace global industry arrangements—forms of segregated difference (where people are held on the basis of nation of origin, socioeconomic status, and other factors) that modulate from place to place (Flynn and Cannon 2009; Morris 2017). These residential enclaves combine the idea of assessment facilities with workers' company housing, becoming key sites where migrants undergo the labor-intensive process of asylum as value is extracted from them as resources.

A similar sequence of events characteristic of other human extractive booms (Gilmore 2007) occurred in Nauru's refugee industry development. Because the securitized dwelling style is part of the routinized operation that follows the discovery of resources, the Australian Immigration Department has a professionalized Detention Services Division. This made it possible to impose readymade processing centers in Nauru from the beginning. Detention Services Division staff schooled in the art of industry design, refugee policy advisors from mainland organizations like the Jesuit Refugee Services, Life Without Barriers, the Victorian Foundation for the Survivors of Torture, and academics from refugee legal and psychiatric departments across Australia were charged with designing the profitable new field of industry exploration.

During my fieldwork, all migrants lodging asylum claims were enclaved in one of two newly built processing centers in the heart of the country's phosphate fields, presided over by the Australian companies Transfield Services and Wilson Security. The RPC 2 facility was used for single men eighteen years and older, and RPC 3 for families, unaccompanied minors, and single adult females. RPC 1 was for foreign refugee industry workers in modular accommodation. Locals who worked in the industry were prohibited from living at the sites, which reflected forms of domestic comfort not often found by local islanders. These were part of the many segmentations in the labor force reiterated in segregated residence, income differences, and differential access to resources.

Accommodation arrangements were sparse, in particular in RPC 2, which consisted of open-ended canvas tents with groups of men bunking on camp stretchers. The tents had electricity, and most, but not all, had fans inside. RPC 3 was made up of large, predominately, but again not entirely, air-conditioned vinyl marquees for accommodating families. Single women were provided with shared donga modular dwellings with double bunks. Both RPCs had basic recreational and dining areas. With only 120 square meters (1,291.7 square feet) of space in the marquees at both facilities, some of which housed up to 22 people, sometimes more, in a space partitioned only by vinyl walls, daily life, one asylum seeker said to me, "was hard and gave no privacy." Limited breeze came through the raised pinnacles of the phosphate atoll, producing an intense heat from which there was little respite. Because none of the tents had their own bathrooms, everyone had to use communal toilets and showers. This meant that, in the case of one compound in RPC 2 (the Alpha Compound), over four hundred men shared eight toilets, two urinals, and ten outdoor showers without doors. After a great deal of back-and-forth with the Nauruan public about the dangers "the refugees" presented, shortly before my arrival in Nauru, the RPCs were made open for asylum claimants to come and go between designated hours. Some unaccompanied minors seen as low-risk were also placed in foster care setups with local Nauruan families under community processing arrangements.

Previously, during the 2001–2008 phase, migrants had their asylum claims processed in the securitized setting of Nauru's state house compound and another facility in the phosphate fields. The processing sites were secured, and access was strict, requiring authorized permission, accredited security, or visitor passes. All of this eventually morphed into an open-center model in 2005 that allowed asylum seekers to come and go on designated times and days. When Nauru's operations restarted in 2012, Australia's Detention Services Division staff and refugee policy advisors proposed an open-plan center to the Nauruan government. "Processing people on an island doesn't present the same fears of absconding as on the Australian mainland," an Australian offshore team manager remarked to me in Canberra when describing the history of Nauru's first settlement design. Most asylum seekers in Nauru presented no security threat; the majority were simply trying to reach the dream of Australia, the Lucky Country. Nauru's many planners contended that a closed model was far too restrictive and espoused the same threat narratives and anxieties that informed the offshoring of asylum to Nauru. They decided that incorporating the large-scale edifice of a securitized facility with the purportedly liberalizing principles of Australian "community detention" (CD) models fit perfectly with the offshore operations.[14] The planners believed that making contact between asylum seekers and Nauruans a feature of the design might counter local fears of Nauru's new arrivals, simultaneously nullifying some mainland liberal opposition. Both governments also thought that instrumentalizing an open-center model could indigenize Nauru's processing site into a sustainable operation well into the future if need be, as a *regional* rather than offshore processing arrangement.

But, as I soon found in my discussions with many Nauruans, the new wave of industry design was not to the majority of the public's liking. Sentiments toward asylum seekers and refugees as threats and Orientalized Others were little different on Nauru. Although both were new resources for the island, no local resident I spoke with was immune to the debates that circulated outside of the country. It would have been hard not to adopt stances on the offshore arrangement as Australian media is the go-to across the atoll. Blaring ABC broadcasts are in no short supply, with the occasional Nauruan transmissions spliced in. Most residents have broadband cable and enjoy easy access to popular and social media that circulates news about the country's asylum system or those more globally. Many locals also closely follow the debates in Australian media about "asylum seekers," "boat people," "refugees," and the war in the Middle East. The asylum seeker and refugee have come to emerge as key scare figures, entangled in global political campaigns that find traction from depicting "floods" of unwanted border arrivals. The refugee industry has also worked hard to sell the idea of spiraling numbers of Taliban-persecuted refugees and representations of "a global refugee crisis." Both images propelled the fears of asylum seekers and refugees that took shape in Nauru.

The revenue of phosphate has also left its legacy in an exceptionally well-traveled middle-aged population. Now, owing to the country's resurging economy from the refugee industry, Nauru's cosmopolitan links have reinvigorated with the reinstatement of the once-bankrupt Air Nauru. Flight destinations extend from Brisbane to Suva and Pohnpei. Popular global media narratives project Nauru—and often Nauruans—as dangerous and backward. Many Nauruans feared the asylum seekers and refugees. Threat narratives that spin around asylum seekers and refugees outside the coral atoll injected into their concerns. I heard the phrase, "We don't know who these people are. They could be Taliban for all we know," from several Nauruans on multiple occasions. "I've read about these refugees online, they'll take our jobs, they'll make trouble"—these were some of the other fears expressed by local residents, along with, "We don't know who these people are. They could bring disease." Or, "You know what some of the media have said about the people they're sending us? They're dangerous. They could be Taliban for all we know."

Starkly, these anxieties about refugees had much in common with local responses to phosphate pollution. On several occasions, groups of Aiwo District residents, where the core production and export of phosphate takes place, joined together to lobby for relocation of the facilities to the windward side of the country. To single out their concerns, local residents put together a health and environmental impact assessment in collaboration with a Nauruan medical practitioner. Finding extreme impacts of the phosphate industry on people's environment, health, and living standards (Thoma and Tstitsi 2009), they rallied together and produced a signed petition for the relocation of the factories from their backyard. These relocation campaigns had little effect and were characteristic of the quick subsidence of collective actions around phosphate in Nauru. The structures of the phosphate factories are more permanent than the modular infrastructure for processing asylum seekers; the former are set up under the imperial long-term ambitions of the British Phosphate Commission, whereas the Australian government initially envisaged the latter as a short-term operation. Importantly, the expenses for Nauru's phosphate industry are incurred by the Nauruan government and not, as is the case for the refugee industry, Australia. This combines with a sense of

FIGURE 9.   Phosphate extraction fields with the refugee processing centers in the background. Photo by Julia Morris.

company loyalty still present among many of Nauru's older generation, along with disagreements and doubts about who is responsible for contamination. By contrast, lobbying efforts for RPC relocation, with its Australian financial backing, were markedly successful.

Steeped in the refugee politics that circulates globally, and, ironically, the politics that had offshored asylum to their island, the majority of locals vetoed the idea of an open-center design. Sentiments like "They might be dangerous" or "How many are they sending us!? We're a small island. Have you seen what's been happening in Europe?" all formed part of the general consensus. Some argued that the very culture, behavior, and religion of asylum seekers would clash with Nauru's own culture, behavior, and denominations. Others questioned the arrival of Afghanis in local communities. Paradoxically, it was moral panic related to asylum seekers as threats to Australian publics that had transformed Nauru into a processing site from the very beginning. The same discourses fed into Nauruans' concerns, further segmented by local employment and the industry's ring-fenced enclaves. These practices pathologized the asylum seeker as in need of medical and security screening and managerial control.

Local reactions were inflected with the extractive entanglements of years of high-risk phosphate mining. All contributed to a suspicion about foreign personnel, local government, and the destructive industries that never failed to be part of the island's next chapter. The majority of islanders were all too aware that their land had come to be historically marked by the positioning of toxic industries and found this particularly frustrating. On multiple occasions, Nauruans remarked to me that theirs was an island that carried the scourges of a succession of high-risk industries. This was echoed by heady, but almost confirming, sighs about the toxic risks they saw their new industry presenting. For some, familiar apocalyptic tales of refugees as risk were given greater currency because of their own experiences of living within toxic spaces. With these "toxic biographies" of extraction (Armiero and Fava 2016, 69), for some Nauruans it was almost to be expected that another harmful industry would come to their island, confirming the narratives they had heard about the asylum seeker and the refugee. After all, a few residents pointed out, summarizing environmental racism far more succinctly than me, choosing to locate a new contaminating industry in an already polluted community, one that had been weakened economically, made it very difficult for those with less resources to counteract. For some, these understandings influenced the ways in which asylum seekers sent to their island were seen: as high-risk commodities.

But their recognition of environmental suffering did not translate to a resignation. Rather, I heard phrases such as "not this time, not in our backyard." In this instance, unlike the failed attempts at phosphate facility relocation, the majority of locals took a stand against their new backyard extractions. They advocated for the segregation of the RPCs away from the island's urban rim and into the Topside phosphate fields, and asked for them to be closed facilities, like immigration detention centers in Australia. It was not until 2015, at the calls of Australian activists and a series of high-profile campaigns to end offshore processing, that the Nauruan government agreed to the recommendations of Australian advisors. In February 2015, they opened the RPCs—as per their original design—to in-and-out movement. At the same time, many Nauruans could not understand how children could come to be in the asylum system in their country. Close-knit family ties define life in Nauru, with many generations living in one house or in separate houses on the same plot of land. Many Nauruans volunteered to host unaccompanied children in their homes through a CD-style system.

The location of the RPCs in the phosphate fields is no accident. It goes to show the low regard that migrants of particular races and socioeconomic backgrounds are accorded: as objects of risk and danger, but also of high value. Ali Bhagat

(2019) has similar findings among urban refugees in Kenya, arguing that the Somali refugee population are treated like waste, kept away from mainstream society due to their racialized positions. Simultaneously, however, these modes of exclusion help facilitate capital accumulation by creating a workforce with tenuous claims to rights who are easily subject to exploitation. In Nauru's extractive enclaves, asylum seekers were also kept in the realm of capital accumulation in and through their dislocation. The craggy moonscape of canyons and pits, laid to waste by phosphate extraction, became a new site of destructive accumulation. Asylum seekers were exposed to phosphate's toxic dangers (dust and other frontline toxic exposures), as well as those presented by the refugee industry as value was extracted from their bodies.

The next section turns to the processing operations, which in Nauru were just as, if not more, scrutinizing than in Australia. Few Australian Liberal Party politicians wanted the success of a mainland legal challenge centered on refoulement or undue harm that would end the offshoring setup and provide political leverage for the opposition.

Well-Founded Fear

In Nauru, determining refugee status relied on the same industry procedures made popular globally. All migrants making an asylum claim had a transfer interview in the RPCs to collect biographical information and make a summary of fear. Worldwide, refugee assessment is conducted on the adjudication of "well-founded fear." Well-founded fear is akin to the industry measure of product quality. In this determination practice, the burden of proof is on asylum seekers to market their veracity. Different to other industry sectors, then, self-representational labor characterizes the refugee industry. This is part of the system of dispossession, whereby people's ability to move is taken away and then partially returned through carefully crafted accumulation strategies. Specific refugee determination personnel use each asylum seeker's narratives of persecution and physical attributes in deciding whether an individual's fear is well-founded.

In Australia, refugee determination is a government practice led by the Australian Immigration Department, who also conduct RSD in Nauru. Because of concerns over the offshoring setup, a number of external Australian refugee lawyers also looked over Nauru's asylum cases in an advisory capacity. Following the work of the Australian Immigration Department, UNHCR Canberra, and international advisors, Nauru has an RSD registry, inaugurated in 2013. Nauruan or Australian employees logged each new arrival into the registry database. These notes supplemented the bio-data collection made during the pre-transfer assessment interviews on Christmas Island.[15] Separate physical and mental health tests for de-

FIGURE 10A. Processing phosphate. Photo by Julia Morris.

termining torture and trauma (T&T), along with PTSD, self-harm, or other mental health concerns were also conducted and logged.

At this stage, those lodging asylum claims were provided with an Australian refugee defense lawyer or claims assistance provider (CAP), who would support them with Nauru's new asylum process. The refugee lawyers or migration agents were contracted through the Sydney-based firm Craddock Murray Neuman. The legal team operated on fly-in-fly-out rotation cycles of what in Australia are commonly termed "RSD missions" when conducted at distant processing sites in the Australian outback.[16] In Nauru, CAPs lawyers provided advice on refugee representation, including how asylum seekers should collate photos, maps, and medical and psychological reports that emphasized veracity of fear and persecution. Craddock also had what they termed a "shop front" in RPC1, where they led group information sessions on the process.

FIGURE 10B.   A new courthouse for asylum claims appeals. Photo by Julia Morris.

RSD support was also conducted with the assistance of a contracted interpreter. In Australia the provision of an interpreter is an important part of the Australian Migration Act, subsection 427(7). Depending on location, interpreters from TIS National, the Immigration Department's contracted firm, are the norm across Australia's main processing sites, which was extended to Nauru's offshore industry context. Many fly-in-fly-out interpreters in Nauru are specialists in credibility-of-fear translation work and are often well versed in the legal jargon, having worked around Australia and in other offshore contexts and/or originally come to Australia through the asylum system themselves.

Lived Experiences of Assessment

It was apparent that for many migrants I spoke with who were awaiting asylum claims, the actual facility setup was largely superfluous. While the built environment was certainly affective in producing ideological differentiations between the asylum seeker and local and foreign workers, what those undergoing assessment stressed to me was how the RSD system itself produced an affectivity that translated to any environment. These "affective atmospheres" (B. Anderson 2009) characterized the experiences that many people shared with me. "I felt like I was still in a jail wherever I was," said Raphael, a young Iranian man from a village outside Tehran, who had been in Nauru for two years by that time. We sat together at the boat harbor with our legs dangling off the concrete wall. It plummeted down into the depths of the ocean's blue-green waters. The boat harbor had become a place where I would often speak with asylum seekers down for the day from the RPCs. Many were keen to cool off in the ocean breeze, which otherwise barely found its way through the stifling heat of the atoll's pinnacled interior. Shouts and excitement surrounded us as a group of Iranian men cannonballed into the surf.

Raphael gazed out onto the horizon as he told me about his life and the experiences he was going through. I was worried that recalling these experiences would be difficult, but Raphael was adamant that he wanted to talk about his preoccupations with someone outside the industry's everyday. He confided that it gave him practice relating the chronology of events he had experienced. Conversations like ours, he said, were not a high-stakes context that might determine his movement elsewhere. For Raphael, informal chats like these helped him process, create distance, and prepare for the countless interviews he had to undergo. He described the anguish of the asylum process, saying that he could put up with the camp confines, but what often overpowered him was the turgid limbo of uncertainty: "You can't plan, you don't know what the future will be, it's hard to keep on going in that kind of situation. I feel like I can't be useful in any way. I'm just wasting away here, without any idea of what my goals can be." Although several asylum seekers complained about the RPC environments, it was, like Raphael, the lived experience of going through assessment that provoked far greater anguish for many—what Melanie Griffiths (2014) describes as "the temporality" of the decision-making system, indeterminate in length. The major issues generating most people's anxieties were the lack of clarity around their claims processing and futures, and their frustrations at being blocked from moving to Australia. This is a kind of slow violence that is difficult to pinpoint, part of the gradual brutalities that migrants surrounded by the weight of refugee legal systems endure over time. However, these toxic experiences are certainly not invisible to those they impact. Recounting narratives of trauma was an incredibly retraumatizing experience for many migrants I spoke with. But stories of trauma are intrinsic to the asylum system, on which an individual's status is based. As a result, extraction takes an extremely intimate form, premised on the extraction of people's personal experiences.

Several of those I spoke with in Nauru, certified or awaiting their claims, had very similar responses to those in Australia about their experiences going through these screening procedures. They described the retraumatizing effect of having to collate past dreadful experiences into an objectified form. "It was horrible to go through," Luke said to me in another boat harbor moment, articulating the harms that encroached on his and others' lives in intimate ways. Originally from Afghanistan, Luke was by then living in Nauru under a ten-year refugee visa. As we sat together by the great expanse of sea that separated us from Australia, he described how he had been told by his appointed legal support that "visuals were particularly powerful, printing off pictures to show what [he had] experienced, getting doctor's examination records." He noted that this was not something he would do unless under extreme duress, adding, "it makes me relive it all again and again." I could only wholeheartedly agree with Luke and others about the casualties that this kind of processing re-rendered. As Didier Fassin and Estelle d'Halluin have argued, for the dominated, the body "has become the place that displays the evidence of truth" (2005, 598). In a climate of distrust, RSD practices have become ever more scrutinizing over the years (Harper, Kelly, and Khanna 2015). Migrants must prove their suffering through medical expertise and new forms of scientific rationality. Medical certificates and evidence of psychological and physical scars are accorded greater veracity than people's verbal accounts (T. Kelly 2012)—or indeed, I would add, basic desires to move elsewhere.

As Luke makes clear, an important aspect of the determination process is the assessment of marks on the human body and psychological suffering. Luke, like others, had to show evidence of mental and bodily scarification to stress the authenticity of suffering, redoubling the amount of harm he had already been through as part of the asylum process. "Intense," "exhausting," and "scrutinizing" were some of the many words I heard used to describe refugee determination in Nauru. In-country screening procedures have become more elaborate, rendering autobiographical accounts superfluous to the veracity of physical and psychic signs of accredited violence—what Webb Keane (2003) refers to as a "representational economy." This gives an insight into the labor-intensive process of asylum, whereby, to follow Marx, the accumulation of value is premised on extracting unpaid labor—or labor that is differently unfree. The work that people must go through in order to move from the Global South to Global North is elaborate and rests on medico-scientific techniques of proving the validity of one's suffering. These are part of the changing conditions of exploitation, whereby racially delineated people are simultaneously excluded—disconnected from wider society and the rights accorded to citizens—and also incorporated into a polity for capital accumulation.

In all mental health screenings, including PTAs on Christmas Island, IHMS, Immigration Department, and other workforces inspect those making asylum claims for signs of torture and trauma. Bodies are read not only as potential carriers of disease but as palimpsests of persecution. The refugee T&T sector, as it is popularly known, has gained incremental authority as a psychological subdiscipline.[17] The T&T sector developed in Australia in the 1980s at the time when the country's refugee industry was beginning to burgeon. Led by industry pol-icy advisor Paris Aristotle, a key figure in the offshore industry's development, directors from the T&T sector are powerful lobbyists in driving government ref-ugee policy and industry spending. In Australia, T&T agencies operate as a body of eight NGOs across each state and territory under the umbrella network, the Forum of Australian Services for Survivors of Torture and Trauma (FASSTT). FASSTT is the government's contracted network for specialist counseling ser-vices for those who are awaiting and receive refugee legal status. It is now stan-dard practice that the Immigration Department provides T&T counseling at each processing site across Australia's states and territories. One FASSTT CEO explained this in interview to me: "It's in recognition of the fact that no matter how you view the arrivals, there will be a proportion of those who are genuine who have suffered persecution and trauma . . . this is specialist work." Because of the political authority of T&T and years of crossover training and capacity building, T&T classification is a standardized part of the assessment process. Sources of refugee torture and trauma can include political repression, living in a situation of war or state terrorism, the escape path, and the experience of liv-ing in a refugee camp. For Nauru, FASSTT setup a specialist offshore counsel-ing agency, the Overseas Services to Survivors of Torture and Trauma, run by counselors experienced in refugee work in other offshore and popular industry sites. Although detailed case files were kept confidential, information on all mi-grants who attended T&T sessions was shared between IHMS, the Australian Immigration Department, and other interested parties.

Many migrants I spoke with undergoing RSD in Nauru knew that this was the case. They commented on the intensity of life under assessment, pointing toward the particularities of a metallurgical practice that involved human lives. Mahmoud, living in Nauru with refugee status, originally from Tehran, de-scribed to me the importance of clinical evidence in the adjudication of asylum, which made the reality of life in and out of assessment "tiring" and "exhaust-ing." "There's always someone looking at you, always. Monitoring what you're doing, where you're at, everything counts," Mahmoud described. Mahmoud's comment that "everything counts" speaks to the behavioral economy induced by the assessment process, in which human bodies *could be* read as sites of refugee-ability. Trauma, as Jay Marlowe found in his work with Sudanese men resettled in Australia, becomes "a form of currency" that people must use in their "claims for recognition and access to vital resources" (2018, 73). This master nar-rative of refugeehood can overshadow the multifarious experiences that indi-viduals more readily identify with.

It is unclear whether psychological distress, scars, and T&T demarcations all noted on the journey to and in Nauru's processing system helped or hindered refugee assessments. But it made the determination system an exhausting and in-escapable experience that itself often induced psychological oppression. Exhaustive scrutiny and panopticon living are the reality of life in this mode of assessment. Those undergoing RSD were also in an asylum system for many months—if not years—all of which compounded the tense registers that suffused the offshore environment around an indeterminate future. High aggression and outbursts were everyday parts of the pressure-cooker environment. Others were incredibly depressed and did not see the point of going through the effort of an asylum claim, particularly if it ultimately meant a Nauruan rather than Australian refugee visa. Many never expected to end up in—let alone be assessed as a refugee for—Nauru.

Maya was one of my closer informants. Iranian, in her mid-twenties, always upbeat and engaged in every opportunity she could find: a proactivity that she confided in me might show suitability for resettlement to Australia, and could be a hopeful ticket out of Nauru for her and her family. We often hung out at the boat harbor, where she helped teach younger children to swim. She would press me for stories about Australia and what places like Bondi Beach were like, bringing my mobility privilege to stark light. Once, Maya invited me back to her family's home in one of the refugee resettlement compounds, nestled in an active mining site. Piles of phosphate rubble surrounded the single-story, modular family-housing units of the settlement zone, where she and 150 others lived as part of Nauru's toxic entanglements. Bulldozers plied up and down the slope around them, carrying the waste from the phosphate extraction zone. I commented on the loud noises of the mining that echoed across the housing complex. She shrugged it off, saying that they had reached an agreement it would stop before dark.

I never asked Maya about her background, beyond the brothers, sister, and mother I had met and knew she was supporting. Maya made references to her family's Christian beliefs on the odd occasion, and on her discomfort with the theocratic Iranian Muslim state she had left behind. But this time, over freshly grilled fish (prepared in the style of her homeland, she proudly pointed out to me), Maya started describing her experiences. Leaning back in her chair, she told me how she and her family had managed to get out of a violent domestic-abuse situation: a father and authoritarian grandparents who threatened to denounce them as seditionists to the local authorities. Her mother had distant friends in Sydney. As Christians in a Muslim-majority country, and with fears that family members might find them in other cities, Australia seemed like a far better option than other places in the region. After precarious weeks spent crossing through India and Malaysia, and months hiding out in Jakarta trying to evade capture by Indonesian police, they paid the AU$10,000 to take a boat in Indonesia bound for Australia. They were told by the broker that they would go through the asylum process in Australia to receive an Australian refugee visa.

Even though Maya knew she might be subject to a processing procedure or even short detainment in Australia, it seemed preferable to the domestic abuse their family had left behind. Their boat's interception, the move to Christmas Island, and the transfer to Nauru were all crushing blows. Now she was stuck in limbo, with her family of five, unable to return, and faced with an unknowable future.

The mobility regime that Maya describes navigating underlines the inordinately high financial and human price—and obvious geographic and racial bias—that is regularly experienced by people in the Global South. In order to move elsewhere, Maya and her family had to pay financial and human costs far greater than many people in countries in the Global North would do. Maya's experiences underline the links that Besteman (2020) has shown exist between identity documentation, border control, race, and place. Racialized foreigners, who find it next to impossible to obtain documentation, must perform within particular legal narratives to move elsewhere. These narratives gain purchase through the labor and capital of pathologized displays of bodily and psychological suffering. The refugee regime—including who has to go through the demeaning asylum process to move elsewhere, the particular locations where people can claim asylum, where they are sent for asylum and resettlement, and the excruciating waiting process—is directly implicated in this system of border control and capital accumulation.

Nauru's offshore industry did not enable a novel series of toxic harms. Rather, to bring Appel's insights from the offshore oil and gas industry to bear, "it enables the continuity of practices that . . . go back over one hundred years across the world's [industry] frontiers" (2019, 63). The experiences of uncertainty that Maya described throughout this process are so well recognized that they have become naturalized as casualties endemic to the industry. Numerous studies and oral histories chronicle the experiences of individuals who live with this type of human extraction: having no work rights, subjected to demeaning NGO representations, and in a waiting game—sometimes for several years in various forms of detention—before any decision is made (Coffey et al. 2010; Fiske 2016; Griffiths 2012). In Australia, psychiatrists refer to "protracted asylum seeker syndrome" (Sundram and Loi 2012): a pathological condition connected to the toxic effects of asylum. This condition is characterized by powerlessness, depression, and identity crises as a result of the uncertainty of one's situation, the demands of demonstrating past trauma, and the experiences of racism connected to the othering of asylum seekers and refugees. Much like the toxicological "body burden," these cumulative wrenching harms, "stored, and later transmitted in somatic memory" (Agard-Jones 2013, 11), can accumulate in people's bodies over time. Often that violence is deeply hidden in people's bodies, and only visible quantification can transform an injured body into a political fact (Armiero and Fava 2016), such as the self-harm, hangings, asphyxiations, and polypharmacy overdoses catalogued in Nauru (Hedrick et al. 2019). In this sense, the lived experiences of Maya, Luke, Raphael, and others I talked to speak for themselves. Their everyday encounters form part of the "elongated exposures to violence" (Davies 2019) and neglect experienced by certain populations and geographies who are rendered vulnerable to sacrifice.

The Politics of Refugee Veracity

In Nauru, the actual processing operations were more labor-intensive than in Australia because, as the next chapter shows, the level of scrutiny for checking that refugee determination complies with relevant laws was far greater. During my fieldwork, the formal refugee determination operations were conducted in special interview rooms in RPC 1. Assessments were audio-recorded and conducted by Australian DIBP RSD personnel. Nauruan RSD officers led some occasional portions, such as interviewing individuals or family groups, but only under close supervision. In these assessments, CAPs lawyers and interpreters were present for substantiating each person's asylum claim to assessors. Often, mainland refugee legal advisors, UNHCR Canberra, and other nongovernmental assurance teams would quality-control the procedure, discussed in the next section. During the screening process, usually several hours long, each asylum seeker's persecution fears were better established. They were quizzed on their fear, harm, and threat of persecution, and proving the experience of suffering became the way to access mobility. Photos, maps, and medical and psychological reports could all be brought in as further evidence.

As part of the scrutinization process, asylum seekers had to prove that there was not an area in their home country where they might be safe. Country data included everything from the conflicts in particular geographical regions to the threats faced depending on one's ethnic or social grouping. A country of origin (COI) information analysis substantiated this aspect of the assessment, including with state intelligence information. Claims of statelessness, of which there were many in Nauru, could also be validated through the COI aspect of the refugee assessment. Country research was also sometimes used by RSD officers when evaluating possibilities for the application of the "cessation clause," based on whether or not flight circumstances may no longer exist. Interpreters were often familiar with the home regions of many asylum seekers in Nauru. At times, I was told, this could help or hinder the fear assessment if an interpreter was pushed to make clarifications to the refugee determination teams.

Because of government concerns of refoulement and Australian legal challenges, the refugee processing operations developed for Nauru brought in "complementary protection." This expanded the criteria for a successful asylum claim in Nauru beyond the five Geneva Convention grounds of persecution. For example, risk of arbitrary deprivation of life, the death penalty, torture, and cruel or inhuman treatment or punishment might fall within what RSD experts call the "threshold of fear." A number of exclusion clauses applied to lodging an asylum application in Nauru. Migrants could put forward an asylum claim in only one country. For example, if they were previously processed in Indonesia and were traceable through UNHCR RSD registries, a claimant might be denied. Any asylum seeker who had committed a criminal act in the past, even if very minor, could also be denied certification.[18]

After receiving all relevant information, RSD officers made an assessment on each migrant's credibility of fear. Because of Nauru's controversy and both governments' fears of legal challenges, determinations were sent to the mainland for what was termed "quality assurance." Much like the routine phosphate samples sent to mainland laboratories, as part of the offshoring arrangement, people's asylum cases were extensively controlled by industry personnel using enterprise-specific standards. If adjudicated as exhibiting well-founded fear, and found to be a refugee under the Geneva Convention definition, all migrants received a Nauru refugee certification, including a refugee residence permit for Nauru. Between July 2014 and October 2017, the period that covered my fieldwork, 1,062 asylum seekers received positive refugee certifications out of a total of 1,216 decisions. Two hundred and thirty asylum seekers were deported to their country of origin or a suitable alternative. In total, 87.3 percent of asylum seekers received positive responses, which is, I was told, a high "success" rate compared to countries worldwide.

Nauru is only 21 km², and many locals were reluctant to have too many refugees living in the country. Storage sites that held dry phosphate heaved over in capacity; land availability was tight. This offshore arrangement was also never envisaged to be permanent. The Australian government's deterrence spectacle extended to a presentation of border enforcement, but not to the resettlement of refugees in Nauru in the long term. Nor did resettlement prove to be feasible when later attempted. Therefore, the Australian and Nauruan governments looked to persuade those granted refugee status to move elsewhere in the long term. During my fieldwork, resettlement packages for refugees were available from Nauru to Cambodia, which fomented new supply-chain relations and patterns of exchange. Because of the political currency of the deterrence spectacle, the conditions were negotiable. At the time of my fieldwork, the Australian government offered an apartment in Phnom Penh with a paid year of rent (contracted with IOM and then with Connect Settlement Services), a Cambodian bank account with AU$10,000, private medical care, Khmer language classes, a monthly salary for six months until local employment could be found, and job seeker's support. While I was in Nauru, Cambodian personnel were also in residence attempting to market this package at the RPCs and resettlement districts. In total, only ten refugees took up the Cambodia deal from Nauru and Manus Island in total, and just one Rohingyan man from Nauru ended up staying in Cambodia. In return, the Cambodian government received AU$55 million in development aid, and AU$3.5 million went to support each refugee who agreed to the arrangement.

These attempts combined with the work of staff in the state IOM Nauru office, set up onsite in 2013. At all times, asylum seekers could opt into one of IOM's AVRR package deals. "Fly home" arrangements were marketed throughout the RPCs in controversial posters that read "Missing your family? Talk to IOM," but also by resident IOM personnel avidly working to drum up more customers for their business.[19] But at the time of my fieldwork, the majority of migrants operated in standoff with the Australian government in the hopes of reaching Australia. Some I spoke with were also scared about the prospect of life in Phnom Penh. Like in campaigns against Nauru and Malaysia, Australian activists and humanitarians utilized colonial tropes of "third-world abuse" and human rights violations to critique the Cambodian arrangement.[20] For those who stayed in Nauru, resettlement programs, as chapter 5 details, looked to integrate them into the small island nation. Once given refugee status, they were assigned resettlement housing around Nauru by Australian contracted caseworkers. However, all refugees wanted to be in Australia, not in Nauru.

The next section turns to migrants whose asylum claims were denied and who appealed these decisions or were deported from Nauru. In Nauru's asylum system, there were elaborate reassessment rounds that extended the longevity of the offshore industry. Many screening procedures were driven by legal considerations that no asylum seeker be refouled to a place of danger, which might mean industry closure. In this section, I also show how the institutionalization of refugee legal practice contributed to the development of Nauru's offshore system. The law, I argue, played an important part in solidifying Nauru's toxic landscapes of accumulation, in particular when it comes to indigenizing projects between sovereign states. This relates to Nauru's specific colonial history around extractive projects, in which the island has been subject to capitalist rearrangements in order to give power to Australia's economy. As a result of the phosphate dependency years, Nauru already had the sociolegal structures in place for one system of value to slip into the footprints of another—even as the transformation of trade systems from phosphate to refugees engendered collective violence.

The Refugee Appeals Process in Nauru

Refugee appeals, under the system of a "refugee tribunal," are an intrinsic part of asylum operations worldwide. Refugee tribunals proliferate on a global scale, with trained tribunal members involved in development projects that seek to promote and build asylum systems internationally. These global systems are dependent on the logics of border inclusion and exclusion, looking to distil the "deserving" from "undeserving." Under the system known as "merits review," refugee tribunal members "stand in the shoes" of the decision maker to determine each asylum claimant's veracity afresh (Vrachnas et al. 2012, 324). Australia's refugee appeals system is regarded with high authority among industry professionals: a "world-leading merits review process" that surpasses even UNHCR's processing operations in the field, which are said to be "far less sophisticated or comprehensive" (Crock and Martin 2013, 138). Australia has a statewide Refugee Review Tribunal (RRT), established as a statutory body in 1993 under the country's Migration Act, with branches in each of Australia's states and territories.[21] Under the mainland practice of merits review, trained tribunal members reassess each migrant's asylum claim. If denied an appeal from the tribunal, asylum seekers in Australia have a third avenue of assessment through judicial review. Under section 476 of the Migration Act, judges at the Federal Circuit Court, Federal Court, or High Court reassess each migrant if it is decided that a legal error arose in the tribunal redetermination.

In Nauru's first processing operations, Australian Immigration Department staff, contracted into refugee determination, also reprocessed those whose asylum claims were denied. There was no external system of refugee tribunalists or judicial courts for conducting merits reviews. Nauru has an established court system set up under German colonial administration and progressively expanded under the British Commission. The state judicial structure consists of a District Court, Family Court, and Supreme Court, housed in a courthouse attached to the government buildings. In a country that has relied on extrajudicial authority since colonial rule, lawyers are a handful in number; no one is judicially trained. Following independence, a semiprofessional system of Australian Victorian bar-trained pleaders (known as "bush lawyers") was established to offer Nauruans more participation in their country's legal system. Yet few are legally proficient. Instead, the government employs foreign personnel to do Nauru's legal work and provide the judiciary with magistrates and judges. With the support of New Zealand legal funding, judges are recruited from overseas. Respected Australian and Fijian judges sit on Nauru's bench, along with dedicated Fijian professionals who strive to reorganize the country's legal system, which was virtually abandoned after the phosphate heydays. The majority of Nauru's Supreme Court cases relate to phosphate land disputes, with backlogged queues for lodging a decision-making complaint. Before 2012, Nauru did not have refugee tribunal courts or judicial court jurisdiction for asylum appeal.

Here was another instance where the institutionalization of refugees within international legal practice contributed to the development of Nauru's offshore system. Like other neocolonial contexts ripe for social engineering, Nauru became a laboratory for operationalizing RSD expertise. This was a "unique opportunity" for establishing a legal system that is "truly world class," Nauru's Australian deputy secretary announced in their paper presentation "Establishment of a New National Refugee Determination System: Threats and Opportunities; the Case of Nauru" at Monash University's Access to Asylum Conference in Italy (Vohra 2014). Neither the Nauruan nor Australian governments wanted to be accused of refouling a refugee, which would threaten the offshoring arrangement. In Nauru's phosphate laboratory, samples are collected hourly from products, and chemists analyze cadmium content, bone phosphate lime, and moisture levels—to meet international buyers' needs and evade penalty charges. Here, the global optics leveled on quality-controlling industry operations meant that Nauru's processing system also required enhanced decision making, even more so than in Australia.

Because Nauru had no history of refugee legislation or resettlement, the Nauruan and Australian governments solicited professional advisors to interpret international refugee legislation and formulate an ideal vision that fit in with the political strategies of Australia's regional migration management plans. Two emerging professions in international refugee and migration law found government utility for their expertise. Here, they could distil the foremost principles of UNHCR's international legal system to plan and build a processing system on a national scale. Over the years, under the auspices of UNHCR, specialist training and development work in refugee law and practice has created a vanguard of "refugee experts." The formation of the Nauruan asylum system drew on these global networks of transnational professionals, and advice was elicited from many quarters. Engagements between international and national agencies, academics, and UN intergovernmental and government divisions focused on strengthening Nauruan legal structures, infrastructural services, and national capabilities to appropriately house the operations. Ideas were discussed in prestigious research centers like the Kaldor Centre for International Refugee Law at Sydney's University of New South Wales and the University of Oxford's Refugee Studies Centre, as well as at industry conventions and more informal fora.

Like latter-day Prometheans, refugee industry professionals found the chance to explore their theories about an asylum system's optimum architecture, evolved into directives for the Nauruan project. Little different from eighteenth-century impulses that saw the imperial Pacific as a laboratory for scientific thought, this "unspoiled, living archive . . . offered unprecedented opportunities for comparative assessments and the testing of hypotheses" (Howe 2000, 33). They sought to form a just asylum system as that concept stemmed from international legal ideas about "credible fear." "RSD is like a diagnostic test," one industry legal advisor said to me in interview in Australia. "You would not expect doctors to deploy a diagnostic test that did not maximize the chances of making the correct diagnoses and which did not contain the necessary safeguards to do so." A modern vision of refugee diagnostic testing that was fair, effective, and independent and sieved out the "genuinely persecuted" was the ideal. When they compiled Nauru's Refugee Convention (2012), the operational planners made sure to provide for the establishment of both a Nauruan Refugee Status Review Tribunal and judicial appeal system in the country's new refugee legal system for anyone desiring reassessment. Unlike Australia's tripartite reassessment process, they also added in a fourth round of Australian High Court appeal. Later, the design would be championed at legal conferences as a cutting-edge framework that could contribute to refugee assessments "throughout the region" (Vohra 2014).[22]

Meanwhile, in Nauru, local motivation for legal acquiescence also stemmed from European claims to technological and scientific superiority. The colonial claim that law is a sign of civilization and rationality has an enduring legacy in Nauru, as does the reliance on foreign legal assistance. Even after independence, the country continues to use the Queensland Criminal Code, the appeal court remains the High Court of Australia, and judges and legal personnel are still recruited from overseas. Many in the Nauruan government saw economic benefits in the offshoring arrangement. Ironically, in light of Australian activists' narratives of islander savagery, many Nauruans also maintained an ecclesiastical belief in the virtues of international refugee law, and the idea of providing sanctuary to refugees. Having an asylum industry was, for many islanders I spoke with, a marker of a politically self-determining nation, of Christian values, and of civilization—against racialized visions of who should not belong. Nauruan bureaucrats consented to an influx of Australian officials into Nauruan government positions, including those familiar with international refugee and human rights law. As immigration and refugee management services are well-institutionalized industry sectors in Australia, many of the requisite industry players and bureaucratic administrators easily expanded their institutional fabric to Nauru. The formation of the Nauruan refugee system drew on these global networks of transnational professionals, slotting into a legal system that already revolved around a culture of fly-in-fly-out advisors. They worked on rebuilding and reordering the remains of the colonial infrastructure of phosphate extraction in service of a neocolonial extractive project around refugees.

Departing from Anglo conventions, the advisors excitedly trialed a three-member Nauru Refugee Status Review Tribunal. Three tribunal members from Australia's Refugee Review Tribunal flew over from Melbourne and Sydney for the second phase of reprocessing asylum seekers. The new tripartite system of Nauru was heralded as particularly progressive because most review hearings in Australia and Europe favor one tribunal member. In Nauru, if denied the first time through, migrants were afforded "the luxury" of being reassessed by not one but *three* Australian tribunal members. The Australian industry planners believed that having refugee merits reviewed by three independent and professionally trained refugee decision makers ensured maximum operational fairness. To have a tripartite tribunal demonstrated that Nauru was governed by fair Western ideals. They also included a panel of four barristers contracted to provide refugee defense for the third judicial review stage. For the Australian planners, bolstering Nauru's review tribunal with additional members and bringing a panel of Australian barristers for judicial presentation were further proof that technological advancement could be maintained. An even fairer process sought to demonstrate Western visions of justice in a place that some of Australia's campaigners against offshore processing labeled as operating outside the rule of law.

Operating from a pool of mainland Australian Refugee Review Tribunal members, under contract with the Nauruan government, the team of fly-in-fly-out tribunal members reassessed each asylum seeker over two-week sitting periods. Rather than making their decision as per the one-member system in Australia, the tripartite system allowed for the team to caucus each other over the credibility of human fear and potential of refoulement. The team completed their reassessments within a period of ninety days, providing written reasons for negative or positive decisions.

If denied again, all asylum seekers had a third recourse—to a Supreme Court hearing—if granted eligibility by the tribunal members. With New Zealand funding, the Nauruan government has put great efforts into reinvigorating their judicial system in recent years. In January 2014, a high-profile ruckus saw the dismissal of the resident magistrate and Supreme Court registrar Peter Law, followed by Chief Justice Geoffrey Eames. Law disputed a Nauruan government decision to expel two Australian businessmen: one ran the local radio, and both had trodden on the toes of government members in their small-town business dealings, running sidelines out of the Menen Hotel bar. At the time, Australian activist campaigners against the offshore operations latched onto the decision. They drew on colonial imaginaries of backwardness, circulating media reports of failed-state savagery that compared Nauru to the Congo (see, for example, Clarke 2014). These events were at the point when asylum appeals were on the horizon, with more migrants receiving asylum adjudications from the tribunal stage.

A high-profile protest at the RPCs in July 2013 also saw 153 asylum seekers charged with criminal damage for having burned down RPC 3. This was not the first time protests had erupted, but it was certainly the most extreme. Planes with asylum seekers had arrived in Nauru since September 2012, but RSD was slow to get off the ground: there were lawyers to contract and translocate, tribunals to set up, legislation to enact, locals to train to make the operation "regional," in addition to the general uncertainty of the Australian government about what to do with the asylum seekers in Nauru, now that they had pursued the offshore spectacle of deterrence. With chants of "We're refugees not criminals," "We want to go to Australia, we should be free," and "Nauru Guantanamo," RPC1 was dramatically burnt to the ground, as groups of asylum seekers demanded to know when the processing of their claims would begin. They demanded the start of RSD, the improvement of conditions, and other standard operating procedures from Australia, such as back then refugee defense lawyers. The disaster was the greatest catastrophe to happen in Nauru at the time (over AU$60 million in damages to properties that were uninsured). The disaster costs were enormous: 5 people were sent to hospital, and 153 asylum seekers were charged with damages. They were all represented by legal defenders flown out from Melbourne for several months at exorbitant cost, and eventually given Nauruan community service. However, the value of advancing the company town district far outweighed the violent consequences entangled in offshore processing.

The Supreme Court, already backlogged with phosphate land-dispute cases, was faced with the immensity of taking on the RPC rioters, in addition to the final asylum appeals load. To counter threats to end offshore processing, and in anticipation of the new workload, in August 2014, the Nauruan government appointed a new Supreme Court bench of not just one but, again, a *three-strong* judicial team. Fiji's former vice president, Joni Madraiwiwi, who sat on the Truth and Reconciliation Commission in Solomon Islands in 2008, took up Nauru's post as chief justice. Mohammed Shafi Khan, a former Queensland, Victorian, Australian Capital Territory, and Fiji barrister, and Jane Elizabeth Hamilton-White, a former Queensland barrister and principal magistrate of the Solomon Islands, were also appointed to the bench. The following year, in October 2015, they appointed Filimone Jitoko, senior law lecturer at USP and High Court judge, as the new Supreme Court registrar. Shortly before Jitoko's appointment, before asylum seekers started receiving appeals decisions, an entirely new refugee courthouse was built for the final appeals stage; it opened to proud fanfare during my fieldwork. Now, the country had courthouses dedicated to refugee *and* phosphate extraction disputes. "Despite criticism from some overseas media outlets with no knowledge of our system and the past problems, we have held fast to the commitment we made to the Nauruan people when we were elected, and the result is a more accountable legal system," Nauru's minister Adeang said at the time (RON 2015a).

In Australia, defense lawyers are not usually trained barristers but migration agents who specialize in refugee law. They do not have practice jurisdiction in supreme courts, nor do their contracts cover them for this third judicial round in Australian or offshore processing. Instead, for Nauru, fly-in-fly-out Australian contracted barristers, all well versed in credibility-of-fear representation, supported migrants' asylum claims. Here, receiving a negative decision from the Nauru Supreme Court met with one final route for appeal, unlike the conventional three rounds in Australia. Under Nauru's Appeals (Amendment) Act 1974 and Australia's Nauru (High Court Appeals) Act 1976, Supreme Court appeals were at the time determined by the High Court of Australia and not domestically.[23] Nauruan citizens could lodge an appeal on a lower court decision to the Australian High Court and fly to Canberra for their appeal hearing. If denied three times, all asylum seekers in Nauru had a fourth round of asylum appeal through the High Court of Australia.

In Australia, the High Court is the third and final appeals possibility for someon making an asylum claim. But in Nauru, this added a fourth part close to the intense reassessment process. During the High Court hearings conducted in Canberra, no asylum seekers could be physically present, as is the way in Australia. Instead, contracted Australian barristers provided representation for asylum seekers, defending them in Australia in front of a bench of seven justices. Decisions of the High Court on asylum appeals were final. There were no further reassessment rounds once a matter was decided by the High Court, and the decision remained binding on all other courts throughout Australia.

But it cannot be said that the hazardous effects of refugee processing systems stop here. Again, migrants from the Global South are subject to cumulative forms of toxic exposure far disproportionate to those experienced by the majority of their Global North counterparts who seek to move elsewhere.[24] These nation-state hierarchies that unevenly organize life—where nationality becomes a proxy for race and class—traveled to Nauru with the offshore refugee industry.

Toxic Accumulation

At the tail end of this elaborate and excruciating assessment process, asylum seekers denied in Nauru's extractive setting were deported on chartered flights to their home regions. For those asylum seekers who raised the topic of removal to me, deportation was a humiliating and deeply unsettling possibility. It foreclosed why they were pushed to leave their home countries and make the lengthy precarious journeys that segued them to Nauru. Some had been financially supported by networks of family and friends, and had spent months, often years, in their attempts to reach Australia. These momentous journeys had, for all, culminated in a treacherous Indian Ocean crossing, followed by lengthy entanglements in the offshore industry circuits. For some, deportation meant the real possibility of being returned to harmful situations, socioeconomic devastation, and the very conflicts they had tried to escape. These could be environments that were unfamiliar or hostile, and where suspicion and stigmatization would be attached to their return. Other asylum seekers I spoke with in Nauru were concerned about how they could repay the spiraling debts that supported their journeys abroad. This combined with feelings of disappointment, failure, and shame, and the hostility they might face from family and acquaintances if they were deported. Even then, deportation so often does not conclude a migrant's journey (Hiemstra 2019). Those asylum seekers who touched on deportation with me pledged that if they were deported, they would simply migrate again, desperately willing to re-engage in the refugee business and its toxic toll.

Rejected asylum seekers were certainly cast as criminal, threatening, or unwanted foreign Others, treated like waste, and expelled in a similar manner from Nauru. Yet, unlike in Zygmunt Bauman's (2004) terms, where people are rendered abject waste, the bodies of rejected asylum seekers became recurring sites of accumulation. Industry players like IOM and charter flight agencies, such as Adagold Aviation (specialists in mining and resources projects in remote locations) and Skytraders (once known for shipping chilled meat), were among a number of providers who found financial profit from this end of the supply chain. They facilitated the transferral of asylum seekers between Nauru, Australia, migrants' countries of origin, and other nearby regions. In the 2014–2015 financial year, the Australian Senate reported expenditures for charter flights added up to almost AU$17 million for Nauru alone. These unprecedented corporate profits point to the ultimate political value extracted from Nauru's offshore frontier. Deported asylum seekers—and the entire assessment cycle—allow Australia to show its power and reaffirm political subjectivities of the natural citizen versus a foreign racialized Other. Refugee assessment offers a way to manage people, whereby particular racialized migrants are represented as a toxin that should be disposed of. This is in spite of the very real toxicities that accumulate in migrants' bodies in the service of political economic accumulation. Disposability then is not just a byproduct of capitalist production; profit is further secured in the wasting of certain racialized and criminalized populations.

Moral capital was also secured in the disposing of populations by industry advocates. In their activism, advocates linked deported asylum seekers to the industry's global political economy through a depoliticizing frame. From the outset, Australian campaigners based their lobbying efforts to relocate Nauru's refugee industry on classic colonial discourses of islander "underdevelopment" and "savagery." Australian activists gave visibility to the toxics risks that the offshore refugee operations presented, but in ways that were concerned with the liberation of third-world refugee victims. They broadcast images of legitimate refugees deported from Nauru in publications like Amnesty International's *Islands of Despair: Australia's "Processing" of Refugees on Nauru* (2016) and the Edmund Rice Centre's *Deported to Danger: Investigation into the Fate of Deported People*

(2016), and in numerous Australian and global media reports. Using photos of brutality and horrific narratives sent in by or sourced from rejected asylum seekers, activists reinforced the veracity of the refugee as a suffering victim saved by first-world compassion. Asylum was also represented as a benevolent operation, rather than a migration governance system premised on the adjudication of fear. Starkly, these representations misrecognized the shared ravages of dispossession, exploitation, and oppression between asylum seekers and Nauruans in favor of the fetishization of refugee suffering. This is not to deny that many asylum seekers have been through violence, as previously described—and could very easily reexperience it on return. Instead, it is indicative of the governmentalizing power of a system premised on hierarchies of separation, whereby the West is continually instituted in a positional superiority over its Others. These hierarchies are facilitated here through the representation of the asylum seeker and the refugee either as suffering or risky bodies.

As the next chapter details, activist praxis fueled new levels of toxic risk that encouraged migrants to perform in particular ways: to draw in the interest of Australian liberal publics, who were attracted by narratives of refugees as vulnerable and Nauruans as savage. The international legal system of pathologized suffering also informed the perception of many migrants concerning the roles they should play to obtain asylum in Australia. Many asylum seekers in Nauru saw ingratiating themselves with Australian activists and emphasizing helplessness and Nauruan savagery as key to moving to Australia. The effects of basing a politics on these moral imperatives, however, is that it legitimizes the regimes of control and practices of violence of the overall refugee industry. Instead, this mode of envisioning Nauru as an underdeveloped backwater in counter to the "modern West" revives a colonial discourse that justifies new modes of Australian investment in the refugee industry. The civilizational discourse of underdevelopment and morally legitimate suffering has proven very useful to the global refugee industry, which is perennially substantiated on the basis of these hierarchies. Under a policy of deterrence, discourses of brutality are also profitable to the Australian government's border spectacle. Meanwhile, because of the political economic imperatives involved in sustaining the supply chain, risk creates surplus value for the mobile global refugee industry, cyclically tasked to carry out the operations in boomtown contexts like Nauru on a regular basis.

SECURING THE OFFSHORE INDUSTRY

There were remarkable differences between refugee and nonrefugee industry environments on Nauru, which made the values attached to the offshoring arrangement starkly apparent. The immense concern of the Australian and Nauruan governments in sustaining the system—unsusceptible to legal challenge—made the former function almost as if a city in a city, exuding the sheen of health and safety regulation in contrast to the nonrefugee environment. I walked around phosphate plants ravaged with dust and rust, sharp and jagged edges teeming with tetanus possibilities. Asbestos coursed through roofs, as a hangover from British Phosphate Commission days and Nauruan independence glory years. Food lay out of date in schools and the largely Chinese-run retail shops, with little need or will for firm business regulation. Electrical wiring systems often fizzled; power cuts and incidence of electrocution were all too frequent. But over the course of my time on Nauru, at the cusp of two industry eras when more migrants received refugee status, moving from the RPCs across Nauru's urban fringe, I lived through a noticeable operational shift. Refugees interacted more routinely with nonrefugee spheres, transforming the company town state into one preoccupied with risk adversarialism.

Asbestos reparations began with the local church roof and across successive buildings around Nauru's urban hub. Laminates marked with Transfield appeared across the dwindling phosphate industry sector and other public service divisions: "Are there any uncontrolled hazards? Take FIVE to Keep FIVE. Think START: Stop, Think, Assess, Review, Talk." Australian industry personnel led information

FIGURE 11.   New driving safety checks in Nauru's Aiwo District. Photo by Julia Morris.

and industry-training sessions for Nauruan public service departments, firefighters, police, and more, on how to meet Australia's occupational health and safety (OHS) requirements, write incident reports, and take part in health and safety liaison inspections. Police roadblocks and breathalyzer checks became routine under the training guidance of Australian Federal Police. All were dramatically out of place on Nauru's main ring road, where common practice is to dexterously juggle a family on one bike, and where overburdened phosphate lorries swerve at top speeds, drivers with cans of ACE in hand, in flagrance of phosphate commissioner–developed laws.[1]

A warning sign "Watch out for children playing" went up on the road by the Anibare refugee resettlement housing complex. One weekday morning, I headed out on a run around the phosphate extraction fields, circumnavigating the refugee processing sites, before returning past mined-out limestone pinnacles. A Transfield truck pulled up beside me, distinctively marked with flashing headlights tacked to the side, as per refugee industry OHS protocol. Two jovial refugee managerial workers stuck their heads out. One handed me a luminescent vest, saying, "We have OHS meetings every week. Several people have issued reports about a low-visibility runner up here. One driver said he almost hit you. Next time you go running, make sure you have this hi-vis vest on." Like the oil company town culture Diana Davids Hinton describes, community life in Nauru "ran according to company rules" (2008, 370).

In chapter 2, I looked at the metallurgical practices that migrants undergo as part of refugee status determination, tracking some of the on-the-ground realities of this system on people's lives. I showed the extractive effects of this process, in which objectification and retraumatization are central. This chapter draws on my ethnographic fieldwork, moving against simplistic assumptions that depict Nauru as a "black site" outside of international oversight. Offshore contexts are frequently depicted and indeed *can be* financially successful because they operate as havens outside of international accountability (Maurer 1998; Palan 2006). In Nauru, the offshore trope has become commonplace. The "racist rhetorics of representation" (West 2016) surrounding Nauru are replete with colonial imaginaries of Western salvationalism extending to the Conradian darkness of the "savage" world. Headlines like "Out of Sight: Out of Mind: Human Rights Abuses at Nauru's Immigration Detention Centre" (2015), and "Nauru, Refugees and Australia's 'Torture Complex'" (2016), books such as *Offshore: Behind the Wire on Manus and Nauru* (2016), and academic networks like Researchers against Pacific Black Sites conjure a distancing racialized imaginary. This depiction is heavily embedded in colonial genealogies, whereby white Australian humanitarians sweep in as saviors. However, in counter to these depictions, as my opening vignette makes clear, an extreme amount of risk managerialism went into attempting to secure the offshore industry project. Drawing on my findings, I argue that because offshore refugee processing has been exceptionally politically and economically valuable for the Australian and Nauruan governments and their industry contractors, but also exceptionally risky—financially, politically, and in terms of human safety—risk managerialism, including an array of inspectorates, were intrinsic to company town development. These "elaborately choreographed routines," as Appel also finds in her work on the many safety rituals of Equatorial Guinea's offshore oil environments (2012, 692), are intended to transmit the feeling of a sanitized and protected environment to workers, residents, and visitors. They are part of the day-to-day corporate practices found across the world's mineral frontiers that endeavor to protect industry assets.

Industry personnel may envision "the achievement of a new kind of legitimacy through their participation in regulatory processes" (Kirsch 2014, 185), deploying claims to legal and medical standards to stifle criticism and resistance. But asylum presents conditions that differ from other forms of resource extraction. In Nauru, contracted organizations could not avoid the hazards that a human extractive sector presents. Mental health destruction, self-harm, hunger strikes, and fears of violent protests dominated the industry's every day. These risks were unusually destructive because of the moral strength of activist networks, which contributed to making Nauru an exceptionally risky operational environment. Interventions by activists rested on a moral deployment of the body of the refugee as suffering and vulnerable. Although these concerns are certainly real, the stereotype of vulnerability informed the perception of many migrants concerning the roles they should play to obtain asylum in Australia. In the context of a harsh policy, in which asylum seekers' and refugees' movements were limited to the island's confines, many migrants in Nauru saw ingratiating themselves with Australian activists and emphasizing helplessness and Nauruan savagery as key to moving to Australia. These troubling representations reveal how migrants' bodies remain entangled with the forces of capital—and are disproportionately subject to objectifying practices that intensify the risks to their bodies.

Another surprising finding of my fieldwork was that some of this was the case with phosphate processing in the British Phosphate Commission era. An incredible amount of risk managerial practices went into securing phosphate commerce—an industrial environment also suffused by ecological, financial, and reputational risks. Yet here lay, for farming enterprise, cut-price phosphate, and overall, the sustenance of the global agricultural economy. The success of the phosphate business justified the expenditures. So, too, with refugees. The Australian and Nauruan governments transposed their concerns from losing mineral to migrant commodities, wherein lay a much-promoted political policy. High political economic factors were at stake for both governments. The Australian political party at the time might lose power, as when the Rudd Labour government pulled out in 2008. Billions of dollars had been poured into the industry project, as later chapters elaborate, to farcical extent. The Nauruan government might go bankrupt, as it had from phosphate wealth exhaustion previously. Pressingly, Australian refugee industry workers were almost all employed under Australian contracts. Asylum seekers fell under workplace "duty of care." No firm wanted to be liable for the industry lawsuits that erupt from noncompliance or accidents in the workplace. "Mundane" health and safety practices are an integral part of the industry's "modularity" (Appel 2019), which operationalized to control the financial and toxic effects of Nauru's company town. Ultimately, technologies of "audit culture" (Strathern 2000) look to provide accountability and legitimacy for problematic practices but do little for the real dangers of a carceral context. While the political economic expediency of these moves is readily discernible, this again begs the question: Who is subject to a politics of exposure as these industries coalesce? Despite the plethora of risk management practices, I suggest that risks endemic to a human processing industry can be little constrained, no matter how much regulation is attempted.

Part One: Company Town Safety

In Nauru, traces of health and safety regulations predated the refugee industry, owing to the work of the colonial phosphate industry. The later BPC years of the 1950s and 1960s were a time when the associated risks of phosphate industrial operations became the subject of international concern. An increasing number of industry safety standards and regulatory auditors developed worldwide to protect workers on extraction sites. The push behind much of the improvement drive was to minimize workplace errors so as to maximize productivity and promote peace between capital and labor. The parallel rise in trade labor unions, followed by duty-of-care legislation and personal injury claims, motivated employers to reduce the human and financial cost of workplace injury. Instead, the dominant workplace trend gradually moved toward enhancing industrial practice through an increased focus on safety and other workplace enhancement regimes (Smith and Leggat 2005).

For the BPC administrators, practices of industrial regulation demanded adherence. In Nauru, a large percentage of the workforce was Australian and thus governed by the Australian occupational health and safety guidelines developing at the time around mining risks. Workers' Compensation ordinances provided for the compensation to workers for injuries sustained on the job. Until 1968, Nauru also remained a UN Civilizational Trust (it was previously a League of Nations Trust). First the permanent mandates and later the trust commissions took a particular interest in Nauru because of the "peculiar circumstances" of the mandate (Viviani 1970, 49). At the same time, other countries sought monopoly over Nauru's high-grade phosphate—"always on the look-out for opportunities of misrepresenting this country," argued the British MP Sir Maclean at a debate on June 17, 1920, in the British Parliament. The Australian government was sensitive to criticisms of local exploitation, making the ministerial statement in 1922 that "the working of the phosphate deposits is in no way prejudicial to the interests of the natives, who, on the contrary, have never been so well off as they are under the present Administration" (cited in Viviani 1970, 49). Like the League of Nations before, the UN received regular reports from the administrators, phosphate workers, locals, missionaries, and other visitors in the event of discontent. They conducted annual and later triennial visiting missions that focused on the health and well-being of Nauruans. The phosphate commissioners were often called to task to display the benefits of their administration for locals and validate the continued mining, which was expressed through the paternalist tradition of the benevolent company town. This was also a time when indigenous rights movements had risen to critique imperial practices of exploitative resource extraction and advocate for self-determination. In Australia and

FIGURE 12. British Phosphate Commission–era road safety in Nauru. Photo courtesy of the British Archives at Kew.

the Pacific, liberal quarters called for the nationalization of mining into the hands of the Nauruan people. By giving the company town the sheen of pleasantry, phosphate commissioners attempted to attract Australian workers, and deflect attention away from the cut prices they gave themselves—often the subject of UN debate.

As chapter 2 made clear, phosphate processing comes with a range of pollutant effects, not to mention bodily and ecological risks. The British Phosphate Commission worked with the World Health Organization (est. 1948) and the South Pacific Commission (est. 1947) around the development of health and safety programs. They also provided annual reports to the International Labor Organization (est. 1919) that justified their good works. They emphasized the BPC's high labor standards within an aesthetic urban environment, following the principles established in paternalist company towns more generally. The BPC introduced several risk-mitigation measures to prevent the leachability and dispersion of hazardous chemical elements abundant in superphosphates. For example, an electrostatic dust precipitator reduced the amount of phosphate dust produced; workers also wore fume hoods to protect against associated toxins that might minimize production rates, or worse yet, curtail this offshore extractive boom. Waste management infrastructure controlled the disposal of waste. The phosphate commissioners established a state system of rubbish collection, working with the Nauru Local Government Council in the 1950s to arrange inter-district "village pride" competitions to promote cleanliness and hygiene. The BPC administration carried out regular servicing and repair of administration and Nauru Local Government Council buses, trucks, utilities, cars, and other plant and heavy equipment. All districts were sprayed regularly with residual insecticides spread by power-driven misting machines. To ensure they had a stable and problem-free working context, Nauruans were provided with extensive welfare programs, including local hospitals, school systems, athletic clubs, picture houses, and social and educational clubs. Booster injections against all major diseases were administered, complete with annual X-rays for the entire population at the hospital built by the BPC administration.[2]

UN inspectors remarked on the "good health of the inhabitants" and that the amount of cadmium dust associated with phosphate mining was "insignificant" (United Nations 1965). "The extraction and export of phosphate is by efficient modern methods," assured the Australian administration in response to concerns about the impact of the mining site on Nauruans (Australian Government 1959–1960). Although the UN Trusteeship regularly critiqued the phosphate administrators' distribution of funds and lobbied for greater local inclusion in the mining operations, they commended the "high standard of living and social services available to Nauruans" (United Nations 1965).

These insidious forms of risk managerialism and corporate social responsibility (CSR) engineering are familiar to scholars of toxic risks looking at the manufacturing of ambiguity (Auyero and Swistun 2009; Kuchinskaya 2014; Murphy 2006). Strategies, actions, and discourses are operationalized to generate uncertainty about the connections between chemicals and bodily reactions, and ultimately maximize industry profits. Certainly, local Nauruans were not immune to pollution in their country. The majority were well aware that that phosphate industry did emit toxins. However, the invisibility of scientific data, weighed against the visibility of the industry's avowed benefits. This conditioned a response to exposure among many Nauruans that was shaped by a trade-off of health for short-term economic progress and material rewards. Such acclimation to "the banality of toxicity" (Ahmann 2018) was—and continues to be—compounded by the spectacle of phosphate as the fuel of Nauru's modernity, supporting the foodways of people living in far-off regions.

I spoke with many of Nauru's older residents, who reminisced with fondness over these BPC years, making comments like, "Everything was clean and orderly," "Dust wasn't an issue," "The drainage system was state of the art." Beatrice, one of Nauru's oldest residents, looked almost misty-eyed as she spoke to me of the "village pride–style" competitions across Nauru's company town quadrants. Ironically, I met Beatrice at a sausage-sizzle event at one of the refugee industry workers' compounds, organized by Transfield Services, the then chief contracted management firm in Nauru's refugee industry. Designed to coincide with an Aussie rules football match and raise money for local community organizations, the sausage sizzle was one of many events vital to the reconfigured corporate benevolence across the industrial town. Beatrice and I quickly got chatting and exchanged phone numbers. This was so often the way in a context where my young white gendered identity opened many doors for me, coming from, in this instance, a place of maternal concern and islander hospitality. One week later, I was sitting on a woven pandanus mat in a gazebo in Beatrice's backyard, sipping from a coconut freshly picked by her husband, and speaking about her childhood memories of the later BPC years.

"Back then we were proud of our nickname, Pleasant Island," Beatrice recounted. "Now, it's just kind of ironic. We use it and laugh. Have you seen the T-shirts they sell on the market? The 'Pleasant Island' ones? People [by which she meant largely Australian industry workers] buy that stuff as a joke." I actually had, I remarked, without mentioning to Beatrice the sniggering Australian refugee industry workers I had also spotted lining up to buy one.[3] She sighed. "The place is a dump. No one cares anymore." She swept her arm in a wide arc. Her yard, like so many others, was littered with the refuse and beer cans that characterize the Nauruan landscape. None of the home maintenance is provided by the phosphate administrators, as used to be the case before, which created an imperceptibility surrounding phosphate's toxic effects. Even as we spoke, flumes spouted from the phosphate plants in the distance, while a pack of wild dogs ran past her door. (A problem that refugee industry firms were trying to sort out.) The stark contrast between the elaborate risk-prevention regulations of the BPC days and the phosphate dangers encountered in Nauru now made the hazardous nature of the business immediately discernable. Predicting such eventualities, a sizeable faction of locals stood against Nauruan independence in 1968. They pushed back against the move toward self-determination, arguing that conditions would be more favorable if the island stayed under Australian administration and the Trusteeship mandate.

Subsequently, when the Nauru Phosphate Corporation took over the mining, there was little interest in maintaining industrial manufacturing protocols. The BPC pulled out with little in the way of industry transition, support, or guidance, leaving the operation at the hands of the newly inaugurated NPC. As many Nauruans became overnight millionaires, in-house regulations slid into abandon. "Aiwo was atrocious in the '70s and '80s, it was just dust up to your ankles," a RONPhos executive recounted to me of this time. "There was no legislative requirement nor were people particularly concerned with the environment. Economically it was just unimportant." a RONPhos executive recounted to me of this time. The electrostatic dust precipitator was very expensive and labor-intensive, requiring specific expertise. He continued: "Each day you could see the dust slowly, slowly, starting to come out the chimney at the factories. It started accumulating in the water tanks and in the drains." My neighbor Sean, a phosphate worker, described this: "I remember for us as kids, it was like snow. Dust floating down when the cantilever was in motion. It was up to your ankles. We would play in the stuff. For our parents, it wasn't like that. Growing up right here in Aiwo, people had to close their gutters because they couldn't drink water from the roofs. It was just thick with it. Nauruans, life expectancy, fifty-five. God knows what stuff we've been drinking, inhaling."

Those Nauruans I spoke with about the NPC and RONPhos-era contrasts insisted that the contemporary phosphate town was an improvement to earlier NPC days. However, living in Nauru's Aiwo District, it was clear that in-house regulations were not a priority. In a country where phosphate still constitutes the third-biggest revenue sector, concerns are often not something to talk about too loudly, nor are they financially useful. The majority of Nauruans knew all too well the risks of phosphate extraction. Workers knew that they were systematically exposed to dangerous substances while working in the phosphate mines and plants. Buada residents knew that the easy cash afforded by backyard extraction was "killing the land," and many locals feared the respirational consequences of living in a factory district, even as they benefited from the phosphate wealth. John, a phosphate executive, commented: "People in the environment and medical departments sometimes say, "Oh maybe we should stop mining, look at something else, we've done enough damage, it's time to move on." They try and carry out a health study. But then the government just shuts them up because they want the money. And everyone else wants the money. So, with Nauru, the environmental, the health impact takes a back seat to economic progress. I'm an environmentalist and it breaks my heart because I'm destroying my island. But when it comes to mining, money wins." Sitting in his office, where he had a paperweight made of phosphate on his desk, I found John's comment a stark admission of the active blinders placed on better understanding pollution in the country. Yet, I soon noticed that others spoke openly about the inaction of government authorities when it came to pollution. Sizable numbers of local residents also found it monotonous to engage too long with the subject. This was part of "an everyday praxis of not noticing" (Ahmann 2018, 145) compounded by an attunement to long-term exposures (Shapiro 2015). Given that life for Nauruans has for centuries revolved around the monoeconomic boom of the phosphate industry, islanders have long learned that accepting pollution is a condition of survival locally. Overall, the reliance on phosphate has placed many people in a position where bodily and ecological risks are rendered subservient to capital. In Nauru, toxins have accumulated over generations, but residents are living through a net reduction in active phosphate extraction and a new boomtown heyday from the refugee industry. Thus, "lag acts on the sensorium" (Ahmann 2018, 146), contributing to a local quiescence to hazardous industry.

Part Two: A Corporate Mindset

> Everything needs to meet Australian standards because Australia is building it and it's country-funded and might have a liability otherwise. So, disability ramps will be installed, just like with all things that would be required if this was taking place in Australia.
>
> —Refugee industry contractor, Nauru, June 2015

There were several reasons for the elaborate risk world I encountered in Nauru. Fieldwork made clear that the many forms of risk adversarialism were partially related to the remaking of Nauru as a company town, led by Australian firms for whom risk management has become the mainstay of industrial practice. The changes that ensued in Nauru are symptomatic of industry practice meant to secure smoother conditions for extractive accumulation and enhance workforce productivity. Five-step incident prevention drills like "START," health and safety training protocols, and Comcare health and safety quality controllers are just as ubiquitous across other industrial environments, from offshore hydrocarbons production to oil sands extraction or wherever the next big commodity boom is found, giving a sense of the naturalization of refugees in the field of industry practice.

Whereas I thought nothing of jumping on the back of a motorbike or running without wearing a hi-vis vest, far outside the optic of my university insurance protocols, for refugee industry workers, safety rituals are an important part of the "day-to-day sociomaterial practices" (Appel 2015, 266) that allow manufacturing to continue, and provide accountability against hazardous industrial work. It was the resource-rich sector of refugee processing, in some respects little different to other hazardous extractive industries that enabled one contracted offshore industry executive to say to me with utter confidence: "We're not doing anything extra special or different offshore, other than people working in that part of the business are very aware that it's under the spotlight. The kind of things that we do there are no different than what we'd do if we were working anywhere else . . . the health and safety, the risk and audit, these are all important to the performance and culture of the organization." The executive's comment that "we're not doing anything extra special or different offshore" calls attention to the elaborate safety regimes that go with hazardous industry work, what Appel (2012) shows to be entangled in corporate profit, liability, and risk. It was in some respects only natural that when asylum processing restarted in Nauru, workforces familiar with high-risk offshore oil rig contexts like Transfield, Canstruct, and Wilson would successfully tender for offshore refugee industry contracts and extrapolate elaborate corporate safety practices to Nauru. The high-risk nature of offshore refugee processing enabled businesses well versed in other hazardous extractive contexts to expand to this new industry sector, bringing similar workplace procedures not out of place, I was so often told, in their work in offshore mineral processing and other extractive zones. Another industry executive explained: "We recognize that we operate in dangerous areas. The challenges also are that we're operating in countries where the roads aren't great, seatbelts are unheard of, lighting isn't used, driving conditions can be very troubling, so we're trying to work against that culture almost to say, 'Forget that, if you want to work for us, you've got to wear your helmet, use lights, etc. Your vehicles will be checked more often.'" I might not have noticed these exacting attentions to detail in Australia, but in Nauru this safety culture operated in extreme counterpoint to life outside nonindustry spaces. For example, I would catch a lift with Australian refugee industry workers who would strictly keep to speed limits, check I was wearing my seatbelt, and all had attachable headlights for trips up through the former phosphate now refugee processing fields. In contrast, catching lifts with locals and phosphate workers, I would sometimes climb over rusted bumpers, and have trouble even finding a seatbelt, let alone putting one on. During my visits to the phosphate extraction fields, I would be taken up industry machinery, no hardhat or mask required—or even available. But this was definitely not the case with refugee industrial operations. In contrast, like in the BPC years before, the refugee industry district sparkled with the rose-tinted gleam of occupational health and safety and duty-of-care regulation.

As noted before, Nauru is now a "regional processing country" (rather than "offshore") and hence a company town–style island. Living there was like living in the heart of the industry once the centers opened for in-and-out movement. Not only are the political economic risks incredibly high—few industry executives wanted the loss of an offshore contract or the end of the business under their watch—but so, too, are the physical risks for workforces and those in the processing stages. In many respects, the safety culture that enveloped Nauru was a reflection of the attention to risk and liability that has grown across the industry in recent years, but particularly in the much riskier offshore industrial environment with its powerful activist scene.

The Spectacle of Risk: "End Offshore Extraction"

More than anything, offshore risk was firmly entangled in the constant exposure of activist campaigns. Refugee campaign groups (made up of incensed Australian citizenry, refugee industry personnel, and migrants) like Refugee Action
Coalition; Refugee Action Collective; Buddies Refugee Support Group; Welcome
to Australia; Grandmothers for Refugees; RISE: Refugees, Survivors, and Ex-
detainees; and Australian Churches Refugee Taskforce all organized high-
profile campaigns and rallies to close Nauru and Manus, and "bring refugees to
Australia." Within and alongside these campaign groups came many different
strategies and high-profile players. All engaged in their own in-alliances and
feuds around the best methods for successful organizing.[4] This varied from
abolitionist-style efforts that included public protests to staged boycotts and di-
vestment campaigns of contractors and their affiliates, to organizations and individuals contracting with the Australian Immigration Department in the
hopes of reforming from the inside out.

During my fieldwork, Australia's mainland human rights and refugee lawyers
were constantly engaged in High Court challenges to bring offshore processing
onshore. This included an International Criminal Court submission against the
Australian government for crimes against humanity in 2017.[5] The rhetorical narratives of advocates in this field can be quite direct, calling into visibility the toxic
effects of sending migrants offshore. Their strategies are set within the moralizing
framework of refugee vulnerability and Australian salvationalism from the alleged darkness of Nauru. In one instance, renowned Melbourne human rights
lawyer and refugee advocate Julian Burnside retweeted a photoshopped image of
then immigration minister Peter Dutton as a Nazi.[6] Similarly, journalists in Australia's liberal media (the ABC, the *Guardian*, and the *Sydney Morning Herald*)
were also central campaigners. Some had former refugee camp volunteers in their
teams and felt strongly about the shrinking spaces of Australia's asylum system. In
this way, the knowledge economy of refugees fomented a particular disposition
around whose lives are more (or less) worthy of being saved (Fassin 2010).

Within the government, several key spokespersons emerged, giving vocal political backing in support of the refugee industry. In particular, the Green Party
senator Sarah Hansom-Young, remains a prominent refugee advocate. There are
also several advocates against offshoring inside the Liberal and Labour parties.
The amount of standing-committee hearings and commissioned reports on Nauru over the years speaks volumes to the debates that take place within dominant
government chambers. Some NGOs and individuals are vocal proponents of ending offshore operations. Others took offshore contracts specifically to conduct
subversive activism, in a context long rife with whistleblowers and snuck-in activ-

ists (Morris 2022). The number of leaks, whistleblowing, and Australian Freedom of Information (FOI) requests and disclosure logs across the years makes clear the focus of the many organizing efforts. This also explains the automatic suspicion that I came under during my fieldwork. I was frequently assumed to have activist intentions—and given stern warnings by Nauruan administrators against it.

The campaigns that received global media attention were those saturated in claims around industry standards and a moralizing rhetoric of refugees at risk and Australian salvation. Australian activists waged lengthy efforts to expose any ways in which the industry fell afoul of Australian health and safety or other key operational standards. Frequently, they used the framework of refugee vulnerability and rescue to capture critical attention. This reactivated the colonial dichotomy of barbarity and civilization, constructing "refugees" and Nauruans as racialized victims or villains. But while humanitarian representations suggest the contrary, asylum seekers and refugees in Nauru were by no means passive victims. Rather, individuals and groups strategically mobilized in a variety of ways as part of a "politics of survival" (Fiddian-Qasmiyeh 2014).

In Nauru, some refugees took on as many roles as they could in local and corporate workforces, willing to present themselves as proactive contributors to the Australian economy. Others looked to ingratiate themselves with authorities and individual helpers as a survival strategy in the context of an unknowable future. This was also, some migrants informed me, a good tactic if—and when—competition eventuated for resettlement places outside of Nauru. Such strategies were not a pie-in-the-sky dream. During my fieldwork, a small number of refugees received resettlement places in Canada under the radar, through private sponsorship. These tendencies show how migration regimes can operate in quite discretionary ways, as much as through hierarchies of valuing some lives over others (Ticktin 2011). Many migrants also kept their heads down, embarrassed at the situation and hoping that the Australian government would cave. Within the enduring power of this arrangement, still more refused to be involved in any government initiative, closing the doors of Australian-funded businesses and boycotting all NGO-run programs. A smaller number of asylum seekers and refugees engaged in constant battles against the Australian and Nauruan governments through high profile #CloseNauru campaigns. They worked with some of Australia's activists using social media to facilitate collective action.

Possibilities for political action were severely curtailed in Nauru. Many asylum seekers and refugees experienced overwhelming sensations of isolation and arbitrary policies. As chapter 2 detailed, many feared being returned to their country of origin and struggled with the uncertainty of their future. People experienced what they described as routinized violence and neglect—an "undifferentiated exposure" of living "in the throes of slow violence" (Ahmann 2018, 143).

This led some migrants, as environmental anthropologists of other toxic environments find (Fortun 2001; Petryna 2002), to crystalize such slow-motion imperceptibilities into deliberate formulations of urgency. Protests and strikes were a powerful way for asylum seekers and refugees to mobilize support in Australia and internationally and try to effect change.

Several asylum seekers and refugees in Nauru described to me how they circulated videos, photos, and narratives to Australian activists, where they graphically detailed past experiences of violence to leverage for moving to Australia. They often used rhetorical tropes of escape from Islamic fundamentalism, refugee vulnerability, and Australian democratic-state welcome, combined with civilizational discourses of "underdevelopment" and "the rule of law" leveled on Nauruans. They also constructed websites like "Offshore Processing Centre Voice" and the Facebook group "Nauru's Refugees' News," posting on other social media sites relevant to furthering mobility endeavors. "Well, what else can we do to get there?" Jamil, a staunch self-labeled activist refugee from Iran, asked me on one occasion, as we stood at the side of yet another bucolic Australian-funded "refugee day" in Nauru, designed to integrate the "new multicultural community."

Although none of Australia's more vehement activists were physically present in Nauru, they were perhaps the most omnipresent force in stirring the small country's lifeworld, cofacilitating protests in Nauru, which chapter 4 further explores. During my fieldwork, activists in Australia were often on the phone with refugees in Nauru, planning campaign strategies to end offshoring and bring refugees to Australia. Several of these key individuals in Australia have been involved since the industry's mainland processing days, when the operations took place deep in the Australian outback at sites like Woomera and Sherger. This small but devoted vanguard of middle- to older-aged white Australians remain vocal media spokespersons. For many of the activists I interviewed in Australia, the notion that "asylum seekers are not criminals" but they were often held in similar institutional setups provoked a great deal of anger. These kinds of reactions were also the case with many asylum seekers and refugees I spoke with in Nauru. The frustration of being held in a carceral arrangement led to regular protests and popular signage in Nauru, such as "We're refugees not criminals," and "Freedom is a right not a crime, we want justice," in a world made high-risk in response to a disastrous border enforcement policy.[7]

One of my strongest impressions from fieldwork in Nauru was of the invisible yet powerful role that Australia's activists played in Nauru's lifeworld. Nauru faced no shortage of media coverage on its refugee processing operations. Threats to the offshoring arrangement were in no short supply. Protests and riots were a constant feature, the frequency of which increased when Nauru was in the global media spotlight. I experienced—and discussed with my interlocutors—multiple activist exposés while conducting my fieldwork in Nauru. It was often the subject of discussion among Australian refugee industry workers, who were in constant exasperation as to how to respond. Many industry personnel I spoke with had fears of what migrants in Nauru might do in collusion with Australian activists to attract publicity. When Nauru's global publicity was at its height, industry workers pleaded with people not to self-harm, self-immolate, or worse. There were several periods when a number of mental health counselors arrived in Nauru. They had been flown in at the instigation of industry firms, in an attempt to pacify the country's newly determined refugees and encourage them to make the best of their time in Nauru—or accept a resettlement deal in Cambodia. This was all deeply paradoxical, as rather than allowing for the movement of refugees onshore, the Australian government chose to spend more money in indefinitely maintaining the offshore policy to satiate a politically riled faction of the Australian electorate.

Other incidents came to be locally termed "Nau-rumors," denoting their operational frequency. Despite living in Nauru, I—and others—would often learn of incidents in the country through Australian and global media or refugee industry newsletters and listservs. For example, the latest rumor that circulated in Australian media was about Nauruans and Australian workers waterboarding and beating refugees. I asked around. Media exposés were sometimes greeted with an eye roll.[8] I would be met with similar responses. On this occasion, an NGO worker said, "No, the same thing," shaking her head. On another occasion, a clinician referred to the "suicide attention-seeking card." "You always have the jokers," they continued, discussing their work up on Nauru's refugee processing hill. "It's like the boy who cried wolf sometimes [with] those who resort to desperate means. They tell the Australian newspapers and the activists. You don't want to take the risk of not believing someone who's threatening suicide, but it's often because they get publicity on it in Australia."

"Pregnancy is just a way to get transferred to the mainland," another said, starkly glossing over the violent inequalities that might induce someone into such desperate measures. To me, it was horrific that particular reproductive choices or bodily self-destruction were "commonplace hazards" in the workplace. But these realities were very much part of the industry: the violent consequences of containment and offshoring on people's lives. They were also ones that were given, at times, problematic visibility by Australian and Nauruan-based activists to garner sympathy and mobilize support from publics outside of Nauru.

I discussed some of these issues with one of Australia's more vocal activists, Jenna, at her home in Brisbane, which also doubled as her office. Photos of Che Guevara papered the walls, and the shelves were lined with books on neoliberalism, anarchism, and socialism. Jenna was characteristic of the activist demographic I had met—the white liberal middle-class Australian *Guardian* readership, able to afford the time to devote to refugee campaigns and incensed at how their country could treat asylum seekers. Jenna frequently interrupted our interview to receive texts and calls from others across Australian and offshore activist teams. Having moved from oppositional politics elsewhere, she referenced Angela Davis several times, describing "the prison industrial complex around refugees," and reflected on her organizing practice:

> It's really difficult because the media wants certain things. Even with the *Guardian* and the *Sydney Morning Herald* it's really tough because if it doesn't fit their agenda, it doesn't get published, you don't get a story. Even with the sympathetic media that does the politics-of-pity thing. I just got some photographs last night and I sent them on to the media, knowing that the media's not going to do anything with them because they don't show the media what the media wants to see. The Vietnamese got hold of a camera and they took selfies—like any other sixteen-, seventeen-year-old boys—and they have all these selfie photographs. And we're sort of going, "Nooo! Take pictures of guards beating you up." But they took selfies. Selfies of "oh here's me in my room," and "here's me near the fence," you know, 'cos they're kids.

Despite the clear ethical concerns, Jenna and others worked with asylum seekers and refugees in Nauru and the global media to collate photos of self-harm and stories of waterboarding and sexual abuse at the hands of employees and Nauruans to leverage against the offshore arrangement. Some migrants employed their own bodies to translate their experiential knowledge of the violence of border enforcement operations into the mainstream legal language of refugee suffering as a strategy of opposing injustice. This often had the controversial effect of exasperating barriers between migrants, locals, and industry employees. Each were pitted against the others, as chapter 4 further details, which obscured the shared conditions of exploitation endemic to this industry arrangement—and the broader system of controlling people's mobility.

For Jenna, the moral value of organizing in this arena was paramount. Jenna was certainly not paid in monetary terms. In fact, she and others devoted much of their time and finances to refugee activist work. Ironically, part of the reason why the Australian government moved toward offshoring asylum was because having the operations in Australia made migrants more accessible to organizers. Woomera and Scherger, two of the government's former processing sites, located in the far-flung outback but still on Australian territory, were both marred by riots, escapes, and fires (Jupp 2002), which made it especially difficult to head off activism. But even in the Equatorial Pacific, living in Nauru was like living in a panopticon because of activist efforts that operated at the extreme of extraterritorial oversight and suffused the country with insecurity.

A Higher Risk Profile

Price in the ecosystem services marketplace, Morgan Robertson (2007) suggests, reflects the neoliberal preference for governance over government. Commodities are not self-evidentially given value but instead hotly worked out with and between civil society actors. Deciding whether to operate in a context requires calculating components of risk and value. Operational risk and ethical and financial value all factored into any organizational decision to operate in the mainland and offshore refugee marketplace, be it from NGOs or commercial firms. Organizations all conduct risk assessment profiles to verify if the money, time, personnel, and reputation of refugee and offshore work is justified. Several industry personnel informed me that the hazards that come with refugee work were firm detractors from pursuing a contract in any processing environment—offshore or otherwise—even if they did "similar work" elsewhere. Take the words of this security firm executive whose company chose to work in the naturalized sector of prison incarceration but drew the line at migrant detention:

> If we're moving into a new geography or if we're going into a service area we've never done before, that is, irrelevant of where it is around the globe, we look at it through a risk perspective. So, what are the risks? The contracts should consider all aspects of risk including ethical risks, potential risk of human rights violations, etc. Working in immigration is a no-go for us. We do similar work elsewhere. At least in prisons, people pretty much accept prisons, but you don't have the moral outcry like you do with refugees. And the thing with immigration is that people are being assessed as to whether they're likely to get visas. Depending upon a country's policy, that will determine how easy it is for different groupings to get visas or not. If government policy changes on that, then that will change the risk profile on what you're managing. If, all of a sudden, the national government turns round and says, "Right, we're not going to give any more visas out," then the asylum seekers know it's simply a waiting game before they get returned to wherever they're coming from. It becomes a very different sort of scenario.

This official, like many others, evoked notions of risk. Risk was largely related to the particular hazards of human assessment and the moral values around refugees, which resulted in an outpouring of organizational and public support. The executive referenced the protracted nature of RSD—"the waiting game"—that leads to higher volatility, what Griffiths (2014) refers to as "temporal uncertainties." In the context of an uncertain future and a far-flung operational context, the propensity for individuals to snap is extreme, which the industry director pointed to as shaping "a very different sort of scenario [that] changed the risk profile." This, I was told, suffused the industry environment with fiscal instability.

When it came to the offshore refugee industry, the high risks attached led many organizations to drop by the wayside or take on behind-the-scenes roles, paving the way for others to enter the industry. Initially, the Salvation Army held the AU$74 million contract for RPC management on Nauru. In January 2014, they lost the contract, following a series of incidents of mismanagement and improperly trained staff, combined with a large migrant protest in July of 2013, which resulted in the burning down of one of the RPCs. Once-small firms like Transfield Services (later under the distancing name of BroadSpectrum), an asset management company not familiar with the sector, bid for the small and controversial offshore contract: AU$24 million for the initial period. Transfield found great success over the years, expanding into a multimillion-dollar corporation through long-term government contracts in defense, health, and infrastructure in remote and offshore locations. Transfield executives saw the lucrative nature of immigration services from other outsourcing competitors like the British outsourcing company Serco. However, executives knew they could not compete with businesses already in the Australian industry sector, deciding the offshore industry might be a good entry point into the growing market. The government's mainland facility contractor, Serco, held off from bidding. So, too, did GEO Group, the correctional firm who manage many of Australia's prisons, as well as immigration detention centers in the United States. Both had concerns around working in a remote and potentially volatile context. But Transfield went for Nauru's relatively small and controversial contract. Managing Nauru's offshore sites, the firm earned kudos from both the Australian and Nauruan governments by employing high quotas of local workforces and partially subcontracting security to a newly set-up local firm. They recruited refugee specialist workers from Australia and cultivated an active company town culture, focusing their efforts on promoting an image of corporate responsibility and public participation. The firm sponsored local events and the football team's jerseys, donating surplus RPC food and loaning equipment and labor, particularly when contracts were up for renewal. These responses sought to minimize the primary social visibility of violence in this industry and increase the firm's symbolic capital through demonstrations of being a good neighbor. Instead, they emphasized positive contributions to the community, in order to gain and maintain support for their practices among local residents, politicians, and regulatory agencies. These were all attempts to manipulate public perception of local conditions in order to promote the political economic interests of corporate providers and government entities—as is found around the world in extractive mineral sites (Golub 2014; Kirsch 2014).

"What Transfield Services did was very very clever," an Australian Immigration Department official noted to me in interview when describing the tendering process. "They put in above and beyond their requirements, demonstrating their ability in the industry, and they've made an AU$24 million contract turn into a one-billion-dollar contract as a result. We could soon see that these guys have got the capacity and they're pitching us a product that fits with our political mantra." Such discourses were also extremely convincing to a local population that continued to watch phosphate mining jobs dwindle, Ferraris and Land Rovers rust—covered by the overgrowth of jungle vegetation, and their young people leave because of lack of employment opportunities.

A revolving-door syndrome characterized the offshore industry environment. Predictably, organizations would receive then lose contracts as part of an ever-intensifying arrangement, structured by efficiency, risk, and the maximization of value(s). When G4S lost their offshore contract on Manus Island after a highly publicized 2013 migrant protest, Transfield expanded their work to both offshore sites. They took on the AU$1.2 billion twenty-month Manus contract in March 2014. Shares in Transfield rose 45 percent with the contract, contributing up to 20 percent of the company's revenue. In 2016, Save the Children lost their contract to provide welfare services for children and families in Nauru, following several incidents of alleged activism on the island. Transfield also expanded their contract to that role, recruiting former Save the Children employees into their firm. These are just some of the "strange bedfellows" complexes that developed in the high-risk offshore refugee industry (Morris 2022).

But while offshore work was extremely profitable, an important factor that reticent tenderers cited was the extensive public and media scrutiny that came with entering into the offshore industry environment. Protests were held outside organizational premises on a regular basis, in particular, those of contracted commercial firms. Grassroots organizations such as Corpwatch, Human Rights and Business, No Business in Abuse, and Cross Border Operational Matters (xBorderOps) drew attention to the moral decrepitude of offshoring by lobbying shareholders of contracted corporations. In March 2014, following concerted boycotting efforts from activists and artists, the high-profile Sydney Biennale announced the severing of their forty-one-year ties with Transfield Holdings, the parent company of Transfield Services, as a founding sponsor of the event. Shortly thereafter in August 2015, as part of the HESTA Divest campaign, Australian activists successfully petitioned the superannuation fund HESTA to sell its 3.5 percent share in Transfield, valued in excess of AU$23 million.[9] This was followed by NGS Super's divestment, which provides superannuation for private school teachers, also in August 2015. Just one month later, Transfield announced its new name change to BroadSpectrum after losing the license to the Transfield brand earlier that year. The hashtag #BroadSpectrum immediately started trending, since moral rhetoric played an important role in the voicing of opposition. As one user tweeted at the time:

> #BroadSpectrum is quite a fitting new name for you @TransServices given your Broad Spectrum of human rights abuses towards #asylumseekers.

The anticipation of these sorts of campaign practices deterred several major global industry players from bidding for offshore contracts. Before going with the Salvation Army, the Labour government initially approached the Red Cross to take on the offshore management contract. In many Immigration Department officials' eyes, the international NGO had the expertise, as the Red Cross was already an active player in Australia's refugee industry, as well as in other European countries. The Australian Immigration Department contract the Red Cross to manage asylum seekers in rented community detention housing across Australia's states and territories—a practice that is highly controversial as part of Red Cross' "professionalized engagement" (Lindberg 2020, 220) in carceral sites around the world. Alongside this, the Red Cross fund staff to regulate risks in Australia's immigration detention centers, advising the government on safety improvements. However, despite having the requisite curriculum vitae, the Red Cross also has high-level political connections. Senior cabinet ministers occupy prominent leadership roles in the NGO. Many saw operating offshore as a reputational risk, advising executives in the Red Cross against offshore work. It was on this basis that several industry players changed their names or created new companies just for operating offshore. After I conducted my fieldwork, in the wake of the high-profile Nauru Leaks *Guardian* campaign, the majority of contracted offshore firms announced their decisions not to renew contracts. Wilson Security, Transfield Services (by then BroadSpectrum), and Connect Settlement Services all abandoned working in Nauru's refugee industry in close succession.[10]

Scholars studying mining conflicts around the world have noted how companies use "audit culture" to shift the focus away from destructive extractive practices (Kirsch 2014; Strathern 2000). Instead, industry contractors' gesture to "international standards," which imply they are doing the "right thing." Organizations use audit culture to create the illusion of reform and avoid real constraints on their operations that would limit financial successes. For those who held offshore contracts, a lucrative industry with a higher risk profile motivated a world saturated by prudence and foresight. Previous high-profile industry disasters like the Nauru Riot of 2013, the death of Reza Barati on Manus Island in February 2014, the loss of large rolling contracts (G4S, Salvation Army, and Save the Children), stories of alleged abuse, shareholder consequences, the drowning of a refugee, and more, were all firm incentives for offshore industrialists to develop an intensive corporate culture of risk regulation. Risk showed itself in contractual bidding, but also in the "productive life" (Zaloom 2004) of the Nauruan offshore, as a constitutive element involved in the upkeep of the offshore refugee operations.

On one occasion, I sat with Travis, an Australian security employee in Nauru. We were helping to man the Nauru Rotary Club's film screening fundraising event for Nauruan tweens at a local community hall. *Finding Nemo* was on in the background, projected on a shambolic put-together canvas. This makeshift screen was a leftover from the RPCs, which had their own projector and inflatable cinema screen, then in use for the weekly film club, as yet another attempted practice of corporate accountability. As with most local events, the food was all donated out-of-date goods from refugee industry providers, no longer usable at the processing centers as soon as the best-before date hit: boxes of mixed-leaf salad, white and wholegrain buns, and a selection of pork, veggie, and halal sausages. I asked Travis about this extreme fastidiousness—the expiration date was just two days ago, so the food was still fresh. I found mixed-leaf salad and wholegrain buns to be like gold dust, rarely obtainable in Nauru's supermarkets. I thought back to one of my regular boat harbor acquaintances, Khadija, who came down from the RPCs to swim while she awaited the outcome of her asylum claim. Without fail, she would offer her packed lunch around to everyone sitting by: sometimes kiwis or carrot sticks, often intricately Bubble Wrapped, all flown in from Australian suppliers, remarkably fresh and never out of date. Travis remarked: "You can't have workers and asylum seekers getting gastro. Companies in Australia get sued for things like that. I mean, our firm, or the Immigration Department, will get huge claims directed at them if anyone gets sick. And, you know how it is; it's such a hot environment. That kind of thing will just be picked up on pretty quickly." Travis's comment calls attention to the extremities of offshore industry regulation, so visible against the lack of regulation outside refugee industry spheres. Suing for "gastro" and employee liability culture was next to nonexistent in local business practice in Nauru. What Travis's comment also signals was the role of the extraterritorial campaigns to end offshoring in Nauru's refugee industry world—what the executive earlier referred to as being "under the spotlight." As much as activist campaigners were part of making the business higher risk, they were also part of its regulation. The "hot" offshore environment, where most days failed to go by without media and legal exposés, served to induce a risk-adverse culture that operated to the extreme. Certainly, underneath the infrastructural façade, nightmarish experiences were encountered by those across Nauru's offshore industry context. But because of the high-value nature of offshore work in Nauru, realities of risk justified the need for more financial investment. This gave rise to a safety-saturated environment that enabled industrialists to advance the offshoring arrangement.

Australia's "Safest Workplaces"

Workers deployed to refugee processing sites are exposed to the risks that come with the mental and physical pressures of containing and managing people. Increased uncertainties, mental health deterioration, and violence are characteristic of these toxic industry environments. Migrants are exposed to institutional confinement, long and protracted bureaucratic waits, restricted visa stipulations, and behavioral guidelines, which creates pressure-cooker environments. This results in occupational risks much higher than other sectors. Nowhere were these dangers more acute than in Nauru's offshore context. Dreadful tragedies in the processing and resettlement districts such as a spate of self-immolations in the summer of 2016, including the death of Omid Masoumali, who set himself alight during a UNHCR mission, exemplified the inescapable human consequences of Nauru's offshore industry. This was despite the incredible amount of effort to achieve the goal of risk avoidance or reduction. During my fieldwork, the total number of recorded self-harm incidents rose to 216 at the RPCs in the 20-month period between July 1, 2013, and May 25, 2015, in addition to 355 prescriptions of psychotropic antidepressants (Australian Government 2015).

For some workers in these industry environments, occupational risks were related to the ethics of their involvement and were psychological and constituently physical in nature. This was particularly the case for those employed in the main elements of refugee determination work, whose daily tasks revolved around preparing asylum seekers for hearings or questioning them about nightmarish pasts so as to determine the authenticity of their suffering. Refugee defense lawyers, doctors, RSD officers, tribunalists, and interpreters all referred in interview to the vicarious trauma of collating, listening to, and judging human brutalities. This included such everyday working practices as adjudicating an individual's self-harm, acting as ciphers, relating frightening experiences, and helping migrants locate photos and documents to validate their trauma narratives.[11] "I have to have counseling, I have to, that's what helps me through," one Immigration Department RSD worker told me on this point. "If you don't, then you're a psychopath."

I spoke with interpreters in Nauru, some from similar regional backgrounds, who had arrived to Australia under refugee status themselves, and felt a deep affinity with asylum seekers in Nauru. For them, relating narratives of suffering was no easy feat, nor was being involved in people's deportations easy for many industry personnel. "I deal constantly with self-harm and threats of suicide, very much so," one Transfield worker said. "And when they've not been accepted as genuine, I have to play a part in helping them accept that reality. Sometimes that's meant taking someone to be deported after I have built up this trusting relationship." A mental health counselor also made the damaging tolls of offshore work explicit in interview: "The compromises that people are in, and every day going to work to do bad things to others is making them feel ill. I had a client who had breast cancer say to me, 'I believe that I will be punished for what I'm doing by getting my breast cancer back.' . . . It's a toxic environment and it sends people mad." This was corroborated by another practitioner, who struggled with un-tangling whether helping asylum seekers and refugees at the facilities overrode an ethically problematic context: "You have this constant battle of wanting to do good within the system, and that was one of the best ways to help, and yet feeling complicit, just by being there." Others felt like they were directly enforc-ing a dehumanizing policy regime, detailing the ways in which they found them-selves acting "like jailers" as they imposed forms of social control. A former Salvation Army practitioner described, "One guy wasn't supposed to play chess, and so I had to take the chess board away. In any other normal situation, what right do I have to do that to someone? And yet here I was enforcing these really punitive policies within the camp. Really just nasty things."

Although this is often explained in terms of the "unintended consequences of humanitarianism," I found that industry personnel were usually aware of these pitfalls. The majority had been schooled on humanitarian paradoxes at elite in-stitutions, had been through ethics training sessions prior to deployment to Nauru, and referenced well-worn texts, like Fiona Terry's *Condemned to Repeat*, in conversation. Rather, this all goes to show quite how professionalized the ref-ugee industry has become, where these workplace risks have been naturalized into industry procedures. The Immigration Department's contracted corporate counselor Davidson Trahaire Corpsych, also a regular in offshore oil and gas rigs, started a fly-in-fly-out service for industry workers in Nauru's offshore sites. Be-tween October 2011 and December 2015, the Immigration Department spent AU$17,043,906 on corporate counseling contracts, far more than any other gov-ernment division (Australian National Audit Office 2016). All offshore industry employees had counseling provision in place, even counselors themselves, fol-lowing their fly-in-fly-out stints.[12]

As with other human-industry sectors, many occupational risks were also physical. When discussing their work with me, or more commonly in social drinking circles at the end of the day, refugee industry workers, foreign and Nau-ruan, described the high-risk nature of this kind of work. Physical attacks and destruction to property by asylum seekers and refugees were common due to the sheer frustration they felt at their situations. Industry workers discussed dealing with protests, physical threats, and bodily harm. Some described learning how to administer a "grip and hold" on someone if attacked, and industry protocols for self-harm, lip sewing, and starvation. Many Nauruans left phosphate mining and other employment for the better conditions and higher pay of the refugee industry. But it was not easy work, I was often told, and it was one of few choices in such a company town arrangement.

I would frequently ask local islanders what it was like working at the RPCs, as almost all had worked there or had relatives employed there in some capacity. In one almost focus group–style setting that emerged impromptu in my neighbor's backyard, a group of four Nauruan workers described their experiences of industry life to me. Shaking his head, Jacob, a security worker at the RPCs, went on to detail how some asylum seekers, not wanting to be in Nauru, took to actively making derogatory comments, gestures, and actions toward him and his colleagues. "It's horrible doing that kind of work," his friend Drew chimed in. Drew had recently resigned from the same position. "Some of the asylum seekers were smearing feces all over the RPC walls, leaving all the taps on to waste the water and make Nauru go into drought. They don't care. I stopped working there. I couldn't do it." Some asylum seekers and refugees would single out and taunt Nauruan workers in particular, using the moralizing representations that found purchase globally. Mona, an occasional cleaner, nodded at her colleague's comments as we discussed their working life, adding: "It's not nice working up there. Some of the things people do. Refugees throw their shit on the wall and say to cleaners, clean this, it's your job, isn't it. It's an easy job, but you get abuse all the time. Many locals have been sacked 'cause they've retaliated. You get abused and you have to step back, you can't do anything, everyone is in fear of the asylum seekers. They're pissed off 'cause they can't go to Australia and the media laps it up." Mona's latter point speaks to the disproportionate risks of this industry sector on local islanders. I was told on several occasions by Nauruans, migrants, and Australian industry workforces alike how some migrants would jeer at Nauruan employees then threaten to contact the Australian media about "refugee maltreatment" if approached. These forms of differentiation show how the industry relies on systems of racial inequality, where certain landscapes and the people who live there are disproportionately exposed to harm.

A number of anthropologists discuss mining in terms of a "resource curse," meaning that resource extraction often disadvantages the local communities where the natural resources are located, while the corporations who own the means and modes of production reap large profits (Ballard and Banks 2003; Filer and Macintyre 2006). These disadvantages to local communities usually include a lack of other development, internal political tensions, human rights abuses, and cultural loss. Polluting industries promise major economic development and financial incentives to already impoverished communities. In actuality, these corporations generally offer very few jobs that community members can occupy (Allen 2018; Fortun 2001). In Nauru, the economic devastation of the country created a favorable political and economic climate for industry players to operate in. Having more Nauruans employed in the industry had the advantage of cheaper labor (Nauruans were paid AU$4.25 per hour, while the majority of Australians were on AU$80,0000—AU$100,000 per year, with air fares, accommodation, daily living allowance, and "hazard pay" on top, all tax free). It allowed corporations to point to high local employment and display the alleged benevolence of their work for Nauru's economic development.[13] Workers from outside Australia, it was also thought, might not be so entangled in the industry's activist politics, thus reducing the operational risks of the environment. Importantly, for contracted companies and the Australian government, it further reduced the prospect of organizational liability for high-risk industrial practices. Large-scale menial facility employment and lower-run administrative positions brought jobs for Nauruans, later used as a public defense when problems emerged further down the line.[14]

Although offshore contracts were lucrative, refugee industry workers operated on long fly-in-fly-out cycles. During my fieldwork, six weeks on and two weeks off was standard among offshore workers. Unless high on the occupational ladder, most employees from refugee security, teaching, and resettlement agencies bunked two in a donga room. Shifts were usually long: forty hours a week, with one day off in-between. Commonly, most people I spoke with used "off days" to sleep and recharge. Many told me how they would spend their two weeks off surfing in Bali or camping up Brisbane's Gold Coast to "detox" from the challenges of offshore work, starkly also bringing into focus the privilege of their mobility. During my time in Nauru, I would constantly come up against the strategies and spaces used by industry workers to sustain themselves in a toxic industry environment. On days off, I would find them holed up at the Thursday Ladies' Night in the Jules Bar or at the popular tuna buffets and karaoke nights at the Menen Hotel. At these nights, industry workers would amp up bubble-gum pop at full blast and dance with unbridled escapism; in one instance, a group of Australian-Iranian Farsi interpreters took over the sound system, blasting out the Arabic pop starlet Fairouz. Later this was described to me as "a way to keep going," based on what Murphy (2006) describes as "coping regimes" in sites where toxic exposures are not always so viscerally discernable.

I regularly spent time with Australian industry workers at the sides of these "let your hair down" events, to which I was often specifically invited and picked up from my Aiwo residence. Most invariably had strong opinions when conversations turned to experiences of their jobs. "I don't usually tell a lot of people in Australia that I work in Nauru," confessed Lizzy, a Brisbane-based English-language teacher for asylum seekers and refugees in Nauru, as we sat with a group of her colleagues at the side of the Jules Bar. "People usually think I'm a sadist either way and don't agree with what I'm doing. Either I'm a jailer killing refugees or a do-gooder helping illegals." This was not uncommon for me to hear—how the representational framing of rescue or deterrence came to bear on people's (workers' and migrants') everyday experiences. Like Lizzy, some workers I spoke with expressed feelings of isolation. This is not to revert into humanitarian apologia, but to show that the working environment was also toxic for workers in a context where many were morally wracked about their involvement.[15]

At events like the Jules Bar night we were at, I would observe Wilson Security workers swap numbers with Save the Children social workers in efforts toward this kind of diversion. Many staff frequented the Nauru Hash House Harriers weekly walks, which was how I met Lizzy and her colleagues. Many also plunged in the harbor for a swim or a surf or swapped frothy DVDs to keep themselves busy. "I just come away and want to punch someone. I have to read trashy books, Mills and Boon that kind of stuff. I have to do that, just to make sure that I don't go mad," answered Melissa, a Transfield Services employee, picking up Lizzy's conversation, as we got into talking about their escapism strategies from the harrowing every-day work. "Britney Spears is my go-to," her colleague Beth added. They, like others I met working in Nauru, came from social-work backgrounds with a professionalized interest in refugee work. Working with refugees, in particular, carried a great deal of feel-good value, wrapped into Western cultural logics of "rescue" and the moral economy of humanitarianism. For many, the financial incentive and interest level of working in a small Pacific island also factored in strongly, amid elements of Conradian dangers.[16] For a small minority, the desire to enforce a punitive policy that they agreed with—of "stopping illegals"—was also a deciding factor in their decision to work in Nauru. This is to say that forms of political, financial, *and* moral value all accounted for industry involvement, even as it came with the high risks of damaging tolls and ethical compromises that were described to me on multiple occasions as a "moral sickness."

Others came from work in refugee camps, military conflict zones, and Australian immigration detention centers and found the work "easy to deal with." I met former Serco private prison operators and Wilson Security personnel who moved to Save the Children; there were Red Cross and Salvation Army personnel who worked for the corporate management firm Transfield Services; and so forth. Several welfare and resettlement employees said that they were used to working in a securitized environment, and some were familiar with "grip holds" and deescalating self-harm threats, including using Hoffman cut-down knives. For some of them, it was a "natural" part of the working day to be on constant alert and know how to "deescalate volatile situations." "I'm used to this, I worked in immigration centers on the mainland and on Christmas Island," said an ex-Serco worker now working for Save the Children on one occasion. "This is nothing like Iraq, nothing," commented another ex-army and now facility security worker, pointing toward some of the "humanitarian-security complexes" (Duffield 2001) that are a part of this industry.

But while the work might be "nothing like Iraq," that some employees came with experience in conflict zones and others were versed in grip-hold techniques emphasizes the routinization of violence within industry procedures. Writing of financial traders in Chicago's Board of Trade Futures market, Zaloom notes that the daily practices of the working lives of traders "encourages the production of subjects who can sustain themselves under high-stakes conditions and thereby draw profit from economic risk" (2004, 366). Like Zaloom's traders, risk here has also produced subjects who could sustain themselves under high-stakes conditions. However, as the high-risk nature of this business makes apparent, contracted workers did not always profit from their practices. Instead, the surplus value of frontline workers' labor circulates from Nauru to Australia into the hands of political elites, as does the production of humanitarian imaginaries.

Industry personnel classified Nauru's refugee processing operations as high-risk because of the particular health consequences of the offshore refugee industry, as well as the media scares that shaped extreme levels of risk. With the constant threat of media coverage and industry exposés, workforce personnel were monitored so closely that safety saturation often bordered on the extreme. Security personnel wore cameras on their vests at the RPCs, recording all their actions in case of accusations of abuse. Industry workers filed minutiae incident and injury reports on anything related or unrelated to the industry and underwent regular performance reviews. "There are guidelines about everything now, about emergencies and what's to be done in the case of any event," Simon, a Transfield Services facility manager, told me after I inquired about the fastidious level of detail in the industry. "It's a very vulnerable environment for protests. The system operates in this ultimate Kafkaesque bureaucracy, there's organization to the nth degree, everyone always has their eyes on you. It was very confronting when I first got here. You can't put a foot wrong here. The next thing you know, it's on the Australian news."

While offshore facilities might "promise distance from political entanglement" (Appel 2019, 56), as Simon makes clears, enacting most of this commodity chain on a small Pacific island fails to remove the offshore refugee industry from its most publicized negative effects. In fact, Nauru's operation as a Commonwealth workplace was the specific point of argument for groups of legal campaigners hoping to bring the offshore processing site to Australia.[17] Legal firms and networks like the Australian Lawyers Alliance put together class action suits for offshore breach of duty of care, making submissions to the numerous parliamentary inquiries that enveloped the offshore industry over the years. Lawyers from the Melbourne-based Alliance in particular FOI-ed incidents reported to Comcare, as the federal workplace health and safety inspectorate, in the hopes of successfully ending offshore processing. Barrister Greg Barnes argued: "Nauru is a Commonwealth workplace, it is part of the extended geographical jurisdiction of the Work, Health and Safety Act. There is a duty of care that is owed not only to workers and contractors in Nauru in the detention centre, but also a duty of care owed to any person who comes on to that site, and that of course includes asylum seekers. The Department of Immigration, to be frank, is probably running the most unsafe workplaces in the Commonwealth" (quoted in Carter 2016). The Australian Lawyers Alliance argued that many of the incident reports they had received from industry workers, asylum seekers, and refugees in Nauru were not referred to Comcare, the Australian regulator of work. Comcare health and safety inspectors were regular parts of Nauru's risk mitigation operations. However, by putting pressure on the Australian Immigration Department and contracted firms to comply with health and safety guidelines, legal teams hoped that it would be next to impossible to conform Nauru's corporate landscape to that of Australia. Ironically, it was partly the scrutinization of offshore processing by legal firms and industry professionals (including asylum seekers and refugees) that not only produced new risks but also extreme spaces of offshore regulation. Advocates regularly flagged ways in which the operations fell short of Australian standards. Because of the immense amount of political economic value invested in the industry, these points of arguments against offshoring had the effect of continuous safety saturation in offshore operations.

The final section in this chapter looks in more depth at the monitoring inspectorates that extrapolated to Nauru. In the BPC era, UN missions and the Civilizational Trust governing body took a particular interest in Nauru's phosphate town regulation because of the "somewhat unique commercial enterprise" (Ellis 1946, 10). Now, the peculiarity of the refugee business prompted peak interest among global regulatory players. The amount of on-the-ground regulation of Nauru's offshore industry sites was extreme, drawing attention to the concentration of values in offshore operations and the political economy of the industry's risk-management practices. The firms that I will go on to describe have taken on a fetishistic power as "modes of organizational and regulatory control" (Power 2007, 20) over the risks endemic to migration management environments. Like the actuarial culture that Michael Power describes, these organizations are part of the industrial assemblage through which human threats are quantified and then curbed, so as to optimize industry practice. The global migration control industry owes its existence in part to the work of these agencies and their recommendations for minimizing catastrophic human consequences. Through their work, risk creates value for the circulation of more industrial flows.

A "Transparent" Supply Chain

"Frontier life," Michael Watts writes, "is characteristically volatile and turbulent, associated with forced commercialization," (2015, 217). The oil frontiers that Watts describes are risky because of corporate cost cutting and collapse of government oversight and regulatory authority. He details:

> The oil companies in Ecuador and Nigeria had substantial autonomy and license to do what they wanted and without recourse; they had the backing of the military and indeed had their own security forces; their operations were congruent with a long lineage of local demonic capitalists (whether rubber barons or slavers) and acted rather like authoritarian local governments. In the space created by a history of prior violence and a slick alliance in which enormously powerful companies can act without local or global accountability—the state ensures this unaccountability in-country and the lack of a body of international law at the level of global responsibilities. (Watts 2001, 8)

The situation Watts describes resonates with Nauru's initial uneven development—chosen as a site because of its aura of deterrence, distance from activist activity, and deep colonial entanglements. However, the distinguishing marks of Nauru's refugee frontier became *increased* industry transparency, not secrecy. As with the UN Civilizational Trust regulation days of Nauru's phosphate era, there was an extreme amount of on-the-ground oversight from the restart of the offshore refugee industry in 2012. Because of the project's controversial nature and significant private sector involvement, Nauru had to be in line with Australian workplace standards—or as far as that was possible on a remote Pacific island of only 21 km². Having decided to push ahead with the scheme, neither the Australian nor Nauruan governments wanted the political or economic devastation of a High Court challenge that saw its reversal. As per the *Report of the Expert Panel on Asylum Seekers* and stipulations of numerous industry personnel, representatives from international and state monitoring bodies required authorization to go to Nauru and tour the many locations of the refugee processing and resettlement operations. The Nauruan government made crucial efforts to ensure that the refugee industry assemblage extrapolated to their country. Keen to have individuals trained in refugee social work, psychology, and law to keep the operations to a high standard, they agreed to many of the Australian workplace procedures, most from the very beginning. As refugee processing has developed into a high-risk enterprise over the years, more organizations and individuals have come to take an interest in the industry's regulation.

When I arrived in Nauru, the offshore refugee operations had become an object of intense international interest. Médecins Sans Frontières (MSF), British legal academics, and Australian clinicians all made an appearance during my fieldwork. Fly-in-fly-out inspectorates of Australian Comcare health and safety personnel, the Commonwealth Ombudsman, the Jesuit Refugee Service (JRS), the Geneva-based International Committee of the Red Cross (ICRC), the Suva-based ICRC, the Australian Red Cross, the Office of the United Nations High Commission for Human Rights, UNHCR, and other individuals and interest groups were all firm fixtures around the company town district. A JRS nun was in permanent residence, as was a Fijian human rights lawyer from the Pacific Islands Lawyers for Human Rights Network, employed by the Nauruan government. The Nauruan government also employed Australian refugee lawyers and an RSD quality assurance lawyer on their team, all of whom worked closely with UNHCR. In order to cushion against financial loss and adverse publicity, Nauru went one step further than Australia. Having already signed the Convention against Torture (CAT) in 2001 in the first industry heyday, they ratified the Optional Protocol to the Convention against Torture (OPCAT) in January 2013.[18] On the basis of ratifying CAT, the UN Subcommittee on the Prevention of Torture (SPT) came to Nauru to inspect the industry's operational environments during my fieldwork (a Bristol human rights lawyer, a Manila psychiatrist, and an Oslo psychologist), touring around all Nauru's places of human confinement: the police station, prison, disability center, RPCs, and refugee resettlement housing.[19] Even a Danish parliamentary group requested entry to Nauru, but were denied due to local concerns as to the motives behind their curiosity.[20] The Nauruan government had encountered problems in the past after granting visas indiscriminately. Genuinely trustworthy, and boastful of the country's refugee processing operations, government officials invited organizations like Amnesty International, but also people Angelina Jolie, who received an invitation from President Baron Waqa. Tours of the RPCs were also common in Nauru's refugee industry. The Nauruan government and Nauruan RPC managers maintained great pride in the workings of what many viewed as *their* facilities. They often gave dignitaries showcasing tours, and—if time allowed—tacked on a visit to the phosphate factories.[21] The government and facility management were also keen to be guided by international expertise from others well versed in the industry.

At first, not all locals understood that others outside Nauru might not be as enamored of their island as a site of refugee processing and resettlement. But years of Nauru "prison island" stories, accusations of local savagery, snuck-in cameras, and extreme Australian and refugee activism against the arrangements alerted the Nauruan government that granting someone access to the country could jeopardize the operations. Nor were they particularly willing to grant access to the majority of industry players when narratives of violence and Nauruan savagery predictably followed in their wake.[22] It was this culture of trustworthiness that made Nauru subject to phosphate wealth predation, contributing to their first boom days before the bust.[23]

The Australian government staff who were advisors to the Nauruan government were all too aware of which agencies the Nauruan government should allow in, and which were likely to enter with activist agendas. Similarly, many Nauruan bureaucrats became well versed in Australia's refugee industry politics, requiring little assistance in identifying the major activist proponents. Familiar activist faces of the Australian campaigns to end offshoring became red-listed names in Nauru. Australian industry personnel who took a vocal stance against the offshore arrangement, such as Amnesty International, Human Rights Watch, and the Human Rights Commission (HRC), were later not granted entry to the country.[24] "Why would we let them come here?!" said Oliana, a Nauruan government worker. I had asked her about the recent visa refusal of a high-profile HRC official to publicly enter and conduct an inspection of the country's facilities. "Look at this stuff they write, they just want to bring everyone to Australia," she continued, referencing headlines like "Nauru, Australia Intentionally Torturing Refugees," Amnesty reports such as *Nauru Camp a Human Rights Catastrophe with No End in Sight* (2012), and Human Rights Commission publications like *Time to Rethink Offshore Processing of Asylum Seekers* (2014).

Oliana, like so many islanders in Nauru, was well aware of—and often bemoaned—the colonial histories at play here. Representations of risk connected to Orientalizing colonial imaginaries of Nauru as a site of danger, synonymous with "unaccountability" and "dark island archipelago." These "racist rhetorics of representation" (West 2016) structured the island's patterns of industry development through to the audit culture that I observed saturating industry life in Nauru. According to Marilyn Strathern, audit regimes reconfigure governance thorough "a veritable army of 'moral fieldworkers' . . . when transparency of operation is everywhere endorsed as the outward sign of integrity" (2000, 2). So, too, the case in Nauru, where practices of monitoring became crucial to the avoidance of significant structural change using "the virtuous language of responsibility, sustainability, and transparency" (Kirsch 2014, 185). Indeed, the high value and risk attached to Nauru's industry works led the Nauruan government to request the advice of regulators who would only develop strategies to manage risks, not deflect the endeavor from the business goals. Because access was so coveted, and the majority of staff morally invested, the workforces that came to Nauru implemented far more extensive advisory work than elsewhere.

The final section in this chapter discusses some of the local forms of risk management in Nauru. Impassioned local Nauruans played an important role in monitoring Nauru's offshore environment—in spite of representations to the contrary.

On Company Town Responsibility

Local managerial practices made clear how much the elaborate systems of health and safety I encountered tied into the high-value, high-risk refugee industry. As my opening vignette detailed, the culture of health and safety standardization that spread across Nauru during my fieldwork was noticeably stark. As with so many of these industry schemes, they all connected to the Australian and Nauruan governments' fears of the curtailment of the offshore arrangement. The Nauru lifeguards were one of the more notable local examples. At the time of my fieldwork, Nauru operated on a four-day open-center schedule, but the timings sometimes differed. I often sat at the boat harbor on open-center days, chatting with asylum seekers down from the RPCs or refugees from the resettlement compounds. Most were not versed in the island's jagged maritime terrain or were too excited about being outside of the facilities to pay it any mind. Cannonballing off the sides of the boat harbor and swimming out past the harbor entrance were popular pastimes. For many people, the chance to jump in and cool off from life at the sweltering RPCs in Nauru's phosphate interior overshadowed concerns about the sharp-edged corals. A number of asylum seekers had never swum before—coming from landlocked countries or circumstances where swimming was not a priority—and I witnessed some narrowly averted catastrophes. The new Nauru lifeguards team was always quick to work: a group of young enthusiastic Nauruan men, trained in CPR and rescue techniques through their Australian lifeguard certification, were constantly plastering and bandaging hands, feet, and knees.

As with so many of the other risk-management initiatives, Nauru's Surf Life Saving Club did not exist before the refugee business was resurrected. There were no lifeguarding patrols or stations at local swimming spots. This is not to say that drownings or other incidents did not occur. The currents off Nauru are treacherous. There are only a few spots where locals venture to swim, and even then, most people stick close to the shore. However, most islanders are well versed in the rip tides and corals, and the majority are strong swimmers. With no local instigation and little prior reason or financial ability, the Nauruan government had not set up a lifeguard division. When the RPCs reopened, the then Salvation Army contractors and the Australian Immigration Department decided that it would be more cost-effective to task a local group with looking after asylum seekers and refugees at Nauru's popular swimming sites. Previously, the Australian government had sent security staff with surf lifesaver qualifications to keep watch over the beaches when asylum seekers were out from the state house compound.

For the second industry resurgence, the Nauru Surf Club piqued the interest of the Salvation Army. The club was started in 2011, in the industry gap years, by an enthusiastic Australian phosphate worker, a local resident of Nauru with a Nauruan wife and family, and wholly devoted to islander life. Although made up of adept swimmers, the Nauru Surf Club was not a lifeguarding squadron, but a group of keen trainee surfers who hit the waves at the end of the day. Lifeguarding or "surf lifesaving" is a firm feature of Australian coastal life. Because most of Australia's major towns are coastal, most states and territories have lifeguarding services set up in popular swim spots. Surf Life Saving Australia (SLSA) is Australia's main coastal water-safety authority. Made up of over 311 affiliated Surf Life Saving Clubs that operate across Australia, SLSA is the largest volunteer lifeguarding movement in the world. The entry-level qualification to become a SLSA surf lifesaver is the Bronze Medallion in Public Safety. The Bronze Medallion course is tough. It is usually run over a period of six to eight weeks, and it involves both theory and practical training and a final assessment of patrolling and lifesaving skills. Surf lifesavers must be competent swimmers, skilled in rescue techniques, resuscitation, and first aid.

When refugee processing restarted in 2012, the Nauru Surf Club had only just developed. The group had no sponsorship, only a few secondhand boards donated from Australian charities, and an old bus from the Nauru Police Force. In early 2013, the Salvation Army obtained funding through the Australian Immigration Department to fly trainers over from SLSA who trained and assessed over forty locals as professional Australian lifesavers. In April 2013, the Nauru Surfing Club inaugurated as the Nauru Surf Life Saving Club, a SLSA-accredited nonprofit. Several locals in the club reached a level where they could professionally train others as Australian lifesavers. Like other SLSA clubs, the Nauru branch soon expanded into other activities, including a program of swimming lessons at the boat harbor through an Australian-style Nipper junior lifesaver program. But while Nauru's new lifeguarding squadron started building steam, it was still a leisurely pastime. There were no lifeguarding patrols or stations at local swimming spots. Everything changed dramatically two years after the refugee industry restarted.

On June 22, 2014, a Pakistani man, newly living in resettlement housing under a refugee visa, drowned in the strong undertow currents at the Gabab Channel. Two

FIGURE 13. The Nauru lifeguards. Photo by Julia Morris.

Nauruans ran in to save him, one of whom also drowned in the attempt. At the time, the incident was covered by all the Australian papers as evidence of the dangers of the offshore arrangement. The Australian government took quick action to ensure that no similar drownings occurred that might jeopardize the operations. The time of the drowning also coincided with the start of the open-camp arrangement, along with migrants receiving refugee status and moving into resettlement housing around the island. To protect their human assets, the Immigration Department financed the professionalization of the Nauru Surf Life Saving Club, thus ensuring a regular lifeguarding presence for Nauru's swimming hubs. In 2015, all lifesavers became paid public servants within the new National Emergency Services Department. This new department merged all safety and emergency agencies, expanding from Fire and Rescue and Ambulance into the Life Saving division.

I swam most days down at the boat harbor: a place that was often abuzz as a hub of island life. Transfield staff notified the lifeguards each week of open-center days. Teams of Nauru lifeguards were always stationed from 11 a.m. to 7 p.m. at the Gabab Channel and boat harbor swimming spots, with rescue boards, jet skis, and soon a new umbrella emblazoned with "Nauru Lifeguards." Lifeguards would usually be present even outside of open-center days, but they were on active duty at open-center times. The Nauru lifeguards did rescue several young local swimmers. At other times, they ran projects in schools, teaching children about rip current safety and protocols. But asylum seekers and refugees' safety formed the core of their work—and was the reason for their growth. Waiting lists were long to become a lifeguard, and the dedication and effort that many put in was impressive. I met former government administrative employees, phosphate workers, and several asylum recipients employed as lifeguards. Some had completed more specialist certification courses (like Ocean Survival and Powercraft Aquatic Rescue training) or flown over to Sydney to work with Surf Life Saving New South Wales lifesavers on Bondi Beach. The latter option was restricted to Nauruans; refugees were strictly barred from Australian entry.

At other times, the refugee risks that lifeguards regulated intersected strongly with the political economy of the global media spectacle. On several occasions, I watched some of Nauru's young, motorbike-riding refugees jumping off the boat harbor's sides, venturing into waters that Nauruans, very familiar in the currents and corals, had warned them to avoid. With little incentive to follow the regulatory code, and angry at the offshoring arrangement, some refugees in Nauru leveraged the global media attention centered on refugee victimhood. In the words of one refugee I spoke with, "If they put me in prison, who cares?" and "They can't touch me, I'll contact the Australian papers." On one occasion, I observed three young Iranian men, all refugees, who arrived at the Anibare boat harbor. Jumping and shouting, beer cans in hand, they ignored the lifeguards' pleas to "quiet down." The lifeguards grappled with what to do. "We knew if we called the police, they'd just tell the campaigners in Australia that the Nauruan savages took them away and locked them up. Or maybe even that we assaulted them," one lifeguard told me later, as we stood beside the boat harbor, discussing what had just happened. "Some of these refugees just think they're above the law," another lifeguard added. The event did in fact end with the arrival of the police, who took the three men to the station, but released them shortly after with a verbal reprimand. I talked about this later with one of my closer informants, James, also Iranian and living in Nauru as a refugee. He said, "Yes, for some of them it doesn't really matter. They just want to get to Australia. It's not nice for the Nauruans, but they don't care about that."

I mention this ethnographic moment because it was indicative of the particular level of risk that forcibly containing migrants on an island could present when their rights and identities have become entangled in Western colonial imaginations. It is absolutely understandable for anyone who has been placed in a position of powerlessness and lacks opportunity to exhibit anger and aggressiveness. But the imbalanced optic leveled on Nauru gave disproportionate visibility to these injustices in terms of refugee suffering. This was recognized by refugees on the island, some of whom folded their experiences in the language of colonial tropes to attract Australian humanitarian interest. Some also wielded their humanitarian authority as "suffering refugees" over Nauruans. Even enterprises developed for workplace risk fought to control these sorts of tensions.

The lifeguards were important examples of the amount of regulation that went into ensuring the safety of—and thus securing—a high-value, high-risk commodity. They joined other Australian regulators such as the Red Cross, Comcare, the SPT, and the Commonwealth Ombudsman as important parts of risk avoidance within the offshore operations. In fact, it was because of the Nauru lifeguards' success in securing the processing site that they also helped develop risk-avoidance strategies for other offshore processing regions, helping with the first PNG lifeguarding service in Manus Island. Nauru lifeguards flew out to Manus Island, at the time the seat of the Australian government's other offshore site, working to develop their lifeguarding force for asylum seekers and refugees' safety.

Company Town Responsibility II

Not only was every aspect of Australia's regulatory industry applied to Nauru, but internal controls also flourished. A number of local voluntary regulatory schemes emerged across the industry heyday, prior to and during my fieldwork. Like other countries with entrenched detention center estates, Nauru had a number of visitor schemes in place for interested locals keen to keep a watchful eye on the handling of industry operations. As has been described, many locals took jobs in industry workforces because of the moral economy of this kind of work, with the very goal of helping refugees. Resident Kirbati, Fijian, and Marshallese nuns from the local Catholic convent made constant visits to the RPCs, as did Nauru's president. It was also common for local social groups to make regular visits back and forth. Soccer games were held most Friday evenings at RPC 2 between Nauruans and asylum seekers.

As chapter 4 shows, global discourses of risk impacted on some Nauruans' perceptions of refugees, and vice versa, on refugees' views of Nauruans. Some Nauruans were intimidated by the dangers that asylum seekers and refugees might present, entangled in global narratives of terrorism and criminality. Meanwhile, some asylum seekers knew Nauruans through representations of savagery and backwardness. To combat these imaginaries, the Nauru Rotary Club attempted to set up a buddy scheme between locals and asylum seekers at the RPCs. On notable occasions, the RPCs would break into local life. For example, Nauru Independence Day, January 24, 2015, was marked by visits from the Itsi Dance Group and Culture Department Choir. On the other hand, Angam Day, the biggest event of the Nauruan calendar, made the RPCs abuzz with local activity: storytellers, craft weavers, a stick-dance group, and string-figure players. I was even asked if there was anything I could contribute to the weekly industry calendar, which put me at a loss, as I strove to distance myself—as much as possible in a company town—from the CSR whitewash.

Addressing the harms of the offshore arrangement was not the purpose of these initiatives. Rather, these projects looked to suppress self-harm and violence through the disciplinary whitewash of musical and artistic talent shows, discussed in more depth in chapter 5. Part of the work of some of these engaged individuals, such as church groups, was in furthering risk management, albeit benignly, in the Foucauldian tradition, as a technology of power. According to this view, initiatives encouraging emotional expression act as disciplinary devices that attempt to mold individuals into the ideal docile body (subservient and compliant), removing the propensity for behavioral transgressions beyond the confessional space (Morris 2020). This is not to say that this is the case in reality, or that asylum seekers in Nauru inhabited a state of false consciousness, but that these sorts of practices attempt to regulate the behavior of individuals. Indeed, company town events were all actively encouraged as ways to assuage the violence so common to RSD operations. But with the extreme amount of global media coverage of Nauru as a lawless territory, some locals took it upon themselves to investigate the stories circulated by activist campaigners, creating their own forms of local regulation. Here, locals lived with a higher level of alertness of the uncertainties that the industry operations presented in everyday life.

I soon met Jake, a phosphate truck driver by profession, but a self-labeled human rights activist on the side. Jake's name often came up when I asked my Nauruan acquaintances about any activism associated with the phosphate industry: it turned out Jake tackled the toxicities of both of Nauru's industry sectors. I had seen Jake's name in the credits of photos of refugee protests that were posted on social media by Australian activists. His Twitter handle and bio also signaled that he was a Nauruan human rights activist. I gave him a call, and he enthusiastically agreed to come over to my house to talk about his local activism.

As we sat in my living room, Jake described to me how, at first, he was excited to help out with activism in Australia against offshoring asylum to Nauru. He disagreed with it from a moral point of view. He would keep in touch with some of the leading Australian activists, and they would inform him when they heard a "Nau-rumor," which he would go to investigate:

> A lot of people are pretty angry about the lies that refugees spread. Like one time, there was a refugee couple and they crashed their motorbike. Some locals stopped to help them. They told the media that it was the Nauruans who did the scratches to them! The locals said, "We should never have helped them!" That's when I decided to get in touch with the Australian refugee rights groups to check out any allegations and see if they're true for myself. Really, to help them and find a way for us to work together. Because this system, it just isn't right, but neither is the way they're attacking us for it.

I remarked at how invisible the Nauruan perspective was in favor of the suffering/savage framing strategy. Jake answered with a sigh and a shake of his head. "Those activists in Australia aren't activists," he said. "They just take the refugees' side. There's nothing I can do against that, so I stopped speaking with them."

Like Jake, other locals tried to combat these representations through social media. A small group of Nauruan university students set up the Facebook group "Refugees on Naoero—Nauru" to respond to prominent Australian media reports. One of their posts reads as follows:

> Most refugee & advocate claims on Nauru fabricated to achieve goal to get to Aust. So called "reports" based solely on these claims #fact.

> Fact Check:

> —Theyre [sic] not being neglected medically. They have their own psychologists. Medical Personnel are at IHMS. There's also free medical attention from the "inadequate" (As privileged people with 1st world standards put it) RON hospital where they also have to meet the demands of the locals as well. Otherwise you wouldn't be receiving these "leaked" reports.

> —They're getting free food, allowances, free electricity (With their own generators for subsequent power cuts), free water even bottled water is provided (Although its [sic] the dry season. They still receive water from the desalination plant. Also apparently the provided bottled water are wasted through procurement management and if they were procured successfully, wasted anyway within the centers. Since workers have been giving them away or selling them to the Chinese)

—They're not locked up. They're free to come in and go as they please since last October. How else do you think they're sending these photos, videos, messages to everyone?[25]

However, like Jake, the young Nauruans' Facebook group, and government and local "fact checking" tweets, earned little publicity in Australia. Rather, discursive practices continued to construct Nauru as a site of lawlessness and brutality, outside the scope of accountability.

In the report of the Expert Panel on Asylum Seekers, Australia's operational planners stressed that "effective oversight and monitoring are critical elements of any regional approach" (2012, 34). Yet, for advocates and officials in Geneva and Australia especially, it was in reality the presence of majority-white Australian and European monitors that created a more transparent and just asylum system. This is part of colonialism's continued legacy of racism in international legal institutions of governance. It illuminates the tensions that unfolded in the system of liberal governance that Nauruans were supposed to learn: that is, how to evaluate humans in terms of deservingness. Ironically, despite the compliance of many Nauruans in constructing a "civilized" institution, often seeking out extra forms of operational regulation, they emerged as villains in the saga. Their efforts to integrate industrial best practices were overshadowed in terms of "underdevelopment" and "the rule of law." The exasperation evidenced by community tensions was grasped onto by Australian activists and used to reinforce the goal of #RefugeesWelcome Australia.

The presentation of offshore exceptionality of course continues to obscure the inherently hazardous nature of the industry operations as a whole. Nauruans were represented as uncivilized and unable to effectively take part in operations allegedly appropriate only for a white Western liberal democratic polity. Such representations powerfully render the overall system of asylum in depoliticizing and civilizational terms. Instead, the negative aspects of an entire industry of human assessment were glossed over by the symbolic glorification of Western forms of operational regulation. Such efforts "to optimize" toxic industry operations that centered on human lives raise all manner of ethical concerns that resonate with the uneasy world of prison reform. As Angela Davis (2003) and others have warned when discussing the "prison industrial complex" and "double-edged sword" of prison reform (Feeley and Van Swearingen 2004), generating changes that produce a better incarceration system can instead contribute to its bureaucratization and financialization. Meanwhile, the organizational scramble to regulate Nauru's refugee industrial world reveals quite how institutionalized this business has become in recent years: operating through "a formal 'loop' by which the system observes itself" (Power 1994, 28), without acknowledging its own peculiar perspective. The very idea that there can be standards for assessing human suffering calls attention to the practices of abstraction and valuation that go into the naturalization of violent industry practices around the world, and the workforces that are a part of this process. Even with a politically savvy strategy, activist campaigners had the countereffect of reinforcing the moral economy that contributes to the development and attempted standardization of refugee industry sites around the world. Global threat narratives and hyperbolic representations of "floods, waves, and surges" of "overwhelming refugee numbers" (Strom and Alocock 2014, 454) also reinforced the Australian public's perception that the movement of asylum seekers and refugees should be militarized against, further reproducing cyclical consequences.

As chapter 4 shows, many locals frequently felt the brunt of the offshoring arrangement, but faced barriers to organizing against the industry. Actually, the majority of Nauruans wanted refugees to be allowed to settle in Australia, for differing reasons, but they were disregarded by members of the government who felt that the economic benefits outweighed the industry's toxic consequences.

RESOURCE FRICTIONS

Massive waste, corruption, and ecological devastation in oil-producing communities was matched by none of the rewards of petro-development . . . The oil bust produced a right and proper resentment among oil-producing communities across the delta.

—Watts (2001)

Dogabo Scotty mentioned on 30 July 1946 "It is hard for one to speak his mind openly here as one is liable get in the bad books with the local authorities." We speak about freedom of speech where democracy rules but it is not so here. Before . . . the people were absolutely and unquestionably united. Now they are so divided that it is a very rare thing to find the people agree upon anything.

—Nauru Philatelic Bureau (1983)

Culture played an important part in the segregations that arose across Nauru as risk became entangled in the uneasy interactions of migrants and locals. Scandals such as Australian media campaigns elicited not only anger but also fear in local residents, government, and industry personnel. The dominant presentation on the global media scene remains that of the suffering and fearful refugee. In reality, many locals I spoke with were scared of refugees and what they might do to attract publicity in collusion with Australian activist campaigners. On one occasion, I caught a lift to the USP campus with a local staff administrator. "I don't pick them up anymore," she muttered, pointing to a group of Iranian hitchhikers standing outside Nauru's Anibare Lodge resettlement housing, immediately discernable in tight jeans against the heady Equatorial heat. "Accountability. If something happens and I crash, who knows what the Australian media will say."

These same fears were often voiced to me by local islanders. I developed a close relationship with Judith, a school caterer, after I helped out at a local school event through my involvement with USP. She would often take me on her rounds of Nauru's elementary schools, dropping off premade lunches, as we nattered about life in Nauru. Our conversations were frequently punctuated by the topic of refugees, a subject on which Judith had a lot to say, with security being a top concern. "The thing is, we don't know what they might do next. So many of them are desperate to get to Australia, they'll do anything. We don't know where they're coming from. They could take us hostage. Make bombs from phosphate," she speculated. Noticeable worry lined her face during our conversation as we handed out sandwiches from the window of Nauru's secondary school's lunchroom canteen. For Judith, like many Nauruans I spoke with, her experience of asylum seekers and refugees in the country was deeply entangled in the Australian political rhetoric that drove the offshore asylum arrangement. She would often use words like "illegal" and "terrorist," heard from Australian news media reports that stigmatize the refugee/the asylum seeker (generally conflated) as criminal, terrorist, and welfare scrounger. These broader concerns form part of the Euro-American "mythology of dangerous immigrants," made up of "deeply held suspicions about charity for illegitimate recipients, fears of cultural difference, and the dangers of the resident foreigner for . . . civic life" (Besteman 2016, 302, 141). Like the situation of Somali refugee resettlement described by Besteman in Lewiston, Maine, these insecurities also gained footholds in Nauru's cultural and political context. However, they were shaped by the racist forms of representation that underpin Nauru as a former colonial economy and to the present.

Wider anxieties intersected with the recognition paradigm pulled into action by migrants confined to a small Pacific island, wanting to be in Australia. For working-class residents in Nauru such as Judith, life was deeply intertwined with the chronic instability and violent ravages of the phosphate and refugee industries. The moral power of liberal activist representations, which prioritized the toxic repercussions of the industry in terms of refugee suffering, brought safety risks qualitatively different than those in other industry contexts. The material entanglements of a human and mineral extractive industry sector layered to heighten Nauruans' fears of resource volatility—the explosive potential of phosphate combined with that of refugees, as voiced by Judith. This was a concern I heard from Nauruans on multiple occasions. Anxieties about the risks presented by "the refugees" were made all the more apparent when the refugee industry transitioned from processing to resettlement operations, with migrants moving across Nauru's districts as refugees.

"I'm so worried about having the refugee children in our school," a teacher at Nauru's secondary school said on another occasion, joining me and Judith at the canteen. "We don't want to touch or go too close in case they say we hit refugees. And natural things like kids pushing each other on the playground. The next day it's in the Australian news." But, as with countless other examples, this teacher's fears were confirmed several months later, captured in Australian headlines like "Nauru Government Denies Refugee Children Are Abused in Schools" (Lauder 2016).

On the other hand, Maya, my close Iranian informant living in Nauru as a refugee, told me how she was fearful of walking by herself on the streets because of what she had heard from media reports about Nauruans. Like Judith, Maya's fears of Nauruans also intersected with global media representations that were based on a similar postcolonial politics of black and brown Others: of, in Maya's case, Nauruans as savages. These racist articulations, driven by overlapping values, fused to produce antagonisms between "refugees" and "locals." Migrants also experienced extreme stigmatization by locals on the basis of myths that spoke to nativist and racist fears of cultural difference. This was redoubled by the liberal allegations specific to Nauru that pitted Nauruans against refugees on a sliding scale of savagery and vulnerability. Maya's anxieties about Nauruans—and her quotidian experiences of these shared beliefs about "the refugees"—coexisted alongside the harsh labor conditions and colossal health repercussions of the industry on migrants. All of these global and localized forces combined to manifest in conflicts similar to extractive projects around the world.

Anna Tsing (2005) uses the concept of "friction" as a metaphor for describing the conflicting social interactions that develop from resource-extractive projects for distant markets. Tsing discusses the development of environmental movements that arose to defend the Kalimantan rainforests in Indonesia, and the communities of people who live within them, which were also imbricated within the system of cultural production. Drawing on Tsing, this chapter focuses on the uneasy relations that developed between local residents and migrants—and within these bounded groupings—from Nauru's latest extractive project. Forcibly combining a range of people from different backgrounds on an island sparked extreme social conflicts, as did discursive representations. Tensions were embedded in the rhetorical drive of the Australian government's deterrence policy and global media imaginaries: of Nauru as an inhospitable environment and of the asylum seeker and refugee as threat. But these resource frictions were also entangled in the activist representations that looked to contest the offshore operations.

Orienting the Pacific

When I arrived in Nauru, fear of and anger at "the refugees" were at a peak. The refugee riot of July 19, 2013, was firmly imprinted on many locals' minds even two years later, when I conducted my fieldwork. Many in the Nauruan public saw their role as generous hosts to those fleeing conflict and persecution. As much as Nauruans were entangled in the financial economy of the offshore arrangement, many were also enveloped in its moral economy. Many Nauruans held a feel-good belief that they were helping to stop the loss of lives at sea and were in fact protecting refugees. This understanding bore deep parallels to the phosphate heydays, when many Nauruans proudly saw themselves as global providers within the food supply chain; this was a much-promoted government and industry angle at the time—of islanders supporting the agricultural fecundity of lands far distant. In the new refugee industry era, government and industry public relations campaigns promoted a humanitarian frame because of significant local fears about the arrangement. When the operations began in 2001, headlines in the Nauru papers read, "Australia Asks Nauru for Help," and in 2012, they were "Nauru Again Assists Australia with Asylum Seeker Issue." The latter article continued: "Nauru is supportive of the RPC. Over ten years ago, the then Pacific Solution provided a great deterrent for people smugglers and stopped the unnecessary loss of many innocent lives. The Nauru Government is confident that can happen again" (Mau 2012).

When the asylum seeker protest at the RPCs took place, some locals took to the streets, angered at the ingratitude shown by asylum seekers in the RPCs, particularly when it was heard that Nauruan workers had been attacked. Others, like Jake, the Nauruan activist, fearfully watched from vantage points on nearby phosphate outcrops, using smartphones to film the incident to send to Australian media to prove what was really happening. Government ministers went on the local Nauru Radio to calm everyone down and ensure that nothing more serious happened. "I couldn't understand how they could do this to us. After the kindness we showed," one Nauruan said to me of this event. In fact, many Nauruans I spoke with maintained great pride in the RPCs. They were angry that the asylum seekers would burn down the RPCs, into which Nauruans had put a great deal of hard work and care. By the time I arrived, almost two years later, Nauru's urban fringe was populated with over five hundred refugees, all of whom were discontented with the arrangement. Large-scale incidents like the 2013 riot, but also other occurrences such as protests, self-harm, hunger strikes, and suicidal threats, intensified as the operations continued. Without a move toward Australian resettlement (something all migrants I spoke with in Nauru hoped for), and with Phnom Penh holding little interest—and for some, active fear—the level of risk and insecurity was extreme. Activist campaigners in Nauru and Australia were engaged in constant battles against the Australian and Nauruan governments through high-profile #RefugeesWelcome and #CloseNauru campaigns. This was also the case with several Australian workers in the industry who purposely took a job in Nauru to help build a strong base of evidence to challenge the offshore arrangement.

One popular strategy that some migrant and workforce activists in Nauru took was to circulate narratives of the squalid conditions in the country. They took photos of Nauru's hospital, its schools, its RPCs, decrying how they were inhumane, and circulated these to Australian activist campaigners. They promoted this angle to Australian media outlets and visiting international advocates, including the Amnesty International and Human Rights Watch refugee mission in 2016, in the hopes of mobilizing support for Australian resettlement. These representations were later proclaimed in headlines such as Human Rights Watch and Amnesty International's "Appalling Abuse, Neglect of Refugees on Nauru: Investigation on Remote Pacific Island Finds Deliberate Abuse Hidden Behind Wall of Secrecy" (2016), and their subsequent report *Islands of Despair* (2016).

Many Nauruans received these sorts of representations with a great deal of anger when faced with the welfare system set up for refugees on the island. In reality, in Nauru, refugees were something of an "occult" kind of commodity (Comaroff and Comaroff 1999). Because of the exceptional political and economic risks that losing the project presented, they were controlled, like high-grade phosphate deposits, to the operational extreme. Throughout my time in Nauru, I was constantly in awe at the sheer amount of money spent by the Australian government on furthering the processing operations, and on once again sustaining the small country's political economy, with deep political and ethical implications.

Outside of the investments into the industry operations, boxes of mixed-leaf salad, wholegrain bread, halal-certified meat, smoked salmon, and fruits and vegetables—outlandishly out of place on Nauru's import-reliant and largely spam-filled shelves—were shipped in weekly from Australia for asylum seekers and foreign industry personnel, to be prepared by chefs flown out from Australia. The leftovers rejected by the occupational health and safety regulations found their way into local events, as Nauruans were often firmly positioned as second-class citizens. These instances recall the BPC company town enclaves that once positioned the white man—and expediencies of phosphate extraction—high above the native. The resettlement houses where refugees lived also all had air conditioning, wireless internet, and flat-screen televisions, all powered by separate Australian-serviced generators that never went out, unlike Nauru's temperamental power systems. Specific water salination tanks and Australian-run delivery services provided all refugee residents with fresh water supplies on a round-the-clock basis. Nauruans relied on the often-erratic arrivals of Nauru Power and Water Services' workforces, who were providing for the country's water needs from a dwindling supply of largely broken-down trucks.

Nauru's education and healthcare systems were similarly import reliant, underfunded and undersubscribed, and largely staffed by newly qualified or retired Fijian and Filipino teachers and clinicians. Teachers, doctors, and nurses worked in run-down facilities, struggling to juggle multiple wards with dilapidated resources or classes with over fifty children. But at the processing centers, the Australian government funded a private healthcare and education system, with mosquito vector-control systems and plentiful medication. The RPC school had interactive whiteboards and specially contracted teachers from Brisbane, who flew in with lists of differentiation strategies for meeting the needs of diverse learners and refugee in particular. The medical center had cardiac-emergency bays, a separate mental health wing, and family wards. Government ministers or those lucky enough to have industry connections could sneak in to use the facilities, but for the most part they remained restricted for asylum seekers only. Refugees resettled in Nauru then attended their own private healthcare clinic, on the side of the hospital constructed by the Nauru Phosphate Corporation. The latter was to be replaced by a new hospital, construction of which broke ground during my fieldwork. Once children entered the Nauruan education system, flown-out Australian teachers supplemented every school across Nauru, with a new primary school later adding to the company town growth spurt. These infrastructural developments looked to secure the extractive arrangement well into the future.

Extractive industries have a history of carving out discriminatory labor practices along carefully designed racial/ethnic hierarchies. Accounts of company enclaves emphasize the tactical efforts to control labor along ethnoracializing schemes and ensure compliance among the workforce (Appel 2019; Ferguson 2006; Vitalis 2007). Nauru's industry arrangement was novel in another way, in that the segregations that developed from industry hierarchies and activist praxis went against the Australian and Nauruan governments' goals of sustaining the operations into the future. The majority of Nauruans I spoke with were angry at the dissatisfaction shown by migrants in campaigns like those incarnated in the *Guardian*'s Nauru Leaks and *Islands of Despair*, through websites like "Offshore Processing Centre Voice," and the Facebook groups "Free the Children NAURU" and "Nauru's Refugees' News." I heard comments such as, "I would be treated much better if I took a boat to Australia and got sent back here as a refugee"; "They're rude about our schools and then look, the Australian teachers fly in. If we complained we'd get nothing!"

"It's always the refugee sympathy angle," Judith said to me on one occasion, pointing to the newly published books about Nauru as an example of the ease with which mainland publics took up the suffering-refugee line. She continued, "Some of these people have never even been to Nauru! All they care about are refugees!"

On my first day in Nauru, I went to the state communications provider, Digicel, in the hope of connecting into the country's phone network. I was turned away and told that no sim cards were available at the moment. I had to wait—it could be next week, I was advised, depending on the flight schedule. Transfield Services had bought up the last batch of sim cards for asylum seekers at the RPCs. This kind of experience was a regular occurrence as part of the industry hierarchies that unevenly organized life in Nauru. Every Sunday, refugee industry workers congregated at the weekly Sunday roast up at the RPCs, again recalling the British Phosphate Commission clubhouse segregations of Nauru's colonial yesteryear, from which Nauruans were firmly barred. These sorts of instances helped me understand the seething resentment of life as a local.

A major fear of most locals in Nauru was that of accountability, as noted above. These fears of activism combined with Nauruans' existential anxieties toward the refugee population as risky and deviant, contributing to "the social reproduction of a matrix of racist differentiation" between Nauruans and refugees (Gutiérrez Rodríguez 2018, 19). In attempting to make the offshoring system and their plight visible, some refugees resorted to drastic means of staging graphic refugee beatings, attacking each other and then filming the aftermath, with footage circulated to Australian organizers as evidence of Nauruans beating refugees. Some would post photos on activist-maintained Facebook pages or on the pages of people like the Australian Green Party senator Hansom-Young, the government spokesperson of the push to end offshoring. In their reports and publications, Australian liberal media outlets and activists promoted the emotive tropes of the suffering refugee versus the savage Nauruan. Although well-meaning in their attempts, these representational practices looked to restructure the world of Nauruans, defining them as dangerous as a way to facilitate the resettlement of refugees to Australia.

The reports and imagery circulated by refugees in Nauru bolstered a system of knowledge production that has a colonial history in Nauru's exoticized region. Nauru's historiography is suffused by an imaginary of Pacific cannibalism that sustains the defamatory discourse we see into the present, including books such as *Cannibals and Coconuts* (1929) and *Life and Laughter amidst the Cannibals* (1923). Some of the earliest representations of the indigenous people of Nauru constructed islanders as childlike and savage in a state of nature: "a wild place indeed," wrote Louis Becke in 1897. "Their German masters try to keep a tight rein upon their blood-letting proclivities, and the seven clans with which the island is peopled are no longer allowed to slaughter each other with a free hand." Now, Western imaginaries of Pacific Islander savagery converged with the Australian government's representation of Nauru as a place of asylum-seeker deterrence. As they had done in the past to justify their phosphate extraction mandate, external actors wielded the resulting narrative about Nauru to once again rationalize their own political economic interests.

When faced with these sorts of organizing strategies, many Nauruans feared that some refugees might attack the fuel farms, attack their families, or far worse, knowing that "the refugee as victim" versus "the savage islander" held immense global sway. On one occasion, I sat at the phosphate administration offices with Georgia, my close companion who was a phosphate worker and occasional refugee worker. The conversation took the usual turn, and the civilizational discourses leveled on Nauru came up again. "Fat. Lazy. Refugee beaters. That's all they say," said Georgia, referencing a new article in the Australian *Guardian* that she had just pulled up on her computer. "I get so angry at the refugees, they just spread lies about us. I used to give them free clothes, buy things they'd sell. Then look what they did to us. Telling lies. Saying we're all rapists. The riots and fires, I don't want anything to do with them. And we don't know what they might do next. They're dangerous. We just don't know. It doesn't matter to them." Georgia's response was characteristic of many of the local fears that I was privy to. These sentiments were made particularly acute when, later that day, I overheard a group of teenagers shout dramatically, "Fuck the refugees," as they cycled down the street. The mobilizations of imaginaries of Nauruan savagery escalated these frictions.

Some activists often marshaled incidents such as schoolchildren fights or heightened tensions as evidence of Nauruans abusing refugees. Whenever an incident involving an asylum seeker or refugee occurred in the country, it was widely publicized by activist divisions in Australia, in close coordination with those in Nauru. Sexual assaults between asylum seekers in and outside the RPCs were circulated by Australian media reports that obfuscated the perpetrator, insinuating that it was a Nauruan. In reality, few locals wanted to go near "the refugees," scared of what might eventuate, like the Nauru secondary school teacher I mentioned above. Even locals employed to manage human risk, such as the lifeguards, referenced accountability. In interview, a manager of the Nauru lifeguards commented:

> We wanted to offer swimming lessons to children from the RPCs, but are so worried about what will happen with the whole "get to Australia" thing. We're trying to get one of the refugee contractors to supply a carer. Many of the kids at the RPCs want to be a part of it, but if they get bullied or bashed surfing, it could create problems when there's all these other mainland agendas. We have to be so mindful of politics here. Nauruans are often used as levers for another purpose. It's always, "Look what the Nauruan did to me." We don't want the club tainted with that.

The material entanglements of the phosphate and refugee industry sectors often figured into my conversations on accountability hazards. Another local said to me, "I'm also worried about refugees having access to materials to make bombs. They come from fighting areas, we heard and we've seen these places on TV. We know they can do things and don't know what they might do here. If they're released and they have access to other material from the shops, they can mix it, and make their own bombs. There's a lot of real fear with that. We don't know these people and they don't know us." As the latter comment signals, resource frictions also related to the particular narratives fixated on both commodity forms. With phosphate, many Nauruans held a mixture of feelings about prolonging mining, attached to understandings of the extractive consequences. Fears of cadmium emissions combined with the very real dust flares that enveloped local backyards. In the refugee industry, fears of human toxicity brought refugee racial politics to the fore. The notion of the refugee as a Taliban threat or deviant combined with the particular human risks of the offshoring arrangement, resulting in deep social segregations. Locals lived each day with fears about the origins of migrants, tales of "strange customs," confusions regarding refugee resettlement efforts, and suspicions and rumors promoted by activist campaigners between Nauru and Australia. Both the phosphate and refugee industries thus converged to heighten the anxieties experienced by the inhabitants of this fence-line community.

This is not to say that close friendships did not develop on an individual basis outside of the relations developed by the global flows of resource capital. Many locals, asylum seekers, and refugees in and outside the RPCs became firm friends through working together or through other social contexts. I often encountered deep acts of kindness between locals and migrants outside of the forms of subjectification connected to sovereign territoriality: not as "Nauruans," not as "refugees" or "asylum seekers," but as *people*. Some would share home-cooked meals with one another and help out with community projects. They would hang out at the boat harbor together, host dinners, and invite each other round for birthday parties, genuinely enjoying each other's company. Several Nauruans purposely bought refugee-sold goods on the market, even when these were far more expensive than in the stores. On one occasion, I went to the small market in front of the Civic Centre hub for my Saturday afternoon shopping trip. I got chatting with Sarah, a local political figure, but also an incredibly good cook, as likely to be found in government corridors as selling freshly baked goods on the market. She excitedly told me about a new project she had going, waving over Aisha, an older Iranian woman, also a regular market vendor, who was living in Nauru as a refugee as of several months earlier. They animatedly told me about their plans to launch an Iranian sangak flatbread project, but this one made "Nauruan-refugee style." With a bit more sugar added to the whole wheat, they said, "we're sure to turn Nauruans round to a healthier lifestyle." They were referencing the processed white loaves popular across Nauru.

Yet, these human-to-human relations became quickly enveloped in the industry's politics of subjectification. As chapter 5 details, industry personnel, employed to improve company town culture, actively encouraged these sorts of friendships. They would include what were termed "positive refugee community stories" in the local industry newsletter, *RPC Community Update*, put together by the Australian Immigration Department. These "refugee community stories" actually had the reverse effect of intensifying the partitions between "refugee" and "Nauruan." Sadly, interpersonal relations were also distorted by the politics of activist frames and the

Australian government's spectacle of deterrence. In reality, these social interconnections could have presented efforts of joint activist mobilization, as many Nauruans also disagreed with the offshoring arrangement. Friendships were also starkly ephemeral. Even when relationships developed, I always questioned how long they would last—or even if strategic interests lay behind them. The in-country protests made clear the interests of migrants in going to Australia, rather than staying in Nauru, and the fragility of the offshore arrangement as a whole.

Tragically, because of global media representations of difference and discrimination, conflicts did occasionally develop between some migrants and Nauruans in the country. Often these were in anger at activist narratives, which continuously stirred and shaped life on Nauru. Nauruans always reminded each other not to rise to the bait because of the media representations that would predictably eventuate, but for some, restraint was not so easy to manage. Some conflicts were also in relation to small-town occurrences, suffused with the racial fantasies of the imagined racialized Other. I was privy to women's gossiping circles where the topic of conversation centered on titillating rumors of the sexual prowess of "the refugee men." Racialized sexuality came to bear on how Nauruan women saw refugee men, also entangled in a colonial politics characterized by sexualized portrayals of the Other as "sexual demon" (Gray and Franck 2019). Although Nauru is a matrilineal society, a masculine culture is central to the national imagination, rooted in the colonial politics of European values and practices promoted by early missionaries.[1] Some Nauruan men found the long-term residency of refugee men threatening to their own virility, as ideas of racialized masculine threat intertwined in islander imaginaries. Accusations also circulated of refugees trespassing on private property and picking coconuts from private groves, which compounded the anger of many locals.

The context of dashed hopes and an unknowable future made for further conflict. During my fieldwork, a group of younger, motorbike-riding refugees, newly moved down from the RPCs, took to circling Nauru's ring road at high speeds. They held little visible concern for what local police officers would do—an indifference I confirmed when I asked some of the men if they were worried about being caught speeding. My question provoked much amusement in a context where it was well recognized by migrants and Nauruans alike that, globally, the moral weighting favored refugee over Nauruan. And, invariably, I did observe that conflicts were depicted in the global media through the more powerful trope of islander savagery, as in the following headlines in the *Guardian*:

"Refugees Attacked 'on a Daily Basis' on Nauru, Human Rights Groups Say" (Davidson 2016)

"Nauru Refugee Left with Horrific Head Wound in Attack Dismissed by
   Police" (Doherty 2016)

I often followed up on media representations in conversation with local islanders. Judith had a lot to say on the subject: "Be nice to the refugees, the government's always saying this, don't touch them, they'll just contact the Australian
media and you know what they'll say. But why do they have to be nasty about
us!?" She and others pointed toward how media representations mediated
people's relations, and the sharp reprisals experienced by locals because of the
toxic government-sustained arrangement.

   On another occasion, I took a hike to a swimming hole in Nauru's interior.
Three inebriated Nauruans floated in the pool with cans of beer in their hands.
Mosquitos and the stench of liquor quickly sent me away. "You're not going to
stay!? It's because we're savages, right?" one called out. "I'm a savage, I'm a savage, that's what they always say," another chimed in. I use this example to illus-
trate how islanders—as much as migrants—became entangled in the forms of
subjectification based on the industry's politics of recognition. In his classic study
on the impact of the media on Eskimos and on local communities in Papua New
Guinea, Edmund Carpenter (1973) makes similar findings. He describes the destructive potential of media myths, which can lead to media-induced distor-
tions of human behavior. Here, too, locals became trapped in the discursive
universe that shaped their resource-rich lands. The media shaped social relations,
and at times embodied behavior. In turn, the trope of island savagery also impacted on the feelings of migrants in and outside the RPCs and affected Nauruans and migrants' relations. These relationships rest on the foundation of Nauru's
colonial state formation and capitalist development, where access to resources
(capitalist markets, citizenship, and sovereignty) are the irreducible element.

Experiencing the Orient

During my time in Nauru, migrants held in the country shared many of their
perspectives of life on the island with me. These conversations often took place
at the boat harbor or at local events. On several occasions, I was also invited for
tea and for meals, and we would chat about everyday experiences. Several migrants I spoke with, awaiting or having received refugee status, also voiced concerns of living in a new and unknown locale. The popular media narratives and
representational tropes of Nauruans as savages—promoted by activists—
exasperated these fears, as did the Australian government's language of deterrence. Some refugees in Nauru were far less experienced in living in a new place,

particularly one far off territorial cartographies that held "torture complex" and "dark site" scares. They feared venturing into the country's urban hubs once it was time to leave the RPCs.

At local events, I would often bump into three young Iranian women in their early twenties, wide-eyed and excitable, down from the RPCs. Our interactions began when we found ourselves lining up together at the start of the annual Nauru Coca-Cola Cup 10K. We laughed and joked together about taking part in what was their first race. From then on, I would spot Fatima, Frieda, and Nastja at most local events. Each time, we would catch up about local island life. It became an in-joke that I was their group photographer as they invariably asked me to take their photo. I would act out a mock photo shoot, much to their amusement, as they posed with smiling faces, and we chatted on the side. Despite—or perhaps because of—the journeys they had been through that eventually took them to Nauru, they were curious about my experiences of living in the country as a single woman from abroad. We never spoke about their past histories—nor did I ask—but they would make occasional references to experiences they had been through.

Frieda was streetwise enough, having lived for months in Jakarta, and Tehran before that. She captured aspects of the fears of asylum seekers and refugees in the country, as set within the gendered image of the woman as victim. She asked me on one occasion at the side of a community event, "You walk alone? Outside? Really? Even at night? Have you heard some of what's said about Nauruans?" Frieda, like others, knew little about the place she found herself in on the basis of the regional cooperative arrangement. She was also fed Australian media narratives of Nauruans as threats, which mediated her and others' social relations. "I didn't want to come down to Nauru from the RPC for a long time," her friend Nastja said at one point. "I didn't know what they'd be like with everything I've heard." Like the forms of differentiation experienced by Nauruans, the built environment of the RPCs and industry provisioning also mediated the refugees' and asylum seekers' encounters with local islanders. Prison-style buildings not only produce understandings about who people held in them are (Moran 2015), but they can also produce affective understanding about those who exist outside their walls, and from whom those inside should be protected. For Nastja and her friends, the securitization of the building was designed to keep them away from "the native," as much as Nauruans I spoke with experienced the RPCs as protecting them from "the refugee." Despite the many public relations schemes described in chapter 5, Nastja also told me she had read headlines like "Refugees Attacked 'on a Daily Basis'" and "Refugees Not Safe in Nauru, Bring Them to Australia" on the computers at the RPCs. These narratives of savagery, which define Nauruans in a binary of islander inferiority versus Australian civilization, impinged on and shaped her encounters.

Neither was being a refugee the reality that many migrants had envisaged. No migrants I spoke to in Nauru had factored in or indeed heard of UNHCR's system of third-country resettlement—the supply chain segue that had sent them to Nauru. As Nastja made clear, those certified as refugees found themselves in a complete unknown on the basis of claiming asylum to Australian coastguards. They thought that their asylum claims would be processed by the Australian government: a belief often held from misguided discussions with brokers and boat captains in Indonesia or Sri Lanka. The idea of international human rights law also accorded a great deal of authority. Many migrants I talked to felt a strong sense of entitlement and notions of social justice around the idea of being a refugee. Some spoke of terrifying experiences that should by law, they said, make them refugees. They thought it starkly unfair that despite being certified as refugees by the same Australian Immigration Department officials, represented by the same Australian defense lawyers, and managed by the same contracted organizations, in an industrial enterprise extrapolated from Australia, their residency was tied to Nauru—or the option of Cambodia. For many migrants, watching twice-weekly jets bound for Brisbane, eating food flown in from Australia, being told about expat workers' holiday breaks up on the Gold Coast, and sometimes even brought back souvenirs were all experiences that rubbed salt in the wound of their dashed hopes about a life in Australia. I was often quizzed about life in Australia and could see in my interviewers' eyes their frustrations as I answered their questions.

Many migrants I discussed these experiences with had been living in Nauru for several years in anticipation that the Australian government would change their policy. Many hoped that the political party at the time would cave and slip them in under the radar (as in the 2001–2008 phase). Many also hoped for the success of activist campaigns or Australian legal challenges. With each month then year that passed, the majority I spoke with were sick and tired of the unknowns, of being unable to acquire visas for elsewhere, even for a short visitation. Many were also cosmopolites, used to living in urban climes like Jakarta, Tehran, and Colombo. It was easy to identify Nauru's new refugee residents, the majority of whom placed a great deal of importance on their everyday appearance, contrastingly strongly, Nauruans often remarked, against the local populace. A number of Nauru's younger refugees looked as if they were about to emerge onto a shopping mall strip: immaculately dressed, with slick hairdos, penciled eyebrows, and fashion air-freighted from Dubai—mail-ordered or sent in via care packages to Nauru's main post office.

I was often told by several of Nauru's younger refugees that there was nothing for them to do in the country. There was no cinema. There was no shopping mall. The gym outside of the RPCs was of poor quality. Fruits and vegetables were extortionately priced. They had to mail-order particular foods unavailable in the local stores, which sometimes took months to arrive. The place was, in the words of one refugee, "a dump." Meanwhile, many Nauruans flew in and out to visit relatives in Brisbane and Fiji. They returned clutching shopping bags filled to the brim with goods unavailable on Nauru's shelves: a stark reminder of the boomtown wealth of the refugee industry. Australian workers operated on their fly-in-fly-out cycles, of which the majority frequently complained. At social events, I commonly overheard Australian employees bemoan the trying nature of those six weeks in Nauru. They would swap anecdotes about the brought-over treats from Australia that made life more bearable (bags of Maltesers, Haribo, and the like), as did the salary increases of "hardship allowances." Usually, these conversations were purposely conducted out of earshot of migrants, but this was not always the case.

Many migrants in Nauru also held on to a utopian vision of life in Australia as per the salvational imaginary promoted by humanitarian campaigners. Ironically, this fantasy of the civilized West was connected to the very Orientalist fantasies used to justify their oppression: a racist nomenclature of migrant Others who threaten the civilizational order. Yet, the portrayals of the West as the space of progress factored into many migrants' belief systems. The majority I spoke with saw Australia as a golden land of beautiful landscapes and experiences where, on arrival, the Australian campaigners would support them in many of their endeavors. As a research student at USP, I was often asked about the quality of Nauru's university campus. My interviewers rolled their eyes, asking, "What is the point of a second-rate education? It's not like Australia." "Nauruans are unclean, obese, don't know how to keep fit, not like on Bondi Beach," I was told on several occasions. These narratives were characterized by portrayals of the Nauruan Other as "backward," heightened by representations of refugees in need of rescue from oppressive cultures.

Several migrants I spoke with firmly believed that refugee welfare provisions in Australia were astounding, and that they would be supported in achieving their goals by Australian humanitarians. In one of these conversations by the boat harbor, I commented that I actually found Australia to generally be a bit misogynist and racist, particularly when it came to refugees. I was corrected by my interlocutor, who looked at me aghast. In this instance, it was clear that the #RefugeesWelcome utopia had a great deal of sway. It was less clear what the reality of that dream would be if it were ever attained, nor what many refugees' reactions might be when faced with scanty welfare support, questionable resettlement housing in remote suburban locations, waiting lists several years long, and a racial politics toward refugees that was similar to that in Nauru.

Some frustrations among refugees also related to the power structure of vulnerability and welfare dependency that is part of refugee citizenship. Several refugees I spoke with were angered at the resettlement housing choices made by Australian caseworkers contracted in Nauru. They wanted to be on particular sides of the island or with the friends they had requested. In Nauru, land is tight. Knowing the land's high bartering value for the Australian Immigration Department enticed several entrepreneurial locals into leasing former phosphate extraction land for refugee industry projects. (For some persistent hagglers, up to AU\$8.50/m^2.) But with the refugee scares that enveloped the community, few locals were interested in the prospect of "a refugee" living next door. As detailed, these fears had already resulted in the segregation of asylum seekers, who were relegated to their own offshored in-country sites in the RPCs. Some leasing properties were enclaved in far-flung locations; one (the Ewa Resettlement Accommodation) was directly surrounded by a phosphate extraction zone.

Anger and fear were everyday realities in Nauru. I observed several outbursts of sheer frustration. For example, the annual World Refugee Day celebration was marked by Luke, who was living in Nauru as a refugee, throwing a chair across the room. This was but one instance of some of the pressure-cooker flare-ups that enveloped Nauru. Being in a position of vulnerability was not easy for many people to deal with. This was particularly the case for parents, who wanted to be seen as in control of sustaining their family but were now faced with the paternalism of infantilizing refugee welfare schemes. Many refugees resented the refugee buddy scheme, World Refugee Day, and the refugee art displays that soon took over the country. These placed people in demeaning positions as "the suffering" or "the empowered" refugee, even as others mobilized these stereotypes in activist campaigns. James, my closer Iranian informant, said to me that he appreciated how warm so many people in Nauru had been to him, providing him with new clothes and bringing around nice foods. At the same time, he disliked having to be reliant on others and his inability to set himself up in the way he had envisaged. He felt like he was constantly tiptoed around or talked to as if he was a victim.

For others, living in Nauru as a refugee was a constant source of embarrassment, particularly after assuring relatives they were going to "make it big" in the Lucky Country. Having to request care packages for delivery to Nauru was a complete reversal of the pledges they had made to relatives of their upward trajectories when they left for Australia. Employment was fairly easy to come by because of small-business funding packages from the Australian government, as chapter 5 details. However, it was not in the form that several refugees I spoke with had imagined. Many questioned the point, unsure of where it would lead, particularly as the businesses they set up (principally catering services and beauty parlors), largely catered to the Australian workers contracted to service them as part of a self-perpetuating cycle. All refugees received weekly welfare checks from the Australian (via the Nauruan) government, unless in employment. For most, however, this was insufficient to send anything to families back home, and, for almost all, for furthering their goals of building a future life. "How can I build a livelihood here for my children?" Ruben, a middle-aged Rohingyan man, living in Nibok as a refugee, asked me. "The education system is awful, and what am I supposed to do? Deliver Rohingyan takeaway each day to the Immigration Department?" Many Nauruans I discussed this with also echoed these future uncertainties behind closed doors, saying that "the refugees should be in Australia" and "that's where they would fit in." "There are not enough possibilities for them here" and "It was never supposed to go this far with refugees permanently resettled here" were common refrains. However, at the time, the Australian and Nauruan governments pushed against the relocation of this toxic industry to Australia.

Outside the Australian government's placative efforts that looked to prevent protests (flat-screen TVs, air conditioning, sim cards, and so forth), those certified as refugees were also sometimes afforded lesser rights as refugee citizens and were valued differently because of their marginalization as "refugees." Most of the refugee discrimination related to the public anger or fear many Nauruans felt against refugees because of global campaigns portraying islanders as savage. On several occasions, I observed Nauruan employees apply "no refugee" segregations on a discretionary whim. In one instance, I sat at the Nauru police station, awaiting the printing of my Nauru driving license. A woman walked in. She requested the same procedure I had just been through—a theory test and an application to drive a car—sliding over her refugee visa. The officer at the desk looked her up and down and said, "You know refugees can't drive cars on Nauru. You can have a motorbike, that's allowed, but not cars." She looked aghast and produced her Iranian driving license. "But look how far back it goes!" Firm evidence, she said, of her driving proficiency. The officer refused to budge on the matter, despite her argument that she knew other refugees with Nauru driving licenses, all eligible to drive cars. I later spoke about this with a refugee resettlement worker at a Hash House Harriers expat walking event. She shook her head, telling me that refugees *could* in fact drive cars in Nauru. As resettlement workers, they had a lot of trouble with police officers "refusing people because they were refugees," something they were trying to sort out through government consultations.

On another occasion, I was at the post office. In front of me, an Iranian woman was being served, asking if her package has arrived from Dubai. She had recently moved down into resettlement housing from the RPCs, she told me, asking me with great interest if I was from the Australian media. After I replied that I was not, she moved on to explain how the package was from her family and held products unavailable in Nauru. The post office employee was long in the search. Five minutes went by. "I think they hide our packages, I'm sure of it. So many times, we get second-class service here. They're so quick when it comes to others. Just wait when it's your turn," she whispered to me. Later, rolling her eyes and giving me a conspiratorial nod, she added, "Nauruans are *so* fat and lazy." As the latter part of this encounter makes clear, several migrants ended up directing their anger not at the refugee industry and international legal framework, on which they were reliant, nor at Australian activist campaigners, who were for many hopeful support networks, but predominately at local Nauruans. They read Nauruans through the subordinate postcolonial narrative of savagery that is deeply entangled with histories of extraction.

To counter this, she and others were plied with Nauru buddy schemes, cultural presentations, and documentary screenings, and other industry marketing strategies used to promote refugee and nonrefugee integration. But the global discursive universe, which characterized refugees in victim terms and concurrently portrayed Nauruans and refugees as threats, created perpetual conflicts. These forms of differentiation were compounded by the legal frameworks that classified and defined people with distinct properties (suffering and vulnerable). Enclaving practices segregated refugee from nonrefugee through material and social space, structured according to the system of refugee status determination and resettlement, which ensured the perpetuation of power hierarchies. Industry workforce housing was also set against the RPCs and resettlement compounds and local housing, which brought the entrenched divisions between "refugees," "locals," and "expat" into relief. NGO-led events attempted to bring Nauruans and refugees together, but the RPCs were off-limits to locals without permission, as were the facilities inside them: a well-provisioned school, dining hall, football pitch, and medical center that exceeded Nauru's hospital provisions. These segregations recalled the BPC years, when expat workers lived in special housing, and when the golf course, clubs, recreational halls, cinema, and cricket pitch were all segregated by nationality.

Frictions also occurred internally. Some of these conflicts were related to ethnic tensions presented by combining multiple groups with preexisting, local ethnic animosities into a small island context. Others were related to the psychological burden of the offshoring arrangement, where living up against one another for prolonged periods resulted in extreme tensions. And some also connected to disputes between refugees over activist strategies through which demands for recognition could be successfully made. In Nauru, some of the refugees who were more activist oriented targeted others who refused to take part in the protests that soon took over the country. James, my closer Iranian informant, did not agree with these strategies—or at least thought it prescient to make his disagreement clear to me, distancing himself as an alternative survival strategy. When we discussed some of the media reports that had been circulated about Nauru at the time, he said, "I try and keep away from those guys, stay working, keep my head down. I don't want the Australian government to see me doing that." Maya also commented on this on numerous occasions, preferring to focus her activism on ingratiating herself with local and Australian authorities as per the hardworking refugee ideal. She told me, "No, it's no good. I think the best thing is work hard, build up my CV, take advantage of the English classes, wait and just hope things will change." Some of these individuals had to be moved into separate housing and hotel rooms for their protection. Those who refused to participate in protests were seen as weakening the standoff with the Australian government. Others who chose to accept a Cambodian package or IOM return deal also had to be moved to other accommodation because of the retaliation they experienced.

The next section turns to look at new forms of law and governance that overtook Nauru's streets in an effort to transform fractious relations between refugees and locals. For Tsing (2009), the work of commodity production is partly accomplished by uneasy cultural interactions between participants in the supply chain. Economic processes are never frictionless but can support the business of economic turnover. Here, the risks attached to two homogenized cultures, segregated by industry commerce and media (mis)representations, did not diminish industrial operations. Rather, the amount of industry workforces increased, producing new structures of accumulation. These forms of institution building were devised on the basis of the risks attached to the offshore arrangement. However, like so many of Nauru's financialized forms of social control to sustain the operations, Nauru's newest industry workforce team could barely keep ahead of the risks in order to manage them.

Safe Communities

Like the Nauru lifeguards, the community liaison officers (CLOs) were one of the most visible of the local workforces that was established during my fieldwork. Commonly seen weaving around the main ring road on their new Australian-bought motorbikes, but also in undercover operation, the CLOs, as they were known, became a pervasive feature in the country during the move toward refugee resettlement. The Australian and Nauruan governments developed the new Nauruan Police Force (NPF) in early 2015, amid local concerns over the move of more refugees from the RPCs across the districts and the prospect of open-center circulation. Security firms had already become a popular mode of income on the island. Ten security firms were in operation during my fieldwork, in addition to privately contracted individuals. Many of these firms were either contracted into refugee management or kept an eye on refugees as fear of what they might do grew during a spate of protests. "Are they buying nails?" "Is it possible to make bombs from phosphate?" "Could they attack the fuel farms?" were local concerns I heard regularly. Because of the fears attached to activist mobilizations, several security workers also took to passing by refugee resettlement compounds on their round checks.

At this stage, phosphate and refugee company town growth shared more historical continuities. Before the phosphate trade, Nauru had early forms of community policing via control of the wrongdoers by the chieftains of the fourteen state districts (Itsimaera 1992). But it was under German colonial rule, in the year prior to phosphate discovery, that a formal police force was first set up. Three Nauruans were tasked with company town management across Nauru's districts. As coconut trade was replaced by the higher-value phosphate trade, the policing scheme soon flourished, growing in strength and number. The incoming British phosphate administrators looked to ensure that local frictions did not obstruct the mining operations.[2] In 1910, the Nauru Police Force was formally introduced as a Crime and Trouble Prevention Force.

Under the UN mandate later under the Civilizational Trust terms, the phosphate administrators were tasked with developing Nauru's system of law and governance, a major part of which was effective operational policing. During the phosphate growth years, the renamed Nauru Police Force combined with an additional policing scheme in 1951, still retained to this day, of district constabulary. District constables functioned in addition to the Police Force to assist in the enforcement of the rules and authority of the local governing body, the Nauru Local Government Council. They were deployed by the council on "watch and ward" duties at important locations of the community institutions, particularly around security watch and school truancy. By 1959, Nauru had seven district constables, and the Nauru Police Force consisted of fifty-three officers under the command of a European director recruited in Australia (Australian Government 1959–1960). The force trained in Australian enforcement practice, wore brass-button uniforms, and rode imported bicycles, maintaining peace, governance, and order, to what BPC officials described as "the lasting credit of British enterprise."

The CLOs were the newest addition to the company town governance teams, conceived as a measure that would protect the refugee industry's investments. They were developed by the Australian and Nauruan governments as a refugee policing subdivision of the NPF when it was decided that more manpower was needed to help manage the operations. In the first industry phase in 2001–2008, the NPF had little involvement with the refugee industry. At that time, the industry operations

FIGURE 14.   Community liaison officers on patrol. Photo by Julia Morris.

were not under regional partnership, but operated under Australian jurisdiction. Nor had the system moved into open-center circulation or into statewide refugee resettlement. In the early days, the Australian government largely took on the entirety of the operations, deploying security personnel from their contracted firms. In this period, Nauruans also did not encounter the same level of demonization through discourses of savagery.

The CLOs creation was the effect of several major refugee industry developments that hit the country. In May 2014, the system of refugee status determination had reached the point where migrants were leaving the RPCs under refugee visas and moving into resettlement housing across the districts. Shortly thereafter, in February 2015, the Nauruan government opened the RPCs to in-and-out movement, as the industry planners had initially envisaged. The open-center decision was the result of several activist challenges that continued to threaten the industry's sustainability. Notably, in fall 2014, shortly after the announcement of the Cambodian deal, Australian Green Party MP Hanson-Young revealed that asylum seekers in Nauru had told her that "women were regularly required to strip and exchange sexual favors with guards so they could shower" and "children were forced to perform sexual acts in front of guards" (Fletcher 2014). Then, in January 2015, the Human Rights Commission released their *Forgotten Children* report, which detailed the litany of harm that comes from holding children in immigration detention centers in Australia. Nauru did not explicitly figure in the report. Instead, written statements were taken exterritorialy that denounced the harms of children being in offshore and Australia's holding sites. "This damning report reveals the truth of Nauru and the horrific conditions that children are being exposed to on a daily basis," said MP Hanson-Young (2014) at the time.

As discussed, the Nauruan government had broached the subject of an open center among the public on several occasions, but many locals feared the prospect of permitting the in-and-out movement of rioters and others like them. Local fears continued to surge around "the asylum seeker" and "the refugee" as dangerous. (Verbatim quotes from my fieldnotes of local conversations read: "We don't know who these people are"; "They could be Taliban for all we know"; "I had one of my old relatives worried that they were going to sneak in through the pinnacles and rape us in the night.") These representations, which portrayed the asylum seeker and the refugee in pejorative ways, combined with the risk-based concerns of what Nauru's new residents might do to attract attention to their situation. However, the Australian government's decision to sustain the operations, unless refugees chose to go to Cambodia, induced the Nauruan government to move against their public's fears and agree to the open-center arrangement.

At first, the Nauruan government announced locally that only twenty to thirty asylum seekers per day would participate in the open-center program, initially for three days a week. Government MPs and industry workers held meetings with Nauru's district council representatives and published details in the local paper to alleviate public anxieties. Meanwhile, Australian and global media headlines circulated a different narrative. Their representations retained the connotations of the savage established by early colonialist discourse and the moral elevation of the suffering refugee connected to a history of humanitarian philanthropy:

"Nauru's Move to Open Its Detention Centre Makes It 'More Dangerous' for Asylum Seekers"
—*Sydney Morning Herald* (2015)

"Australia Asylum: Dutton Says Nauru Is 'Safe' for Refugees"
—BBC News (2015)

"Changes on Nauru No Guarantee of Safety"
—*Pro Bono Australia* (2015)

The *Mwinen Ko Nauru Community Newspaper*, on the other hand, offers a window into understanding many of the Nauruan public's fears about the move of asylum seekers into and around the country. The paper notified all local residents of the open-center hours, emphasizing that "the purpose of the Open Centre Arrangement is to enhance the mental health and wellbeing of the Asylum Seekers in Nauru and to assist their integration into the Nauruan Communities" (Appi 2015). The published government statements also stressed the eligibility requirements and low risk presented by all participants:

- Arrangements will be available to families with children and single adult females only, but will be expanded over time to include all cohorts, including single male adults.
- Key eligibility requirements will be in place to ensure all participating Asylum Seekers have:

    1. A current Security Risk Clearance Level Assessment provided by service providers, which demonstrates that the Asylum Seeker is suitable to participate in the Open Centre Program.
    2. A Good Character and meet Good Behavioural Standards, including no outstanding criminal matters or convictions, whilst in the NRPC.
    3. No Asylum Seeker will be allowed to participate if they are currently under a Behavioural Management Plan (BMP) or deemed to be at risk by security providers.
    4. A completed Medical Assessment and Clearance (as advised by IHMS) to ensure they:

        —are suitable to participate
        —do not pose a public health risk

The Nauruan government sought to further emphasize the plight of the refugees as an integration strategy. This framing similarly focused on the suffering refugee but centered the moral contributions that Nauruans were making through their new extractive economy. On one occasion, the *RPC Community Newsletter* (2014) read:

> Refugees have a variety of experiences, and every individual's "refugee journey" is different. Most have faced deeply distressing and harrowing experiences and many have survived a range of physical, psychological and emotional traumas.
>
> Some common experiences of persecution include torture, beatings, rape, disappearance or killing of loved ones, imprisonment without trial, severe harassment by authorities, land confiscation, conflict-related injuries and months, years or even decades spent living in refugee camps or urban slums.
>
> Rarely do refugees have the chance to make plans for their departure: to pack their belongings, to say fare—well to their friends and families. Some refugees have to flee with no notice, taking with them only the clothes on their backs.

The motivating factor for refugees is safety and protection from persecution and human rights abuse, not economic advantage.

The Nauruan government and Australian industry personnel constantly promoted the more general benefits of the industry arrangement. They publicized the many CSR initiatives that had taken over the country. They painted a rosy picture of modernization that avoided depictions of the anger and fear in Nauru, which were the destructive results of this extractive practice. These CSR initiatives recalled the BPC tactics of old, in which the phosphate administrators and administering governments also projected the gloss of company town life. Phosphate industrialists promoted the modernizing practices that brought Nauru into "sophistication" from "a more primitive mode of life," such as the "modern conveniences and comforts" (BPC 1929) of hospitals, schools, and divertive amusements, steering well clear of references to labor strikes or phosphate's toxic tolls. Now, Transfield sausage-sizzle fundraising events for the Rotary Club's Mental Health Unit, new reverse-osmosis units donated by the Immigration Department, equipment for Nauru lifeguards, and later the new hospital and new primary school all found inclusion in refugee industry news, advertised across the *Mwinen Ko* newspaper and sometimes the in-flight Air Nauru magazine.

President Baron Waqa also continued to attempt to warm the country to the new business. In his forty-seventh Independence Day speech on January 31, 2015, he announced:

> Ladies and gentlemen, the Regional Processing Centre for asylum seekers was established nearly three years ago. Since then, it has become a significant employer of Nauruans with 922 locals employed as of to date. The wages from the employees and the benefits generated throughout the economy is enormous . . . My fellow Nauruans, we have a history and culture of welcoming strangers in our land. The suffering some of these refugees endured must have been unbearable, especially those who travelled long distances with young children. Let us make their stay with us to be as welcoming as possible. Treat them as you would treat your friends and families. After all, we were once a people who were deported and dwelled in a foreign land. Let us repay the hardships our forefathers endured, with love—as love begets love. (2015b)

Prior to the open-center launch, community consultation groups spoke with local district representatives to address the public's fears. The Nauruan and Australian governments held meetings in Canberra with the many Australian planning divisions concerning the sort of workforce that could assuage any conflicts and protect both parties' extractive interests. Shortly before the open-center arrangement began, a new police force position was advertised across Nauru. Posters went up in most of the social hubs, the supermarkets, and the Civic Center, and announcements across the papers read:

> The Government of Australia in collaboration with the Government of Nauru has initiated a special training program in Nauru to train locals to be CLOs. The training will be conducted by the Nauru Police Force (NPF) with assistance from Nauru service providers, Connect Settlement Services (CSS). It is a four-day training program that basically prepares each CLO for the Open Centre Arrangement Program, which is expected to take place on the 25th of February, 2015.

Many Nauruans took up the new job—130 at first count—as the new policing scheme set up under the refugee industry flourished, growing in size and number. I spoke with several Nauruans who became CLOs. Some expressed their desire to dispel the Australian media representation of Nauruans as savages. They saw their work in the CLOs as part of the institutional fabric of refugee protection: "to support refugees' integration." All were enticed by the good wages, brand-new motorbike, paid-for petrol, and mobile phone (Alcatel OneTouch, three hours credit, and forty text messages a week), funded entirely by Australian taxpayers. As with phosphate, the political capital earned by sustaining the industry operations was clearly enormous.

Protecting Extraction

> Peace and order, as also the future prosperity of the settlement, will depend first and foremost on the immediate reduction to an absolute minimum of the large quantity of firearms at present in the possession of the natives.
>
> —Representatives from the primary copra extraction firms in Nauru, J.C. Godeffroy & Sohn and Robertson & Hernsheim, joint letter to von Kusserow, the Prussian minister, dated October 1, 1887 (Fabricius 1895)

The CLOs consisted of two branches: the CLO Specials, visually distinctive in luminescent vests and matching baseball caps, and the CLO Normals, an undercover police force stationed in each district. CLO Specials were specifically tasked with asylum seeker and refugee policing, covering open-center hours. CLO Normals were more widespread and maintained a regular undercover presence in the event of any altercations. Officials from the CLO Normals and Specials were attached to specific districts, although CLO Specials moved across district demarcations as they followed the movements of asylum seekers and refugees. All CLOs were trained in patrolling and supervisory protocols by the NPF, including how to conduct round checks, write incident reports, and deal with altercations. All CLOs were also given refugee sensitivity training by Australian social workers from Connect Settlement Services that included covering:

the definition of a refugee (fleeing persecution);
the vulnerabilities of a refugee (possibly traumatized from past experiences);
the culture of a refugee (their different religions and nationalities);
and how to handle the particular conflicts induced by the offshoring arrangement.

On open-center days, the CLO Specials assisted, guided, and escorted asylum seekers down from the RPCs. On one occasion, as I sat at the boat harbor, a group of young Afghani and Iranian men cannonballed into the surf from the harbor's raised concrete walls. The lifeguards ran in all directions, shouting, "We told you guys about the corals! Don't swim around there!" The lifeguards bandaged one man's hand, which was badly cut. A CLO stationed on duty at the side quickly stepped in and took the injured man back up to the RPC for a clinical check before anything more dramatic occurred. As the CLO's quick thinking made manifest, dispelling possible incidents that might be mobilized through global activist frames were important tasks of both CLO branches. Much of the CLO's work intersected with the representational conflicts of the industry's politics of value: the value of refugee recognition, coupled with the political economic imperatives of sustaining the operations. Cindy, a CLO Special, described the risk-managing aspect of her daily work to me: "There was one time when a refugee pinched a child and took a video of the kid crying and said it was Nauruans, they're all bad, the usual stuff. He got the kid to say, 'I want to go to Australia.' Another time, two refugees punched each another and said the Nauruans did it. Me and my friend saw what went on. We wrote an incident report and filed it with the line manager." CLO Specials held weekly intelligence-sharing meetings at the police station with Australian industry personnel. They provided updates on the progress of refugee determination, behavior at the RPC and resettlement houses, and news of potential protests. As part of this era of policing, CLOs in turn shared their intel regarding asylum seekers' and refugees' movements.

All CLOs were trained in the suppression and control of asylum seekers and refugees; ultimately, the goal was to help maintain the government's hold over the industry. They learned to navigate the many side roads that wind through Nauru's phosphate extraction fields in case of an RPC riot or similar incident where they would need to be quickly on hand. Also, Cindy told me, this navigational know-how came in handy for tracing open-center participants' whereabouts after hours. Hiding in the limestone pinnacles became a popular pastime for those at the RPCs, as did staying in other friends' resettlement houses beyond the 5 p.m. open-center cutoff hour. "I don't know their faces yet, so I can't find the asylum seekers too well, but we're trying to find a way to give them ID cards. That will make it easier," Jonah, another CLO, said when I asked around about their workforce practices. Jonah was the friend of one of my local interlocuters who happened to be over when I stopped by for a drink. He sat outside on a deck chair with Tracy, another fellow CLO. Both were keen to talk about their work, which, for them, was a significant example of local efforts to dispel the widespread activist strategy of Nauruan debasement.

In addition to these sorts of tasks, CLO Specials also advised asylum seekers and refugees on appropriate behavioral conduct, particularly with the influx of people in their mid-twenties from the RPCs, for whom revving motorbikes, doing wheelies, and picking coconuts from Nauruans' orchards became common entertainment. "The asylum seekers are always taking the coconuts. Some residents don't like them doing that. That's a big thing we're always on call for," Tracy said. "The problem is also that some of them don't really care," Jonah added. "They just want to be in Australia so there's no respect for Nauru. We're just the fall guys when anything goes wrong." Jonah's comment points to one of the major paradoxes in the CLO policing scheme. Although the program was developed for refugee industry accountability, in reality, the CLOs were the ones subject to liability. CLOs were all well versed in "approaching the refugees," not touching them, and making sure to record any altercation in the event of accusations framed in terms of Nauruan savagery—for example, that they beat refugees.

A Peaceful Refugee Protest

One of the main responsibilities of the CLOs was enforcing new rules developed for refugees in the wake of a series of high-profile protests in February and March 2015. Protests have happened across the course of Nauru's industrial history. In the BPC phosphate extraction years, labor strikes among the Gilbert and Ellice islanders and Chinese workers brought in for mining the phosphate lands were not uncommon occurrences. With the new influxes of asylum seekers wanting to be in Australia, fires and protests plagued the country on a regular basis. Protests are common in migrant-holding facilities in Australia and worldwide (Moran et al. 2013), and no less so in Nauru, in a context of extreme tension. As more refugees moved into resettlement housing, protests became a regular feature of company town life. The protests of February and March 2015 were some of the higher-profile actions staged by refugees against their blockade from Australia. At the first protest, a group 150 strong walked down the main road in Nauru's

Nibok District with banners, cameras, and activists in Australia on the phone. They blocked the road, turning back cars. The Nauru Police Force was called in for unlawful assembly.

In the phosphate industry years, Nauruan policemen were sent on regional training programs to Narsove Police College in Fiji, and then the Australian Police College in Manly, New South Wales. Their capacity building focused on policing strategies such as fingerprinting, photography, first aid, and court procedures—all designed to maintain order and well-being in the company town. In the refugee industry years, policemen's training was revamped and adjusted to the specific threats that the high-risk operations presented, functioning as instruments of frontier management for the industry. By the time of the first refugee protest, the NPF were well trained in riot and disorder management, personal protection, and sexual assault investigation through Australian and regional development programs.[3] They knew about the protests beforehand, from their refugee intelligence-sharing networks. They had also practiced how to escort protestors and conduct crowd control in police training camps in Honiara. They had constructed guidelines on peaceful protest protocol, requesting a written submission that alerted the police force as to the number of people that intended to participate, as well as the venue, the time, and date. Ignoring the protest protocol, refugees took to the streets from the resettlement compounds. Some threw rocks at the police, injuring three officers, and one of the new Australian-funded NPF Land Rover jeeps, goading local police to arrest them. Others took photos with banners reading, "We are refugees not slaves" and "End the discrimination," and a young girl holding a cardboard cross with "Freedom or die" written on it. These images were circulated to Australian activists.

I spoke with James and Maya about the protests. Both had taken jobs in Nauru, refusing to take part in the protests or quit their employment, despite the insistence of some self-labeled activist refugees. James described receiving threats from other refugees in the housing block when he refused to take part in protest activity or quit his job. Maya similarly said that she tried to keep away from anyone involved in the protests. As detailed, for some, the threats of physical assault were so bad that the Australian government funded hotel rooms to keep them away from the danger others presented. This was of course starkly paradoxical as the violence was ultimately the effect of the overall industry arrangement. The offshoring arrangement itself is what pitted people against each other in ways that sustained and legitimized the violence.

At the second riot, the following month, a much larger group of refugees took to the streets. Some placed children in front of them as human shields, taking photos of scratches and bruises for global media appeals. They staged videos where they turned the cameras on after they had goaded and attacked police and

Nauruans. They recorded the subsequent retaliations of Nauruans, some of whom put up their hands to protect their faces, while protestors shouted things like "They're attacking us!" "Refugee beaters!" These videos were later uploaded by activists from the Refugee Action Coalition Sydney and circulated around Australian media teams, catapulted to new heights of visibility as evidence of Nauruan attacks against refugees.

"Government Urges Community to Be Calm amidst Refugee Protests," read the local *Mwinen Ko* paper headline in March 2015. Nauru's minister for justice, David Adeang, appealed on the local radio: "These troublemakers are not innocent victims and should not be portrayed as such. They are trying to manipulate the media and public, and we will not play their game." Meanwhile, the Refugee Action Coalition Sydney released the following statement in 2015: "Up to 300 refugees, women, men and children, from all refugee camps across Nauru have defied the Nauruan government and police attempts to ban refugee protests and staged a peaceful protest this afternoon." They said that the refugees were "punched in the face or pushed to the ground" (Solah 2015), announcing that more rallies were planned. Later that day, the *Guardian* Australia read, "Almost 200 refugees, including several children, have been arrested on Nauru for protesting in the island's capital, as video has emerged showing refugees being assaulted as they protested peacefully at the weekend" (Doherty 2015). Other global media outlets soon followed: "Refugees have staged demonstrations in recent days to protest against conditions on Nauru and their treatment at the hands of locals" (Fox and Bolitho 2015).

At the end of the protests, 183 refugee protestors were arrested for assaulting local police, damaging property, and unlawful assembly. One Nauruan was charged with assaulting a refugee. All protesters were later released on bail. Arrest and the threat of imprisonment meant little. The arrest of any refugees was usually mobilized by activists as evidence of refugee cruelty. In the wake of the protests, the CLOs were charged with new tasks. Not only did they continue policing activist moves, but all refugees had to alert a CLO when they needed to refuel their motorbike. None could go near the fuel farm or power station in case they tried to mobilize activist efforts.

The community policing was an important example of the amount of symbolic capital that sustaining the operations held for the Australian government vis-à-vis allowing migrants to go to Australia. Although Nauru soon suffused with industrial hazards that spread from the RPCs across the country, the value of the deterrence spectacle far outweighed the exorbitant financial—and human—costs. This was particularly the case for the Nauruan government, who ignored their public's requests to urge the Australian government that refugees be resettled in Australia. As a result, like the many health and safety schemes, the amount of regulation that went into Nauru was extreme. An entire community-policing division was devised and grew, as an extension of the system from the phosphate colonial years, on the basis of the risks attached to this offshore industry arrangement.

Certainly, as practices of accountability, none of the policing practices or elaborate incident report–writing systems, such as those of CLOs like Cindy, had much effect in combatting victimization tropes that popularly appealed on the global stage. The Nauru Police Force, on the other hand, was given widespread publicity, figured in terms of police brutality and as evidence of Nauruan savagery, such as in this 2015 teleSUR report with accompanying refugee statement:

> Police Attack Refugees on Nauru Protesting for Freedom
> "The Nauruan police told the refugees to stop protesting, however after they refused and continued the peaceful protest they were attacked. As violence broke out, the Nauruan police and locals began pushing and punching the refugees. One male refugee was punched in the face by a Nauruan police officer wearing hard knuckle gloves and then later dragged away by another police officer," the refugees stated.

Many Nauruan police officers were incredibly upset over these global representations. Several I spoke with resented the amount of work they put into the fractious company town operations. They were always on call at the RPCs and across the resettlement districts because of conflicts between migrants or between migrants and locals. To address allegations that they had assaulted the refugees, some Nauruan police officers gave local and Australian media interviews. They released a public statement that told how they were "sick of the lies told about them and the fabricated allegations of refugees" (RON 2016c). In an opinion piece for the Australian *Daily Telegraph*, President Waqa (2015a) wrote: "Our police and people have been wrongly accused of being violent towards refugees. Anyone who knows the spirit of the Nauruan people knows that we are a peaceful people; yet driven by the political agenda of refugee advocacy groups and so-called human rights lawyers, these lies have been spread by certain journalists who relish the opportunity to use Nauru as a punching bag." But few of these perspectives achieved wider media recognition. Meanwhile, the language of Nauruan savagery gained popular appeal.

Australian advocates for refugees took to finding developmental loopholes that might end the operations. "The Nauruan police force does not have the capacity, experience or resources to prosecute incidents of child abuse," wrote legal academics from the Kaldor Refugee Studies Centre in Sydney in response to the later Nauru Leaks exposé (Hoang and Gleeson 2016). However, because of the political capital of disallowing refugees' resettlement in Australia, backed by a disinterested public in the Australian hinterlands, these sorts of allegations—tinged with discourses of Nauruan underdevelopment—only led to an ever-rolling cycle of more NPF Australian training programs. After riot and disorder management, personal protection, sexual assault investigation, and forensic photography, standard Australian child-protection training sessions soon extended across the country.[4]

Nor did implementing a resident industry police force particularly improve local relations. Conversely, the policing scheme created more spaces of control for governing people's lives within the conflictual relations in which the company town developed. Although one of the shared goals was to unite refugees and residents through a local liaison team, refugee policing solidified hierarchical relations of power and boundary setting that disrupted human relations. Refugees were positioned as vulnerable or as dangerous, while Nauruans became instruments of governance. These epistemic constructions were simultaneously reinforced through the narrative strategies that promulgated the idea of the Nauruan as savage and the refugee as vulnerable or violent. At best, the CLOs, like other regulators like them, were also a part of securing and reproducing the hazards attached to the refugee industry.

The Militarization of City Life

Not only did the economic force of the refugee industry dominate life in Nauru, but the industry also produced new spaces of governance. This led to what Mike Davis famously discusses in the Los Angeles suburbs as the "militarization of city life" (1990, 223), which operated beneath the state façade. With the popularity of the CLOs among locals, the Nauru Police Force expanded the round checks of CLO Normals to focus on assisting them with pressing community problems of the boomtown developments: more locals and Australian workers with money to burn, and wealth disparities coming to the fore across the island. Not everyone in Nauru had access to the wealth associated with the refugee industry. Those without land to lease to industry providers or capital to tap into industry business opportunities (supermarkets, car rentals, security firms, and so forth) were more disconnected from the boomtown growth.

During my fieldwork, several of my Australian and local acquaintances had their houses and businesses broken into or vandalized; the increase in petty theft a noticeable occurrence. Since the coming of the refugee industry, new cars and motorbikes once again sped around the atoll: a sports convertible, a Harley, a Mini Cooper were some of the flashier vehicles I spotted that stood out against the island's small-town confines. In combination with a reignited booze party scene and other boomtown consequences discussed in more depth in chapter 6, vehicles swerved at high speeds. President Waqa (2015b) attempted to curb some of these predilections, beseeching the public: "Today we face many challenges with lawlessness creeping into our society. Crime is on the rise. Stealing, public disorder, drunkenness, driving without a license, dissemination of obscene pictures and articles, rape, among others is destroying the fabric of our society. Coupled with our lack of care for our environment by openly littering in public, we indeed have a very challenging future if we as individuals do not sit together and address these issues."

In an effort to reinstate the governance days of the phosphate era, new regulations were enforced, and old BPC laws resurged. The BPC had introduced Nauru's 40 mph speed limit in the colonial phosphate days, along with liquor prohibition and motor traffic ordinances, at the instigation of local chieftains, concerned over the marked influence of overindulgence in the local community. Until 1967, it was unlawful for a Nauruan to consume or be in possession of any intoxicating liquors. The vast majority of cases tried before the courts of Nauru prior to 1967 were liquor-related offences. Now, in the refugee industry heyday, the government placed customs taxes and tariffs on alcoholic beverages. After requests from local police, Australian officials from the AFP and Transfield Services assisted with breathalyzer training. CLOs were brought in to bulk up the law enforcement efforts. If CLOs saw someone speeding or driving under the influence, they made note of the culprit or number plate, leading to a possible fine or court order. The CLOs' daily work soon included writing incident reports or calling the police, particularly around accidents, fights, drunken behavior, and commotions that happened among locals. The CLOs also policed other regulations instated post-refugee industry, including motor vehicle registration and inspections under the Motor Traffic Act 2014.

The final section turns to the resource wars that developed in Nauru as Nauruan opposition politicians found value from the media airtime afforded by refugees. All sought control over Nauru's resource-rich lands, which riled internal tensions. Meanwhile, this produced narratives ripe for activist campaigners and, in unintended ways, the Australian government.

Resource Wars

It was striking how the figure of the refugee in Nauru, as one of intense global interest, first exasperated and then further securitized the body politic. In Nauru, refugees presented an opportunity for local oppositional movements to flourish. Nauru's small-town politics generated immense interest in the short time since 2012, when the refugee industry began. Political instability characterizes Nauru's ever-rotating government chambers. Yet, during my fieldwork under President Waqa and Minister Adeang, and given the Australian government and international development interests, the political system remained stable. This was even as the country saw regular upheavals, largely owing to the refugee industry. However, with the growth in activist mobilization efforts against the offshore arrangement, opposition MPs, forming always-shifting alliances, waged wars through Australian media. They used Australian media interest in refugees to encourage international and local support, utilizing the moral capital of refugees in their seizure for power. Australian and global media reinforced the local Nauruan opposition's presentation as human rights defenders and the Waqa government as corrupt, "a mix of dictatorship and fear" of immense proportions, said Nauruan opposition MP Matthew Batsuia on Radio New Zealand in May 2015.

These media battles were crystallized in a series of high-profile local protests that broke out across the country in 2015 during my fieldwork. In Nauru, with only one media station, the majority of the public rely on Australian news. In 2014, before I arrived on the island, the opposition MPs at the time, Roland Kun, Matthew Batsuia, and Kieran Keke, threw accusations of corruption against the Waqa government on ABC's *Pacific Beat* and Sky News. Giving phone interviews from Nauru or their Australian and New Zealand residencies, they criticized the January 2014 dismissals of Chief Magistrate Peter Law and Chief Justice Geoffrey Eames, accusing the government of "gagging members of parliament" (ABC 2014a).[5] "They don't want criticism, they don't want scrutiny—they want to turn Nauru into something like North Korea," said Keke to the ABC, a media outlet strongly in support of ending the offshore arrangement.

In a chaotic parliamentary standoff, in May 2014, the Waqa government suspended the three MPs for using foreign media rather than parliamentary debate to criticize local decision making. Then, in early June, two more opposition members of the nineteen-seat legislature were suspended, Squire Jeremiah and former president Sprent Dabwido, after becoming unruly in Parliament, and calling for Waqa's and Adeang's resignations. An Australian media battle waged between the ousted Nauruan MPs and the Nauruan government; it was given widespread coverage in Australia at the time as evidence of the Waqa government's repression, and the need to resettle the refugees in Australia.[6] Tropes of islander savagery again rendered the Nauruan government wild, and Nauru was widely represented as lacking humanity, in contrast with the civilizational imaginary of Australia.

In May 2015, when I arrived in Nauru, the MPs remained suspended. The government had made the controversial move of blocking Facebook. Locally, rumor had it that several teens had taken to circulating indecent photos through Facebook forums. Until the development of internet child-protection protocols and more police training in cyber security, the ban would stay in place. Others

I spoke with thought that it was to stop the mobilization efforts of activists between Nauru and Australia. Neither rationale was quite clear, but the ban had
little effect, as everyone (refugees, residents, and Australian personnel alike) soon
circumnavigated the flimsy firewall—and instructed me how to do the same
on my own laptop. The Australian media, on the other hand, asserted that the ban
was evidence of Nauruan savagery, as did the opposition MPs. Around the same
time, the Nauruan opposition fed the ABC widely aired corruption allegations
against the Waqa government, released in an ABC report entitled "Dirty Business."[7] They contended that Australian phosphate industry tycoons had helped
Adeang and Waqa in their seizure of power, seeking control over the country's
remaining mineral resource supply. The opposition alleged that Adeang and
Waqa had received bribes by Getax, one of Australia's leading phosphate firms.
In exchange, they had promised to promote privatizing Nauru's national phosphate mining corporation and sell Getax phosphate at lower-than-market rates.[8]
In collaboration with the Australian refugee industry, the five ousted MPs alleged that the Nauruan government had created "a culture of secrecy" and called
for resignations. The conflicts came to a head in June 2015.

The opposition MPs organized a group of young supporters to blockade the
Parliament buildings, where I was watching a Parliament sitting at the time.
Everyone excitedly looked through the curtains at the drama that was unfolding
outside. A fire extinguisher was let off, followed by a firework cracker, as Squire
Jeremiah led his supporters toward the Parliament doors. Earlier, on a morning
run, I had seen Dabwido and Jeremiah in the Meneng District, lobbying a small
group of district supporters. Both Dabwido and Jeremiah had been parliamentary
members for the Meneng Constituency before their suspensions. In Nauru, a culture of tongue-in-cheek rivalry continues between the district constituencies.
School and sporting fixtures, parties, and other local events all play around with
competitive district pride. The majority of politicians are descended from district
chiefly clans, from which political rivalries are more acute, but often no less jovial.
Now that the Meneng District had only one parliamentary representative compared to other constituencies, the suspended opposition MPs, keen on regaining
power, organized a group of younger male supporters from Meneng to blockade
the Parliament. They used familiar tropes that appealed to Western audiences,
such as abuses of human rights and a culture of secrecy.[9] Wearing printed T-shirts
that read "Meneng Boyz," they turned up at the Parliament during the sitting and
demanded Waqa's and Adeang's resignations.

All CLOs were reassigned from regulating refugee relations to the new high-
risk spaces, along with the NPF, by then well versed in protest protocol. I, and
many locals at the Parliament sitting, went outside to watch the happenings,
which later became the talk of the country. Protests have happened throughout

FIGURE 15.   Blockading the Nauruan Parliament. Photo by Julia Morris.

Nauru's extractive history: teachers blocking the runway for the 1994 *Leonardo: A Portrait of Love* premiere-bound jet, the ousting of then president Rene Harris in 2002, and frequent protests from Aiwo residents at the phosphate dust blowbacks; however, they are still relatively uncommon. Nauru has a reputation among other Pacific island states of Pleasant Island kindness, and it's even known under the acronym "NAURU: Not Angered Unless Really Upset." On that day, the small-town excitement was palpable. iPhones and iPads were out. Several members of the Nauruan opposition were on speed dial with Australian media teams, shouting things like, "Step down, corruption," which was later splashed across the Australian news as evidence of Nauru's lawlessness.[10] The event was a spectacle of global media proportions. I later received Australian refugee industry listserv notifications about it, alerting me of fears for refugee safety.

The Australian government stayed publicly out of the small-town disputes, refusing to give media statements, except to say that it was a matter for the Nauruan government, and that President Waqa assured them that the rule of law would be followed. Behind the scenes, Australian government officials were less calm, anxiously focused on securing "the future prosperity of the settlement," as with the ten-year coconut war of Nauru's district clan rivalry of yesteryear. During the protest wave, Nauruan and Australian government workers I spoke with were constantly on the phone with Canberra personnel, checking the situation, worried that they might be forced to move the asylum seekers and refugees to Australia. Even with the semblance of regional cooperation in this industry arrangement, asylum seekers and refugees in Nauru would come under the Australian government's full responsibility in the event of prolonged political instability. The government might be forced to revert the operations to Australia, making them "look like fools," I was told by Australian workers in Nauru. This was what all refugees I discussed this with secretly hoped. They knew that even if they were sent to Christmas Island, which was an excised Australian territory and still over 1,500 km from the Northwest Cape, it would be easier to mobilize with Australian human rights lawyers and activists from there.

Another major concern of the Australian government was that the families of the opposition MPs owned the Meneng District land, where most Australian worker housing was located. The majority of Australian Immigration Department personnel, defense lawyers, teachers, social workers, visiting international monitors and dignitaries resided in and beside the Menen Hotel. In the weeks after the protest, tensions were at their height. Phrases such as "Human Rights Abuses" and "Waqa Government Corrupt" were emblazoned on placards stuck to lampposts and trees across Meneng District. Many Australian industry workers I talked to during this time were petrified that discontented landowners might try to reclaim the Australian-leased land in an attempt to rile the Waqa government into abdication. At the time of the protests, all Australian workforces, asylum seekers at the RPCs, and refugees in the resettlement compounds had meetings about the political situation. The Australian companies enacted strict curfews, particularly within the Meneng District, from where the opposition MPs mounted their coup d'état push. Some industry workers moved into housing inside the RPCs themselves. In-country Australian administrators closely liaised with Canberra and the many interested internationals about the on-the-ground situation.

The Nauruan government was also worried that the oppositional factions would sabotage their boomtown endeavors, with the Australian government forced to send asylum seekers and refugees elsewhere. In order to secure their capital gains, and in anger at the opposition's use of Australian media, the Waqa government revoked the passports of Kun and Dabwido.[11] Dabwido and Squire were temporarily arrested, and Batsuia charged for vandalism. But, happening in such close succession, the responses to limit the opposition were only leaped onto by Australian activists and media and used to reinforce subsequent civilizational representations.[12] All of the events were displayed as evidence of Nauruan state despotism. Nauruans were defined as savages in terms of their political organization, represented as diametrically opposed to the civilized governance systems of Australia.

In the aftermath, the MPs and their supporters (later known as "the Nauru 19") waged an extraterritorial media campaign, circulating photos of the blockade and speaking on Australian media about the lack of democracy and the "culture of fear" in Nauru. The Nauruan opposition MPs quickly became heavily utilized by Australian activists as evidence of Nauru's lawlessness, reinforcing the presentation of Nauru as unsafe for the refugees. Liberal media outlets called on the Australian government to "get these refugees off Nauru fast." The Australian media ignored the fact that the opposition MPs also supported the offshore processing arrangement, on which the state economy was reliant. It was, after all, Dabwido who had renegotiated the 2012 arrangement. Rather, they focused on amplifying the presentation of Nauru as a site of lawlessness and darkness, enlisting the oppositional MPs as part of the strategies for making claims against the offshore operation. These tactics also made use of former chief justice Geoffrey Eames, by then residing back in Melbourne and resentful of his judicial dismissal. This was captured in headlines in 2015 like the ABC's "Nauru Rule of Law 'Nonexistent,' Former Magistrate Says."

The power of both insurgents and political placeholders can be found not in the causes that the two factions claim to espouse, but in the value accorded the figure of the refugee as commodity. As much as Australian liberal media outlets and Nauruan opposition found reciprocal utility, the Australian government looked for conflict-management approaches, seeking stability over the offshore arrangement. The prolonged immobilization of refugees in the country created a fractious environment vulnerable to resource predation, resulting in deep political instability locally. Activist strategies and liberal Australian media portrayals were not effective in achieving the immediate goals of resettling refugees in Australia. However, they did solidify a primitivist ideology around Nauru, which made the offshore operations more precarious. In July 2015, amid the wave of Nauruan political battles, the New Zealand parliament passed a motion by New Zealand's Green Party that expressed concern about Nauru's political situation. Two months later, the New Zealand government suspended their state funding of Nauru's justice sector, to which they had contributed AU$1.1 million per year, citing diminishing rule of law and human rights. Although the funding was eventually reinstated, and increased over the years, the suspension was given widespread coverage at the time as evidence of Nauru's disintegration into rampant lawlessness. The reinstatement was not.

While the popular global presentation is of the refugee as the downtrodden, everyday Nauruans have clearly borne the brunt of much of the social costs associated with a toxic industry. Migrants have certainly experienced catastrophic effects, but the log of grievances endured by Nauruans is also extreme and rendered invisible. This includes countless accusations of refugee rape, assault, child molestation, and the stirring of the body politic. Although the refugee industry has greatly enriched its beneficiaries (Australian and Nauruan politicians, the contracted private sector, and landowning elites), Nauruans and migrants have both retained the offcuts of these processes. Representations of the Nauruan as savage and the refugee as vulnerable in contrast to the "modern" West make these mutual experiences of exploitation disappear from record. Instead, media and activists outside the country question the legitimacy of the project, using the same discursive practices of colonialism around the inferiority of Pacific Islanders. This frame is bolstered by the oppositional figure of the suffering, at risk refugee. The self-representational labor of migrants—and activists' organizational strategies—makes this framing morally egregious to dispute. So, too, among Nauruans, migrants are also subject to abstraction and valuation as refugee commodities. Such market developments erode a recognition of shared histories of exploitation and forms of social organization that move outside of colonial discourse and political economic structures.

The practices of migrant-versus-native separation observable here certainly have a deep imperial history (Sharma 2020). But while maintaining racist segregations were crucial aspects of colonial rule and extractivist projects, in Nauru's postcolonial context these forms of differentiation hampered efforts of industry advancement. Chapter 5 turns to look at some of the industry marketing campaigns that took over Nauru in an effort to unite refugee and local and consolidate the industry's mode of capital accumulation well into the future.

EKAMAWIR OMO

Eid Celebration:
Everyone Welcome
Market stalls—Food, Crafts etc.
Listen to music and try food from all over the world
Performances
Where: Civic Centre Conference Hall
When: July 25, 3 p.m.—7 p.m.
Come together and celebrate Nauru's diversity
See you there
Connect Settlement Services

Eid Celebration, Civic Centre Conference Hall, Aiwo District. July 23, 2015. It's 3 p.m. and the Civic Centre is a hive of activity. Nauru's CLO Specials, wearing their high-visibility vests and matching baseball hats, are in abundance. But today is not just your average company town event. Hours have been extended and extra buses are on hand for the Eid celebrations put together by the NGO Connect, the newest Australian contractor on the local refugee industry scene, tasked with refugee resettlement in the small island nation. Posters have been appearing in most of Nauru's social hubs over the past week. Capelle's Supermarket, the Menen Hotel lobby, school staff rooms and corridors all bring tidings of the latest event on Nauru's bustling new multicultural calendar. Thanks to Connect's proactivity, most weeks are usually accompanied by some sort of industry-led entertainment. Movie nights and sporting activities are the mainstream fare, but now Diwali and Nayrouz are marked with yearly national celebrations and attempts to encourage Nauruans to learn about and participate with their new island residents.

"Nauru really has become a multicultural community and it's important we celebrate that," an Australian social worker says to me with a smile. Henna decorates her hands, and a multicolored frangipani is artfully tucked into the side of her loosely pinned bun. "Nauruans can really benefit so much from the refugees. Their cultures and skills are so valuable here." She goes on to add, "Now they're underway with building the new hospital, a couple of us have been trying to arrange for some of the refugees to decorate a wall or two. Something bright, colorful, something that expresses the rich cultural backgrounds we have here. Many of them love drawing."

She's obviously had a hand in the Civic Centre's new décor. For this Eid celebration, art from asylum seekers at the RPCs is in abundance, tacked onto freestanding billboards arranged around the room. Overall, a great deal of organizational effort has gone into today's event. World Refugee Day, just a few months before, was a bit of a washout. Attendance was poor, and the event was marked by an Iranian man throwing a chair across the room. Many people hightailed it, screaming in panic.

The Eid organizational committee must have taken some of this on board. Since the beginning of Ramadan, Ramadan information sheets have papered the country's noticeboards, instructing locals of its significance. "Ramadan, the month of fasting for Muslims, is a special month of the year for over one billion Muslims throughout the world. It is a time for inner reflection, devotion to God, and self-control," Connect's multicolored typeface informs.

Over the last few weeks, Australian community engagement officers from Connect, Transfield, and the Australian Immigration Department have also been driving around the country, trying to encourage Nauru's diasporic communities to put together displays that celebrate ethnonational ties in the spirit of Nauruan multiculturalism. It appears their work was fairly successful, even if the majority of attendees are industry contractors, asylum seekers, and refugees. The former

FIGURE 16.   A Save the Children worker getting henna-ed. Photo by Julia Morris.

snap on camera phones, queue for elaborate henna designs, or buy souvenir gifts to take back to Australia. Most of the latter are bored, though some are keen to show their proactivity in the hopes of resettlement in Australia (they later tell me), painstakingly painting industry workers' hands or manning market stalls.

Elsewhere, circular tables piled with nationally representative wares dot the carpeted space. On a table labeled "Nauru," a coconut-bra mannequin and a string-figure collection are featured. There are also postcards of smiling faces on sunset beaches and a plastic package of kava on one marked "Fiji." Outside, a halal-friendly "barby" is manned by an Australian High Commission employee. At the Taiwanese table, a small development team prepare papaya salad samplers as advertisements for their Healthy Nauru campaign. Kiribati was a bit late on the action. "Kiribati! I forgot Kiribati" an Australian Immigration Department Eid planner later exclaimed, after I remarked on attending the Kiribati community's Independence Day celebrations. I later panicked at my unintended industry development role.

Clusters of tables hold piles of information booklets: "What is Eid?" "Where are Nauru's new communities coming from?" Inside, glossary definitions for "Internally Displaced Persons," "Taliban," "Islamist Rebels," and "Warlords" provide further insight. An excitable Save the Children worker stands nearby, breathlessly waving at any of her "clients" she recognizes. Balloons and flags litter the room. At the back of the hall is a world map, with "Where are Nauru's new communities coming from?" written at the top. Pin markers are tacked around to denote countries of origin. A colorful wall hanging is festooned in the background: *Ekamawir Omo*: Connecting Communities."

I start wandering around the hall with Tessa, a young Afghani woman, living in Nauru as a refugee as of two years earlier. She's been tasked with introducing the concept of Eid to interested locals. The Connect team have been gradually recruiting more refugees and Nauruans into their workforce as cultural liaison personnel. Several Australian workers tell me this local recruitment practice is very helpful in mediating between sometimes-fractious relations. As with other strategies of settler colonial governance reignited across Nauru, these recruitment practices remind me starkly of forms of indigenous collaboration advanced by the British Phosphate Commissioners to secure their extractive mandate.

A video screen cycles PowerPoint images of Iraqi sweets, Muslims at prayer, a map of Mecca. We stand and watch. Tessa is a bit more doubtful about her role in company town cohesion. "I'm just doing this because otherwise I'll go crazy, get stuck in my thoughts," she whispers. "And it looks good on my CV for one day going to Australia."

We do a round of the room, investigating the cuisines on offer. There's a fair amount about. Signs with "Iraq Food," "Rohingyan Food," "Afghani Food," and

"Arabic Food" are taped onto large wooden tables. The food all looks suspiciously similar: samosas, roti, and curry are heavily represented. Other tables heave under the weight of shiny plastic women's high heels and flats, the latest perfumes, Victoria Beckham and Prada handbags: mail-ordered in from Dubai.

One of Connect's main projects has been encouraging refugee integration, not just through photography and film, but also through employment and financing local refugee enterprises with the support of the Australian Immigration Department. Catering is the most common venture as refugees circulate through the island's socioeconomy through forms of local consumption. It is now standard practice for larger government events to feature Rohingyan cuisine alongside the local coconut fish, meat, and chow mein plates. Instead of BBQ or Chinese takeaway, Nauru's Hash House Harriers might be seen feasting on lamb shawarma and akhrot chutney at their post-hash circles. Connect staff, who more often than not are seated on every one of the country's event-organizing committees, whisper a reminder: "Here, take some menus, share them with your friends." Takeaway delivery direct from the Fly Camp refugee housing means that falafel and kofte are only a phone call away.

A few curt taps on a microphone direct attention to the front of the room. Connect's long-skirted Australian multicultural coordinator announces the day. A garland of brightly colored pipe cleaners crowns her head. "Hello, everyone, thank you for coming, we're so pleased that it's such a great turnout, where we're all here together to celebrate what a diverse place Nauru has become." She proceeds, relating the benefits that Nauru's new refugees have brought to the country. An elderly Iranian man approaches the microphone, *taqiyah* atop his head; he softly begins recounting the history of Eid. Hardly audible, he recites a monotonous and all-too-dry monologue, his words barely discernible. People quickly lose interest, starting to chatter.

A young Connect worker catches my eye and sidles over. Bright eyed, midtwenties, she's fairly representative of the NGO demographic that coexists alongside the older, grandmaternal contingent. Connect's workforce has rapidly expanded over the last few months as a result of the RPC open-center circulation and the steady move of refugees across the country. She's one of the many case managers employed in transitioning refugees from the RPC to life in Nauru. She happily chats away, keen to interact with a different face outside of the team: "Lots more asylum seekers are being processed now so there are plenty of job openings here, but many of my colleagues in Australia don't want to do it. They don't agree with offshore processing. It's pretty ethically compromising. Connect are letting me try it out for a few weeks. Working in Nauru definitely isn't for everyone. I'm going to see how I cope with the emotional side of it. But my family were refugees, working with refugees is really important to me. I want to help." Our conversation tails off as the boom box kicks in, signaling the start of the afternoon's official entertainment. The young Nauruan DJ shifts to a thumping beat as he mixes from an electronic setup to rival any mainland player. Youth music engagement is another major vehicle for Nauruan-refugee integration. Connect has arranged funding through the Australian Immigration Department for a few young Nauruans to buy large-screen Macs and music- and video-editing software. A small group of Nauruan, Iranian, and Afghani teenagers are pretty into it. With the encouragement of youth-engaged Australian NGO practitioners—the types usually nicknamed something onomatopoeic, like Rizzo or Snap—the group has already put together several tracks that express in rap and song some of the challenges they have faced. Their efforts are impressive, visually backed by music videos featuring Australian Connect workers seductively dancing in the sea breeze, chiming in with the choruses. The young rappers are out in force for today's live performances, patiently waiting their turn at the side as Nauru's dancers get first dibs in the program.

A group of young girls wearing hula skirts and bikini tops step onto the makeshift stage. The three teens form part of a troupe who often feature at local events as Nauru's cultural dance ensemble. Most dance styles were wiped out when missionaries came to Nauru and encouraged the German colonialists to pass a series of laws that stamped out what they termed the "lurid movement" (Delaporte 1920). The British Phosphate Commission sought to change this somewhat, to display the benevolence of company town administration. Under the recommendation of anthropologists Paul Hambruch, Camilla Wedgewood, and Honor Maude, they encouraged the revival of dance and craftwork. Post-independence, the Nauruan government worked with the anthropologist Solange Petit-Skinner on similar projects, concerned that phosphate wealth had stamped out any vestiges of Nauruan tradition. At industry events like today, the coconut-bra mannequin and string-figure collection are always brought out from the dusty vaults of Nauru's Culture Department, along with the group of young Nauruan girls. In fact, since Nauru has reemerged through the refugee industry, dance offerings have seen a revival and the emergence of new fora outside of Independence Day and the odd birthday celebration, reworked and reinvigorated into a new company town pride. These sorts of cultural displays never fail to be followed by a nostalgic sigh among local residents about Nauru's lack of culture. "You really notice it against the vibrancy of the refugees," is a comment I often hear, emphasizing how "refugees" have become essentialized locally as carriers of diversity.[1]

As the hula dance reaches a close to a chorus of camera flashes and applause, the beat boxing teens get their moment, crouching low as they rap to the turntable's beats. Connect's dynamic youth coordinator leads them in a James Brown–style number. The lyrics focus on strength and empowerment. Each of the teens showcase their breakdancing moves to wild applause. As the music sidles into Arabic pop, a group of Afghani men are encouraged to take to the stage in an elaborate circular dance. Closely flanking one another, they progressively speed up to the rhythmic cycles, a few whoops thrown in for good measure.

"It's great to see them all enjoying themselves," the Connect worker whispers in my ear. "Their faces are so similar to those guys I work with back at Diversifat in Brizzy. I recognise this dance from our Eid celebrations." She sighs. "Their hand movements are so gentle, don't you think? Beautiful, just beautiful."

In this chapter, I draw on my observations from the field to examine industry cultural events designed to stimulate and sustain the refugee economy in Nauru. As previous chapters made clear, resource frictions enveloped Nauru throughout the industry's operations. In close succession, similar cultural projects around refugee celebration and multiculturalism as in Australia were made relevant to Nauru's 21 km^2 territory. Taken together, these industry projects were part of an extravaganza of cultural production that attempted to transform refugees into a national identity. Cultural practices, major events and exhibits, and artifacts endeavored to make refugees into icons of a new national island tradition that would establish Nauru as a refugee resettlement hub for Australia. Events like the Nauru Eid celebration looked to reconcile refugees and locals to the realities of long-term resettlement in the country, while also building a bedrock for the industry to be sustained well into the future.

In recent years, scholars have focused attention on commodities as the subject of cultural analysis. Cultural spectacles and promotional narratives of prosperity attempt to secure popular allegiance to risky modes of accumulation (Apter 2005; Barrett and Worden 2014; Coronil 1997; Sala 2009). In *The Pan-African Nation: Oil and the Spectacle of Culture in Nigeria* (2005), Andrew Apter examines how the oil-boom state of Nigeria utilized its petroleum wealth to organize cultural spectacles that displayed Nigeria's newfound riches as a rapidly developing petrostate. Cultural production was integral to the project of nation building, whereby colonially influenced cultural performances were reinvented as "authentic Nigerian traditions." These cultural transformations erased the violence of colonial legacies and masked a decline of the country's productive capacities, which eventually contributed to the extreme poverty and inequalities of Nigeria's present.

The cultural strategies developed around the refugee industry can be read in close parallel. In Nauru's refugee-dominated political economy, industry marketing events like Eid and World Refugee Day were powerful cultural strategies for the Australian and Nauruan governments. Like the "politics of illusion" that Apter describes in oil-rich Nigeria, cultural techniques formed part of a "false historical consciousness" that repackaged Australian- and ultimately European-influenced cultural performances as Nauruan (Apter 2005, 245, 15). By mish-mashing cultural traditions into an aesthetic of "Nauruan multiculturalism," the Australian and Nauruan governments looked to develop Nauru as an extractive site at the center of Australia's border enforcement archipelago. This banner of multiculturalism overshadowed the richly multicultural social and cultural landscapes that already coexists in Nauru. Before refugees, the industry argument went, Nauru was a homogeneous nation. Refugees gave Nauruans the opportunity to join the cosmopolitan nations of the world. Multiculturalism in this view depended on preserving the role of refugees in the Nauruan and Australian political economy. In the meantime, this "model of mystification" (Apter 2005, 15) sought to gloss over the violence, protests, and toxic realities of Nauru's controversial offshore industry context.

It is not surprising that Nauru relied on many of the same forms of representation to produce a national culture as Australia. In fact, the cultural imaginary utilized in Nauru drew on a logic of refugee protection as benevolent that has been refined across industry frontiers. During the past few decades, refugees have saturated modern social life and thought through new forms of public consumption (Gatrell 2013). Art and theater performances, interactive games, virtual reality, community events, books, lesson plans, and meetings with refugees have all emerged as methodologies in the global refugee industry to represent displaced persons and reach new audiences (Johnson 2011; Malkki 1995; Morris 2021a; Rajaram 2002). It was precisely this model of understanding human movement through discourses of suffering, empowerment, and welcome that Nauruans were supposed to embrace, even as media representations and activist strategies promoted a narrative of local savagery. As this and previous chapters show, however, the problems of a human extractive industry were not disguised—and were only exacerbated—underneath the dizzy prosperity of "refugee protection" and "multicultural harmony" projected to locals and refugees.[2] The spectacle of multiculturalism also failed to address the inability of refugees to move beyond the small island nation. The desire of refugees in Nauru to be in Australia—and not in an imagined multicultural island community—led to continued operational failures. In Apter's terms, refugee "prosperity was illusory, producing signs and images of national development that somehow fell short of the mark" (2005, 218).

Yet, the significant initiatives and struggles in the politics of cultural production are not unique to Nauru's extractive frontiers. Nauru was a veritable cultural laboratory used to promote forms of social life synonymous with the global refugee industry. The contradictions of the refugee industry are simply in starker relief in Nauru. Overall, I argue that the spectacular failures that plague Nauru's refugee industry are down to three main cruxes. First, cultural events like

World Refugee Day structure individuals' interactions in relation to the very seg-
regational schema of "the refugee" that enflames public xenophobia and compassion fatigue. Unfortunately, this differentiating framework is also what binds
the industry reliant on framing people as refugees and migrants' legal claims.
With the authority of this sociolegal paradigm, it is also how many migrants have
come to identify their experiences. Second, the multicultural projects in Nauru
were entangled in flaws that develop from forcibly resettling migrants in a small
island context. Migrants sent to Nauru had little interest in engaging with the
industry's attempts at integrating them into Nauruan society. Finally, efforts by
industry organizations and the Nauruan government to influence community
perceptions came up against the Australian government's global spectacle of deterrence. Ultimately, the alliances developed between Nauruans and refugees
were superseded by the Australian government's theatricality of enforcement.
Globally, events like the Eid Celebration were never promoted to the Australian
public, because that would negate the entire spectacle of deterrence. Simultaneously, popular activist representations of the refugee as helpless victim converged to set a scene of suffering and violence. These cultural representations
continue to link Nauru's extractive frontiers to global spaces of refugee consumption. Depictions of the risky/at risk refugee body affirm the fantasy of Australia
as a bounded white nation, with refugees as exotic objects for exclusion or salvation. Yet, as I see it, illuminating shared conditions of exploitation and solidarity is a productive step toward dismantling a violent regime. By analyzing
how refugee culture functions in practice, this chapter uncovers how dominant
ways of thinking about human movement might be fostered by refugee culture.
Failures to imagine an alternative system of free movement can be partially rem-
edied by understanding how images, performances, creative texts, and other
cultural productions have worked to stimulate and sustain the refugee industry.

World Refugee Day Goes Offshore

At the instigation of mainland contractors, well versed in the resource frictions
that plague the business ("It's similar to what I encounter in Brisbane" commented one contracted Australian refugee resettlement worker), World Refugee
Day found its way to Nauru in 2014. Initially, when the first asylum seekers arrived to Nauru in 2001, the Nauruan government ran many of their own public
relations strategies to win Nauruans over to the offshore processing arrangement.
When HMS *Moonera* came to port, the Nauruan government organized flower-
decked dancing troupes to sing in traditional costume for the new arrivals. Later,
government personnel and community groups crammed school, scouting, and

visitors' trips to the processing facility in the former state house buildings, all of which sought to dispel local fears and satiate some avid curiosity. At this point, the operations remained on a processing-only setup, with no move toward refugee resettlement. Then president Rene Harris stressed that "these people will be staying for around three months, not exceeding four months . . . and will reside at the topside or other areas that have been chosen . . . our foreign friends are undoing medical check-ups and there is no serious or contagious illness that will affect or be a threat to us . . . the people are all definitely leaving Nauru to go to other places and none are allowed to stay in Nauru. These people will not be of harm to our daily lives" (Republic of Nauru 2001). At the time, there was little need for community cohesion projects for the temporary and largely self-contained business of processing the refugees and then resettling them elsewhere. Nor were there the same resource frictions that enveloped Nauru in the industry's second instantiation from 2012—the effect of interdicting the resettlement of refugees to Australia. In Nauru round two, the standoff between the Australian government and refugees saw those certified at the RPCs move into resettlement accommodation around the country from May 2014.

To make refugee resettlement a viable prospect, the Nauruan government introduced the celebration of World Refugee Day as an annual event one month after refugee resettlement began. World Refugee Day is the global refugee industry's biggest marketing event of the year, in which the refugee finds visual and oral definition. World Refugee Day developed out of World Refugee Year—a yearlong global publicity drive in 1959 designed to encourage public support for resettling refugees at a time when interest and awareness were low.[3] Most major refugee-hosting and resettlement countries now commemorate World Refugee Day, keen to celebrate the benefits of refugees to incite public support. In 2000, the United Nations officially inaugurated World Refugee Day on June 20 as a global celebration, drawing together UNHCR's global marketing work with that of Refugee Convention signatory states worldwide. Some countries, particularly those with strong refugee philanthropic groups, such as Australia, also celebrate Refugee Week, which encases Refugee Day in a weeklong publicity drive. From the United States to Kenya to Taiwan, refugee cultural celebrations have gained popular marketing appeal on an international scale.

At the time of Nauru's first inauguration of World Refugee Day, in June 2014, local anger and fear toward asylum seekers and refugees were at a peak—blowback from the RPC riot of July 2013. Following the recommendations of Australian industry personnel with experience in refugee publicity work, the Nauruan government first instated World Refugee Day Nauru, keen to deflect local attention away from the industry's otherwise shaky legitimacy. The first World Refugee Day Nauru was marked by a public holiday, just one week before

Phosphate Commemoration Day. Phosphate Commemoration Day, celebrated on 1 July, commemorates when the Nauru Phosphate Corporation took over phosphate mining from the British Phosphate Commission. Phosphate saturates social life in Nauru, even though the ruinous legacy of phosphate capitalism on the island is glossed over. Nauru's airport lounge and hotel lobbies herald phosphate as a marker of national pride. Wall hangings and murals across government corridors all attest to the miracles of phosphate. Phosphate Commemoration Day itself is a state holiday, an official dinner for phosphate industry workers, and a company awards ceremony.

From phosphate to refugees, annual celebrations soon heralded a new living commodity that had brought about the country's economic resurgence. A broad array of cultural forms built on the precedent of the phosphate mythologies that flourished during the industry's golden age. Global imaginings of refugees as suffering bodies established a set of cultural frameworks that shaped how refugees were presented to local islanders in Nauru. For the first Refugee Day, an elaborate program was organized by the Nauruan government in collaboration with industry contractors to celebrate refugees and win public support for the offshore arrangement. In the lead-up, local schoolchildren were encouraged to write refugee poetry in competitions run across the school districts, recalling the specific narratives attached to refugees in their prose. Some teachers took time off from earth sciences classes focused on how Nauru's phosphate was formed to put together lessons where they discussed what makes a refugee.

On the day itself, a full-day program of events opened with a morning refugee commemoration parade around the airstrip. Industry workers and a small number of asylum seekers from the RPCs marched with a banner reading "World Refugee Day" out in front. The minister for education, Charmaine Scotty, handed out specially printed T-shirts to the procession participants that read "World Refugee Day Nauru 2014." A display of marketing materials was put together at the Civic Centre to warm locals to the refugee industry. Transfield Services and Save the Children workers compiled a selection of refugee art from the RPCs that bore a striking resemblance to the state murals heralding phosphate. Locals, asylum seekers, and refugees were all invited to attend the day, with additional company-bus services available for Nauru's living forms of propaganda. Afterward, a soccer match was held at the oval in Denig between a refugee team and Nauruan team and given widespread local press coverage.

Following the daytime events, industry workers organized an official dinner commemorating refugees at the Centennial Hall, attended by local luminaries, Australian offshore workers and Immigration Department officials, and refugees from the resettlement districts. After the playing of the national anthem and opening prayer, Minister Adeang delivered a welcoming speech on behalf of the government of Nauru, emphasizing the significance of World Refugee Day. He recognized and welcomed Nauru's new refugees moving down from the RPCs across the island, and his welcome was echoed by the acting Australian high commissioner. Adeang discussed his friendship with a refugee couple who had helped him in his household renovations. He stressed the importance for everyone to extend their warmest welcome to refugees moving into Nauru proper. Adeang also reiterated why the Nauruan government had decided to bring the industry operations to Nauru. He focused not on Nauru's immiseration but on the country's efforts at helping Australia combat people smugglers to save more lives at sea. Adeang also mentioned the upcoming celebrity visit of Angelina Jolie, who had accepted President Waqa's invitation to tour Nauru, which so many Nauruans were excited about. Following the speech, two Afghani men were ushered forward to discuss their journeys to Nauru, thanking the government and its people for their hospitality. The day closed with a musical finale of local dancers and a refugee song.

World Refugee Day II

Nauru's second World Refugee Day was more lackluster than the first. At the first World Refugee Day, there were only forty-one refugees living in Nauru, twenty-nine families, and twelve under-eighteens. The anger and fear that overtook the country were not yet at their peak. But as more migrants received refugee status and moved down from the RPCs—278 refugees in November 2014, 456 by February 2015, then 506 by June 2015—resource frictions coursed through the company town districts. The numbers of refugees moving into Nauru from the RPCs was small. Yet, in comparison to Nauru's wider population of 10,500 people, these influxes were significant for the country. In this context marked by stark unpredictability and constant flare-ups, local and refugee discontent was at a peak. Neither the majority of islanders nor asylum seekers or refugees felt well disposed toward celebrating refugees as part of Nauruan life. Nor did World Refugee Day Nauru 2014, 2015, or 2016 influence global perceptions of the country in the ways that the Nauruan government had hoped for.

Under the marketing power of a vast refugee industry sector, Australia celebrates an entire Refugee Week. At this time of year, Australian public relations teams gear their marketing work to battle against public apathy and resentment by stressing key angles, such as the value of diversity and the economic benefits of refugees to the country. Similar cultural programming to that used in Nauru illuminates the nightmares experienced by refugees, expressing visibly the value of giving money and supporting refugee resettlement in Australia. But across the offshoring years, and throughout my fieldwork, industry pressure also centered on the horrors of offshoring asylum to Nauru and Manus Island. During Australian Refugee Week, dioramas of boats and stories from refugees who spent time in the Nauru or Manus RPCs hoped to encourage public support for ending the offshoring policy.[4] This critical response to the fledgling offshore industry in Nauru made it difficult for the Nauruan government to publicly celebrate refugee resettlement alongside other dominant resettlement countries in the international system.

Many industry personnel flew in and out under the radar, but none gave endorsement to Nauru's operations. None of the celebrities that lend their brand power to the refugee industry at an international level endorsed the country's arrangement with Australia. Schoolchildren wrote poems about the war-torn journeys of refugees to the safety of Nauru in excitable preparation, but Angelina Jolie eventually rescinded her acceptance of Baron Waqa's invitation. UNHCR personnel advised Jolie's entourage against the visit. They knew that their goodwill ambassador would be subject to activist derision in Australia if she went to the country, potentially tarnishing their and her brands. UNHCR themselves only added a brief acknowledgment of World Refugee Day Nauru on their website. In fact, rather than rehabilitating the public image of the offshore refugee industry, the first World Refugee Day Nauru was widely critiqued in Australia.

In response to the Nauruan government's "Happy World Refugee Day 2016!" tweet, these were some of the immediate replies at the time:

> @Republic_Nauru @MSMWatchdog2013 ^^If only "celebrating World Refugee Day" meant no more refugees incarcerated on Nauru . . . you could do this
>
> @Republic_Nauru stop assisting Australia in violating refugee rights. Then we can celebrate together.

While Refugee Week Australia 2015 focused on ending offshore processing and celebrating the benefits of refugees to Australia's socioeconomy, the second iteration of World Refugee Day Nauru, which I attended, was a bit of a washout. The country still had a public holiday, one week before Phosphate Commemoration Day. But on the day itself, no contractors organized a refugee commemoration parade or elaborate full-day program as the year before. There was no crowning dinner for refugees or invited dignitaries. Connect and Transfield industry workers quickly put together a small display of refugee art at the Centennial Hall. Booklets that presented information on Nauru's refugee demographics were stockpiled on the side. A well-worn map with major refugee countries of origin around the world (one I had often seen at events like these) was tacked to the back of the room, but attendance was poor. Groups of local children ran in and around the exhibitions, many in the hopes of free food (like takeaway samples from the Iranian refugees). "Last year was much better," a Connect employee assured me at the event. "This year we just didn't plan it in enough advance." She continued: "We're trying to empower people not as refugees but as part of the *Nauruan* community. Nauru really is a multicultural community and it's important we celebrate that." It was this goal of "empowering people not as refugees but as part of the Nauruan community" that formed an important part of Nauru's new cultural strategies, which sought to gloss over the deleterious effects of the offshore industry arrangement.

Celebrating Multicultural Nauru

The move toward multicultural diversity was a trend that developed since tensions mounted locally, but also as resettlement started across the country. Australia has an elaborate industry sector of organizations tasked with encouraging resettled refugees to join the labor market and bolster the Australian economy (known as "refugee resettlement providers"). Because negative sentiments and misunderstandings about asylum seekers and refugees are commonplace in Australia, resettlement providers are also well versed in public relations. They make efforts to configure people not just as refugees but also as carriers of "cultural diversity" to promote local integration and bolster arguments about the importance of refugee resettlement. In December 2014, when more migrants received refugee status, moving down from the RPCs across Nauru, the Australian Immigration Department awarded the AU$32 million contract to the newly formed Australian NGO consortium Connect Settlement Services. Following a merger between Melbourne's Australian Multicultural Education Services (AMES) and the Brisbane-based Multicultural Development Association (MDA), Connect became the newest offshore contractor tasked with "a new corporate profile as the expert in managing cultural diversity," delivering "meaningful individual and community outcomes for refugees starting a new life on Nauru" (Republic of Nauru 2015b).

Given the tensions that arose from the offshore arrangement, the Australian multicultural workers decided to try something different after the clear failures of mainstream industry events like World Refugee Day. In an effort to warm Nauruans and refugees to the prolongation of the offshore operations, they drew on popular Australian imaginaries to configure Nauru as a "multicultural" country in full harmony. The newly formed NGO consortium for offshore refugee resettlement, Connect Settlement Services, was made up of two Australian industry giants, AMES and MDA. AMES in particular played a seminal part from the very beginning of the Australian government's postwar refugee resettlement operations, growing into the largest state provider of refugee settlement services. In Australia, competition is fierce for the provision of resettlement services. The Australian government seeks to expedite the transition of refugees into Australia's social and economic life. The Australian government also proudly upholds this aspect of their industry operations, counterbalanced against the system of deterrence. Industry professionals consistently cite Australia as a global leader in refugee services that other countries should emulate.

AMES was a major player in the early industry surge. In the 1950s, Australia's nascent Immigration Department placed emphasis on the assimilation of refugees, with little in the way of resettlement support. People were expected to integrate themselves into the "Australian way of life" (Stratton and Ang 1994, 18) largely under their own steam. Early arrivals were placed in Migrant Reception and Training Centres and given some language tuition, of which AMES played a part, though a small volunteer teaching agency housed in dongas in Melbourne. As global circuits of human movement increased and citizenship became available to migrants outside of Europe, the Whitlam Labour (1972–1975) and the Fraser Conservative (1975–1983) governments harnessed and institutionalized multicultural policies in the 1970s (Castles 1992). In heralding a culturally diverse society, successive governments sought to deflect attention from the country's past "white Australia" policy and ongoing legacies of settler colonial violence. Instead, the promotional construct of "a unified nation of diverse cultures" (Hage 2002, 429) became central to the imaginary that propelled the postwar growth of Australian settlement during the last decades of the twentieth century. This declaration of Anglo-Australian diversity provided the national ideological counterpart that helped drive the later Hawke Labour government's (1983–1991) economic ideology of unifying capital and labor.

Within the institutionalized fabric of Australia's multicultural policies, an increasing number of refugee settlement services and life-skills programs actively encouraged the integration of migrants from the Global South in particular. Alongside this, the valorization of ethnic culture and depictions of cultural diversity reinforced the new conception of the national Australian identity that purportedly broke with the identity of the past. Multiculturalism instead became a proxy for difference, "recoding and recasting racisms with . . . the coded evasions of 'political correctness'" (Lentin and Titley 2011, 3).

AMES was a crucial part of the industry funded to advance Australian refugee cultural and multicultural policies. AMES soon grew into AMES Australia, the lead partner of the Humanitarian Settlement Services Consortium in Melbourne with over two thousand volunteers and one thousand staff across the metropolitan region. MDA is a newer organization, developed in the late 1990s but now contracted for the majority of refugee resettlement work across Queensland, in addition to management of community detention centers. The directors of both organizations are figures prominent in shaping Australian refugee and multicultural policy. Along with contracted schemes, such as English language tuition, employment, and housing services, both organizations lead regional community events around the stated goal of multicultural celebration. After winning the off-shore bid for Nauru, the partner contractors brought the same cultural schema utilized in Australia to market refugees to Nauruans—and refugees to life in Nauru. As with their work in Australia, the second part of AMES and MDA's joint offshore contract focused on encouraging refugees to join the Nauruan labor market.

Increasingly dependent on maintaining a human import-driven economic model, Nauruan political leaders incorporated the foreign refugee industry's perspective of development into their own discourse. Refugee harmony and development featured prominently in Nauruan media and encouraged the perspective that the operations of the refugee industry could be compatible with national interests. In their public relations campaigns, local leaders associated refugee resettlement with the advanced expertise of developed nations. The national discourse on development and modernization was framed by the ongoing promotion of the importance of refugees to the country and the role that Nauru played as a safe haven for refugees. In announcing the newest addition to the local industry firms, Nauru's secretary for justice Lionel Aingmea said: "We believe we should assist refugees to become resilient and independent of services as soon as practicable. Connect's partner, AMES has over 50 years' experience in teaching English and vocational skills to refugees. Connect will work more collaboratively with the Nauru Government settlement team to ensure both refugee and Nauruan communities are working in harmony" (Republic of Nauru 2015b). Minister Adeang echoed Secretary Aingmea's sentiments in Nauruan media and parliamentary debates, stressing the significance of the task ahead but saying that Nauru was willing to be guided by Australian expertise.

By the time Connect arrived onto the offshore industry scene in December 2014, Nauru's residents had been subject to extensive public relations efforts designed to communicate the moral values of the operations. Initially, many locals were keen to find out more about the asylum operations, which had been on and off again since 2001. But this interest dwindled in the wake of global media representations and activist actions in the country. From the initial concept to move from processing to resettlement, in-house planning units set up a Community Consultation Committee (CCC), recognizing that firm local support was needed to make the move toward resettlement a success. The CCC was made up of a small group of local islanders (teachers and government representatives), who attended all major Australian-Nauruan government meetings in Canberra and Nauru. They participated in some of the RSD training and were instructed on Australian-style integration programs. The Australian government flew them to Australia, touring them around AMES's refugee resettlement housing in Mel-

FIGURE 17. "A culturally diverse nation." Photo by Julia Morris.

bourne and MDA's similar facilities in Brisbane, both of which had already been showcased on multiple occasions to leaders of government and nongovernmental resettlement programs around the world. Like the CLOs, the CCC members were tasked with local public relations. They, and other government agencies, would often organize info tables at local events, many of which I attended, to speak with concerned Nauruans about the specifics of refugee processing and resettlement. But as the operations progressed and refugees in Nauru grew increasingly frustrated about being on the island, many Nauruans became less convinced. "If they're fleeing persecution, why are they so picky?!" "Why are they rude about Nauruans when we're providing protection!?" were the questions I commonly heard in conversation.

When Connect resettlement practitioners started working in Nauru, public relations schemes on the benefits of refugees dramatically expanded. By June 2015, 506 refugees had moved across the country, and 655 asylum seekers were still awaiting processing in the RPCs, with most able to come and go as part of the open-center arrangement. To herald Nauru's rapid industry developments and alleviate the rising tensions from the offshore operations, Connect multicultural workers began to regularly display not only the commonplace narratives of refugees but also the diversity of refugees. They drew on popular Australian imaginaries to produce a fairy-tale narrative of multicultural harmony in Nauru and the future this promised for the small island nation. Now, events like World Refugee Day but also Eid, Diwali, and Nayrouz were all publicly marked with national celebrations. These events attempted to encourage Nauruans and refugees to learn about and participate with each other through the language of "multicultural diversity." Posters went up across Nauru's districts on the approach of major ethnic festivals or dates of industry significance, inviting locals to partake in not only World Refugee Day but also an extensive program of public celebrations that Connect staff made into public blockbuster events.

These cultural programs, which elevated refugees as agents of cultural transformation and material change, stretched to a remarkable array of fields, finding their way into projects for schoolchildren and youth. Education has always been an important part of refugee industry public relations strategies internationally, from the early days of World Refugee Year. Refugee Classroom Resource Packs, teaching aids, role-playing, board games, and now online UNHCR simulation games are prominent tools designed to entertain and educate a younger generation, particularly in major areas of refugee resettlement or where public sympathy is low.[5] Again, Nauru's colonial foundations around global extractive industries shaped the country's industrial fabric in the present. As a legacy of phosphate colonial days, Nauru still uses the Queensland education system. Years of educational consultancy have led to a national curriculum remarkably similar to Australia's but made specific to Nauru through aspects such as a focus on dominant local industries—in particular, the processing of phosphate for export. Now, in Nauru's new industrial era, educational consultants have reinvigorated Nauru's curriculum in line with the state's new dominant industry sector—refugees.

In 2014, before refugee children entered Nauru's public school system, Nauru's Year Sevens learned about the historical development of phosphate mining in their backyard. As part of the social studies unit "From Rock to Resources," they were taken on field trips to the extraction sites on the phosphate hill. Meanwhile, Year Sixes studied the processes that makes a refugee. In their social studies class, they charted the historical developments of the refugee industry operations from the first 2001 *Tampa* arrivals and took field trips to the RPCs. In their social studies unit "Forced to Go," they learned about the commodity trail from persecution to protection from a case study of a refugee's journey to Nauru. They practiced exercises where they imagined themselves as a refugee moving toward salvation in Nauru. The previous semester, they had focused on human rights, discussing some of the European-derived laws and major organizations in the field of refugee protection. In the refugee education unit, students drew on this industry knowledge, with its apolitical framing and exaltation of

Western liberalism, to talk through the morality of their country's role in protecting refugees. They did not discuss deportation, the human consequences attached to offshoring asylum, or forms of incarceration; nor did they discuss the resource frictions that enveloped Nauru. Instead, lessons focused on the fairytale narrative of persecution to protection made popular in institutionalized refugee curricula around the world.

Before refugee children moved from the private school at the RPCs into Nauru's public schools, extensive work went into the redevelopment of Nauru's education system. The Australian government flew employees from Nauru's education department to Australia for refugee training sessions and curriculum consultancy in advance of the resettlement operations. The rhetoric of multiculturalism became central to Nauru's new nation-building project. In scoping through the curriculum, Australian refugee education experts recommended the removal of the refugee curriculum unit for the 2015 academic year. Like their parents, asylum seeker children at the RPCs had lived through the realities of life before Nauru and at the RPCs, including the self-harm that took place at the centers on a regular basis. Most children, like their parents, also had their goal set on resettlement in Australia, not in Nauru. Some had been encouraged by their parents to participate in the protests and activist campaigns that gained headway over the last years. As a result, in their discussions, the Australian and Nauruan education teams agreed that, with this new cohort entering into the schools, it would be insensitive to include a focus on refugee ontologies. They removed the "Forced to Go" unit for the 2015 year and downscaled the annual refugee poetry competition. Instead, that year, the Australian consultants created a new course unit for Year Tens on Multicultural Studies, which sought to downplay the salience of the refugee category through a generalized celebration of multicultural diversity.

These practices of socialization became an important framework for crafting a vision of a modern Nauruan nation rooted in the values promoted by the industry. The commonalities with cultural projects that propel the expansion of extractive industry sectors around the world are noticeably stark. One can see how refugees have been harnessed to fuel a national imagining of morality and modernity in much the same way as the "fantastic illusions" (Wenzel 2014, 213) of other resource sectors globally. Indeed, much like commodity fetishism, this kind of refugee fetishism obscures the massively consequential impacts of the industry, and not just in its offshore guises. But the smoke-screening strategy was somewhat irrelevant, in that local islanders in Nauru were already exposed to the realities of refugees not wanting to be in the country. It was this understanding that constantly undermined the efforts of refugee resettlement workers as they sought to gloss over the deep segregations and rifts that charged through Nauru.

The imposition of multiculturalism also overlooked the richly multicultural social and cultural landscape that already exists in Nauru, with the island's mix of Pacific Islanders, Chinese, South Asian, Australian, and New Zealander migrants. For Nauruans, back-and-forth migration has long defined everyday life on the island. Many islanders are incredibly well traveled as a result of an economy characterized by global export and development aid. But in cultural pageantry, such as in the Eid celebration, people were asked, contradictorily, to perform multiculturalism through a hardening of assumed national identities. Such practices produced even more segmented borders premised on national stereotypes and territorial demarcations.[6] But in a way, these segregations define the entire system of sovereignty that sent asylum seekers to Nauru in the first place.

This points to a tension that Dace Dzenovska (2018) also finds when examining the remaking of Latvia under the banner of political liberalism. Western European "tolerance workers" were part of the reeducation efforts to encourage the "not-yet-European" Latvians to break free of Soviet communism and nationalism. But, as in the Latvian context that Dzenovska describes, what was peculiar about the multiculturalism project in Nauru was that values of inclusion were being institutionalized alongside practices of exclusion. Migrants were segregated as refugees through most other means, including visas, policing, specialist housing, industry services, and workforce refugee training sessions. Migrants who a month earlier had been watched by local security guards and were then living under the charges of CLO police forces were now expected to celebrate their combined diversity with Nauruans. Nauruans, meanwhile, remained the subject of global media commentaries that depicted them through tropes of savagery, some of which were promoted by asylum seekers and refugees in Nauru as a strategy to reach Australia. The goal of the Australian refugee resettlement workers was to forge a collective national Nauruan identity that dispelled these deeply rooted labor segregations. However, not only were they Australians flying out to Nauru to facilitate this endeavor, and so most were unfamiliar with the region, but their efforts also glossed over the institutionalized structures of inequality that undergirded the offshore arrangement. In particular, they ignored people's refusal to be part of the Nauruan nation-building efforts. This politics of denial lent an uneasy air to imagined community life in Nauru. It only superficially suppressed refugees' mobility desires, which were given forceful promotion elsewhere.

Embedded in these multicultural practices was the underlying understanding of the West as a civilizational space. The nation-building efforts in Nauru, advanced by predominately white Australians, suggested that Nauruans lacked sufficient recognition of their "diversity." Nor did Nauruans allegedly exhibit the harmonious relations synonymous with other (Western) countries of refugee resettlement (such as Australia). This was of course deeply contradictory, as Nauru's offshore industry was founded on the racism exploited by politicians in Australia. But the social and cultural programs were pressed forward as another means of advancing Nauru as a civilized place of refugee resettlement, and civilizing refugees in habits of decency. Such politics exemplify the simultaneous racist logics that refugees and Nauruans were subjected to throughout the industry arrangement.

The next section turns to some of the regular events organized by Australian Connect resettlement workers that attempted to advance the Nauruan multicultural community. In their initiatives, Connect employees tried to introduce new patterns of behavior considered more favorable to the operations of the industry.

The Beach House

Mirroring their welcome hubs in Brisbane and Melbourne, the Connect consortium put together "the Beach House," a rented Nauruan property near Anibare Bay. At the Beach House, Connect staff replicated their work in Australia, attempting to organize what they termed "community connection events" for refugees and locals. Connect workers devised a long list of sporting and entertainment fixtures, including swimming, basketball, volleyball, youth soccer, cricket, aerobics, and film nights. Every fortnight, staff organized a Family Film Night, recalling the public relations strategies of old. In the phosphate years, Nauru had two cinemas set up by the BPC: one for foreign industry workers, the other for Nauruans. This was one of the BPC's many strategies to maintain a positive image of their role in the community, stifling opposition to their polluting practices. Both cinemas fell into abandon when Nauru gained independence and the BPC lost their ability to mine. The newly instated Nauruan government, flush with phosphate wealth, later built a brand-new cinema at the Civic Centre. However, during the phosphate bankruptcy years, the doors of the new Republic of Nauru cinema closed. Apart from the odd screening at the top of the Civic Centre sponsored by Digicel—a phone company brought to Nauru in the refugee resurgency years—the country did not have a program of film events. But thanks to the refugee industry, the movie-night trend was reignited from the colonial phosphate industry heyday.

Brightly colored posters went up regularly on the major display boards outside supermarkets and shops across Nauru prior to each event: "for free with the whole family," "free refreshments," "bringing the community together." Nauru's Australian resettlement workers inflated a blow-up screen and set up the surround sound–system weekly at different sporting ovals across Nauru's districts in an effort to bring together refugees and locals. I regularly went to check on the interest level of these industry events. Few people attended. Often the events were canceled.

FIGURE 18. "Bringing the community together." Photo by Julia Morris.

Occasionally, small groups of local children would walk across the sports grounds for free popcorn, as a desultory breeze passed through the palm trees.

But Connect staff were undeterred, and indeed remarkably enthusiastic. Aerobics nights were soon added to the busy schedule of community connection events. Held on Friday evenings, the aerobics classes also recalled similar colonial-era efforts. In the BPC years, "keep fit" classes were organized for locals at the newly built hospital as part of the civilizational paternalism of the BPC's mandate. This time round, through the proactivity of refugee industry workers, aerobics classes sought to warm locals to a new extractive project, and migrants to resettlement realities. Weekly, Madonna and 1980s disco pop blared from Connect's educational hub in the Menen Hotel—a separate space from the Beach House, designed as a small learning center for reading and English language classes. Posters decorated the room with "Join the party" and "Connecting communities" as the taglines. Eager resettlement workers practiced high kicks and star jumps in leotards at the front of the room, expectantly waiting for refugees and Nauruans to appear. Based on my conversations with Connect employees, and certainly every time I attended, no locals ever showed. Occasionally, one or two refugees stopped by. Nauruans I spoke with said that they were tired of these kinds of community engagement projects—their efforts at kindness were only ever met with global derision. The few refugees who turned up did so, they told me, to take their minds off their desires to go to Australia. "It keeps me busy" and "It's something different to do from sitting with everyone else talking about the future" were two responses I got at the end of one aerobics class in the Menen Hotel's side room that consisted of me, a middle-aged Iranian woman and her teenage daughter.

On the other hand, some of Connect's cultural projects were incredibly "successful," albeit certainly not in the way the Australian government had envisaged. The youth music project I encountered at the Eid celebrations was one of the most popular of Connect's many programs. In attempting to get locals and refugees to embrace the industry arrangement and project an ethos of multicultural harmony, Connect workers arranged for the Australian Immigration Department to fund an impressive big-screen Mac and video-recording setup for some of Nauru's musically talented youths to collaborate with refugee teens. Under the guidance of a youth engagement practitioner with experience in music integration projects from similar work in Australia, the group put together several collaborative tracks, complete with high-quality videos shot down at the Anibare boat harbor. Young Nauruan musicians contributed backing beats overlaid with lyrics composed by a group of refugee teens, all keen rappers and beatboxers. But a twist occurred in the Australian government's plans for developing a vision of a multicultural Nauruan nation conducive to the offshore setup. The group collaborated not on celebrating the multicultural harmony of Nauru, but on voicing their opposition to the offshoring arrangement. Each of their tracks focused not on the Nauruan harmonious ideal, but on the exclusion of refugees from Australia. The group drew on the representational tropes of suffering and persecution synonymous with the refugee industry, but in ways that projected a unified front supporting refugee resettlement in Australia.

I spent time with the group of teenagers during my fieldwork as they edited their tracks and performed at local events. Rory, a Nauruan in his early twenties, was highly proficient in music production and editing work, a skill he had advanced during his time studying in Suva. He had already set up a small business locally, composing musical tracks for birthdays and other special occasions. In their Connect-initiated collaborations, Rory produced backing beats, over which Taj and Jamal, two Afghani teens, and soon close friends of Rory's, rapped their personal narratives: brutal conflicts in their homeland, the severing of their families, and their dreams of setting up a new life *in Australia*. They enhanced their main song with a music video shot at the Anibare boat harbor. The video featured close-up shots of Taj, Jamal, and other young refugees and Nauruans, along with a number of younger Australian Connect workers dancing wistfully in the background, all staring out to sea toward Australia.

Firm friendships were forged through the project, and their work was of impressive quality. However, their efforts clashed with the Australian government's broader social and cultural discourse of border enforcement and deterrence. Instead, their work gravitated toward the refugee industry's circuits of value that see refugees moving from third-world periphery to democratic core. This highlighted the unique challenges for the Australian and Nauruan governments in furthering the offshoring arrangement. Rather than orchestrating a Nauruan multicultural community, all the local teens became deeply engaged in the injustices attached to their friends' Australian exclusion, wanting to participate in their struggles to find refuge from conflict-driven countries in Australia. "I just hope Australia can see this," Taj excitedly said to me. "I really want to help them," Rory added, "hopefully get the Australian government to change their mind. This isn't right what's happening here."

The teens were all keen to upload their music videos to YouTube. Weeks of work and thousands of Australian dollars had gone into their making, and the young participants were very proud of their recordings. Yet, despite the success of the project in engaging local youths with the moral value of refugee resettlement—albeit for Australia, not Nauru—the Australian Immigration Department would not authorize the video upload. Unfortunately for the group, their efforts remained caught up in the Australian government's spectacle of deterrence, and so the videos were not allowed airplay outside the island. The Australian government brought offshore processing to Nauru in the first place as a Debordian spectacle—a "circuit breaker" (Expert Panel on Asylum Seekers 2012, 12)—that would dissuade future boat arrivals, which is what garnered their electorate's support. Funding music collaborations that voiced the injustices of exclusion from Australia—not to mention sound systems for Eid celebrations, pop aerobics classes, yoga, and the like—sat uneasily with the Australian government's presentation of hardened maritime deterrence. As a result, the images of Nauruan-refugee solidarities were not aired beyond the island. Ironically, it was the obfuscation of these kinds of alliances that also fed into the global activist sphere and back into the enlargement of the offshore industry. The representation of Nauruan savagery promoted on global media platforms exasperated local/refugee resentments, which underpinned the barrage of multicultural social engineering projects.

The second section turns to the efforts of resettlement workers in facilitating the entry of refugees into the Nauruan labor force. The socialization efforts described were designed for crafting new social values among Nauruans and refugees conducive to the industry's expansion. The final part of Connect's work was intended to communicate to both refugees and locals that refugees could create opportunities for Nauru's redevelopment—not only financially, but also through corporeal labor. Paramount to these projects was the development of self-sustaining myths about the importance of refugee labor to the nation. These practices celebrated Nauru's newfound significance in the international political system as a refugee resettlement nation. Yet, as I go on to detail, refugees did not want to resettle fully in Nauru, structuring their labor power in relation to the Australian market economy.

Sow the Refugee

> If we were to propose a motto for our economic policy, we would suggest the following one, which dramatically sums up the need to invest the wealth produced by the destructive mining system in order to create reproductive and productive agricultural wealth: "sow the oil (sembrar el petroleo)."
>
> —Suarez Figueroa (Coronil 1997)

In his masterful account of Venezuela's oil boom, Coronil refers to the state's metaphor of "sowing the oil" so as to turn oil money produced by the destructive mining system into "productive agricultural and industrial investments and, thus . . . transform Venezuela's vast but exhaustible oil wealth into permanent social wealth" (1997, 134). Coronil suggests that the "oil illusions" produced by state leaders are tied to the particular qualities of the commodity. In Nauru's refugee industry, the vision of the oil economy's "petro-magical" effects that Coronil identifies was here adapted to the particularities of a human commodity. A principal part of the work of refugee resettlement organizations, especially the offshore contractors that came to Nauru, was to transition migrants who received refugee status into units of human capital. Like the oil development initiatives described by Coronil, the Nauruan and Australian governments sought not just to extract political and economic capital from refugees but also to utilize their labor power in the rapid growth surge of Nauru's refugee industrial present.

Workers in the offshore refugee industry found themselves in a unique situation, however. In Australia, the majority of refugees with whom they work are keen to enter into the labor market. Many often juggle multiple jobs in order to sustain themselves and their families in the face of employment discrimination and a lack of transferability of qualifications and skills, illuminating the struggles of refugees to translate their body power into valorized labor (Rajaram 2018). Yet in Nauru, the Connect refugee resettlement employees encountered a new problem: people who wanted to contribute their labor power not to Nauru's industrial developments but rather to the country from where the contracted Australian workers had just arrived. Thus, the refugee resettlement workers flown out from Australia had to also take on the task of marketing life in Nauru to refugees who were determined to be resettled in Australia.

From the initial decision to move refugees from the RPCs into the wider Nauruan community, the Australian government hired Australian refugee resettlement workers to prepare for the transition. None of the resettlement workers I spoke with had been to Nauru before. However, their job was to integrate refugees into a new country, and market that move to both refugees and Nauruans in the process. Together, the Nauruan and Australian governments put together a Government of Nauru Settlement Team that, along with the Community Consultation Committee, would better nationalize the industry and encourage Nauruans to be more invested in its operations. As with the CLOs, Nauruan recruits provided the Australian workers with cross-cultural mediation and skills conducive to the smooth running of the industry.

Like the CCC, the Settlement Team members were trained by AMES and MDA. The Australian Immigration Department also flew the Nauruan team members to Australia and toured them around the country's refugee resettlement operations, where they observed Life Skills for Living in Australia programs for newly arrived refugees. Under the recommendation of Australian personnel, the Nauruan government created an entirely new state department tasked with overseeing the country's resettlement efforts, the Department of Multicultural Affairs. With the numbers of people moving into local resettlement housing from the RPCs, Minister Adeang's portfolio expanded. He became not only the minister for finance and minister for justice and border control but also the minister for multicultural affairs. In his new portfolio now lay the Community Consultation Committee, the Settlement Team, and the CLOs, in addition to the assessment operations in the RPCs.

Connect also employed a number of local staff, along with their fly-in-fly-out Australian labor force, to assist with promoting refugee integration locally. "Connect is working closely with the Government of Nauru Settlement Team and other service providers to offer a solid foundation of cultural knowledge for refugees living in Nauru to equip them for productive, positive and integrated settlement experiences," Connect's community engagement manager said (Republic of Nauru 2015c). Because the new refugees would soon be interacting with Nauru's state institutions on an everyday basis, Connect also led education and information sessions on refugees across the country. Connect and other flown-in practitioners provided sensitization training to teachers, clinicians, local law enforcement, and others, in order to "assist with refugee's integration and awareness about their new surrounding" (Republic of Nauru 2015c).

A series of training programs led by Australian resettlement workers and local Nauruan recruits were a key part of the refugee industry's socialization projects. All migrants who received refugee status took part in an integration

FIGURE 19.   Learning about refugees. Photo by Julia Morris.

program straight out of Australian refugee resettlement design schemes. The three-part induction package—the Nauruan Cultural Orientation program—was led by the local settlement and Connect workforces and was designed to provide an introduction to aspects of Nauruan life. By now, through the open-center arrangement, next to all refugees were already familiar with life in Nauru. Many of those still living at the RPCs and awaiting their asylum claims took the Transfield company buses to go shopping at Egigu or Capelle's supermarkets. They spent time with friends locally, went to the boat harbor swimming spot, and took part in events like the annual Coca-Cola 10K. However, the life-skills programs were an extra precaution to better ensure the integration of refugees into Nauru. If Nauru was to be a model of refugee resettlement, it stood to reason—external industry consultants thought—that the island adopt the refugee industry design of Australia and other dominant refugee resettlement nations. The racializing logics of these industry initiatives were clear, whereby refugees and Nauruans were simultaneously subjected to programs that emphasized a higher type of Anglo-Australian civilization.

All newly certified refugees were taken on a household induction of their resettlement accommodation allocated by Connect personnel. They were given home-safety demonstrations on electrical fittings, TV remotes, and air-conditioning. A bus tour around the country followed, where groups of refugees were shown key institutions of everyday interaction, such as the supermarkets, post office, hospital, government buildings, schools, the university campus, and childcare and nursery facilities—all accompanied by tips for life in Nauru. They were made familiar with the public and private transportation networks, including the private bus service that operated alongside phosphate company transport. Along with the country's Christian churches, which some refugees already frequented, Nauru's newest refugees were also shown the new mosques that had been built within the resettlement compounds, complete with multilingual signage as part of the state's new multicultural commitment.

An optional three-day Settlement Life-Skills Orientation capped the resettlement scheme. During the Life-Skills Orientation, industry professionals from across Nauru came together to deliver presentations to all new refugees. An enthusiastic local team led the Nauru publicity efforts to convince refugees of the value of becoming part of Nauruan society and outline the responsibilities that it entailed. Even though the refugees who had left the RPCs were no longer under full corporate liability, the industry remained at risk from Australian activist campaign threats. Refugees were still a high-value commodity that required protection in the eyes of Australian and Nauruan practitioners. The talks featured local subjects chosen on the basis of refugee risk, including health and safety hazards, such as tidal currents, food sanitization, and traffic safety. The Nauru Police Force spoke on the rights of Nauru's new citizens, the role of the police, the CLOs, and local laws and customs. They detailed the new speeding and driving-safety policies, including the breathalyzer and driving-license checks that had become commonplace in the risk-averse country. Refugees could use the public medical system, but they also had access to a specialist private clinic that operated in a renovated ward and was run by IHMS under a second contract for refugee healthcare. Healthcare workers also presented the plans for the brand-new AU$27 million hospital funded by the Australian government, with the goal of bringing development contributions to the country and convincing Nauruans and refugees of the benefits of this third-country resettlement arrangement. Meanwhile, the hospital also provided a more insidious form of governance: keeping asylum seekers and refugees on the island by reducing the need for medevacs to Australia.

Teachers from across Nauru's school districts explained the country's education system, which had been specially bulked up by Australian teachers chosen because of their familiarity with working with refugees. Transition programs in advance of the arrival of children from the RPCs ensured that the school environment and curriculum would be well adapted to their needs, everyone was informed. USP administrators spoke on the higher educational courses on offer, now subsidized for those with refugee status. Women's Affairs representatives discussed women's connection programs including links to the community, childcare, volunteering, and work experience possibilities. Connect and all personnel stressed the employment prospects for refugees in the Nauruan labor market, providing details on the various Nauruan workplace environments and small business packages available.

The Life-Skills program added to the increased number of visits to the RPCs from local groups that took place from 2014, in particular Nauruan women's groups, school refugee awareness-raising trips, and men's football friendlies. In the move toward refugee resettlement, cultural and language sessions and Nauru documentary film screenings also occurred on a more regular basis in the RPCs to acclimatize those under assessment to life in Nauru. "We will do our best as Nauru Government representatives and work alongside Connect to assist the refugees in any way, to make them feel welcome and know that they are safe here on Nauru. The Nauru Community are keen to welcome refugees who can contribute to the community in a positive way," the new Nauruan settlement manager assured everyone on local media (Republic of Nauru 2015c).

Mobility Futures Australia

Refugees were inundated with a plethora of initiatives to integrate them into the folds of capital accumulation in Nauru, while simultaneously playing a role in Australia's political economy. However, rather than succumbing to these value-driven circuits, many refugees attributed new forms of value to their labor power, advancing their aspirations of moving to Australia. As a researcher in Nauru, I had constant opportunities to speak with refugees about their thoughts on Nauruan resettlement. On many occasions, I was told by those slated to take these programs that none of the promotional efforts were convincing. Almost all refugees continued to lobby or hold out for resettlement in Australia. Behind the scenes, several refugees mocked the Nauru marketing attempts to me, making comments like, "In Australia people are fit, they work out, they eat healthily. Everyone here's fat." "The place is a dump. How can they tell us to keep ourselves clean!?" Others recognized the efforts the Nauruan government was making in a financially desperate situation but thought it a failed endeavor. All of those I spoke with who took the Nauru orientation package did so because they were hoping for resettlement in Australia. Instead, refugees refashioned local drives to extract value from their labor, explicitly positioning themselves within Western circuits of political economic and moral value.

Marcus, an Afghan man, newly living in Nauru with refugee status, made some of these efforts clear. At the Eid celebration, he commented to me that "it's all Australian firms who are leading it anyway. It's like I'm going through the same thing I would be in Australia. Just here, not there." Every refugee I spoke with went through the orientation, like Marcus, to cultivate the image of the "hard worker" that might enable their life in Australia. Several refugees pointed out to me that the completion certificate could be useful for eventual resettlement in Australia. "You never know who can help you with reaching Australia. It's better to do everything you can and show you want to contribute," Alessandro, a Sri Lankan man also employed in Nauru under a refugee visa, added to the Eid conversation I had with Marcus.

Several refugees also went through the program to show evidence of their cultural sensitivity toward Nauruans. This was sometimes a prerequisite for job applications in Nauru, and refugees I spoke with thought it would look good down the line for Australian moves. Local job specifications in Nauru, particularly with Australian firms willing to employ refugees back into the refugee industry, often required (in one direct example) "a demonstrated ability to engage with community members from refugee and local communities" and "a strong understanding of Nauruan culture and respects the local people and their practices." No refugees ever attended the Cambodia marketing presentations led by flown-over Phnom Penh teams or, later, by a young resident Cambodian promoter. The Cambodian promotional attempts were capped by a locally screened video of Australia's then immigration minister Peter Dutton, who stressed the "wealth of opportunities" of life in "fast-paced and vibrant" Cambodia. Like the IOM offers marketed around the RPCs, these deals were only clandestinely taken by a few refugees. They had to be moved away from other refugees for their own safety because they were targeted as weakening the refugees' position in the standoff with the Australian government. The Nauru cultural training programs certainly reflected the promotion of social practices and values encouraged locally by the refugee industry. However, refugees shaped the Nauruan orientation package into an Australian orientation, making themselves relevant for Australia's mainland circuits of accumulation. For many, the Nauruan orientation held utility for possible resettlement in Australia, as did Nauruan employment.

Progressive Industrialism

The Beach House also acted as a job seekers' agency for Nauru's new refugees. Australian Connect case managers individually discussed each refugee's financial situation and occupational backgrounds with them, putting together a list of employment prospects around Nauru. Australian-funded microfinance packages were available for setting up a small business on the island. Job advertisements also regularly went up in the Connect offices for positions that might be of interest. These efforts converged with the propagandistic value of portraying refugees locally as harbingers of economic development. An ever-evolving publicity campaign stressed the importance of refugees to modernizing the nation. Connect teams visited local businesses to entice them with the benefits of employing a refugee. Connect, other industry contractors, and government departments also promoted positive examples of refugees making a successful transition to the Nauruan workforce. Using the framework of multiculturalism, the Australian companies advanced the image of "the model refugee worker" and the diversity-compliant local business. They stressed the enthusiasm and work ethic of Nauru's refugees through regular "Refugees in the Workplace" segments in the refugee industry newsletter, which was disseminated across the country.

Local workforce reception was divided on the benefits of refugees to the nation, I soon found. The dwindling phosphate sector was not so keen to employ refugees in their workforce. Nauruans still retain great pride in their phosphate operations. Along with the refugee industry, the phosphate industry is the one workforce where Nauruans are guaranteed a job. Nauru's phosphate companies maintain high local employment rates in keeping with local government directives: of the total workforce employed at RONPhos in 2015, during my fieldwork, 93.5 percent were Nauruans. This is a postcolonial reversal from when next to no Nauruans were employed in the phosphate industry. Refugees were not counted as foreign workers, as part of Minister Adeang's approach for encouraging local employment. However, some Nauruans held deep fears that "refugees might take their jobs," reflecting the culturalist narrative popular globally. With fear about how they might be perceived locally, phosphate executives would only approach refugees in the event of no uptake from Nauruans.

Some local employers viewed refugees as coming with demanding expectations from visions of life in Australia or previous experiences in cosmopolitan metropolises before. One phosphate executive remarked in interview: "There was this one guy we had, he wanted an office, 24/7 internet access, a car, a satellite phone, and a secretary. And he was adamant about it! I told him others with the same job just take the RONPhos bus. I mean, I don't even have that stuff. You get these over-the-top expectations from some of the refugees who see themselves as above others because they're treated like that here. The air-con and private healthcare, and all that." In interview, another local company manager described refugees as "drifters," "shopping about," with little interest in furthering Nauru's future growth. He described how in the instances when he had hired a refugee, the individual had moved to a different job a few weeks later, without the incentive for career development.

Rather starkly, the one sector where Nauru's two resources did habitually meet was in local attempts at rejuvenating the country's phosphate-depleted landscape. A small number of refugees took jobs at the Nauru Rehabilitation Corporation's half-hearted garden center allotment designed for environmental development. They—and a few potted plants—represented the ironies of Nauru's abortive agricultural and human developmental endeavors. Both germination efforts failed to flourish as land and life were extracted in Nauru's phosphate and refugee industries, and products and desires circulated elsewhere. As this signals, some of Connect's efforts were "successful," albeit only at surface level, as no refugee ever wanted to settle permanently in Nauru. Those who worked in these kinds of positions did so to generate surplus value for the own future aspirations that lay firmly beyond Nauru. Instead, they advanced forms of capitalist value accumulation that fit with their desires.

Meanwhile, among industry workforces in Nauru, some refugees were seen through tropes of "guaranteed hard workers," which increased their socioeconomic value locally. The Taiwanese, for example, preferred hiring refugees at their agricultural farms. Their agricultural team decided that refugees worked much harder than Nauruans, who often showed up late or sometimes not at all. Many Nauruans have a general laissez-faire attitude to Western concepts of work. "That's island life" is a commonly heard aphorism. "We take it slow here," Georgia, my close Nauruan acquaintance would say to me, laughingly making references to some of the truisms of "lazy islander" colonial tropes. These so-called negative traits have long been stereotypically associated with Pacific Islander culture in contrast to Western concepts of time management, efficiency, and individualism—descending from the values promoted by colonialists concerning the legitimacy of their extractive mandates. In conversations, Australian company workers would stress a similar kind of colonialist civilizational framework: that only by adopting the attitudes of Australian workers could Nauruans hope to advance their situations. These stereotypes, which typified the Australian-brought refugee industry with modernity and progress (as once was the case with the phosphate industry), overlooked local priorities. Families are close-knit in Nauru, and, for the majority, where a great deal of importance is placed. It is not uncommon for Nauruans to take a week off work to prepare for a child's birthday celebration or support a family member in the event of an illness or other pressing circumstances. In this context of different cultural expectations, some industry sectors, like the Taiwanese agricultural development division, viewed refugee labor as a potential boon to the workforce.

Many of the middle-aged and older generation of Nauruans have also lived through the phosphate boom years, when the free flow of phosphate wealth made working unnecessary. During the phosphate industry years, foreign labor comprised most forms of low-wage service employment. As a result, many Nauruans still distanced themselves from pejoratively viewed positions in cleaning, laundering, cooking, and construction, which remained staffed predominately by Kiribati workers. Many refugees in Nauru were classed as low-skilled economic migrants—or found their past qualifications unrecognized when they attempted to access legal channels to Australia and became "low-skilled" by default. Unable to obtain an Australian visa through other means, they had attempted to insert themselves into the Australian economy outside of the regulated operations. Their labor was promoted by contracted Australian organizations as instrumental for maximizing Nauru's growth, as much as their bodily currency brought the state-building efforts to fruition.

Some refugees circulated more explicitly back into refugee industry firms, tasked with securitizing other migrants awaiting asylum adjudications. A few months in, Transfield and Wilson both employed a small number of refugees in refugee welfare and security back at the RPCs—positions that helped produce and reproduce refugees as commodities. Like with the phosphate industry, Australian refugee industry workforces maintained quotas for local employment as part of the development agreement with Nauru.[7] However, many Nauruans I discussed this with found the arduous schedule of the Australian industry workforces difficult. They were unused to the strict regime of Australian requirements or the harrowing work of toxic industry practices. I spoke with Australian Transfield line managers and observed their interactions with Nauruan employees as I sat at the Wilson security compound, which I did on a regular basis. It was one of the few places on the island where I could pick up high-speed internet and observe industry goings-on without arousing suspicion. Australian Transfield line managers were constantly exasperated at the late arrivals or even no-shows of Nauruan workers. Transfield soon offered financial incentives to Nauruans who completed a full week of work, but struggled to maintain consistency. In contrast, refugees represented productive labor for the company: on time, efficient, and accommodating to the demands of their new employers. Ingratiating themselves with authorities was for many refugees a survival strategy in the context of an uncertain future. The power imbalances attached to presentation in the hopes of onward Australian moves meant that some refugees were seen as—and indeed were—"hard workers, always on time." Other refugees acted as human relations personnel for Nauru's resettlement efforts. Connect's employment office was soon filled with employed refugees who advised others on appropriate work in Nauru, producing and reproducing the refugee developmental economy. As more people moved across Nauru as refugees, not only revenues extracted from refugees but also the labor of refugee bodies redoubled state growth; refugees worked in the reinvigorated government office and now also in busy supermarkets and hotel launderettes.

In Australia, refugee welfare support is low and determined on a strict eligibility basis. In Nauru, however, this was not the case, as the Australian government sought to warm refugees to long-term resettlement. The microfinance option took off in popularity, with the Australian government providing credit loans to any refugee interested in entrepreneurial projects. Nauru's system of landownership is such that 75 percent of family members must agree for any new form of land development. With lengthy family genealogies, this can mean obtaining the agreement of hundreds of people. Internal disputes make local business ventures difficult to get off the ground, particularly when land has become such a precious commodity due to leasing for phosphate and now for the refugee industry. Instead, it is a popular Nauruan practice to lease land to foreign business holders. Chinese retailers, in particular, have maintained a strong presence in Nauru since the phosphate colonial labor days. At the encouragement of Australian resettlement workers, some Nauruans leased their land for refugee business ventures. Rohingyan and Iranian takeaway, beauty salons, and a Persian restaurant became new features in the country. On several occasions, I was handed flyers by Iranian women at local refugee integration events with prices for eyebrow threading, waxing, facials, and other beauty treatments rarely seen in Nauru, at least not since the phosphate boom days. Sewing machines were available at the Beach House on Thursdays and Fridays, with wool shipped in from Australia. Some refugees interested in small-scale self-employment took knitting classes with Australian Connect workers. A small group of refugee women knitted blankets, hats, hand warmers, and toys, which they sold at the weekly Saturday market or at industry events.

The social and physical landscapes were transformed daily by the wealth and labor associated with refugees, while also giving way to new ecologies in the production of cultural value. Local supermarket stockists soon started carrying foods to cater to the palettes of Nauru's new refugee demographic, including a variety of spices, tahini, lentils, and halal meat. This was in addition to foods geared toward Australian offshore workers, such as quinoa, whole wheat bread, and a variety of European cheeses. The increased culinary diversity was a dramatic change, several locals and a supermarket owner pointed out to me. Some

FIGURE 20. Australian government–funded refugee business in Nauru. Photo by Julia Morris.

refugees took to gardening beside the resettlement compounds, growing differ-ent varieties of herbs that reflected a new industry environment. Nauruan and Farsi phrases also converged on the streets, shaping a new lexicon that reflected the country's shifting demographics. But while these ecological transitions made visible Nauru's industrialization through and by refugees, no refugee was truly interested in resettlement in Nauru. Rather, the reality of transforming Nauru into a land of sparkling multicultural diversity glossed over the uneven relations on which the wealth was founded.

At the same time, the majority of the refugee-run enterprises predominately serviced the refugee industry workers employed to serve them. Few Nauruans had a taste for spicy cuisine, preferring the cheaper Chinese takeaways readily available elsewhere. Nor did they have utility for knitted hand warmers, which were better suited to—and bought by Australian industry workers for—Australian winter climes. In reality, the skills of the Australian resettlement workers flown out to Nauru were better suited to the Australia from where they came. The foods cooked by refugees were also better suited to the Australian multicultural ideal that the resettlement workers envisaged, where samosas and dhal were already everyday fare.

Several refugees integrated chips and other local preferences into their cuisine and made their food milder, so as to cater to the local demographic; or, as with the sangak flatbread project, they worked to create new enterprising ventures. However, their prices could never rival the local Chinese takeaways, which always undercut any business in town—and shaped the majority of local palates. Many Nauruans purposely frequented refugee-run businesses in sympathy and bought refugee-cooked food and refugee-knitted hand warmers. These gestures dwindled as more protests overtook the country.

Reshaping Circuits of Value

The resettlement teams worked to reinforce identities and practices among refugees favorable to Nauru's industrialization. Yet, many refugees took advantage of employment opportunities through counterprojects that manipulated the industry's development attempts. Instead, they reshaped the system of value that saw them as productive resources for the island, advancing their own onward moves by connecting forms of capital accumulation with their firm desires to move to Australia. This was also an effort to move against the overall valuation system that ranked them low in the eyes of the Australian government.

For all refugees I spoke with, employment in Nauru was only ever a survival strategy in the hopes of eventual resettlement in Australia. All had taken on the work because their positions were with accredited Australian companies or could help with their onward trajectories, which, I was informed, "looked good" for their envisaged Australian moves. It appeared rather chilling to me that refugees would work back in Nauru's destructive refugee industry. However, one Afghani refugee, Isaac, working for Transfield Services, told me how he knew it looked disturbing for him to work back at the RPCs, but that Transfield was a globally—and particularly *Australian*—recognized firm. He could build up his CV by taking a job back in the industry sector. This was the same rationale explained to me by a refugee working for Wilson Security, and also echoed by Tessa, who worked for Connect. "Australian company" and "Australian workforce qualifications" were always the responses given to me.

Similarly, all of the microfinance businesses set up by refugees in Nauru were done so with hopes for future in Australia. Their efforts in Nauru could prove that they had catered to Australian clientele. Nauru's colonial legacies made this easier to facilitate. Such mirroring aspects as the Australian currency, the Queensland education system, and Australian firms in operation made it relatively easy for refugees to use Nauru as a transitory hub for working toward Australian futures. It was on this basis that English language classes took off in popularity, and in fact were oversubscribed, with many Connect workers employed to teach English to refugees in Nauru. Those who were initially not fluent in English became very proficient, taking evening classes alongside their employment—all in the hopes of eventual resettlement in Australia.

Courses at Nauru's branch of the University of the South Pacific, where I was housed, were also extremely popular. Many of Nauru's new refugee residents attended USP open days during my fieldwork. Australian Connect workers collected course descriptions and flyers to distribute around resettlement housing compounds. As I sat in the library looking through Nauru's archives, I was often asked about the courses on offer at USP and whether enrolling in one might have currency in Australia; this made me uneasy about my involvement with the industry operations, and I recommended the advice of others more proficient. As a result of Connect's developmental drives, several refugees did enroll in subsidized degrees and vocational training programs at USP, taking advantage of the opportunities presented by the Australian government to shape themselves as possible citizens for Australia. The Nauruan language classes, on the other hand, had no uptake. Connect workers even had trouble finding a Nauruan keen to teach the local language to refugees.

At the same time, as the popularity of the "hard-working" refugee trope made clear, power imbalances resulted in some refugees disciplining themselves in ways conducive to the industry's value regime: always turning up on time, always proactively engaged. But the refugees I spoke with did this to gain the approval of Australian workers and support their possible resettlement elsewhere. In a context where one-to-one case workers assessed what you were doing, where RSD teams might possibly one day fly in and recommend you be moved to another country, and where forging a close relationship with an Australian worker could be a tactical onward move, several refugees I spoke with also judged that "being seen as a hard worker" was an effective survival strategy in a dehumanizing industry environment. For them, not working and engaging in high-profile protests reflected poorly on future endeavors. The projects of Australian resettlement workers ostensibly sought to integrate refugees into Nauru, sustaining prosperity for the nation through an ethos of multiculturalism. However, employment was only ever used by refugees for pursuing onward Australian dreams. I use the word "ostensibly" because several Australian resettlement workers I spoke with acknowledged this to be the case. Some secretly hoped that the English language courses and other forms of employment would be useful for refugees in the event that the Australian government caved and allowed for their resettlement in Australia.[8] On the other hand, while some refugees focused on making themselves into Australian market subjects, others took advantage of prominent Australian activist campaigns, moving against the Nauruan and Australian governments' public image.

Freedom or Death

Some refugees produced themselves as the empowered dutiful refugee to fill the Australian market niche. Meanwhile, others publicized the tropes of refugee suffering to appeal to Australian moral values. Both played with the fiction's constructions that could support their resettlement in Australia. From the start, many refugees refused to work, attending few of Connect's industry projects. Others publicly gave up their jobs in protest against the Australian government's maritime embargo and the Nauruan government's complicity. They chose to concentrate their efforts on more explicit forms of publicity, working with Australian activists in high-profile campaigns. While contracted resettlement workers attempted to downplay refugee differentiation using diversity paradigms of multicultural harmony, in their organizing, some refugees reinforced the popular image of the refugee as a suffering victim to support their resettlement in Australia.

In February and March 2015, in the high-profile protests that brought about the establishment of the CLOs, groups of refugees came together in a series of labor strikes, closing the shutters on almost all of their Australian-funded business ventures in protest. Many refugees boycotted Nauru's schools, English classes, jobs, and all of Connect's multicultural offerings. Even though the Nau-

FIGURE 21.   Refugee labor strikes. Photo by Julia Morris.

ruan government announced that all refugees who continued to protest would lose their jobs, the majority cared little for these threats in the knowledge that firing a refugee would be construed in Australian media as evidence of the Nauruan government's cruelty. In the first 2015 protest, much to the surprise of Australian resettlement workers, protesters took to the streets, storming the Connect job agency and chanting, "We want freedom!" "We're refugees not criminals!" "Freedom or death!" They issued statements to ABC News through mobile phone communications, with one refugee saying, "We are refugees, we are not slaves. The way that we're living here and the way the Nauru government is behaving with us is just like slaves" (Fox and Bolitho 2015).

Several activists in Australia encouraged these protests exterritorialy. Those activists I spoke with in Australia were certain that the protests, the photos of children holding crosses, and the accounts of violence would galvanize a global movement in support of resettling refugees in Australia. In the aftermath of the riots, Nauru's lone Persian restaurant shut its doors. The Nauruan landowners were no longer willing to rent the building to the Iranian proprietors. Even if they had not explicitly made derogatory statements against Nauru to the Australian media, the Iranian refugee owners of the restaurant were associated with a wider group who figured the country as made up of savages and beaters of refugees. This was evidenced by continued accusations splashed across Australian and global media, such as this statement from an anonymous Iranian refugee in the *Guardian*: "They attack the refugees. You are walking in the street, they say 'Fuck you, go back to your camp.' They throw rocks. They spit at you. This is normal" (Mathiesen 2014).

The Nauruan government continued to release media statements that sought to address these accusations. President Waqa (2016b) spoke on Australian media, announcing, largely to deaf ears, "The refugees are not in detention but enjoy the same freedoms enjoyed by Nauruans, although refugees have better facilities than locals. They have access to good quality education, health services and social support networks." He later wrote opinion pieces in the *Daily Telegraph* (2015) and the *Australian* (2016) in the wake of continuing accusations against local savagery:

> We have hosted the offshore processing centre for Australia, and we have done so with compassion, understanding and professionalism. As a Christian nation, we treat every person—refugee or asylum-seeker—with dignity, even when that respect is not returned. We have worked hard to ensure asylum claims are processed fairly and with integrity.
>
> Despite what you might read, refugees are safe in our country. Many choose to interact with locals and many do not, but that is their

choice which we respect. They have housing, food, education, health facilities, leisure activities—all provided at no charge.

But some refugees—coached by activists in Australia—cause trouble, refuse to send their children to school and encourage others to do likewise, as they mistakenly believe social unrest will help them get to Australia, their ultimate agenda.

This includes fabricating stories of abuse . . .

Media organisations such as The Guardian Australia and the ABC seem surprised when we don't allow them access to our country. After their dishonest campaign against us, they expect us to open our arms and allow them to visit and create more trouble within our borders! . . .

While we understand the importance of transparency we have a responsibility not to cause unrest, incite violence and create potentially dangerous situations.

Nauruans will continue to be good hosts to our refugee and asylum-seeker guests. Our motto is "God's will first" and I believe God's will is to show love and care to all, irrespective of those who may try and tarnish our name or belittle our nation. (Waqa 2016a)

Minister Adeang invited Channel Nine's *A Current Affair* to shoot a segment on Nauru's refugee processing arrangements, and later Sky News too. However, Australian media channels like the *Guardian* responded with accusations that the reports were biased, insensitive and symptomatic of right-wing tabloid fodder.[9]

The Spanner in the Works

Ever present in the offshore refugee industry arrangement was the operational crux of deterrence. Investments in social and cultural programs for locals and refugees only reached the island population. As the music project made clear, the Australian government did not want to show that the arrangement was too nice, because that would negate the entire political economic value extracted from the project. Emphasizing the vast expenditures on flat-screen TVs, Mac-Book Pros, air-conditioning, and overheads for Madonna-themed aerobics classes would only anger the Australian right-wing electorate. Part of the currency of offshoring asylum was the spectacle of deterrence, even if the reality differed significantly. This spectacle coincided with the promotion of refugee suffering and Nauruan savagery by activist organizers. Unfortunately for activist campaigners, in an attempt to convert Australian audiences through a politics of pity, they were also part of the cultural production that fueled the offshoring.

Famous campaigns like the *Guardian*'s Nauru Leaks reinforced the paradigm of the helpless and vulnerable refugee, running up against some of the Australian electorate's compassion fatigue. This presentation also fueled anxieties about the threat of violence that refugees presented, both in Australia and in Nauru. At the same time, these representations added value to the global refugee industry operations and the powerful industry players that had enabled this offshoring arrangement to emerge.

Nor did activists' promotional efforts bring about the resettlement of refugees in Australia, which was their principal concern. Instead, the media campaigns only riled the Australian government, who remained set on victory in the standoff. In 2016, across the course of many protests, then immigration minister Dutton continued the deadlock stance, announcing, "My message to those who protest is that it will not change the government's commitment to the processing and resettlement arrangements in place on Nauru" (Republic of Nauru 2016a). President Waqa echoed this: "My message to refugees here on Nauru is to accept they are here and to understand that the Government of Nauru is doing its best to look after them and keep them safe. Advocates must begin telling refugees and asylum seekers the truth about their situation and what their future holds, and stop goading them into quitting their jobs. There is always hope, but there's a time when you must be realistic and accept the circumstances. Only then can you get on with your life" (Republic of Nauru 2016a). Because the Australian government was determined to outlast the refugees, and the Nauruan government was financially reliant on them, the flare-ups that marked this industry sector only led to more social and cultural projects to ingratiate refugees and locals to the offshore arrangement.

Although locally the cultural imaginary project by industry firms was of a resettlement country where the refugee and Nauruan lived in multicultural harmony, these politics of magical fantasy reared their head as the pivotal flaw in the industry design. As Timothy Mitchell (2002) shows us, projects encounter practical difficulties when fundamental failures are presented as minor complications in the implementation of plans. Nauru only ever operated as a twilight universe of refugee resettlement based on an idealized version of a refugee resettlement country. But it was hollow and artificial, reliant on Australia to send migrants for refugee processing, and filled with, when I arrived, 506 refugees who never imagined nor wanted to construct their lives in Nauru. The imagineering projects ignored the aspirations of refugees to be in Australia rather than in the imagined multicultural community—a crucial flaw in a state-building and community-cohesion exercise. Rather, these public relations events went to the other extreme, actively celebrating and encouraging refugee and Nauruan development locally as part of a utopian industry imaginary. Nauru was recast in multicultural terms, contradictorily driven in large part by Australian culture. As a result, the power, capital, and labor that went into the state-building effort were largely ineffective, superficial at best. Indeed, connectivity efforts often led to more frictions, and strikes added to the protests that shook the industrial frontier, moving from the RPCs across the country.

It is to the resource curse that chapter 6 turns, questioning the future of the phosphate turned refugee company town.

BITTER MONEY

Venezuela had lost control over itself; intoxicated by oil as waste it had become transformed into waste. . . . The identification of both the nation and individuals with excrement became an ever more common short hand expression for everyday problems . . . "somos una mierda," "es que este es un pais de mierda" ("we are pieces of shit," "it's that this country is made of shit").

—Fernando Coronil (1997)

Every one, the Kiribati, the Tuvaluans and so and so are laughing at us. The whole world are laughing because we do not have any more money. Victims of "cheap humor," the "natives who sold their souls."

—"In Times of Phosphate," Mwinen Ko, special issue, 1994

They talk about the glory days. But these, these are the bullshit days. I go to Australia and people laugh when I say I'm from Nauru. Bird-shit island, now this.

—Personal interview, Republic of Nauru, July 2015

When I lived in Nauru in 2015, the country was deep in the throes of a series of conflicts and held a tarnished image globally for their role in the offshore asylum arrangement. Nauru was targeted in the global media through notions of primitivity and debasement. Throughout this book, I have highlighted the voices and experiences of people in Nauru underneath these popular portrayals. Despite continuous stereotyping by media and essentialization in the public imagination, stances on refugees in Nauru were not fully in support or against, as residents had their own complicated relationships with the industry. While some residents clearly prioritized economy over human impacts, many made clear that the refugee industry was not good for the country. Other residents found themselves in-between these positions, with a range of responses to the powerful public discourses, cultural ideologies, and industry's material realities. At the same time, Nauru was constantly changing through political, social, and economic processes—and these changes were compounded by the wax and wane of the refugee industry. Changes in the regulatory climate also brought deep alterations to the country's social landscape, as did regular conflicts and fractious social relations. Meanwhile, residents were constantly asked to respond to a hegemonic national discourse that touted the refugee industry as a socially responsible corporate neighbor and vital part of the local economy.

The history and heritages of phosphate were powerful factors that influenced the ways residents thought about life in the contemporary refugee moment. Because the new social and economic developments were entirely generated by sudden wealth, the new prosperity was seen as fleeting, tied to memories of poverty, austerity, and an uncertain future. Alongside this, the relative ease of running Nauru's refugee processing operations—unlike the Australian government's similar project on Manus Island, which was marred by lawsuits and violence—owed itself to the industry pathways that preceded it. The organization and materialization of the phosphate industry clearly shaped the ease of the refugee industry's arrival. Nauru's refugee project reconfigured colonial infrastructural forms, practices of dependency, and sociolegal affiliations as the country was refashioned as a company town in line with new forms of human production.

Refugees visibly unleashed an unprecedented boom that converted Nauru into a new monoeconomy: from 2016 to 2020, refugee-related revenue were the dominant income stream for the Nauruan government. During this renaissance era, sparkling refugee resettlement blocks, monthly land-leasing payments from the refugee industry, and multicultural cuisine were all testament to the permeation of refugees through Nauru's economy and polity. Air Nauru once again soared overhead with a fleet of five aircrafts, filled with foreign industry workers experienced in processing and resettlement, and locals on shopping sprees to Brisbane and Majuro. As part of the refugee industry euphoria, in 2017, services extended to Kwajalein and Guam, with plans for a return to Norfolk Island.

The Nauruan government continued to "gift the nation" (Coronil 1997) and its charismatic leaders with "magical power" as "agents of modernity" after the decades of phosphate bankruptcy. Headlines in the local news ran with displays of the country's progress:

> "Nauru bank a big hit!": The agency's automatic teller machine (ATM) has been installed and comes online soon while the bank has also taken over the ownership of another similar ATM on the island at the Capelle and Partner store.
>
> Another exciting product available to customers shortly will be a MasterCard debit card which can be used overseas, including Australia. (Republic of Nauru 2016b)

Local leaders promoted a world in which Nauruans and refugees worked side by side to shape a multicultural utopia. "We coexist on our beautiful island with a diversity of nationalities and cultures," said Louisa Waqa, the first lady, in her International Women's Day address in March 2015, as protests broke out across the country. "We have embraced those who have traveled afar or from within the region to be part of our existence. We have opened our hearts and our homes to those who have found themselves on our island. We are truly an island of many nations."

"It should be known that most refugees living on Nauru are peaceful and law-abiding . . . many refugees and their children . . . simply want to enjoy a peaceful life on Nauru," said Minister Adeang as he attempted to alleviate tensions locally in a special issue of the *Republic of Nauru Bulletin* (2016) the following year. This statement was addressed "To Our Guests: Refugees and Asylum Seekers."

"We have taken bold steps to reform our systems of government and strengthen our democracy despite the lies spread by some foreign media like the ABC, who refuse to recognize the advances we are making and continue their dishonest political campaign of attempting to influence Nauru's domestic politics," wrote President Waqa (2016a) in one of several Australian newspaper op-eds.

Between 2010 and 2019, Nauru ranked fourth globally for the highest percentage of refugees in relation to state population, at 3.2 percent. This bore stark parallels to Nauru's first phosphate heyday, when PO_{43} saw the country boast the world's second highest GDP per capita (over AU$50,000 per person per year), after oil-rich Saudi Arabia. But a ravaged pockmarked landscape, cadmium contamination, and respiratory illness, as well as a reliance on imported labor and goods, are some of the many byproducts of the phosphate boom. And as with phosphate wealth, refugee wealth, "the magical elan vital of economic and social transformation" (Watts 2004, 206), proved to be a very mixed blessing.

For Parker Shipton (1989), the Luo concept of "bitter money" best encapsulates the misfortune inherent in new ways of obtaining money linked to forms of economic advancement (like selling lineage land for profit or dealing in tobacco or gold). Bitter money is ill-gotten money that comes from the sale of certain commodities and is thought to be dangerous to its holder. In their discussions of the refugee industry boom, many Nauruans were torn because the economic benefits that refugees brought were accompanied by conflicts engendered by the high-risk operations. Ultimately, the realities of the refugee business were assumed by and felt to the disadvantage of Nauruans, as much as by migrants entangled in the industry. As with other toxic industries, no amount of risk-management could detract from the familiar operational hazards of processing and managing people. Like the extractive industry communities that anthropologists and other scholars describe, torn apart by internal or intercommunity conflicts, harsh labor conditions, colossal environmental impacts, fluctuating prosperity, and contentious health repercussions (Ross 2015; Sawyer

2004; Watts 2001), Nauru again became tied into the repeating destructions of a resource-cursed state.

This chapter closes by tracing some of these consequential impacts of Nauru's refugee industry "boom" period, questioning the impending post-refugee moment that the island is quickly approaching. The figure of the refugee remains a crucial part of Nauru's local economy, feeding the Australian border-spectacle imaginary in the process. Even by 2021, when only 109 refugees remained in the country, the Australian government continued to fund Nauru's "enduring capability" to the tune of AU$811.8 million allocated for offshore management in the 2021–2022 Australian budget—bringing the accumulated costs to over AU$9 billion since 2013.[1] Yet, these budget allocations to Nauru are winding down in a country, and region, that finds itself in a moment of gradual transition. I consider the ways that residents in Nauru are creating new economic possibilities, some of which hold serious environmental consequences for local islanders. My intention is not to paint a picture of a community without future, a community of money-obsessed or alcohol-addicted young people, or a community of powerless, exploited islanders living in the ravages of colonial industry. Alcoholism, mental illness, and other problems do plague Nauru (Hannigan 2002; Khambalia et al. 2011). But, overwhelmingly, the residents I talked to were proud of advancing their communities, rather than continuing to see a brain drain lure young people to working in the refugee industry or to Australia. Instead, my aim is to provide a more nuanced portrayal of the ways that people in Nauru deal with the aftereffects of the refugee industry and continue to hold concerns for the sustainability of their community. I believe it is here that possibilities for Nauru's future lie.

An Ungovernable Space

Yaren District, Republic of Nauru. July 5, 2015. I sit on a rusted bench beside the tennis courts laid out by the British Phosphate Commission. In my sights is the ivory-pillared mansion of the commissioner's clubhouse. Once, I'm told by Australian workers and islanders alike, this glamorous seat was filled with pool tables good-natured banter and was the home of the ultimate Sunday roast. The refugee processing center now has that title.

I listen to excitable screams. It's break time. The shipment is finally on the way out after months of trading standstill. I heard a rumor a few days before. A Nauruan Aiwo resident, fed up with the dust from the phosphate factories, set one of the cantilevers alight. Several years prior, protestors from the frontlines of Aiwo District also burned down the main police station. I put this to my Nauruan companion, Chris. He's an old-time phosphate worker, and I knew he'd be well versed in industry politics. He nodded and said, "People often run up to the kiln area and get them to stop the furnaces and machines. Sometimes they'll stop cooking the phosphate and wait for the winds to change. But sometimes they don't. People have set the conveyers alight before. That's what happened with the old cantilever."

We become engaged in an avid conversation about phosphate dust—how to contain it, some of the repercussions. Chris, like several Nauruan phosphate workers I spoke with, is incredibly environmentally concerned—not unlike many in the refugee industry grappling with the sector's ethical politics. He went into the phosphate business with the goal of addressing the pollutant byproducts—all starkly visible to him as he was growing up in Nauru. As we sat by the phosphate loading bay, he described some of the projects to me:

> People have come up with so many suggestions about the dust. Someone said, "Let's put sprinklers in the chimney," but that still dried it. Before that there was another one. We'd build the chimney up, aim it even higher, and blow the dust as far as we could so it wouldn't fall until it reached the sea. But it didn't work. The winds changed. We didn't always know when that would happen. Sometimes if we had big winds, the dust would blow back down in our faces. We just couldn't build the chimney high enough. BPC had the electrostatic dust precipitator installed when they were running the show.

He drew the process for me on the sand. "The dust went up the tube. See, like this. And when it got stuck and thick, then here"—he drew another line—"the dust moistured down and drained out as fumes."

"Did it work?" I asked.

"Well, things can never be perfect when you're in the mining industry, dust is always part of it, but it was diluted." He then shook his head, sighing as he thought back to the NPC takeover. "Things fell way behind. There weren't the regulators, compliance, penalties, we didn't know so much about it. None of the environmental concern or demand like now. Now it's Zero Dust."

I'd heard all about Zero Dust the day before. After much persistence, I finally landed a tour around the phosphate plant. Immediately, my factory tour guide hurried me over to marvel at the new equipment fresh in from Brisbane: part of the industry's latest approach to the oxymoronic "sustainable extraction." In explaining this new technology to me, my factory tour guide pointed to a long metallic cylinder, tracing an invisible line along its side. "The dust goes to a chamber here. Then it's filtered, over here, before going to the chimney." He gestured up at the ceiling. The furnace was on halt for the moment. "See, right now we get dust coming out the chimney, but if this works then it'll only be smoke."

Back down by the playground, Chris confessed more skepticism about Zero Dust. "When they don't do the mining, that's when we'll get Zero Dust. But if we stop that, we stop the money. No minister, no landowner wants that. They'll never solve the dust."

Shortly after the tragic self-immolations of Omid and Hadon in April 2016, against a backdrop of deepening civil unrest and industry disruptions, Minister Adeang announced that Nauru was looking to expand market opportunities into new regions beyond the Pacific. With a discontented public, immense human costs, and activist campaigners constantly on the offensive, the Nauruan government was forced to move toward new overseas circuits and take on an export-oriented approach. Adeang made a statement to all of those living with refugee status in the country, broadcast on Nauru Television, Radio Nauru, and published in a special edition of the *Nauru Bulletin* (available in multilingual translations). In the speech, he recognized everyone's desires not to be in Nauru, even though for Nauruans it was home. Nauru and Australia were in negotiations with new trading partners to facilitate the resettlement of refugees elsewhere. He emphasized the microcredit loans, the employment services, the educational programs, and the new air-conditioning units installed throughout the refugee processing and resettlement districts. He asked that everyone take advantage of the many available initiatives, using their time on Nauru "constructively and peacefully," respecting "our home, our beloved nation, our Pleasant Island [as] our welcome guests" (Adeang 2016). In the meantime, the Australian and Nauruan governments were at a loss about what to do next, conscious that the country needed to extricate itself from the damaging enterprise or face more uprisings.

Then, activists campaigning for the end of offshoring launched their biggest push. In August 2016, the Nauru Leaks campaign made global waves, published across news outlets from Sydney to New York City to London, and beyond. Working with the *Guardian* Australia, the team of well-known Australian activists brought together a catalogue of over two thousand filed incident reports from when refugee processing first began. Reports of rape, beatings, self-harm, and child sexual assaults were publicly exposed, collated on the *Guardian*'s Nauru Leaks online interactive database, together with graphic imagery, footage, and the words of asylum seekers, refugees, and former Australian industry workers who had become vocal campaigners against the offshore operations. Nauru's offshore industry operations were characterized as an exceptionality, "a dark, wretched Truman Show without the cameras," a "gulag archipelago," rife with "horrible mistreatment," "squalor," "trauma and self-harm" (Farrell, Evershed, and Davidson 2016). Nauru was catapulted onto the global media stage. BBC, CNN, Al Jazeera, *Le Monde*, and the *New York Times* all featured reportages on the incidents and on the global refugee movement. Many local newspapers around the world followed suit.

The organizers' campaigns unleashed a season of activist power. A small Amnesty International and Human Rights Watch team flew to Nauru on a furtive three-day "refugee mission," collating stories of machete chasing, refugee beatings, rape, and squalor. They gave interviews worldwide, on ABC, NPR, and in the *Guardian*. Their subsequent report, *Islands of Despair* (2016) was circulated as evidence of torture on the island and soon cited in a host of publications worldwide. During the summer months, extraordinary levels of action took place in Australia and across the globe. Pro-refugee activists rappelled from the Australian Parliament, dying the fountain in front of Parliament House red, and then held a banner that read "Close the bloody camps now #justiceforrefugees." Others interrupted the Australian prime minister's Question Time, gluing their hands to furniture, shouting, "Justice for Refugees!" and "Let them stay!" Churches hung banners up across Australia in support as high-profile rallies took to the streets. Networks of activists, NGOs, and academics organized author readings of *Offshore: Behind the Wire on Manus and Nauru* (Gleeson 2016), "the true story of Australia's treatment of asylum seekers and refugees," and high-profile screenings worldwide of the new documentary *Chasing Asylum: The Film the Australian Government Doesn't Want You To See* (2016). The ABC released a *Four Corners* program, "The Forgotten Children," which included claims of Nauruans sexually assaulting refugee children, and a local culture of rape, savagery, and violence.[2] Snap actions were held outside Australian embassies and consulates from London to Washington, DC. Segments aired worldwide, all as evidence of the savagery of Nauruans— refugee molesters to the extreme.

At the time, I was living in Berkeley, and my immersion in this media world against offshoring brought the moral power of the figure of the refugee into stark visibility. But a politics of fear and animosity also converged with the activist narrative of the suffering refugee. It was the anti-refugee refrain that pro-refugee lobbyists battled against and that sustained Nauru's offshore operations. In Australia, the discourses of fear and compassion fatigue that led to migrants being shipped to Nauru are fixated on the figure of the refugee. As much as activist campaigners made waves with the push to end offshoring, conflicting yet converging narratives predictably emerged around the statement "We don't want our country 'flooded' with 'Islamic refugees'" (Heffernan 2017). "You're free to go home anytime you like, Australia is NOT your home and NEVER WILL BE :)" read one response to the post "We are here and still suffering #Nauru" from the Nauru refugee–maintained Twitter account @SuchNigel (Such a Human).[3]

In Australia, this was the time of the Islamophobia rise. From the 2015 Sydney shooting to a later 2017 Melbourne car rampage, the Muslim terror angle had become daily tabloid fare. The ultra-right–winger Pauline Hanson had steadily resurged in vocal prominence as the leader of the One Nation Party. Her plans for a total refugee resettlement embargo and a ban on all Muslims entering Australia was given widespread right-wing promotion connected to discourses of Islamic terrorism. "We've seen that these refugees we've brought in are actually terrorists themselves, so let's take a hard stance on this. We don't know who these people are," riled Hanson to nationalist support (Carney 2016). Although the activist campaigners sought to "bring the refugees" to Australia in #RefugeesWelcome campaigns, many in the Australian public were not so receptive. Along with scares of refugees as ISIS insurgents, the discourse of "queue jumpers" also took precedence for many Australians. The imaginary of migrants circumventing the system was especially popular among people already living in Australia as refugees. Many refugees in Australia were also set on disallowing the resettlement of this particular cohort of migrants, who went outside the popular refugee-camp queue narrative.[4] Others supported the government discourse of "protecting lives at sea," believing that Nauru was an important node in the deterrence cycle that dissuaded unregulated maritime arrivals. From this perspective, ending the offshore operations would open the floodgates to a surge of migrants by boat, which lead to extraordinary numbers of drownings—the images of which were made popular by industry supermajors like UNHCR.

Nonetheless, the activist campaigners could only achieve victory if they persuaded the Australian public that refugees should be resettled from Nauru. The tropes of suffering around which the industry found extraordinary moral economic capital enabled unprecedented global exposure. For migrants in Nauru involved in the campaign, promoting themselves as refugees was how they acquired visibility in the context of an uncertain future—even as others were not keen to market themselves in this way. In this sense, the mission against offshoring faced a fundamental contradiction, and one that led to the establishment of Nauru as a refugee resettlement outpost in the first place. Ultimately, these presentations reinforced the paradigm of the vulnerable refugee, rubbing up against some of the Australian electorate's compassion fatigue. At the same time, the humanitarian spectacle gave added value to refugee industry operations, with its powerful industry players, from which resulted the offshoring arrangement. Unfortunately, the campaigns failed to sufficiently convince the Australian public that refugees should be resettled from Nauru to Australia. At the end of the unprecedented season of high-level volatility, the offshore operations held strong.

The Devil's Excrement

But by this time, the Nauruan government and public were well and truly fed up with their national resource. Minister Adeang had been accused on ABC *Lateline* of killing his wife, the entire country was accused of violence against refugees in global media reports, and President Waqa was portrayed as the totalitarian state's evil dictator. Activist campaigners leapt onto anyone who did business with the small country, tarnishing them by association. This even extended to the Nauruan government's Brisbane-based public relations team, who had been employed at the Australian Immigration Department's advice in the peak of media conflicts in 2015 to minimize Nauru's adverse global publicity.[5] A number of Australian organizations were threatening contract termination; the activist campaigns were too much to take and the operational risks too great. Wilsons Security, Transfield (by then BroadSpectrum), and Connect all announced high-profile resignations across 2016. Not only were the willing industry contractors dwindling in number, but other firms operating in Nauru outside the explicit industry operations, such as Bendigo Bank, were targeted as part of an unethical supply chain.[6]

"They call our country a hellhole and accuse our government—which was recently democratically re-elected with an increased majority—of all sorts of things that are untrue," wrote President Waqa (2016a) in the wake of the Nauru Leaks global blockbuster drive. One among many saddening posts on the local "fact checking" Facebook group "Refugees on Naoero—Nauru" read:

> Feeling defeated.
> All I actually hear is bad things about Nauruan people; so much its [*sic*] hard for me to explain where I am from because every second person ends up bashing my country and just assuming that it's "a nothing country" (everyday [*sic*] when I worked at a supermarket I would get comments like this).[7]

But the president's Australian newspaper articles, government press releases, local Facebook posts, increased media invitations (including an entire Sky News crew), and government protestations that "the processing center for asylum seekers is world class and far exceeds the standard of many refugee camps across the world" (Waqa 2015a) earned little airtime outside of Nauru. Nauruans were certainly subject to a torrent of public relations events—perhaps some of the most refugee-sensitized publics I had seen, with refugee-awareness raising and national multicultural festivities on a regular basis. But similar Islamophobic fears also raged among many in the Nauruan public, all heightened by their very real resource conflicts, and a local diet of Australian and global tabloid media that connected the refugee, the economic migrant, and the terrorist. Some local residents had conspiracy theories tied into terrorist imaginaries about what it was that made the Australian government so unwilling to take refugees from Nauru.

The Australian government also wanted to rid themselves of the industry operations. The offshore arrangement, with many refugees on suicide watch, and all refusing to take the Cambodian resettlement arrangement, did not have a sustainable future. Bill Shorten, leader of the Labour opposition at the time, was calling for a senate inquiry, saying that Australia could not "turn a blind eye to what's happening." "I'd ask Mr. Dutton, how many abuses will there have to be before he thinks he should act?" Shorten publicly announced to the press (S. Anderson 2016). The rappelling protestors and refugee-torture allegations continued. In the same period, Australia's National Audit Office released a scathing report about the spiraling offshore expenditures: their second in the span of only two years. The report concluded that between September 2012 and April 2016, AU\$1.1 billion was approved by Australian Immigration Department officers who "did not have the required authorization," and there was "no departmental record of who authorised the payments" of another AU\$1.1 billion spent on sustaining Nauru's refugee company town (Australian National Audit Office 2016). Australian Senate Estimates committees were constantly on the offensive, organizing more public hearings around the refugee torture allegations.[8]

Globally, politicians were also beginning to raise eyebrows. Some, like the British government, had already sent their acting high commissioners for Nauru from Honiara headquarters to observe the operations under the radar. Criticisms of the offshore arrangement did little for the Australian Liberal government's reputational standing, but they also faced an impasse. In the eyes of leading Australian government strategists, they could not now resettle the refugees in Nauru, even if many I spoke with secretly wished this was the case. If they took this option, the Labour Party would have a field day, mirroring the Liberal Party's move on the Gillard Labour closure in 2012. The only solution, they decided, was to extend the geographies of distribution into new frontiers globally. But for the Nauruan and Australian industry partners, looking to promote the refugees to onward markets, the value acquired from their human resources "had, in the magical and mysterious process of being transformed into money, become a putrid and toxic waste" (Watts 2004, 205). Not only had they failed to market refugees and Nauruans to each other, but now they had trouble persuading other countries to enter into the regional industry operations. Wherever the resettlement operations potentially extended, activist campaigners targeted that country's involvement with the same anti-civilizational angles thrown at Nauru. This had already been the case when Cambodia joined the supply chain; before that, it was the Gillard plan for using Malaysia instead of Nauru as a processing hub. Phrases such as "human rights abusers," "dictators," and "refugee attacks" all emerged with sensationalist tabloid flare.[9] Nauru's resettlement extensions, Australian government representatives decided, had to take place in majority-white resettlement countries that had long-standing industry procedures already in place.

New Zealand had previously offered their assistance but at the time was too close for Australian comfort for the spectacle of deterrence to work.[10] The Australian government still had a hard-lined stance to promote amongst their anxiety-driven, anti–boat arrival public. The United Kingdom had just emerged into the Brexit age, enveloped in similar xenophobic fears as those rippling across Australia. Many in their public had little taste for the transoceanic trade in refugees or for the idea of "immigrants" at large (thought of in racially and ethnically contingent terms). Canada had resettled a few refugees from Nauru under the radar. However, they were in the middle of their own refugee politics after media-fueled anxieties surrounding Prime Minister Justin Trudeau's high-profile resettlement of Syrians in the country.[11] There, public interest was also beginning to dwindle as US presidential policies drove migrants across the US border into Canada (the so-called Trump bump) and Canada increased its immigration levels at a record-setting pace.

Then, the Australian government cracked a new and greater trade deal that would send the refugees into new resource frontiers. At the UN Summit for Refugees and Migrants in September 2016, the Australian government agreed with the US government to a "trade deal." In exchange for groups of US asylum seekers in Costa Rica, the United States would take a limited number of Australia's refugees from Nauru. Like Australia, the United States funds extensive regional processing and resettlement operations across Central America. Like Australia, US political parties have also acquired political currency around the promotion of a hard-line approach to undocumented southern-border arrivals (Nevins 2010). Similar regional frontiering projects look to deter and screen out the unwanted from wanted arrivals but have also led to a large surplus of migrants in trading limbo.

With the assistance of UNHCR RSD teams, Australian Immigration Department teams flew to Costa Rica to select Central American asylum seekers for resettlement in Australia. The US government negotiated that the most "complex" and "difficult" cases were only fair for this trade deal.[12] US Immigration and Customs Enforcement teams followed suit, flying to Nauru and Manus to conduct their own enhanced screening procedures. Any interested refugee could put their name down for this segment of the transcontinental trade, with women, children, and families given priority. Those who declined the deal would receive a twenty-year Nauru visa or be relocated to their home region. The lifetime Australian embargo would stay in place for all migrants certified as refugees offshore after

July 13, 2013. The Australian government solidified this arrangement with amendments to the Migration Act. At the same time, they announced dramatic increases in maritime border enforcement over the upcoming years to turn back and decrease the numbers of maritime arrivals.

But populist anxieties still threw up obstacles for the extended supply chain to work. The US Congress caught wind of the trade deal, made under the Obama Democrat administration. Republican congressmen sprang into action. Iowa Senator Charles Grassley, chairman of the Senate Judiciary Committee, and Virginia Senator Bob Goodlatte of the House Judiciary Committee sent a letter to Secretary John Kerry and the head of the Department of Homeland Security, Jeh Johnson, demanding answers about the shipment of the possibly high-risk refugees arriving from Nauru, writing: "The individuals who will be resettled are coming from countries of national security concern. In fact, two of the countries are officially designated by the State Department to be State Sponsors of Terrorism . . . it begs the question why Australia and other countries refuse to admit these individuals" (Grassley 2016). When the news hit, right-wing US media outlets like the *Conservative Daily Post* were up in arms about the Obama trade deal "to grant asylum to 1,800 'high threat' Muslims denied by Australia," railing: "Though the so-called migrants were deemed too dangerous to be allowed admittance to Australia, due to their connections with state sponsors of terrorism, Obama and Kerry have quietly agreed to grant them *permanent residency*, and distribute them throughout American cities and towns, without consulting local governments" (Jeffries 2016). The United States is a highly desirable resettlement destination that the Australian government thought few refugees in Nauru or Australian activists would critique. It also met the white colonial sensibility of Australian activists who showed a constant disdain for resettlement policies in global southern regions. As a significant site of resettlement industry, the Australian government thought that the United States would meet the demands and predilections of Australian industry activists and philanthropists. Under the weight of a large refugee advocacy sector, similar resettlement work to Australia also extends across the United States. Powerful conglomerates of ecclesiastical, NGO, INGO, academic, bureaucrat, refugee, nonrefugee, incensed citizenry, and corporate players also work to persuade publics of the benefits of refugee resettlement against similar fear mongering.

But dramas continued to unfold across the transoceanic trading floor. In November 2016, after the deal had been struck, the shock of a Trump presidency broke onto the horizon. As promised, upon his ascension, he went rampant. Wildly racist, Islamophobic policies went into overdrive: refugee resettlement clampdowns; wall building on the southern border; Iraq, Iran, Syria, Yemen, Somalia, Sudan, and Libya all blacklisted from any entry capacity. Refugee resettlement quotas were halved to 50,000 for 2017 from 117,000 in 2016, and all refugee resettlement programs were suspended for 120 days. The Australian government panicked not only about their offshore refugee trade deal, but also about their transcontinental trading future in any capacity. As one of his first acts after taking office, Trump signed an executive order to withdraw from the Trans-Pacific Partnership, a trade agreement covering twelve countries including Australia, signed in February 2016 after seven long years of negotiations. Meanwhile, the Australian press and Labour opposition had a field day, breaking out the Trump puns with predictable flair, with Prime Minister Turnbull "roasted" on the Nine Network's *60 Minutes* by political editor Laurie Oakes: "Malcolm Turnbull Doesn't Realise He's Been Trumped" (Oakes 2017). "Donald Trumps Australia's Interests" reads another headline (Speers 2017).

However, Australia is a close ally of the United States, what Erik Paul (2006) refers to as the "fifty-first state," and one of the largest military contributors to the US-led coalition in Syria and Iraq. Begrudgingly, Trump agreed to uphold the deal, "the worst deal ever," complaining that he was "going to get killed" politically, accusing Turnbull of seeking to export the "next Boston bombers" (Miller and Rucker 2017). The US refugee import embargo contained a clause that still honored prior trading deals, including this refugee-refugee exchange. But it would only be for a total of 1,250 "extremely vetted" and selected refugees from Nauru and Manus, despite there being double that number on both islands.

For refugees in Nauru, there was transcontinental turmoil about their resettlement destinations. Yet, many were also enwrapped in the same scares that saw them ping-pong back and forth in trading standstill. Nine hundred refugees signed up for the additional screening for US resettlement as soon as the arrangement was announced. Many also watched the xenophobia unfolding across America, petrified, questioning their onward destinations. I received an email from Maya, my close Iranian interlocuter, still waiting in Nauru for her upcoming move to the United States. She was excited about leaving Nauru, but also scared about possible resettlement into unknown worlds of hatred and fear. She questioned her reception as an Iranian and as a refugee, asking what it was like in the United States, where I was at the time. Several refugees in Nauru also remained set on resettlement in Australia. After tireless years of campaigning, they did not want to relent and take anything less than their ideal. Many also had family and friends in Australia and did not want to be sent into a complete unknown far from their support networks and loved ones.[13]

Some activists in Australia also played a significant part in encouraging refugees in Nauru to resist the push toward the United States as a resettlement destination. They instigated the prolongation of the efforts to end offshoring and the #RefugeesWelcome campaigns, encouraging refugees not to relent. Many of the activists and refugees I spoke with in Australia and Nauru suspected—and some secretly hoped—that the transoceanic trade deal might fail. Many also believed that the Nauru savagery narrative—now made visible on a global scale—might yet encourage the Australian government into submission. Unfortunately, this only led to the nightmarish cycle of more human harms, which reinforced Australian public disinterest while simultaneously stirring Nauru's social geographies.

A Renewable Resource Cycle

Two fundamental predicaments arise from this narrative of Nauru. The first is the lasting problem of the refugee complex that makes possible the forms of capitalist wealth to commodify people as refugees. As Albert Ellis once wrote, in what could surely characterize the ubiquity of the refugee industry, "You can't get away from the old B.P.C. . . . . The Commission's personnel both past and present are now so numerous and widespread, with such a faculty of coming to the fore when special phosphate matters . . . have to be dealt with" (1946, 277). Far from refugees being a "natural" resource, my ethnographic work shows that a tremendous amount of work goes into the legal production of "making someone" into a refugee. I have argued that it is important to get behind the commodity fetish and challenge essentializing notions in more critical and perhaps revolutionary directions. But as each chapter has detailed, the particular industry narratives around refugees prove difficult to disassemble. This is all the more acute in an industry where people give self-promotional veracity as commodified bodies, wherein the consumptive practices of nation-states shape constructions of the self. Yet even if migrants want to be made into refugees, what of the enduring effects of refugee idolatry on a grounded and renewable scale? As this book has sought to make clear, high-risk industry operations function starkly to the detriment of those enveloped in the refugee system. Images of refugee suffering and anti-civilizational depictions of Nauruans, what West (2012) refers to in the Papua New Guinean coffee trade as "an imagined primitive," solidify the consumer fetish under an oppositional frame.

As Mitchell (2011) points out, profitable resource projects are not only sources of revenue and conflict for the countries directly involved in their production, but impinge on and shape the body politic in places that have a great demand for utilizing that resource. As much as people who move are subjected to growing calculability, bureaucratization, and regulation, refugees are firmly entangled in the edifice of capitalism as a calculative practice of democratic rule. It was because of the resource spectacle of Nauru's 1,355 refugees, used to satiate an inflamed public, that the Australian government publicly raised their refugee industry quotas in the 2015 budget. They increased the number of bodies for resettlement contractors to transition from points of production (refugee camps and the like) into the Australian market economy.[14] Australian refugee industry funding increased, from refugee resettlement and language training to money for UNHCR's regional expansion, standardizing human mobility processes and regimes on a global scale.

In addition to these budget increases, the Australian government publicly escalated their operations in Iraq and Syria, sending warplanes to join the US-led coalition in fighting, what Tony Abbott termed the "death cult" and "Islamic State terrorist threat" in Iraq and Syria (Peatling and Hutchens 2015). Ironically, this increase in conflict and militarization cyclically results in more human displacement, fueling the resource cycle.[15] At the same time, AU$957.9 million was put into border enforcement to target future arrivals on land, by air, and on sea. Boat pushbacks extending into Indonesian waters, regional border enforcement funding, anti-smuggling marketing campaigns, and fisherman payoffs looked to prevent migrants arriving in unregulated ways outside the state spectacle of refugee resettlement. As part of this spectacle of civilization, the Australian government publicly resettled twelve thousand Syrian refugees from Jordan, Lebanon, and Turkey. With UNHCR and IOM workforce personnel, the government led a "refugee mission" to the Middle East to identify and process "worthy" human lives fleeing the terrorism of Syria and Iraq (women, children, and the families of vulnerable minorities). This constant "discovery" of refugees in particular regions continues to sediment a narrative frame of liberal protection and civilization. It is crucial to the naturalization of industry operations that govern how human life is shaped and sustained. As the refugee industry has grown at unprecedented speed, human movement has been reconstituted on a massive scale in the context of persistent colonial and imperial politics and acute racism and border struggles.

And, of course, the second question is, what of Nauru? The country has now been remade as a refugee company town so that it sparkles like Oman. Nauru's refugees have already reached peak production rates and are rapidly declining in numbers. By 2021, just over one hundred refugees remained in the country. What then of Nauru, whose refugees will be relocated elsewhere? What of the incredible buildings and infrastructure that have become modern Nauru—the hospital, luxury cars, the glass doors of Bendigo Bank, the new ATMs, the Air Nauru routings on the horizon? What of the company town infrastructure? The trained refugee determination teams? The Refugee Day Celebrations? The Beach House? The Rohingyan takeaways? "Imperial ruins" (Morris 2021b; Stoler 2008) already blanket the atoll. The rusted phosphate turrets, the BPC train tracks, the Japanese bomber remains have been added to by turbulent refugee pasts: the burned-out husk of the RPC 3, the boarded-up Persian restaurant, a moldy DIAC—IOM sign still tacked onto the former processing centers from the first industry heyday. These infrastructural forms all gave a sense of foreboding but were also ever-present reminders of declines into poverty.

A Finite Resource?

> With the aging of the industry, abandoned oil camps and decaying oil towns scattered throughout the states of Zulia, Portuguesa, and Anzoátegui have added a ghostly aura to oil's former presence in Venezuela.
>
> —Coronil (1997)

In *In The Time of Oil* (2010), Mandana Limbert follows the temporal uncertainties brought about by the oil boom in the Arabian Gulf, where the inevitability of decline produces a constant anxiety about a coming future without oil, and a return to poverty. In Nauru's refugee company town, the present was not only haunted by the future, but also redoubled by memories of the past. Nauru has seen constant escalation of the lifespan of both the phosphate and refugee industries, but the preoccupation with how long either would last was palpable. In the 1920s there was no sense of urgency, and most people felt that the phosphate would last for "perhaps 300 years" (Nauru Philatelic Bureau 1983). By 1939, a life of sixty to seventy years was first mentioned, with Nauru's peak phosphate extraction rate expected in 1973. In 1980, the Nauru Phosphate Corporation announced that the anticipated life of the phosphate industry would only be fourteen years. These predictions have been stretched out on an ever-rolling cycle as secondary phosphate mining has rampaged into once verdant lands; limestone byproducts are shipped to the Kiribatis and Marshallese, prolonging yet also expediting the inevitable decline.

The impending threat of a future without phosphate fomented a "temporal disposition" (Weskalnys 2014, 220) in which uncertainties about the end of phosphate converged with the end of the refugee industry. In my many conversations with locals in Nauru, depleting phosphate and refugee supplies were spoken of in tandem. Everyone knew—and many willed—that the end of refugees be on the horizon. For the government, this meant obtaining maximum revenue from a dwindling operation, future-proofing Nauru against economic shock. The end of the boom meant the likely disappearance of Nauru as a sovereign state and the ironic possibility of Nauruans one day becoming refugees themselves, as the industry moved away to other global sites of extraction. The visa and taxation schemes, high land leases, and local import duties were part of the drive to generate maximum revenue in an era of future uncertainties. Alongside this, the Nauruan government pushed for a new hospital, new primary school, new higher education center, and public sector training programs to extract maximum local benefits from the Australian government in anticipation of the nonrefugee days that loomed ahead. The hope was that the country would continue to grow after the boom, attracting new industries, so that even modest activity would support their economies.

FIGURE 22.   Imperial debris. Photo by Julia Morris.

Many of my conversations with government bureaucrats revolved around the concept of "future-proofing," the awareness that the renewed economic prosperity was finite. Their economies were not diversified, refugee supplies came from elsewhere, and Nauruans depended for their existence on the large, transient population brought in with the industry operations. Nauru's company town boomed because of activity supplied by the Australian government, but energetic local leadership needed to keep the country growing when refugee activity declined. Several Nauruan government officials said that the current "good times" were "just like the phosphate days," but this time round they needed to invest. "I always make sure that there's something in it for us," a ministerial secretary remarked on this point in interview. "Like when it's education and they're sending in the Australian teachers, then Nauruans need to profit also. Teachers in every classroom, not just for the refugee children. With the hospital, it's not just a hospital for refugees, but one that will benefit Nauruans for when they're not here." This is known in extractive industry circles as the "Dutch disease," which several of my local interlocutors made note of and were adamant about wanting to avoid in this new industry boom. This concept posits that a booming resource sector can pull in a disproportionate amount of labor and shift production away from other tradable sectors. Given their familiarity with the dangers of this kind of overreliance, local representatives were keen to take measures to ensure that any such resource curse be preventable, particularly in an industry sector that was subject to such volatility.

Many islanders voiced fears of repeated bankruptcy to me in conversation, having been through those hardships in the 1990s. However, many were also firmly entrenched in what was described as "a party-town mentality" from the days of the phosphate boom. Several locals made the point that the country had become "dependent" upon the refugee industry, as it once was on the phosphate industry. They lamented the lack of diversification in their local economy. As a result of this monoeconomy, so many of the future-proofing schemes were faced with a resource-cursed mendicancy. This was much to the exasperation of foreign personnel, who continued to staff many of Nauru's main administrative positions. During an interview at Nauru's main hospital, a Fijian nurse expressed this common frustration to me: "We came to work this morning and a party was starting up next door. People don't come to work, they get a friend to sign them in on the time sheets and they still get dollars if they don't turn up to work. Nauruans live like it's the phosphate years. The government just spoils this country rotten. In my country you have to sign in and you work, and man is it tough. The caterers didn't turn up to work last week so we ended up serving food to the patients." I put this to Bernard, an older Nauruan MP, who had been through Nauru's boom-and-bust cycles, including a brief stint as president. "This is just how we do it here, we're proud in Nauru," said Bernard in interview, chuckling. "We were the first Pacific island that obtained independence, and man did we want to show it. Other people came in and did everything for us. We didn't have to lift a finger. It's hard to get over that even though we need to." His remarks illuminate the complex legacies of extraction that have shaped many islanders' boom mentalities in the present. Bernard called my attention to the local Cantilever Boys' song that was playing as we had lunch at the Bay, a popular spot that had sprung up in Anibare with industry activity. The upmarket seafood restaurant was part of the mushrooming company town settlement that existed to meet the interests of Australian workers, and more than once played lavish host to high-powered Australian Immigration Department personnel and industry executives (including Australian immigration minister Peter Dutton earlier that year, captured in the local newspaper posing with a garland of frangipani atop his head). For Bernard, the song's refrain summed up the buoyant optimism of boom times: "Naoero, we do the local style. Naoero, we like the Nauruan style . . . We sit around on a mat, staring at the driveway . . . drinking ice coffee and drinking home brew beer, that's the Nauruan style." Sitting with Bernard in these lavish surroundings made Nauru's tenuous situation clear. Nauru was a party country, again riding on the boom. The question remained though: Would this activity be sustained after the excitement of the boom died down?

Nauru certainly demonstrated the kind of problems common with rapid development in mineral boomtowns (Olien and Hinton 1982). Even when voicing future uncertainties and the need to set the county on an even keel, the new gold rush undermined the success of long-term planning endeavors. Nauru entered into an almost predictable cycle of boomtown repercussions. Loss of local livelihoods was a major problem accompanying the industry boom that was kept from public view by the Australian Immigration Department and DFAT. The continued processing of migrants, even in small quantities, certainly generated wealth and jobs locally in the boom days, but this was also marked by detrimental effects on the social fabric of Nauru. The Nauru Education Department did not maintain dropout statistics since their last census in 2011 (40 percent left school at seventeen, and 1 percent of students attended tertiary education), but it was clear from my institutional observations and many discussions with local personnel that dropout rates remained high, exasperated by easy refugee industry employment. Many high school students found quick or ad hoc employment with refugee managerial or resettlement contractors, so they were dropping out at sixteen. The ease of finding work in the refugee industry in some capacity (which paid several times the salary of government departments) gave high school students little incentive to stay in school.

Also clear was the side effect of the resurged party scene, such as the new bars and popular bingo halls that sprang up across the country. These new forms of consumptive excess tempted older students from school and lured parents from ensuring their children went to school or, at times, even that they were properly fed. Thanks to Nauru's refugee boom, each week AU$3,000 cash prizes, jet skis, and motorbikes were on offer—which the CLOs then had to oversee in their new roles in company town governance. In response to these temptations, and the "Topside brain drain," as one local called it, the Nauruan Education Department created the Nauru Education Assistance Trust Scheme in 2016. They offered AU$5 a day in financial incentives for all students who attended school from preschool to grade twelve. This method was also one born in the phosphate town years. The BPC paid a subsidy to the island's church schools on the basis of attendance and academic progress. At the time, the scheme was heralded as a great success, inaugurating, it was said, an educational system superior to any other Pacific island, where compulsory attendance was achieved.

The Australian government's DFAT office in Nauru mirrors some of the BPC's developmental trends. Australian aid accounts for roughly 20 percent of Nauru's overall budget.[16] Of DFAT's official AU$25.2 million aid budget for Nauru during my 2015–2016 fieldwork, 22 percent was put into the education system: a figure that steadily increased over the years. In order to help build Nauru's educational capacity, DFAT funded teacher training schemes for Nauruans with New South Wales's University of New England in Nauru and in Australia. They increased the number of Australia Award scholarships for Nauruan students to study in fields such as health, education, environmental management, and public policy, with the view to long-term development. In addition to the Australian fly-in-fly-out teaching teams brought in for refugee education, DFAT also funded the building of a new Learning Village, which brought together Nauru's higher education institutions onto one campus. But in reality, in an almost classic example of boom-and-bust failure, well-meaning but beleaguered development teams always waged battle against the refugee industry.

Like in the phosphate town years, during the refugee industry years, the Australian government attempted to project the rose-tinted vision of developmental progress in DFAT reports. They funded economic impact assessment teams to detail the wonders of Nauru's resurged economy and the increased employment opportunities. In their reports, practitioners were told not to detail the surge of Nauruans moving from key local positions to work in the refugee industry. Instead, the emphasis was on the wonders of Nauru's boomtown economy, not its damaging effects. Australian development teams only critiqued these initiatives to me behind the scenes.

Local residents and industry personnel recounted numerous stories to me of the consequences of the high-paying refugee industry on other crucial institutional sectors in the country. I spoke with several younger locals who had dropped out of the UWE teacher training courses because it was too much work, with some of them juggling families. They could obtain easy employment with the refugee industry if times got tight, I was told. Australian industry recruiters argued that working with Australian firms provided transferable literacy and writing skills that could be used for other sectors in the future, which is why several refugees took jobs back in the industry. However, what seemed to be more often the case was that many locals used industry employment to obtain quick cash or, like the Fijian nurse observed, have friends "clock in" and not even show up to work. The many Nauruan security guards I spent time with at the Wilson Security Village were not interested in pursuing transferable qualifications; most were interested in the higher salaries compared to other local industry sectors.[17]

The implications of easy refugee industry employment were already manifold during my fieldwork. Many development aid budgets went unspent because no trained staff were there to ensure the money was spent effectively. During my fieldwork, the Education Department, for example, had an AU$31,000 budget for administration supplies and only spent AU$1,000, which resulted in government cuts for the following year. A great deal of the Australian aid budget also went unspent, rolling into the following year, without government employees to decide how the finances should be allocated effectively. This was similarly the case with the RPC revenues at large, which totaled AU$115 million in 2015. The country remained reliant on expatriate labor and expertise, with almost all institutions staffed by foreign advisors in managerial positions.

The Nauruan government also continued to project the outward display of wealth that had become so commonplace since the phosphate era, which ultimately led to the country's economic crash. In the phosphate heyday, government demands were for full twenty-one-gun salutes abroad. Legendary stories are told of past presidents demanding red-carpet treatment when they indulged in shopping sprees in Melbourne. Not unlike those dreamtime years, in the refugee boom heydays I observed, chauffeured government cavalcades drove around the small country for island events. On a number of occasions, I witnessed gluts of pomp and ceremony as refugee wealth once again abetted spectacular excess. At government events, the president rolled up in a blacked-out chauffeur-driven car, flanked by brass-buttoned police. A Nauruan flag proudly waved from the bonnet. Outlandishly pompous formalities went into the displays of Nauruan grandeur. Lavish spreads always accompanied government events, heaving with imported delicacies that I rarely encountered or could afford in the shops: pork belly roasts, mussels, crabs, salmon (foreign to Nauru's waters), now diversified with Rohingyan and Iranian cuisine on the side. The government spared little expense even in the voiced anticipation of a dwindling future. Part of the tension was exhibiting the outward appearance of wealth to a hyperconsumptive public shaped by phosphate excess, while preparing against another imminent demise. Although government MPs stressed the need to invest, they also tried to replicate the past boomtown years, caught in something of a resource spiral of attempting to dazzle and divert locals away from the bitter curse of the refugee boom.

The phosphate heydays were marked by windfall payments and shopping sprees to Dubai. There were no taxes, import duties, or other tariffs. Free healthcare and education were—and continue to be—provided to all. A major obstacle for the Nauruan government remains the constitutional ease of votes of no confidence, which makes public discontent a constant threat. The Nauruan government did not want to lose sight of sustaining the country after the boom ended, but it also struggled with how to appease a public used to lavish treats and expenditures. They also faced the unsavory reputation of Nauru's early phosphate boom government, who had led the country into bankruptcy. Many in the public still woefully mistrusted the government in any capacity. At the Nauruan government's request, DFAT brought over Australian specialist advisors under the Pacific Technical Assistance Mechanism scheme in fields including health, customs, taxation, and finance. During the early refugee industry years, the Nauruan government had lost out on a number of key revenue generators, particularly in import tariffs and taxation. With the support of the Australian advisors, they initiated several new regulations to ensure that refugees were used in a market-efficient manner, including taxation and customs import duties, but they feared the public reprisal. Worried at the response of the Nauruan people, and to secure the local business interests of representatives—and those of their families, who owned many major establishments in the country—the Nauruan Law and Justice Department made business taxation schemes excludable to all but foreign industry firms. Similarly, visa fees were only charged for foreign workers, asylum seekers, and refugees. The Australian government footed the bill for the latter, which was Nauru's principal revenue stream in 2016: AU$28.6 million that year alone and rising to AU$29.6 million the following year as the Nauruan government took advantage of creating specialist visa categories for asylum seekers, refugees, and refugee industry workers.

The country's small-town context, where kinship and local political ties complicate the landscape, also posed challenges to the government in enforcing regulations. Nauruan families can be so extensive that family connections spread across the island, with as many as two out of every five Nauruans related in some way (Kun, Togomae, and Kund 2003). Local islanders arriving back to Nauru from trips abroad often refused to pay import duties, waving their credentials or asserting family and friendship ties. One of the main supermarkets, Egigu, is government owned, earning profits for officials and their families from taxation and duty exemptions. This was also the case with the locally owned bingo halls and cocktail bars, where small-town family ties run deep. Yet, in Nauru, everything rests on tenuous boom-bust foundations, portending an ominous demise.

"Ladies and gentlemen," spoke President Waqa (2015b), "today we live in a time of great harvest, but challenges and scarcity always revisit us time and again. I ask each and every one of you to set aside a portion of your income for the rainy day and invest as much as you can." But despite President Waqa's words, the government also propelled the national spectacle of wealth, fawning on their public used to hyperconsumption that went along with a culture of generosity and communal obligations. In Nauru, lavish gift giving is a crucial part of social and political life. People commonly request—and expect—money and favors from their members of parliament. Like the phosphate boomtown years, during my fieldwork, government MPs flew planeloads of locals off on spending sprees to the Marshall Islands, celebrating the new destination for Air Nauru's expanding fleet in dreamtime style. Under the spell of fantasies of progress, interested local publics could partake in government-funded trips to Majuro, receiving stipends for shopping-mall and nightclub excursions. This reminded me starkly of the stories

I had heard from the 1970s phosphate boom years. Meanwhile, these lavish expenditures silenced the violence of a history and present made at the expense of the "natural resources" and labor of people relegated to the margins.

Refugee wealth made it difficult to transition to the frugality that many voiced as necessary for securing their economy on a stable plateau. Instead, some locals I spoke with made furtive plans on the side, having lived through past boom-and-busts before. Some juggled multiple jobs in the refugee industry to prepare for a time without refugees. They ensured that their children went to high school in Fiji and maintained close connections abroad. Others maintained properties in Australia or Fiji, bank accounts abroad, or shoeboxed cash under their beds in case the country had another catastrophic fold. Some also ignored the eventualities, with a Pollyanna belief that, as the local saying went, "tomorrow will take care of itself."

A major challenge for Nauru's sustainable development has long been the availability of land, exasperated by the ease of refugee and phosphate lease earnings. Not only is land finite on an island of 21 km², but land has also taken on new valuations tied into phosphate and refugees. As with industry employment, the government struggled to compete with the higher land leases earned from refugee and worker housing and the RPCs (AU\$8.50/m² versus over AU\$12.50/m² for the latter). As a result, enthusiastic ideas for local development schemes met with little success. Attempts at agricultural and development projects across the district locales, including new school projects, playgrounds, and the hospital expansion, ended up being delayed or never took off the ground. Local landowners could easily obtain quick revenue from refugee industry firms. With more migrants moving across the country with refugee status, many landowners held out for refugee land-leasing contracts, rejecting offers of alternative initiatives. In Nauru, development projects were doomed to failure, not because they failed to integrate the knowledge of local participants (Scott 1998), but because the local knowledge of participants involved the acquisition of phosphate and refugee wealth without apparent effort. Unfortunately, the projects that the country found windfall success with have had immense repercussions. Ultimately, these forms of industrial extraction were also limited, as with the government's latest entrepreneurial endeavor to diversify their product lines.

Offshore to Offshore Extractions

Expectations of the end of refugee wealth turned the Nauruan government's attention to their own offshore, bioprospecting mineral extraction of the seabed floor. Like the refugee trade in its early days, seabed mining has taken off worldwide as a new economic growth sector, leading to a so-called Wild West mineral stampede (Kolbert 2021). Seafloor polymetallic nodules are rich in silver, gold, copper, nickel, cobalt, and zinc, and found in sizeable deposits in volcanic hotspots in the Pacific Ocean. Worldwide, undersea minerals are in high demand for the making of cell phones, wind turbines, solar panels, and computers. But this promotion is in spite of the destruction of fragile marine habitats, species, and ecosystems that is the result of intensive scraping of the ocean floor (Levin, Amon, and Lily 2020; Miller et al. 2018). Meanwhile, Japan, Great Britain, Russia, South Korea, China, France, and Germany, among many others, have secured licenses to mine the global ocean's abyssal plains. Since the early 2000s, the Secretariat of the Pacific Community—as of 2011, with EU support—has marketed seabed mineral extraction as a development strategy for Pacific states, organizing high-profile conferences that endorse the new and emerging industry.

In the knowledge that the refugee industry was temporary, the Nauruan government set up the Nauru Ocean Resource Inc. (NORI), an incorporated subsidiary of the Canadian-based firm DeepGreen Resources, to scout out mining prospects in their economic zone. But like Nauru's agricultural and refugee prospects, the country's particular geographical position has resulted in a surrounding seabed barren of high-value minerals for global trade. The largest of the world's deepwater mineral deposits in terms of nodule abundance and metal concentration is found in the Clarion-Clipperton Zone: an area that spans six million square kilometres between Hawaii and Mexico. In 2011, the International Seabed Authority (ISA) gave the Nauruan government 25,000 km² of the ISA Reserved Area, specially earmarked for developing countries as an "untapped" extractive frontier.[18] Exploration licenses for this area are granted by the ISA, with preferential access to developing states. As a result, small Pacific island countries have partnered with foreign seabed mining companies to obtain industry expertise and together take advantage of the extractive trade. NORI, under the promotional steam of the Nauruan government and DeepGreen, has become the seabed mining champion of the Pacific. In 2011, Nauru became the first company to obtain a mining exploration license from the ISA with DeepGreen. As the refugee industry tapered, the Nauruan government put together plans to accelerate the mining explorations into these new resource frontiers.

As with other extractive industries, there are immense industrial byproducts that come with the seabed mining trade. The volcanic hotspots where nodules are found are home to an abundance of ecological communities. Crabs and mussels, luminous octopods, deepsea fish and prawns, and brittle stars are just some of the marine life living in the nodule fields (Tornero and Hanke 2016). The intrusion of the harvesting machines into the deepsea ecosystem destroys the productive vent habitats, like geysers on the ocean floor, killing virtually all of the attached organisms on the vent structure's chimneys. The mining also releases pollutant metal byproducts into the ocean water that not only contaminate ecological life but are also ingested by the seafood that surfaces into the global food chain. In Nauru, the move to another high-risk industry was certainly accompanied by environmental concerns. However, temporal uncertainties about prosperity overshadowed the possibilities of environmental catastrophe. The understandings about the directly experiential realities of phosphate and refugees, combined with the living memory of phosphate bankruptcy, also provided a complex ground on which locals interpreted and understood deepsea mining operations. At least this time, it was felt locally, the turbulence that accompanied this new extractive frontier sat far outside Nauru's frontlines.

Yet, as with Nauru's other industry projects, the seabed mining operations are again outsourced to foreign firms. Deepsea mining work is dominated, like the refugee industry, by foreign industry personnel. It is also an extractive sector that is finite, lasting until the inevitable peak manufacturing rate is reached. It is another way for Nauru to accumulate profits through an armchair revenue scheme. In 2015, the Nauru Justice Department set up the Seabed Ministerial Fund with the SPC-EU Deep Sea Minerals Project team in anticipation of the new royalty windfalls on the horizon. They estimated exporting six million to seven million tonnes per annum from the seabed floor. The Nauruan government would recoup taxes and royalties until drilling depletion. This combines with extensive training, capacity-building workshops, and scholarships for young people in deepsea mining as Nauruans again find themselves entangled in a knowledge economy to enhance the industrial growth of regions far distant.

Refugee Resurgencies?

> Seeing that millions of pounds of the tax-payers' money have been paid out for these two islands, the inevitable question arises as to how long will the deposits last. It is, of course, almost impossible to gauge accurately the depth and extent of the phosphate deposits, but . . . even if the annual output from the two islands reaches the high figure of half a million tons, Australian, New Zealand and United Kingdom farmers have nothing to worry about as regards future supplies of fertiliser for the text two hundred years at least!
>
> —Collinson (1923)

As with the ongoing phosphate mining, which assuages Malthusian food scares in global regions far beyond the island, Nauru may still have a refugee company town role to play. Nauru's international trade owes a great deal to the moral panics around the figure of the refugee. Politicians and the press have made much of the ways in which the asylum seeker and the refugee are figures of fear or welfare scroungers to explain their countries' engrained inequalities. At the same time, politicians widely promote policies of strengthening borders, incarceration, containment, and policing as solutions to the movement of poor people of color across borders. Cyclically, these policies refuel the resource cycle that produces more people as refugees as this form of intimate labor becomes one of the few modes of border entry. Meanwhile, the apolitical refugee frame obfuscates the forms of extraction, conflict, and inequality driven by countries in the Global North that induce people's movements in the first place.

In Nauru, the industry planners developed the infrastructure to sustain and prolong refugee processing, altering the "time-honored 'here today, gone tomorrow' pattern of oil field production" that Hinton (2008, 374) describes. When announcing the US trade deal, Turnbull reiterated that Australia would continue to toughen borders and enhance their Middle Eastern military presence. For Nauru, this means moving to a controlled production output that would extend the island's company town life on a more permanent basis. Nauru, Turnbull announced, would take on a permanent place as a remote processing outpost in the regional deterrence frontier. At the UN Summit for Refugees and Migrants in New York in September 2016, shortly before the American trade deal was publicly unveiled, Minister Adeang said that Nauru had the infrastructure and systems in place for the processing phase, but elicited other countries to join the supply chain on a more permanent basis: "Nauru invites other countries to assist in finding durable resettlement solutions for our refugees. This is the critical missing component. Remote processing is one part of what needs to be a comprehensive migration strategy" (Round 2016). Later, Adeang put forward a supply-chain segue that would move Manus Island's refugees to Nauru's quality assured landscape, famed privately among industry executives for its safety measures. In May 2017, with the imminent closure of the Manus RPCs following the PNG Supreme Court ruling, Adeang said that there was extra capacity at Nauru's processing sites, extending the invitation to refugees in Manus. As with secondary mining, this would enable Nauru to expand their market share, assuming that their primary reserves were exhausted by the end of the year. However, Nauru continues to be financed by the Australian government with the understanding that this operation might be restarted in the future. The Australian construction-turned-managerial firm Canstruct, who took over from BroadSpectrum (formerly Transfield Services) in 2017, had their AU$594 million contract extended in 2021; this equated to AU$10,000 per day for each refugee remaining on the island. The thinking in Nauru is that asylum seekers and refugees are safe investment strategies on account of public anxieties about the perils they represent. This could well induce the gravitation of governments toward Nauru as an offshore processing site into the future.

With the political potency of refugee scares, the human supply-chain setup may prove an attractive assemblage for governments beyond the Asia Pacific. Not only can employees move from camp to camp within a professional network but also the industrial schema modulates to other regions. European governments have looked to the Australian system of processing and externalization. Proposals for establishing offshore processing camps in countries neighboring the EU have spanned locations such as Albania, Morocco, and further afield to Central and East Africa. Elements of this are already in place. The Spanish enclave of Ceuta in Morocco performs some of these operations, interdicting migrants arriving from sub-Saharan Africa. Meanwhile, under the 2016 EU-Turkey deal, Turkey accepts the return of asylum seekers and migrants in exchange for a payment of US$6.6 billion in aid: an initial five-year arrangement that was extended in 2021. That same year, Denmark's Parliament passed legislation to allow the relocation of asylum seekers to countries outside Europe for the assessment of their claims. In April 2022, the UK government announced their plans to pay Rwanda £120 million to process and resettle asylum seekers as part of a similar arrangement. Likewise, the US government funds Central American countries to strengthen the border between Guatemala and Mexico, in addition to the training of border enforcement throughout the region. Meanwhile, the Bangladesh government relocates Rohingyans from border camps in Myanmar to the island of Bhasan Char in the estuary of Bangladesh's Meghna river. Refugees have transformed Bhasan Char from a deserted silt island to a bustling city with over ten thousand inhabitants, funded by Western donor governments—a story with some parallels to Nauru. These sorts of arrangements are in addition to the much-vaulted plans of "refugee islands," "refugeeias," permanent "refugee camps," "refugee cities," and even an entire "Refugee Nation" put forward by white Western elite academics and entrepreneurs (see, for example, Buzi 2015; Betts and Collier 2017; Cohen and Van Hear 2020). Yet, such industrial enclave arrangements are founded on the racialized and class-based exclusion of people attempting to move, generating profits for corporate, NGO, state, academic, and individual actors under the guise of development assistance.

Ironically, Nauruans might also find themselves inserted within the industry cycle on a more permanent basis in a context where the country is imbricated in managing and now potentially *becoming* refugees. Projections of sea-level rises indicate that Nauru is experiencing dramatic ecological upheavals, while ocean acidification is affecting Nauru's coral reefs, fisheries, and marine resources (McKenna, Butler, and Wheatley 2014; Republic of Nauru 2019). Encroaching oceans see Nauru's neighbors pondering future directions. With Nauru's high-rising atoll, the country has up to now been little affected. But who knows what the future holds as Nauru continues to sell the island's limestone rock to Kiribati and the Marshall Islands as part of their coastal adaptation projects. Nauru continues to underwrite the development of other nations, further degrading their environment out of imposed economic need.

This is not to make recommendations about what the Nauruan government should do. Their current industry is obviously immensely destructive, and perhaps on the way out. This remains to be seen, particularly with the global abundance of ever more "raw human materials" for processing, and the symbolic capital of border spectacles. Rather, it is to stress that the government's refugee industrial operations, like offshore mineral and phosphate mining, are hugely damaging, marked by the "bitterness" Shipton describes. Local residents all along the spectrum of the debate over the offshore refugee industry were concerned about the country's economy and the finitude of the phosphate and refugee industry sectors. While many disagreed on exactly how to move the country forward in a way that would be sustainable for generations to come—environmentally and economically—they found hope for the island in the ingenuity of small projects and economic initiatives that could lead toward community revitalization.

Discourses of racial and cultural superiority continue to haunt Nauru. These colonial (mis)representations obscure Nauru's centrality in new global commodity economies. From feeding into and from global food systems through phosphate and to Australian political economies through refugees, portrayed first as "guano island" then "gulag island," Nauru and its people shoulder the humiliation of resource-curse exceptionalism and Australian handmaiden depictions with remarkable jocularity. Yet, as I have sought to detail, Nauru has virtually the same blueprints and builders as Australia and elsewhere. The country's operations are the product of the institutionalization of a global system that fits within the logics of border control. Migrants are included or excluded through differential legal categories based on the adjudication of suffering. The image of the refugee as a voiceless victim allows people to further disregard the structural causes and inequality that make more migrants refugees.

This book has shown that activist campaigns can inadvertently promote representations of migrants as victimized refugees that strengthen practices of border control to new extraction sites. This is not to call into question the pain and suffering of migrants in Nauru as in any way inauthentic, but to highlight the possible convergences of activist representations with egregious government policies. The reality, I found, is that, in this human extractive industry, the effects are manifold, negatively impacting Nauruans, contracted personnel, migrants, and ecological environments entangled in the system. Such developments around a new type of human colonialism have profoundly horrific effects on all populations. It is thus imperative to rethink the circuits of geographical exploitation through which contemporary forms of offshore industry are brought to the fore.

Coda: PO_{43} Meets RSD

I sit with Sylvain, a Nauruan former phosphate worker. He's taken to making jewelry and sculptures from phosphate discards, largely for refugee industry personnel. Sylvain's house is invariably filled with laughter and noise, and I regularly make sure to stop by on my cycle route home. Trudy, his wife, is bubbly and always up for a natter about the latest Nau-rumors and company town goings on. They share a coconut with me, freshly picked, as we look through Sylvain's newest creations. The walls of their house gleam with curved statuettes, necklaces engraved with names like "Kazzy," others in the shape of hearts and diamonds, several in the shape of Nauru. A whiteboard is filled with orders from Australian offshore workers and the date of completion. Sylvain and Trudy are friends with several of Nauru's new refugee residents living in nearby resettlement housing. Some will occasionally pop by to learn the art of phosphate whittling—several hoping for future business ventures, keen to contribute in creative ways to the Australian economy, others simply to pass the time on their extended Nauru stay.

To one side sits a phosphate paperweight carved with the logo Wilson, the subcontracted Australian security firm in the refugee industry: a visible amalgamation of two extractive sectors in one. I assume it's another souvenir for a

FIGURE 23. PO_{43} meets RSD. Photo by Julia Morris.

fly-in-fly-out worker returning to Australia—maybe to give to their line supervisor back in Melbourne. "No," Sylvain tells me. "That one actually never sold." I turn the embossed stone over. A logo I've never seen is carved on the backside, hidden from view on the shelf. A Nauruan employee, I'm told, from one of Wilson's local subcontractors, designed it for his Australian security partner, before they lost their contract to another company town player. Now it sits obscured, backside turned, industry contract annulled. Before I leave, Trudy ties a pendant around my neck in the shape of Nauru, engraved with my name, Julia. She says to me like so many others, "We probably won't see you again, you guys always leave once you've done your work and mostly never come back." I think how stark these words are in portending Nauru's future without refugees. What will be the long-term harms left in the boom-and-bust's wake? Nauru is a country that has, willingly and unwillingly, been subject to the toxic remainders of commercial processes.

Acknowledgments

My passion for mobility was shaped by a childhood lived across continents. Toing-and-froing between the United States, the United Kingdom, and Canada, I had little understanding that this was an exceptional way of life that came with enormous privilege. A nomadic existence was not without its challenges, but all pale in comparison to the harrowing experiences I see many people going through in their quests to be mobile: to follow their dreams, support themselves and their families, and leave harmful situations. My awareness of these mobility injustices, gradually learned from extensive travel and conversations, and research projects with Music in Detention in the UK and Grassroots Leadership in Austin, Texas, incited me to embark on this book and pursue my own long-term research agenda on free movement. Having a third-culture existence led me to question early on the relationship between place, citizenship, and belonging. I become particularly troubled by the divisions people create on the basis of imagined nationalist distinctions. It is these territorializing subjectivities that politicians prey on, which justify the border-making strategies that play out in the world today, and which I came to examine in Nauru. My work is inspired by a never-ending drive to jolt people's understandings to push past bordering demarcations and recognize our human commonalities.

From Geneva to Australia to Fiji and Nauru, many people supported me along my journey. My deepest gratitude goes to the islanders and migrants in Nauru who assisted me throughout this research. Many extended their hospitality and generosity, helping to bring this book to life. Nauru is woefully misunderstood and significantly misrepresented. I have tried to do justice to a fractious context. I am undoubtedly fortunate to have assembled a book so transnational in scope, particularly in a situation where many do not have such ease of mobility, and in an island region where the impending prospect of environmental emigration is a very real concern. Above all, it is these injustices that I am trying to make apparent. To those in Nauru and Fiji whose real names I cannot acknowledge here, I give my utmost thanks. Also, special thanks go to my *roro*-making Suva family, my supportive Nauru facilitators, my bumpy back-of-the-bike, fish- and noddy-catching partners in crime, and especially Tuna Frenzy!

I met many inspirational people across my field sites, working in full conviction toward social justice goals. My thanks go to all of the organizations and individuals across Australia who lent their insights and perspectives on what was uniformly agreed to be an unjust arrangement. Many met with me in spite of threats to their employment. I appreciate everyone's time and support even though I cannot individually acknowledge them here for fear of any repercussions to them. To my Melbourne house-sitting family, I give my special thanks.

When I was an early activist, passionate about migration justice but unsure how to direct my energies, Bob Libal, Elaine Chadron, and the Austin Grassroots Leadership team set me on my path of "following value." mónica tereza ortiz remains my Austin decompressing-with-margaritas partner, whose own writings give me tingles. Most of this book came together among the pine trees of the West Coast. At the University of California, Berkeley, the Center for the Study of Law and Society provided my home away from home. Berkeley's Anthropology Department was my stalwart disciplinary base. Cups of tea and conversations helped me draw together the jumble of ramblings that burst out of my time in the Equatorial Pacific. Laura Nader's support and wisdom gave me the bedrock foundation from which to find my way into a new world of theoretical engagement. I cannot acknowledge enough the warm and generous spirit of academics across the UC and Stanford systems: Anna Tsing was an exceptional mentor and remains a wise interlocutor. Hannah Appel, Yvette Cooper, Susan Bibler Coutin, James Ferguson, Rosann Greenspan, Bill Maurer, Calvin Morrill, Tony Platt, Jonathan Simon, Christopher Tomlins, and Michael Watts all drew me into their world through their scholarship, advice, and support, giving me new insights on the intersections of political economy and refugees. Outside the California Republic, Andrew Burridge, Jean and John Comaroff, Deirdre Conlon, Lucy Durán, Nick Gill, Nancy Hiemstra, Angela Impey, and John Speyer offered early guiding thoughts and fantastic opportunities for a young professional that I will remain eternally grateful for. My West Coast walks and talks with Amin Ebrahimi Afrouzi, Krystal Barghelame, Sean Becker, Kseniya Husak, Kavitha Iyengar, and Stephen Nathan provided critical banter and necessary replenishment. Each heartened me with their admirable goals.

Up the West Coast writing trail, the University of Victoria, University of British Columbia, and—over to the East Coast—the University of Toronto and York University gave me opportunities to present, also instilling in me the conviction that, however disturbing I found my theoretical frame, it importantly jolts public understandings. I look forward to future years of continued engagement. My thanks to Alexia Bloch, Leslie Butt, Sarah Close-Humayun, Jennifer Elrick, Jennifer Hyndman, Helen Lansdowne, Bruce Miller, Stephanie Silverman, and Julie Young, in particular.

I am lucky to have had the time to think this through. For this, I thank a writing-up scholarship from Oxford's Anthropology Department. The Social Science Research Council and the Oxford Europaeum Institute supported my early germinations, in particular Josh DeWind and Ronald Skelton through the Dissertation Proposal Development Foundation and Vincent Chetail at the Graduate Institute of Geneva's Global Migration Centre. All my back-and-forths were met with the cozy fireplace of St. Cross College. And importantly, Oxford's Centre on Migration, Policy and Society and the Anthropology Department saw me through the significant bulk of my fieldwork. Vicky Dean and Nathan Grassi were an indispensable team. Jakob Engel, Alice Gerlach, Michael Melia, Seamus Montgomery, Martha Newson, Steph Postar, Lena Rose, and Olivia Vicol were a great doctoral crew over the years. Alexander Betts, Mette Berg, Mary Bosworth, Matthew Gibney, Fernanda Pirie, and Nicholas Van Hear all provided essential guidance. James Bull and Lucy Caroline Evans, continued companionship. A further shout-out to James for creating the Introduction's phosphate equation for me.

The support and inspirational conversations I had as a postdoctoral fellow at the New School's Zolberg Institute on Migration and Mobility were unparalleled. I cannot thank enough Alex Aleinikoff, Alexandra Delano, Abou Farman, Vicky Hattam, Laura Liu, Anne McNevin, Elliott Montgomery, Nitin Sawhney, Everita Silina, Radhika Subramaniam, and Miriam Ticktin. I owe special gratitude to Rocio Carrero, Sam Fox, Gina Mikan, Cayce Pack, Adam Sirois, and Katinka Wijsman for their friendship and conversations.

Since I joined the faculty at the University of North Carolina Wilmington, a number of colleagues have offered their insights to this book, along with their friendship. I especially thank Florentina Andreescu, Hikmet Kocammaner, Jenny Le Zotte, Christina Lord, Erin Michaels, Aaron Peisner, Menaka Raguparan, Candice Robinson, and Blevin Shelnutt. In my department, I am also grateful for the support of Gao Bei, Herb Berg, Chris Carlson, Shannon Chalmers, Lesley Daspit, Theresa Jackson, Anastasia Kuz-Grady, Dan Masters, and Mike Turner. Since moving to the Wilmington coast, I have been lucky to carve out a supportive community: Alexis, Ashik, Dave, Eric, Jeff, John, Kate, Katie, Lani, Nadine, Phil, Shannon, and Steve are shining stars of this porch-rocker backyard crew. My immeasurable thanks to Chae Kwak for his guidance along the way.

My warm gratitude to Biao Xiang for the insightful conversations and connections provided by a visiting fellowship at the Max Planck Institute's Mobility Lab in Halle, and the exceptional work of Jonathan Kraemer. Important conversations were also enabled through a Princeton-Singapore workshop series with Nanyang Technological University and the fantastic support of Laavy Kathiravelu and Sandra Brunnegger. Similarly, my thanks also go to the wondrous Monica Eppinger and the Saint Louis University Law School, Yale University's School of Environmental Studies and Forestry School, Stockholm University, and the faculty and staff who brought together the UCLA Emerging Immigration Scholars Conference. I also appreciate the comments provided by anonymous reviewers for *Mobilities* and *Extractive Industries and Society*, as well as those from the shining stars that are Heath Cabot, Filipe Calvão, Ann Kingsolver, Jana Lipman, Siobhan Mc-Guirk, Adrienne Pine, and Georgina Ramsay. Parts of the Introduction and chapter 4 draw from my article "Violence and Extraction of a Human Commodity: From Phosphate to Refugees in the Republic of Nauru," *Extractive Industries and Society* 6 (4): 1122–1133, © 2019, with permission from Elsevier. Parts of chapter 2 draw from my article "Refugee Extractivism: Law and Mining a Human Commodity in the Republic of Nauru," *Saint Louis University Law Journal* 64 (1): 59–90, reprinted with permission of the *Saint Louis University Law Journal* © 2019, St. Louis University School of Law, St. Louis, Missouri. I also explored some of my arguments in my book chapter "Making a Market in Refugees in the Republic of Nauru," in *Asylum for Sale: Profit and Protest in the Migration Industry*, edited by Adrienne Pine and Siobhan McGuirk (Oakland, CA: PM Press, 2020, 165–180). Thanks to the National Archives at Kew and Paul Johnson for the permission to reprint the British Phosphate Commission photographs, and to Bill Nelson for his brilliant work in creating the map of Nauru. The research and editorial assistance of Jim Lance, Clare Jones, and the Cornell University Press team has made my arguments in this book all the sharper, and I especially thank Jim for remaining committed to this book over the years. I am also indebted to Adriana Cloud, Mary Kate Murphy, and Michelle Scott for such careful work in copyediting, Brock Schnoke in marketing, and to Amron Gravett for indexing.

It was only with Bridget that I would have embarked on the journey that took me from music workshops in British immigration removal centers to the Pacific. Her support and whip-smart intellectual engagements continue to be indispensable to my trajectories. I was fortunate to have caught her on her own exciting moves to Bristol. I look forward to a continued friendship.

Across landmasses, the Morris and Cooke clans have persevered. I truly appreciate how a sailor-style upbringing has been indispensable to my global outlook and research directions. G&G, always there with Popinjays warmth for my UK returns. Jeremy, Rhona, Oliver, Chloe, and the gang, with countryside rambles. To my West Coast grandmother, Ilse, I owe a great deal of these chapters. My parents, Jenny and Derek, have long been committed to our multiple directions and provided immense support as I teased out my path. As someone who has trailblazed her own exciting directions, my sister inspires me on a daily basis. She fills me with sisterly pride, as does our newest honorary Morris-Littman, Aaron, whom we are so lucky to have in our family. I thank both of them for their love and support over the years, and to the exciting times we all have ahead. Mike inspires endless sparkles and smiles. I'm so fortunate to have met such a dream of a voyaging partner who supports my intrepid ventures.

This book starts and ends with mobile pathways. It is only fitting that I dedicate it to the beauty that can come from a life in mobility.

Notes

INTRODUCTION

1. At time of writing, just over one hundred refugees remained on the island, but Nauru was no longer being used as an offshore processing or significant resettlement site. In 2020, the Australian government moved their offshore industry operations back to Christmas Island, an external territory of Australia and another on-again, off-again phosphate-followed-by-refugee industry isle. Australia simultaneously increased maritime border enforcement and boat pushback policies across the region. In 2022, the Australian government agreed to a long-standing offer from New Zealand. Up to 450 refugees, including the remaining refugees in Nauru and those residing in Australia under temporary arrangements, would be resettled in New Zealand over the course of three years. Nauru continues to be financed as part of a spectacle of deterrence, under the understanding that their operations might be restarted in the future.

2. Unpublished data acquired from the Nauruan government during my fieldwork. The International Labor Organization (ILO) also archives material related to employment statistics in Nauru.

3. All names have been changed throughout to protect anonymity.

4. The ideological purchase of the communist fleeing refugee, the Taliban persecuted refugee, and so forth, illustrates how discourses around refugees, democracy, human rights, and liberal freedoms have mixed considerably in the course of valuation. This global hegemony was set in motion with the industry's institutional rise. The institutionalization of the refugee regime found investor support because of its emphasis on pro-Western values, Euroamerican superiority, and progressiveness (Loescher and Scanlan 1986).

5. "Refugee service provider" and "refugee sector" are the terms used by the Australian government, and "organization" denotes any outsourced supplier of provisions or management, irrespective or their commercial or nonprofit status. Organizations are contracted into the Australian Department of Immigration and Border Protection (DIBP), and tenders are available for bidding, largely online, unless conducted privately under closed tendering processes. Since my fieldwork, DIBP has been integrated into the Department of Home Affairs, which is responsible for a number of different portfolios including immigration.

6. These momentary increases were reduced back to 13,750 people for 2020–25 due to the COVID-19 pandemic.

7. All interviews throughout the entirety of my fieldwork sites were conducted with written and oral research consent forms and university ethics clearance. I refer to few government officials by name and only for historical accuracy, never in an interviewee capacity. I have changed all names of people to protect confidentiality and only refer to companies when I was given written or oral consent to do so.

8. The numbers of so-called UMAs are low compared with cross-border movement elsewhere. In 2011 in a "peak season," when there were 4,565 boat arrivals to Australia, over 61,000 UMAs traveled to Italy from North Africa, Greece, and Turkey, and over 100,000 to Yemen from Somalia (Philips and Spinks 2013). Globally, the overwhelming majority of migration is fully authorized, with only 10–15 percent of international migrants estimated as being outside of regulatory systems, most of whom are visa overstayers.

Within these migration patterns, South-South migration is as significant as South-North migration. Hein de Haas (2009) refers to the egoistic statistical inflation in the Africa-Europe directional context as the "myth of invasion." Heath Cabot (2016) also points out that particular global Western "hotspots," such as the Mediterranean, the United States–Mexico border, and Australian maritime borders, have been constructed as crises epicenters, despite the on-the-ground realities that more people migrate across other regions.

9. AusTender is the online government portal where government contracts are available for bidding and published, unless operating under closed tender: https://www.tenders.gov.au.

10. This is not to make an argument against the specificity of place. Instead, it is an effort to think through how more general processes and forms enable diverse capitalist projects in very different locations, and the frictions that eventuate because of *attempted* abstraction and distancing. Appel is also not making the argument that infrastructural assemblages seamlessly move from place to place. Heterogeneity lies beneath the performance of appearance, and performance is also a work-intensive endeavor that should be taken seriously.

11. Although I do not make explicit mention of camps, this very same argument is applicable to the development of refugee camps as extractive sites around the world (Morris 2021a). See also Bhagat (2019) for an insightful discussion of the political economy of refugee camps, which have become lucrative economic investments for UNHCR, INGOs, NGOs, corporate, government, and other local partners.

12. I largely leave Manus and Christmas Island out of my analysis. There are certainly deep connections to Nauru, such as the company town networks that fomented across these sites. But here I seek to illuminate one place in minute detail, deeply exploring the groundedness of a refugee industrial project in situ. Unlike Nauru, the PNG government did not authorize the same degree of external rule from Australia, including the placement of Australians in local government positions. Indeed, several of PNG's government ministers have been outspoken about the deal. The 21 km^2 context of Nauru, on the other hand, presented a world ripe for company town control, as much as local and pioneer boomtown opportunities.

13. Of these arrivals, 70 percent received successful asylum claims, and of them 586 were resettled in Australia, 360 in New Zealand, 19 in Sweden, 10 in Canada, and 4 in Norway. The remaining 486 migrants were refused asylum and deported to their countries of origin or alternative destinations.

14. In the nineteenth and early twentieth centuries, more than a million people were "blackbirded": tricked, forced, or coerced from places such as the Solomon Islands, Gilbert Islands, and Tuvalu into indentured labor or servitude (Banivanua-Mar 2007). Sugar and cotton plantations in Fiji and Queensland and pineapple plantations in Hawaii were themselves colonized regions that were built on migrant and indentured labor.

15. See also work on the continuities between plantation systems in Australia and contemporary seasonal worker programs, which scholars have argued create an unfree workforce and systemic precarity (Petrou and Connell 2019).

16. Australia has a sizable undocumented migrant workforce (recent estimates place this population at 100,000 people). Generally, most workers arrive in Australia by plane on tourist, student or humanitarian visas but overstay their visas or work more than permissible. In some regions of Australia, as much as 80 to 90 percent of the harvest workforces are made up of undocumented workers (Howe and Singh 2020). Alongside this, the Australian government promotes a number of seasonal temporary worker visas in agriculture and other key working sectors. These visa regimes do not allow for pathways to citizenship and, researchers find, institutionalize precarity (Petrou and Connell 2018).

17. I specifically distinguish the figure of the refugee as the commodity. I do so to emphasize how it is the depoliticized, dehistoricized, and universalized figuration of

the refugee—as much as people's bodies—that is abstracted and utilized by governments, organizations, and individuals for a range of value-laden prerogatives. In some cases, I focus more on the broad array of immaterial forms and fetishizing discourses that propel the refugee industry and other actors. In other cases, my focus is on the material circulation of migrants' bodies as capital. I recognize that both are often inextricably linked in industrial contexts.

18. Scholarship critical of antitrafficking discourses has pushed the envelope much further in this regard. Researchers show narratives of migrants as racialized and gendered trafficked victims (O'Connell Davidson 2015) or of sex workers as exploited and vulnerable (Raguparan 2017) to be highly problematic. The depiction of trafficked victims as racialized Others in need of salvation continues tropes of the colonial civilizing mission, whereby white western intervention is required to save black and brown victims. Meanwhile, such narratives help advance the strategic interests of governments and civil society in controlling, disciplining, and limiting the mobility of certain racialized populations.

19. There is a danger in overstating the belief that freedom of movement is neatly geographically partitioned between the Global North and South. Social immobility occurs overwhelmingly in countries in the Global North, where structural barriers also impede people's life chances. So too, in the Global South, cosmopolitan elites are also endowed with plenty of resources and have the ability to move freely. The North/South representation sustains the colonial superiority mentality that plays out in Nauru's refugee politics. Such binaries also reinforce the unmet promises of white privilege used by Australian politicians as a political strategy of blame making, through which the offshoring arrangement partially finds some public support.

20. See Jana Lipman's (2009) insightful work into Guantánamo's social and labor history. Lipman similarly brings to the fore the experiences of local residents in Guantánamo hidden behind populist portrayals, arguing that framings of Guantánamo as an Agambenian space of exception make invisible Cuba and Cuba–United States imperial ties.

21. Global solidarity movements around refugees were brought to the fore with Russia's invasion of the Ukraine. Whiteness became a means of mobilizing solidarity with huge outpourings of sympathy connected to racialized notions of relatedness. Much Western media coverage of the conflict drew on a hierarchy of deservingness based on Global North/Global South binaries, suggesting that Ukrainians should be valued more by virtue of their whiteness and alleged affinity to Europeans. Unlike migrant nationals from Middle Eastern and African countries, Ukrainians were able to access the right to work, housing, healthcare, and education for children in any EU country. At the same time, reports detail how Black and Asian Ukrainian citizens and long-term residents experienced overwhelming discrimination (Bajaj and Stanford 2022). These dynamics reveal both the geopolitics of who a refugee is at particular moments, as well as the ways in which national boundaries are constantly defined through a racialized politics.

22. Lau (2007) describes the concept of "paper families," in which restrictive U.S. immigration policies and practices against Chinese American communities from the late 1800s resulted in an elaborate system of claiming fictive identities. This included the creation of "crib sheets" outlining genealogies, village maps, and other information that could be used during immigration processing.

23. See Pittaway et al. (2010) on the ethics of "stealing stories."

24. Nauru is also home to a mix of Pacific Islanders, Chinese, South Asian, Australian, and New Zealander migrants from a long history of transnational migration and colonial industrialization. I distinguish between migrants living in Nauru more generally and migrants awaiting or having received asylum claims. This is not to negate Nauruans' many migration histories or to depict the island as insular or homogeneous through tropes of indigeneity and sedentarism.

25. Class, race, gender and language all structure experiences of mobility and citizenship, including who is defined as a "migrant," "expat," "émigré," and so forth. I am conscious that even using the term "migrant" conjures up a world of tropes embedded in processes of racialization and coloniality (Erel, Murji, and Nahaboo 2016), and do so cautiously.

26. Following the Protocol's launch, lobbied for by expansionist commissioners Felix Schnyder (1960) and then Sadruddin Aga Khan (1965), refugees doubled in number, from 2,356,991 to 4,518,659 just ten years later. UNHCR's annual budget soared to over US$500 million by 1980. Most staff moved outside of headquarters or were—and continue to be—recruited specifically for the field. See Morris (2021a) for a deeper discussion of these forms of institutional expansionism.

1. BUILDING THE WORKINGMAN'S DREAM

1. There is a powerful body of literature on the politics of landscape and memory in the transition of low-income regions to prison economies (Schept 2020; Story 2019) and on the overlapping political economies of plantation to prison industries (Gilmore 2007; Oshinsky 1996). I also find synergy here with McKittrick's work on the continuities between plantation pasts and futures, which carry histories of racialized violence that "folds over to repeat itself anew" (2013, 4).

2. Nancy Hiemstra (2019) looks at these tactical forms of distancing in terms of "chaotic geographies" that create a sense of dislocation and insecurity among detained migrants but allow for inordinate profiteering by private contractors. Nick Gill (2009) also examines the power effects of moving detained migrants across facilities on the advocacy and support practices of activists and sector employees.

3. See also research on the placement of toxic radioactive waste sites on the land of indigenous communities in Australia (Green 2017).

4. Margaret Crawford (1995) provides one of the most informative discussions of company towns, from which the title of this chapter is derived.

5. While the island was administered as a colony, the Germans did not want to use the word "colonies," and instead preferred the term *Schutzebiete* or "protected territory." In reality, German protectorates were administered no differently from colonies, with full German sovereignty over the area (Weeramantry 1992).

6. The American Protestant mission first sent Gilbertese missionaries to Nauru in 1887. They met with little success and soon departed the island. However, they did leave an adherent in Chief Auweieda, who conducted small religious gatherings after their departure and prior to the Delaportes' arrival (Maude 1971).

7. Missionary reports, journals, and letters from this time provide a great deal of information on these circulated representations, most of which are available at USP's Suva and Nauru archives.

8. These were highly gendered white heteronormative spaces that have much in common with the regulation of imperial domestic spaces described by Stoler (1995). The comfortable living conditions of Nauru's company town extractive setting combined with the intimate control of labor and domestic life.

9. Robert Vitalis (2007) makes a similar finding in oil company towns, describing the hierarchies of discrimination, racism, and labor inequalities that move alongside oil company town forms. Mining firms often organized drilling in ways that best inhibited the organization of unions, particularly by dividing and subordinating labor by race.

10. See the personal war diary of Patrick Cook, a local Nauruan sent to Truk, kept from December 8, 1940, to August 9, 1945. See also the diary of Nai Fai Ma, a Chinese resident in Nauru during the Japanese occupation, kept between 1942 and 1945. Copies

of both are housed at USP Nauru and the National Archives in Canberra. The National Archives also holds a number of short accounts of this period in the papers of R. Maslyn Williams, who extensively chronicled the history of the BPC.

11. Scouting in Nauru began in the 1920s through the initiative of a German phosphate worker. Harold Hurst, the leader of the Geelong Scouts, then helped fully establish the Nauru Scouts in the 1930s, setting up links with the Geelong Rovers. These sorts of local initiatives were popular with the BPC as corporate social responsibility strategies for their annual UN reports. However, the Nauru Scouts also facilitated strategic networks for Nauruans, which were utilized in the eventual push for independence.

12. The Nauruan government later managed to retain and still lease out the office building to Jacob's Engineering, a NASA engineering contractor.

13. US$70 billion went through 450 banks in Nauru in 1998 (Hughes 2004).

14. The Nauruan government severed their diplomatic relations with Taiwan in 2002, receiving US$130 million from China. In 2005, they switched back to Taiwan. In exchange, Nauru received US$4 million to repay Kiribati and Tuvaluan workers. In 2006, Nauru received another US$10 million to bail out Air Nauru, doubled health care assistance, and a monthly stipend of AU$5,000 to each government minister. The Taiwanese government maintains a full-time diplomatic and developmental presence in Nauru, currying favor with the Nauruan government for UN recognition through a number of agricultural and medical projects and cash funding. Stipend payments continued during my fieldwork. Although this was described in global media as evidence of government corruption, the majority of government ministers were openly generous with their constituents, handing out cash when requested. This also characterizes some of the government's lack of financial foresight in a country defined by the dictum "Tomorrow will take care of itself." See Dobell (2007) for a further discussion on the "diplomatic chess" of Taiwanese versus Chinese recognition in the Asia-Pacific.

15. The ABC documentary *The Howard Years* (2009) details this conversation. The Australian government's negotiations with surrounding countries as offshore sites and their varying responses (including Kiribati, Fiji, and Tuvalu) are also well documented in Australian parliamentary reports.

16. The Migration Amendment (Excision from Migration Zone) Act 2001 excised Christmas Island, Ashmore Island, and Cartier Islands, shortly followed by Cocos Keeling Islands. From 2001 to 2005, the Howard government made ad hoc attempts to excise further areas from Australia's migration zone. Although sometimes thwarted by the opposition and other parties in the Senate, they gradually extending territory excision to over five thousand places (Carrington 2006). The act particularly angered refugee advocates because it did not just interdict boats from reaching Australian territorial waters but also disallowed migrants' asylum claims in excised Australian territories.

17. See the Australian human rights lawyer Julian Burnside's critique of this angle in the 2015 essay "The Drowning Excuse." Available at: https://www.julianburnside.com.au /the-drowning-excuse/.

18. The idea of the RCF carries a long organizational pedigree. Previous incarnations of UNHCR, including the Nansen Office and the Intergovernmental Committee on Refugees but particularly the International Refugee Organization, found great financial success and institutional growth from moving thousands of refugees around the international state system, and to hitherto new geographical contexts. With its specialized staff and fleet of more than forty ships, IRO relocated more than one million refugees from Europe to the Americas, Israel, South Africa, and Oceania between 1947 and 1951 (Amar 2014, 37). See Morris (2021a) for an analysis of the international refugee regime's expansion on the basis of UNHCR's strategic advancement. See Kneebone (2014) for more discussion of the Bali Process.

19. The Green Party instead supported a Tasmanian Solution as a means of keeping refugee processing within Australian mainland operations, while also resurging Tasmania's beleaguered economy.

20. See *Plaintiff M70 / 2011 v. Minister for Immigration and Citizenship*; *Plaintiff M106/2011 v. Minister for Immigration and Citizenship*.

21. Nauru received AU$50 million in aid from Russia for diplomatically recognizing the two South Caucasus Republics.

22. Kevin Rudd was prime minister under the Labour Party between 2007 and 2010. Under a leadership challenge, Gillard assumed the office of prime minister and leader of the Labour party in June 2010. Rudd then challenged the leadership in 2012, not long before the state election, citing the inability of Gillard to achieve party victory in the upcoming election. At the February 2012 leadership ballot, Gillard retained the vote. A second leadership spill took place in June 2013, in which Rudd was elected as Labour leader. Rudd was then defeated by Abbott. See P. Kelly (2014) for a good synopsis of the political period.

23. As Appel (2019, 154) argues in what could very well be applied from oil to the global refugee industry, the measurement of standards is immaterial, and in practice there are no universalizing standards between radically different extractive sites. Rather, the very presence of a standards discourse forms part of the "licit life of capitalism" and routinized violence that renders lawful extractive operations and allow companies to "get away with almost anything." See Morris (2016) for a discussion of the dangers of applying "standards" and "good industry practices" to the governance of migrants' lives.

24. See Beresford et al. (2012) for a critical recounting of the history of colonial-era educational programs directed at indigenous Australians. See also Libesman and Briskman (2018) for a discussion of the continuity of colonialism in social work with indigenous Australians, and Coddington (2014) on the overlapping "logics of enclosure" for indigenous and asylum seeker populations in Australia.

25. In 2002, the US government defined Nauru as a "rogue state" under the Patriot Act, forbidding American banks, mutual funds providers, securities dealers, and others to do business with the country. The measure also blocked foreign banks using these accounts from doing business in Nauru. These sanctions, which cut Nauru off from the entire US financial system, were eventually lifted in 2008, after a great deal of political wrangling.

26. In 2007, the Nauruan government reinvigorated their Cuban ties on a diplomatic visit to Havana, during which time Nauru's foreign minister, David Adeang, extolled Cuban policies and criticized US foreign policy. The Cuban government provides medical training to Nauru and other Pacific island states, reciprocally deploying Cuban doctors to Nauru on an intermittent basis.

27. Under Operation Weasel, President Ludwig Scotty agreed to set up a shop-front Nauru embassy in Beijing, through which the CIA could smuggle North Korean defectors in collaboration with the New Zealand government. When accused by China, both the US and New Zealand governments denied the scheme, pointing the finger at the Nauruan government. Nauru closed their embassies in Beijing and Washington, DC, in August 2003, never receiving the promised amount.

28. Car rental services became a lucrative form of local revenue. Some entrepreneurial Nauruans found great profits from shipping jeeps to Nauru from Japan, from where they were then leased to the Australian government and their private contractors at hugely inflated costs.

29. Waqa, a former schoolteacher, and minister for education, defeated opposition nominee Roland Kun in the 2013 elections, one year after the refugee industry restarted under Dabwido. Kun had been part of the Dabwido government (Waqa was not), but resigned over a disagreement with Dabwido. Dabwido stepped aside to allow for Waqa

to put himself forward as an electoral candidate, following which he was elected into office. In August 2019, Waqa finished third in his electoral district of Boe, which lost him a seat in parliament and the power to stay in office. Instead, Lionel Aingimea, a lawyer and politician, was elected as the new president.

30. IMF and World Bank involvement is often presented in terms of small-state predation. However, a number of prominent figures in the Nauruan government described to me how they actively solicited IMF and World Bank involvement. Well versed in post-development critique and the repercussions of involving the IMF and the World Bank, they were keen on the financial stability that they believed involvement would bring in the long term. The IMF and the World Bank had previously refused to work with the Nauruan government under Rene Harris because of the state's legacy of phosphate corruption. Their reinvolvement with Nauru took much local government persuading.

2. MINERAL MEETS MIGRANT METALLURGIES

1. Nauru's 2019 biological diversity report details the threats to the black and brown noddy that account for this decline, including loss and disturbance of nesting sites, and unsustainable harvesting. Tagged noddy birds have been found as far off as the Northwest Hawaiian Islands, 4,000 kilometers to the north, as local noddy populations dip to worryingly low levels (Buden 2008).

2. Land preservation and redevelopment is of course an extractive industry in its own right, replete with alienating effects and power-laden environmental campaigns (Murray Li 2008; Smith 2007). Such discourses have been used by the Nauruan government and local landowners on multiple occasions (Weeramantry 1992). Amy McLennan (2017) puts the failure to expand community garden efforts in Nauru down to the imposition of agriculture and growing practices in places that likely never had them.

3. AusAid (the Australian Agency for International Development) was the Australian government's international development department. In 2013, the department was integrated into the Department for Foreign Affairs and Trade (DFAT). DFAT maintain an active office in Nauru, staffed by both seconded Australians and Nauruans.

4. Land and life in Nauru are explicitly entangled as commodities. These resource entanglements were noticeably stark in how companies sometimes operated across—and also reciprocally enhanced—the phosphate and refugee industries. In 2012, Sydney businessman Mozammil Bhojani, who held an AU$2.5 million contract in Nauru for the Anibare Lodge refugee resettlement accommodation and the Budapest Hotel for industry workers, was charged by the Australian Federal Police (AFP) after being publicly found to have paid Nauruan officials over AU$100,000 for reduced-price phosphate shipments.

5. The Australian government imported bottled water to Nauru for asylum seekers and all industry personnel, which later became a major source of local revenue from import customs and taxation schemes. They also installed a special desalination tank at the RPCs for nonpotable water, in addition to expanding and largely running Nauru's state desalination setup through refugee industry contractors, at immense local financial profit. However, the financial profits can hardly be said to have benefited the health of the vast majority of Nauruans.

6. In her research, McLennan (2017, 2020) traces the colonial histories surrounding poor nutritional health on Nauru and the rising prevalence of diet-related noncommunicable diseases, including obesity, diabetes, and cardiovascular disease.

7. Antje Missbach (2015) extensively discusses boat pushbacks into Indonesia and the "ebb and flow" of maritime trading economies.

8. Although financially successful, IOM has become a marginalized industry player among the industry sector as a result of their close collaborations—some say mercenary work—with state governments in managing human migration. See Ashutosh and

Mountz (2011) and Andrijasevic and Walters (2010) for critical discussions into AVR programs and IOM at large.

9. At the time, all asylum seekers carried a USB stick with biometric data. During my fieldwork, IHMS was attempting to coordinate their mainland medical records system into a cloud-based system that allowed for data sharing across Australia's offshore refugee industry: between Christmas Island, offshore processing sites, and the mainland.

10. There is a strong literature on the pathologization of refugees as objects of medico-scientific knowledge (Fassin and Rechtman 2009; Malkki 1995; Ticktin 2006) and the cultural constitution of trauma within the asylum process (Marlowe and Adamson 2011).

11. Over the twelve months between November 23, 2012, and November 29, 2013, there were fifty-three medical transfers or evacuations from Nauru to the mainland (JAC 2014). These numbers dropped dramatically over the years. However, in February 2019, the Australian Parliament passed the Medevac Bill into law in a shock defeat to the government. This piece of legislation streamlined the process for asylum seekers and refugees in Nauru or Manus Island to receive medical care in Australia if unavailable on that island, allowing close to two hundred people to receive treatment in Australia. The contentious medevac laws lasted for nine months before being repealed. Those who did travel to Australia under these laws were housed in a mixture of securitized hotels and community detention centers in Melbourne and Brisbane. Some were allowed to move into Australia on temporary bridging visas, while others took up alternative third-country resettlement offers or were returned to their country of origin. In 2022, the Australian government agreed to a long-standing resettlement offer with the New Zealand government, which added to a preexisting resettlement arrangement with the United States.

12. See among many high-profile struggles—including a case where Australian doctors refused to discharge patients back to Nauru—those documented by Allard (2015), Beech (2017), and Hoang (2016). Tremendous activist protest also coalesced around the 2019 medevac legislation to allow for those who had traveled in the 2019 period to Australia to receive medical care to stay in the country.

13. Following Australian court intervention and activist campaigning, by February 2019 all children and their families were removed from Nauru for resettlement in the United States or outside the media radar in Australia.

14. CD has become popular among advocates, catalyzing a whole new wave of industry settlements. Despite CD being described as humanitarian, research has found that incarcerating people in the community is still filled with the dangers that the asylum system presents, all governed by for-profit corporations (Gill 2013; Morris 2017).

15. Depending on Wi-Fi capacity, which can sometimes be erratic in Nauru, refugee assessment databases include the results of each asylum seeker's medical tests, such as those made by IHMS.

16. In Australia, the Abbott Liberal government removed legal defense funding for asylum claimants from the federal budget for 2014–2015. From March 2014, all migrants lodging asylum claims without an immigration permit or those undergoing secondary reassessment through a refugee tribunal are no longer provided with free legal representation through the Immigration Advice and Application Assistance Scheme in Australia. This is unless they meet strict criteria of disadvantage, such as mental health concerns or are unaccompanied minors. In these cases, depending on the discretion of what is now the Department of Home Affairs, individuals are eligible for government-funded legal assistance under the Primary Application Information Service. Because of concerns around these cuts, most of the legal work continues funded by private donors, through trained volunteers, or as part of the pro-bono arm of large commercial firms' work, albeit to a heavily reduced extent.

17. The significant literature on the construction of PTSD as a scientific condition shows how diverse peoples are brought within the same framework of understanding centered on the diagnostic category of trauma (Fassin and Rechtman 2009; Young 1995).

18. Bosworth (2011) and Hasselberg (2016) both detail the trend towards excluding foreign nationals based on minor infractions as a method of state selection.

19. Between 2012 and 2016, the Australian government reported that 540 asylum seekers took up this offer from Nauru (Karlsen 2016).

20. For example, see, on their websites, Amnesty Australia's "Australia and Cambodia Should Scrap Asylum Seeker Deal," the Asylum Seeker Resource Centre's "Fact Sheet: Cambodia Agreement," and a number of posts from Human Rights Watch across 2014, including "Australia: Reconsider Nauru Refugee Transfers to Cambodia" and "Australia/Cambodia: Deal Puts Refugees at Risk."

21. Since July 1, 2015, the RRT amalgamated into the Administrative Appeals Tribunal, with refugee decisions reviewed by a Migration and Refugee Division within the AAT. Other than creating efficiency with staffing and processes, this has not changed the RRT's legislative responsibilities. The tribunal retains its own legislation.

22. See also the "Comparative RSD Systems—Nauru" and "Refugee Processing on Nauru" papers presented at the International Association of Refugee Law Judges 2014 conference in Tunis, and again at the Kaldor Centre for Refugee Law's Annual Conference in 2015 by the principal Australian member of Nauru's Refugee Status Review Tribunal (Mackinnon 2014, 2015).

23. On March 12, 2018, Nauru withdrew from using the High Court of Australia as its highest appellate court. Instead, the government developed a Nauru court of appeal composed of regional Pacific islander judges. Commentators expressed concerns about the motivations behind this decision, while acknowledging the importance of the country to determine its government institutions. The withdrawal came at a time when a group of Nauruans remained under prosecution for anti-government protests (described in detail in chapter 4), as well as during the reassessment of asylum seekers under the appeals process. On the other hand, supporters remarked that using a state court of appeal might streamline a previously scattered decision-making system. It would make appeals more accessible, with asylum seekers and low-income Nauruans able to participate in person, and with a much wider and binding jurisdiction.

24. This is by no means to say that freedom of movement is alive and well for the great majority of people in the Global North. Significant poverty and other mobility impediments exist inside industrialized countries, many of which were brought starkly to light during the COVID-19 pandemic. Historical race regimes and unequal patterns of capitalist organization also explain these systems of mobility inequality in place.

3. SECURING THE OFFSHORE INDUSTRY

1. Car accidents remain one of the most significant causes of death in Nauru. Statistics are difficult to obtain on this front. In one of the last published studies, Taylor and Thoma (1985) calculated that 60 percent of accidental deaths in Nauru involved a motor vehicle, and the mortality rate was five times higher among Nauruans than Australians. During my fieldwork period alone, three people died from motorcycle and car accidents in two different incidents. This included Nauru's director of public prosecutions Wilisoni Kurisaqila and, separately, two teenage Nauruan girls.

2. Colonial-era practices of hygiene and sanitation played an important part in the biopolitical management of populations. Across the nineteenth and twentieth centuries, overseas imperial expansion was entangled with medicine and public health initiatives (Bashford 2004).

3. Satirical takes on Nauru's early characterization as "Pleasant Island" have become tediously predictable at this stage. For example, in September 2020, Amnesty International launched a podcast series, *Witness*, where they investigate "some of the most dangerous and volatile places on earth." Their second episode, focused on Nauru, was called "Pleasant Island."

4. O'Neill (2008) provides a helpful discussion into conflicting forms of refugee activism in Australia.

5. In August 2016, a PNG Supreme Court ruling, spearheaded by Australian lawyers together with a local PNG lawyer, ruled the Manus processing center as illegal and unconstitutional because of the significant Australian government involvement. Instead, migrants at the facility were moved to a nearby air naval base, and then the capital Port Moresby, as successive Australian politicians expressed it, so as "never to reach Australia." The mining-and-energy logistics support firm JDA Wokman—later distancing themselves through a subsidiary known as Applus Wokman—received the AU$44 million contract to resettle refugees in Port Moresby.

6. See https://www.julianburnside.com.au/peter-dutton/.

7. Pupavac (2008) argues that campaigns for the humanitarian inclusion of asylum seekers and refugees often deepen racialized and gendered stereotypes of "good" refugees versus "bad" criminals. This framing can reinforce a victim-villain binary and legitimize other forms of incarceration.

8. It is not part of my intention to uncover what did or did not occur; nor can the toxic exposures of this industry be adequately understood by answering this question. Instead, I am concerned with how conflicts symptomatic of this extractive industry were represented. In this regard, I am indebted to the work of Michelle Murphy (2016), who moves beyond proving or disproving the contested reality of chemical exposures to consider how exposures are materialized and imbued with uncertainty. Making judgments about the claims of injury can become too easily plugged into activist arguments that rank one individual over another or reinforce the need for more labor controls within an overall toxic industry.

9. The website https://xborderoperationalmatters.wordpress.com/tag/hestadivest/ details the concerted efforts that went into this campaign outcome.

10. To further add to this revolving-door syndrome, the construction firm Canstruct in Nauru took over the asylum seeker and refugee management contract from Transfield Services (BroadSpectrum) in 2017.

11. Mares and Newman (2007) bring together advocates' autobiographical accounts of the reasons and challenges behind involvement in the refugee sector. Their collection gives a fuller picture of the traumas of involvement in this industry environment. Numerous personal accounts and reports over the years also speak volumes to the ethical challenges that practitioners encountered (Briskman and Doe 2016; D. Isaacs 2016; Morris 2022; Zion 2019).

12. The graphic novel *At Work in Our Detention Centres: A Guard's Story* (2014) is an illustrated narration of the experiences of a former Serco guard, the contractor for the Australian mainland immigration detention center. It provides a powerful first-hand glimpse of the tolls of this kind of work and resonates with many of my findings in Nauru.

13. In industry sectors where there were insufficient numbers of trained Nauruan workers, Australian contractors, such as IHMS, the corporate medical provider on the island, moved toward hiring foreign workers from the Philippines over Australia as another way to pay lower wages and decrease the propensity for activism.

14. For example, after the high-profile riots on Manus Island in 2014, in which one person was killed, it was local security guards who were convicted in PNG's Supreme

Court and sentenced to ten years in prison. The tragic event was blamed on the lack of industry professionalism of Manusians.

15. Several former industry workers, particularly social workers, published articles, gave interviews, or became high-profile spokespersons against offshoring after their experiences working in these industry environments. Many organizations and individuals engaged in policy advocacy behind the scenes, leveraging their high-profile networks to push back incrementally against the offshoring arrangement. Save the Children's CEO, Paul Ronalds, gave a number of media interviews, defending the NGO's contractual involvement in Nauru on this basis. After Save the Children lost their contract in 2015, the administration became more publicly vocal about their stance, collaborating on later reports such as *At What Cost? The Human and Economic Cost of Australia's Detention Policies 2019.* Their contractual involvement, however, still remains heavily critiqued.

16. As Paige West (2016) shows in Papua New Guinea, the representational practices of nature and culture have a deep history specifically in Oceania. Past colonial accounts describe an exotic world that is alluring and romantic, yet also repulsive and dangerous, but above all prime for discovery by intrepid white explorers. This fantasy jungle world structured the creation of the colonial economy in phosphate mining in Nauru through to the refugee industry as it endures today.

17. See the Australian Lawyers Alliance's 2016 report *Untold Damage: Workplace Health and Safety in Immigration Detention Under the Work, Health and Safety Act 2011.*

18. At the time of my fieldwork, the Australian government had not yet ratified OPCAT. After much civil society pressure, they ratified OPCAT in 2017.

19. As part of the ratifying requirements for CAT, a small monitoring team from the SPT must have unrestricted access to any place of human confinement on an intermittent basis. Under OPCAT, signatory governments are required to set up a further state inspectorate or "national preventative mechanism" (NPM). During my fieldwork, the Nauruan government was debating how best to designate an NPM in such a small island context. They decided that a new position should be created of a Nauru Ombudsman, who would be an expatriate appointed by the chief justice to emphasize that individual's distance. The creation of a Nauruan Ombudsman was something that Nauruan politicians had long been interested in advancing during the Rene Harris government's phosphate-squandering years (Ratuva 2011).

20. Media reports and opposition political statements circulated widely at the time of this denial, such as Human Rights Watch's "What Nauru Is Hiding from Danish Lawmakers," August 31, 2016, and the Guardian's "MP Andrew Wilkie Says Nauru Visa Denial Proves Australia 'Has Much to Hide,'" September 6, 2016. Similar media reports later followed the Nauruan government's disallowing MSF to provide psychological and psychiatric healthcare to Nauruans and refugees in Nauru from November 2017 to October 2018. Shortly before that, MSF had released a report, *Infinite Despair* (2018), documenting the extreme mental health suffering in Nauru.

21. Factory tours and tours of toxic sites are common in industrial settings around the world. In tours sponsored by toxin-producing companies or government agencies, narratives are typically framed within "discourses of safety and containment, industrial progress, and objective science" (Pezzullo 2007, 4), designed to provide good publicity for the company.

22. See, for example, Amnesty and Human Rights Watch reports such as *Australia: Appalling Abuse, Neglect of Refugees on Nauru* (2016) and *Island of Despair: Australia's "Processing" of Refugees on Nauru* (2016); secret filming by BBC reporter Sarah McDonald with the Australian refugee rights activist Kate Durham in August 2002, which culminated in the BBC film *Australia's Pacific Solution* that lambasted Nauru as a

dump; and a June 2013 BBC Newsnight report from Nick Bryant. Bryant was granted media access but relied on the consultancy of refugee defense lawyers and Nauruan government opposition, producing a narrative that targeted the Nauruan government.

23. In the phosphate-wealth heyday, Nauruans became subject to an extreme level of exploitation. For example, real estate agents grossly inflated the prices charged to Nauruan government for investments in Melbourne, making vast profits. The Nauruan government was also advised to invest AU$60 million into banking through the law firm of Allen, Allen, and Helmsley, who disappeared with the money, most of which was never recovered. Similar examples of wealth predation on the Nauruan government occurred across Europe, the United States, and the Pacific (Hughes 2004).

24. The Human Rights Commission was one of the few of Australia's major industry regulators embargoed from Nauru, under much publicity from campaigners. The Nauruan government invited HRC staff to tour the RPCs and resettlement houses, but in an informal capacity. The HRC's formal workforce exclusion from Nauru relates to their public stance against offshore processing. In Australia, their work around migrants at large (not just asylum seekers and refugees) is similar to the Commonwealth Ombudsman in that they audit processing operations, but in line with international rather than national legal guidelines. This has placed them in a somewhat adversarial position to the Australian government. The HRC, like the Commonwealth Ombudsman, have a consumer complaints branch where they receive complaints from asylum seekers about the facilities in which they are housed. The HRC retained this aspect of their work in Nauru through emails or letters, as they do in Australia. They also managed specific human risks in the PTA section—before asylum seekers were sent to Nauru—which operated in Christmas Island on Australian territory. The HRC still conducts regular auditing inspections of the Christmas Island facilities, following the move back to Christmas Island as the regional industry hub.

25. "Refugees on Naoero—Nauru," Facebook, October 19, 2016.

4. RESOURCE FRICTIONS

1. Hypermasculinization has been sustained through sports and weightlifting, in which Nauruans hold Olympic titles. Biersack and Macintyre (2017) discuss the role of sports in the production of Pacific Islander masculinity. Sports was a crucial part of colonial "civilizing missions" to redirect islanders from tribal warfare to colonial warfare and instill a set of values associated with the cult of male athleticism. Sports, militarism, and "precolonial conceptions of an ethnicized warriorhood" merged to articulate a warrior ideal for postcolonial times (Biersack 2016, 199).

2. This is a strategy typical of settler colonial governance, where deploying "native police" became a popular means of protecting investments by bringing order to "disorderly frontiers" (Nettelbeck and Ryan 2017). In Nauru, the native police force enabled phosphate extractors to realize their vision, while simultaneously fulfilling a humanitarian requirement to civilize the populace and bring them under colonial authority.

3. The AFP is stationed to provide in-country support to the majority of smaller island states such as Kiribati, Niue, Tuvalu, and the Marshalls. Not long after the refugee industry first started in Nauru in 2001, the Australian and Nauruan governments established a Nauru Police Force Police Capacity Program. The Nauruan government requested the police training program when brokering the development projects attached to the offshoring industry arrangement. Like the legal governance interests once advanced by the BPC, the Nauruan government were keen to rebuild their police force structures after the phosphate crash a few years before. The AFP maintains a permanent residency in Nauru, where staff assist in training projects as elicited by the NPF. They also fund equipment for the Nauruan Police Force.

4. Nauru also enacted new child protection legislation (Child Protection and Welfare Act 2016), drawing on regional assistance funding under the UNICEF Pacific's Child Protection Programme. This was before all asylum seeker and refugee children were moved from Nauru to Australia.

5. Waqa survived a no-confidence motion in response to the deportations in January 2014.

6. See, for example, "Nauru Opposition MP Roland Kun Labels Government a Dictatorship after Suspensions Upheld" (ABC 2014b).

7. Available at: https://www.abc.net.au/news/2015-06-08/nauru-president-and-justice-minister-allegedly-bribed/6530038. The Nauruan government released the following media statement in retaliation: http://www.naurugov.nr/government-information-office/media-release/nauru-blasts-abc-730-as-biased-conspiring-to-destabilise-govt.aspx.

8. In 2021, Getax was charged by the Australian Federal Police for its attempts to bribe Nauruan politicians to further its phosphate exports business.

9. As is common with strategically thought-out struggles, locals in mining districts sometimes use civilizational discourses that might be seen as racist and paternalistic in conflicts with mining companies (Macintyre and Foale 2002).

10. See, for example, the BBC's 2015 headline, "Australia to Raise Concerns with Nauru about Rule of Law," and the NZ Lawyer's "Rule of Law under Threat in Nauru" of that same year.

11. In a twist to the story, the New Zealand government gave Kun expedited citizenship as a humanitarian entrant in July 2016, after his initial attempts to return to his New Zealander wife were blocked by the Nauruan government. The media headlines that circulated at the time speak to the civilizational representations that course through this context: of the well-organized, advanced culture of the West saving the brown native from an unimaginable fate. See, for example, the 2016 headlines from the *Sydney Morning Herald*: "Escape from Nauru: How Ex-MP Roland Kun Slipped the Net to New Zealand," and from the *Guardian*: "Nauru Opposition MP Secretly Granted NZ Citizenship Flees to Wellington" and "'I Couldn't Crack Up': Nauru Opposition MP Recounts His Dramatic Escape to New Zealand."

12. See, for example, the ABC's report from June 29, 2015, "Nauru Must Be Held to Account for Its Human Rights Abuses."

5. *EKAMAWIR OMO*

1. Augoustinos et al. (2015), Malkki (1996), and Rajaram (2002) all provide important critiques of essentialized and racialized representations of "refugees" as engrained with innate cultural or tribal properties.

2. Multiculturalism is a conceptually and practically messy term that generally refers to the coexistence and state promotion of "other cultures." Lentin and Titley (2011) provide a powerful discussion of how coded evasions of "multiculturalism" gloss over racist structures through the language of cultural diversity.

3. See Gatrell (2011) for a good discussion of the development of World Refugee Year as a global industry promotional campaign. See also Morris (2021a) for an exploration of twentieth-century representations of refugees and marketing techniques that helped establish the conditions for the refugee industry's meteoric rise.

4. Since 2013, Melbourne's RISE: Refugees, Survivors and Ex-Detainees has staged a public boycott over celebrating Refugee Week because of the policy of offshoring asylum. Their boycott has continued in response to the use of refugees as a marketing tool by the Australian government and UNHCR while mandatory detention, conflict, and displacement carries on unabated.

5. See, for example, UNHCR's online refugee-experience game, *Against All Odds*, developed in 2006.

6. This is a major critique of multiculturalism, wherein an "excessive emphasis on diversity" paradoxically serves to "reify differences" (Bloemraad and Wright 2014, 303).

7. In 2015, 817 Nauruans were employed at the RPCs, in comparison to 658 foreign workers.

8. See Morris (2022) for an examination of the ethical challenges and differing rationales of Australian practitioners employed in Nauru.

9. See, for example, Meade (2016).

6. BITTER MONEY

1. This budget allocation covers overall planned expenditures for Nauru and Manus together, including industry contracts. It does not cover the development aid packages for either region through DFAT—nor the many informal financial requests made by the Nauruan government. It also does not cover additional aspects of Australian border enforcement, including regional cooperation deterrence measures (AU$104.4 million), their regional Airline Liaison Officer Program to identify attempted undocumented travelers or asylum seekers flying to Australia (AU$7.7 million), immigration detention on the Australian mainland and the Christmas Island arrangement (AU$1.27 billion), Australian asylum tribunals (AU$54.8 million), and resettlement services in Australia (AU$573.7 million). These figures are available in the Australian 2021–2022 budget.

2. The ABC was later heavily criticized for using old photographs of facilities no longer in use, and footage of men hitting each other with steel poles taken from a YouTube video called "Who Let the Dogs Out," posted by a user known as "NoRulz." The Nauruan government released a response, given next to no publicity (Loop 2016). Earlier that year, the ABC had also been forced to apologize for alleging on a program that a five-year-old asylum seeker boy had been raped in Nauru.

3. Such A Human (@SuchNigel), "We are here and still suffering #Nauru," Twitter, January 25, 2017, 11:48 p.m., https://twitter.com/SuchNigel/status/824162035621593089.

4. The depiction of refugee-camp queue jumping has acquired popular currency in Australia. One (among many) of the Australian government's populist arguments for advancing the offshore arrangement is that asylum seekers circumvent approved channels to expedite their cases. However, many advocates point out that in reality there is no orderly queue, rather, the resettlement system operates as an ever-changing discretionary process.

5. Toward the end of my fieldwork in 2015, the Nauruan government, fed up with bearing the brunt of global accusations, contracted a Brisbane public relations team, Mercer PR. Although Mercer PR was contracted to manage the Nauruan government's negative publicity, Mercer themselves became the subject of activist targets. Their workplace practices in Brisbane were scrutinized by activist campaigners and their other clients publicly named and lobbied to divest.

6. For example, the managing director of Bendigo Bank, Mike Hirst, gave a 2016 interview on ABC Radio about the ethics of their presence in Nauru, followed by a formal statement from the company. In April 2016, Westpac Bank cut all ties with the Nauruan government.

7. "Refugees on Naoero—Nauru," Facebook, 2016. The page has since been removed.

8. See the Australian Senate inquiry "Serious Allegations of Abuse, Self-Harm and Neglect of Asylum Seekers in Relation to the Nauru Regional Processing Centre, and Any Like Allegations in Relation to the Manus Regional Processing Centre." From November 2016 to March 2017, hearings were held across Australia. The committee of senators released their damning report in April 2017. Shortly thereafter, the Global Legal Action Network and the Stanford International Human Rights Clinic submitted a communication to the Office of

the Prosecutor at the International Criminal Court charging the Australian government of crimes against humanity. In 2018, the National Justice Project lodged two class action lawsuits representing the remaining asylum seekers in Nauru and Manus Island, charging that they were subjected to torture, crimes against humanity, and the intentional infliction of harm by the Australian government. As of writing, the lawsuits were still ongoing.

9. See for example characteristic reports and headlines such as "Australia: Reconsider Nauru Refugee Transfers to Cambodia" (Human Rights Watch 2014), "Is Cambodia Engulfed in a Human Rights Crisis?" (ABC 2014), "Australia Is Trying to Get Refugees to Resettle in Cambodia and Unsurprisingly They Refuse to Go" (*Time Magazine* 2015), and "Australia Joins UN Condemnation of Cambodia But Refugee Deal Remains" (*Guardian* 2018).

10. In 2016, the New Zealand government offered to take 150 refugees per year from Nauru and Manus as part of their annual resettlement quota. This offer was declined at the time. The offer was then re-extended by New Zealand and declined by the Turnbull coalition government in the summer of 2016. The offer continued to be renewed over successive years. It was not until 2022 when public attention was focused on the pandemic that the Australian government agreed to accept New Zealand's long-standing offer. Under the deal's terms, New Zealand will resettle up to 450 refugees living in Nauru or facilities in Australia over three years. At the time, only 110 refugees remained in Nauru and 1,100 in Australian processing facilities. This arrangement does not apply to those refugees who remain in Manus Island; instead they have the option to move to Nauru or resettle in the United States.

11. Trudeau promoted a liberal government policy toward refugees, including a 2015 election promise to welcome twenty-five thousand refugees from Syria. Once in power, Trudeau's Liberals switched the name of the Immigration Department to Immigration, Refugees and Citizenship Canada to highlight this concern. In 2017, after then US president Donald Trump put a four-month hold on allowing migrants into the United States on refugee visas and enacted an infamous "travel ban" that barred travelers from seven Muslim-majority countries (later expanded to thirteen countries), Trudeau famously tweeted that refugees were welcome in Canada.

12. The US and Australian governments have made refugee trade deals in the past, including between Nauru and Guantanamo toward the end of Nauru's first industry heyday in 2007 (Dastyari 2008).

13. The volunteer group Ads-Up, was set up by Australians living in the United States to contact refugees arriving under the Australia–United States deal and support them with social contacts, advice, and services. Operation #NotForgotten was also developed in 2019 between Ads-Up Refugee Network Canada, the Refugee Council of Australia, and the Vancouver-based settlement organization MOSAIC to fund private sponsorship places for refugees in Nauru and Manus to move to Canada.

14. By 2018, this had reached peak levels of 18,750 refugees. These figures should be put into context in that Turkey hosts nearly 3.7 million refugees. As a fraction of overall global migration (estimated at 272 million migrants globally), the numbers for Australia are low, even as the figure of the refugee has acquired significant attention and value.

15. Australia continues to maintain a military presence in Iraq and Syria as part of a broad international coalition known as the Combined Joint Task Force—Operation Inherent Resolve (CJTF-OIR). This includes military drone strikes in the region.

16. This percentage has remained relatively consistent over the years, although Australia's budget allocation to Nauru has steadily increased. Nauru's other principal aid donor countries include Taiwan, Japan, and New Zealand. Multilateral partners include the Asian Development Bank, the European Union, UN agencies, the Green Climate Fund, and the Global Environment Facility.

17. The Nauruan government increased public sector salaries in 2015 in order to compete with the refugee industry firms. At the same time, they also lobbied Australian contractors to increase local RPC wages, which were far lower than those of Australian contractors.

18. The International Seabed Authority is an organization formed by the United Nations in 1982 to divide deepwater mineral resource zones in international waters. They enhance and enforce environmental extraction regulations through bodies like the International Tribunal for the Law of the Sea. Under international law, countries control the waters within two hundred miles of their shores. Beyond that, companies, sponsored by a country that is party to the United Nations Convention on the Law of the Sea, must apply for permits from ISA to explore the seafloor, which is termed "the Area."

References

Adeang, David. 2016. "To Our Guests: Refugees and Asylum Seekers." *Republic of Nauru Bulletin* 4(136), May 6.

Agard-Jones, Vanessa. 2013. "Bodies in the System." *Small Axe* 17(3(42)): 182–192.

Agustín, Laura. 2007. *Sex at the Margins: Migration, Labour Markets and the Rescue Industry*. London: Zed Books.

Ahmann, Chloe. 2018. "'It's Exhausting to Create an Event Out of Nothing': Slow Violence and the Manipulation of Time." *Cultural Anthropology* 33(1): 142–171.

Alatas, Syed Hussein. 1977. *The Myth of the Lazy Native: A Study of the Image of the Malays, Filipinos and Javanese from the 16th to the 20th Century and Its Function in the Ideology of Colonial Capitalism*. Abingdon: Frank Cass.

Allard, Tom. 2015. "Somalian Refugee Abyan Becomes a Political Pawn after Abortion Request on Nauru." *Sydney Morning Herald*, October 24. http://www.smh.com.au/federal-politics/political-news/prisoners-island-offers-little-hope-for-new-life-20151022-gkggkx.html.

Allen, Matthew G. 2018. *Resource Extraction and Contentious States: Mining and the Politics of Scale in the Pacific Islands*. Singapore: Palgrave Macmillan.

Amar, Jacques. 2014. "The Law of Return: A National Solution to an International Issue, 1945–1967." In *Postwar Jewish Displacement and Rebirth 1945–1967*, edited by Françoise S. Ouzan and Manfred Gerstenfeld, 34–45. Leiden: Brill.

American Board of Commissioners for Foreign Missions. 1913. The Missionary Herald, 109. Boston: Thomas Todd Company.

Amnesty International. 2016. *Islands of Despair: Australia's "Processing" of Refugees on Nauru*. Amnesty, October 17. https://www.amnesty.org/en/documents/asa12/4934/2016/en/

Anderson, Ben. 2009. "Affective Atmospheres." *Emotion, Space and Society* 2: 77–81.

Anderson, Stephanie. 2016. "Nauru: Australia 'Cannot Turn a Blind Eye' to Asylum Seeker Abuse Reports, Bill Shorten Says." ABC News, August 11. http://www.abc.net.au/news/2016-08-12/cannot-turn-blind-eye-to-nauru-abuse-reports-shorten-says/7728268.

Andersson, Ruben. 2014. *Illegality, Inc.: Clandestine Migration and the Business of Bordering Europe*. Berkeley: University of California Press.

Andrijasevic, Rutvica, and William Walters. 2010. "The International Organization for Migration and the International Government of Borders." *Environment and Planning D: Society and Space* 28(6): 977–999.

Antal, Berthoin Antal, Michael Hutter, and David Stark. 2015. *Moments of Valuation: Exploring Sites of Dissonance*. Oxford: Oxford University Press.

Appadurai, Arjun, ed. 1986. *The Social Life of Things: Commodities in Cultural Perspective*. Cambridge: Cambridge University Press.

Appel, Hannah. 2012. "Offshore Work: Oil, Modularity, and the How of Capitalism in Equatorial Guinea." *American Ethnologist* 39(4): 692–709.

——. 2015. "Offshore Work: Infrastructure and Hydrocarbon Capitalism in Equatorial Guinea." In *Subterranean Estates: Life Worlds of Oil and Gas*, edited by Hannah

Appel, Arthur Mason, and Michael Watts, 257–273. Ithaca, NY: Cornell University Press.

——. 2019. *The Licit Life of Capitalism: US Oil in Equatorial Guinea*. Durham, NC: Duke University Press.

Appel, Hannah, Arthur Mason, and Michael Watts, eds. 2015. *Subterranean Estates: Life Worlds of Oil and Gas*. Ithaca, NY: Cornell University Press.

Appi, Dominic. 2012. "How and When Asylum Seekers Came to Nauru." *Mwinen Ko Nauru Community Newspaper*. August, 29th ed.

——. 2015. "Asylum Seekers Will Be Allowed in the Communities through Open Centre Program." *Mwinen Ko Nauru Community Newspaper*. February, 52nd ed.

Apter, Andrew. 2005. *The Pan-African Nation: Oil and the Spectacle of Culture in Nigeria*. Chicago: University of Chicago Press.

Arboleda, Martín. 2020. *Planetary Mine: Territories of Extraction under Late Capitalism*. London: Verso.

Armiero, Marco, and Anna Fava. 2016. "Of Humans, Sheep, and Dioxin: A History of Contamination and Transformation in Acerra, Italy." *Capitalism Nature Socialism* 27(2): 67–82.

Ashutosh, Ishan, and Alison Mountz. 2011. "Migration Management for the Benefit of Whom? Interrogating the Work of the International Organization for Migration." *Citizenship Studies* 15(1): 21–38.

Augoustinos, Martha, Clemence Due, and Scott Alen Hanson-Easey. 2015. "The Essentialised Refugee: Representations of Racialized 'Others.'" In *The Cambridge Handbook of Social Representations*, edited by Gordon Sammut, Eleni Andreouli, George Gaskell, and Jaan Valsiner, 323–340. Cambridge: Cambridge University Press.

Australian Broadcasting Corporation (ABC). 2014a. "Nauru Parliament Erupts into Chaos after Opposition MPs Suspended for Speaking to ABC, Foreign Media." ABC News, May 14. http://www.abc.net.au/news/2014-05-14/an-nauru-mps-suspended-for-speaking-to-abc/5451366.

——. 2014b. "Nauru Opposition MP Roland Kun Labels Government a Dictatorship after Suspensions Upheld." ABC News, December 21. http://www.abc.net.au/news/2014-12-22/nauru-opposition-mp-labels-government-a-dictatorship/5984104.

——. 2015. "Nauru Rule of Law 'Nonexistent,' Former Magistrate Says." ABC News, *The World Today*, July 10. http://www.abc.net.au/worldtoday/content/2015/s4271171.htm.

Australian Government. 1959–1960. *Territory of Nauru Report*. Canberra: Commonwealth of Australia.

——. 2002. *A Certain Maritime Incident Report*. Senate Select Committee. https://www.aph.gov.au/Parliamentary_Business/Committees/Senate/Former_Committees/maritimeincident/report/index.

——. 2013. Budget Estimates Hearing, May 27–28. www.aph.gov.au/~/media/Estimates/Live/legcon_ctte/estimates/bud . . . /BE13-0039.ashx.

——. 2015. *Taking Responsibility: Conditions and Circumstances at Australia's Regional Processing Centre in Nauru*. Select Committee Senate Report. Commonwealth of Australia, August 31. http://www.aph.gov.au/Parliamentary_Business/Committees/Senate/Regional_processing_Nauru/Regional_processing_Nauru/Final_Report.

Australian National Audit Office. 2016. *Offshore Processing Centres in Nauru and Papua New Guinea: Procurement of Garrison Support and Welfare Services*. ANAO report. Commonwealth of Australia, September 3. https://www.anao.gov.au/work/performance-audit/offshore-processing-centres-nauru-and-papua-new-guinea-procurement.

Auyero, Javier, and Débora Alejandra Swistun. 2009. *Flammable: Environmental Suffering in an Argentine Shantytown*. Oxford: Oxford University Press.

Baird, Julia. 2016. Australia's Gulag Archipelago. *New York Times*, August 30. https://www.nytimes.com/2016/08/31/opinion/australias-gulag-archipelago.html?_r=0.

Bajaj, Simar S., and Fatima C. Stanford. 2022. "The Ukrainian Refugee Crisis and the Pathology of Racism." *British Medical Journal* 376: o661.

Ballard, Chris, and Glenn Banks. 2003. "Resource Wars: The Anthropology of Mining." *Annual Review of Anthropology* 32: 287–313.

Banivanua-Mar, Tracey. 2007. *Violence and Colonial Dialogue: The Australian-Pacific Indentured Labor Trade*. Honolulu: University of Hawai'i Press.

Barrett, Ross, and Daniel Worden, eds. 2014. *Oil Culture*. Minneapolis: University of Minnesota Press.

Bashford, Alison. 2004. *Imperial Hygiene: A Critical History of Colonialism*. Basingstoke: Palgrave Macmillan.

Bauman, Zygmunt. 2004. *Wasted Lives: Modernity and Its Outcasts*. Cambridge: Polity Press.

Becke, Louis. 1897. *Pacific Tales*. London: Routledge.

Beech, Alexandra. 2017. "Pregnant Asylum Seeker on Nauru Flown to Australia." ABC News, February 3. http://www.abc.net.au/news/2017-02-03/pregnant-asylum-seeker-on-nauru-flown-to-australia/8239662?mc_cid=1ba9917e28&mc_eid=7906bcbf06.

Behlmer, George K. 2018. *Risky Shores: Savagery and Colonialism in the Western Pacific*. Stanford, CA: Stanford University Press.

Beresford, Quentin, Gary Partington, and Graeme Gower, eds. 2012. *Reform and Resistance in Aboriginal Education*. Perth: University of Western Australia Press.

Besteman, Catherine. 2016. *Making Refuge: Somali Bantu Refugees and Lewiston, Maine*. Durham, NC: Duke University Press.

——. 2020. *Militarized Global Apartheid*. Durham, NC: Duke University Press.

Betts, Alexander, and Paul Collier. 2017. *Refuge: Rethinking Refugee Policy in a Changing World*. Oxford: Oxford University Press.

Bhagat, Ali. 2019. "Governing Refugee Disposability: Neoliberalism and Survival in Nairobi." *New Political Economy* 25(3): 439–452.

Biersack, Aletta. 2016. "Introduction: Emergent Masculinities in the Pacific." *Asia Pacific Journal of Anthropology* 17(3–4): 197–212.

Biersack, Aletta, and Martha Macintyre, eds. 2017. *Emergent Masculinities in the Pacific*. London: Routledge.

Blake, Chris. 1992. "Environmental Distribution of Heavy Metals on Nauru, Central Pacific, and Possible Relationships to Human Health." Bachelor's thesis, University of North England.

Bloemraad, Irene, and Matthew Wright. 2014. "'Utter Failure' or Unity out of Diversity? Debating and Evaluating Policies of Multiculturalism." *International Migration Review* 48(1): 292–334.

Bogaard, Amy, Rebecca Fraser, Tim H. E. Heaton, Michael Wallace, Petra Vaiglova, Michael Charles, Glynis Jones, Richard P. Evershed, Amy K. Styring, Niels H. Andersen, Rose-Marie Arbogast, László Bartosiewicz, Armelle Gardeisen, Marie Kanstrup, Ursula Maier, Elena Marinova, Lazar Ninov, Marguerita Schäfer, and Elisabeth Stephan. 2013. "Crop Manuring and Intensive Land Management by Europe's First Farmers." *Proceedings of the National Academy of Sciences* 110(31): 12589–12594.

Boochani, Behrouz. 2018. *No Friend but the Mountains*. Translated by Omid Tofighian. Sydney: Picador.

Boochani, Behrouz, and Omid Tofighian. 2020. "No Friend but the Mountains and Manus Prison Theory: In Conversation." *Borderlands* 19(1): 8–26.

Bosworth, Mary. 2011. "Deportation, Detention and Foreign-National Prisoners in England and Wales." *Citizenship Studies* 15(5): 583–595.

Bridge, Gavin. 2009. "Material Worlds: Natural Resources, Resource Geography and the Material Economy." *Geography Compass* 3(3): 1217–1244.

Briskman, Linda, and Jane Doe. 2016. "Social Work in Dark Places: Clash of Values in Offshore Immigration Detention." *Social Alternatives* 35(4): 73–79.

British Phosphate Commission (BPC). 1929. *Report*. Suva: University of the South Pacific Archives.

Brock, William H. 1997. *Justus von Liebig: The Chemical Gatekeeper*. Cambridge: Cambridge University Press.

Buden, Donald W. 2008. "The Birds of Nauru." *Notornis* 55: 8–19.

Bullard, Robert D. 1990. *Dumping in Dixie: Race, Class and Environmental Quality*. Boulder, CO: Westview Press.

Buzi, Jason. 2015. *Refugee Nation: A Radical Solution to the Global Refugee Crisis*. Jason Buzi.

Cabot, Heath. 2014. *On the Doorstep of Europe: Asylum and Citizenship in Greece*. Philadelphia: University of Pennsylvania Press.

——. 2016. "Crisis, Hot Spots, and Paper Pushers: A Reflection on Asylum in Greece." Hot Spots, *Fieldsights*, June 28. https://culanth.org/fieldsights/crisis-hot-spots-and-paper-pushers-a-reflection-on-asylum-in-greece.

——. 2019. "The Business of Anthropology and the European Refugee Regime." *American Ethnologist* 46(3): 261–275.

Calvão, Filipe. 2016. "Unfree Labor." *Annual Review of Anthropology* 45: 415–467.

Carney, John. 2016. "'These Refugees Are Actually Terrorists': Pauline Hanson Demands Muslim Immigration to Australia Be Banned—a Day after 'ISIS-Inspired' Knife Attack in Sydney." *Daily Mail*, September 12. http://www.dailymail.co.uk/news/article-3784572/Pauline-Hanson-calls-ban-Muslim-immigration-Australia-calls-refugees-terrorists.html#ixzz4buJuDZyQ.

Carpenter, Edmund. 1973. *Oh, What a Blow That Phantom Gave Me!* New York: Holt, Rinehart and Winston.

Carrington, Kerry. 2006. "Law and Order on the Border in the Neo-colonial Antipodes." In *Borders, Mobility and Technologies of Control*, edited by Sharon Pickering and Leanne Weber, 179–206, Dordrecht: Springer.

Carter, Jeremy Story. 2016. "Is the Australian Government Failing Its Workplace Duty of Care in Nauru?" ABC News, March 2. http://www.abc.net.au/radionational/programs/lawreport/nauru-asylum-seeker-detention-centre-challenged-over-whs-care/7210180.

Castles, Stephen, ed. 1992. *Mistaken Identity: Multiculturalism and the Demise of Nationalism in Australia*. Sydney: Pluto Press.

Chouliaraki, Lillie. 2012. *The Ironic Spectator: Solidarity in the Age of Post-Humanitarianism*. Cambridge: Polity Press.

Clarke, Melissa. 2014. "Nauru Expels Australian Magistrate Peter Law, Bars Chief Justice Geoffrey Eames from Returning to Country." ABC News, January 19. http://www.abc.net.au/news/2014-01-20/nauru-sacks-deports-australian-magistrate-chief-justice/5207600.

Coddington, Kate. 2014. "Geographies of Containment: Logics of Enclosure in Aboriginal and Asylum Seeker Policies in Australia's Northern Territory." PhD diss., Syracuse University.

Coddington, Kate, Deirdre Conlon, and Lauren L. Martin. 2020. "Destitution Economies: Circuits of Value in Asylum, Refugee, and Migration Control." *American Association of Geographers* 110(5): 1425–1444.

Coffey, Guy J., Ida Kaplan, Robyn C. Sampson, and Maria Montagna Tucci. 2010. "The Meaning and Mental Health Consequences of Long-Term Immigration Detention for People Seeking Asylum." *Social Science and Medicine* 70(12): 2070–2079.

Cohen, Robin, and Nicholas Van Hear. 2020. *Refugia: Radical Solutions to Mass Displacement*. London: Routledge.

Collinson, Clifford W. 1923. *Life and Laughter 'Midst the Cannibals*. London: Hutchinson.

Comaroff, Jean, and John L. Comaroff. 1999. "Occult Economies and the Violence of Abstraction: Notes from the South African Postcolony." *American Ethnologist* 26(2): 297–303.

Cook, Ian, Philip Crang, and Mark Thorpe. 2004. "Tropics of Consumption: 'Getting with the Fetish' of 'Exotic' Fruit?" In *Geographies of Commodity Chains*, edited by Alex Hughes and Suzanne Reimer, 173–192. Abingdon: Routledge.

Coronil, Fernando. 1997. *The Magical State: Nature, Money, and Modernity in Venezuela*. Chicago: University of Chicago Press.

Coutin, Susan Bibler. 2003. *Legalizing Moves: Salvadoran Immigrants' Struggle for U.S. Residency*. Ann Arbor: University of Michigan Press.

Crawford, Margaret. 1995. *Building the Workingman's Paradise: The Design of American Company Towns*. London: Verso.

Crock, Mary. 2003. "In the Wake of the Tampa: Conflicting Visions of International Refugee Law in the Management of Refugee Flows." *Pacific Rim Law and Policy Journal* 12(1): 49–95.

Crock, Mary, and Hannah Martin. 2013. "Refugee Rights and the Merits of Appeals." *University of Queensland Law Journal* 32(1): 137–155.

Cude, Thomas H. Thomas Cude diaries, 1921–1922, 1939–1942, 1945–1947, and associated papers including correspondence, notes, and records. Sydney: New South Wales State Library.

Czeczot, Hanna, and Michal Skrzycki. 2010. "Cadmium—Element Completely Unnecessary for the Organism." *Postepy Higieny i Medycyny Doswiadczalnej* 64: 38–49.

Dastyari, Azadeh. 2008. "Swapping Refugees: The Implications of the 'Atlantic Solution.'" *University of Technology, Sydney Law Review* 9.

Davidson, Helen. 2016. "Refugees Attacked 'on a Daily Basis' on Nauru, Human Rights Groups Say." *Guardian*, August 3. https://www.theguardian.com/australia-news/2016/aug/03/refugees-attacked-on-a-daily-basis-on-nauru-says-amnesty-report.

Davies, Elizabeth Jordie, Jenn M. Jackson, and Shea Streeter. 2021. "Bringing Abolition In: Addressing Carceral Logics in Social Science Research." *Social Science Quarterly* 102(7): 3095–3102.

Davies, Thom. 2019. "Slow Violence and Toxic Geographies: 'Out of Sight' to Whom?" *Environment and Planning C: Politics and Space* 40(2): 409–427.

Davis, Angela. 2003. *Are Prisons Obsolete?* New York: Seven Stories Press.

Davis, Mike. 1990. *City of Quartz: Excavating the Future in Los Angeles*. London: Verso.

Dauvergne, Catherine. 2016. *The New Politics of Immigration and the End of Settler Society*. Cambridge: Cambridge University Press.

De Genova, Nicholas. 2002. "Migrant 'Illegality' and Deportability in Everyday Life." *Annual Review of Anthropology* 31: 419–447.

——. 2013. "Spectacles of Migrant 'Illegality': The Scene of Exclusion, the Obscene of Inclusion." *Journal of Ethnic and Racial Studies* 36(7): 1180–1198.

de Haas, Hein. 2009. "The Myth of Invasion: The Inconvenient Realities of African Migration to Europe." *Third World Quarterly* 29(7): 1305–1322.

Deireragea, Beiyedage. 1995. "Beiyedage Talks to Youth about Angam." In *Spirit of Angam*. Republic of Nauru: Curriculum Office, Education Department.

Delaporte, Mrs. Philip A. 1920. "The Men and Women of Old Nauru." *Mid Pacific* 19(20): 153–156.

Delaporte, Philip, Salome Delaporte, and Maria Linke. 1909. *Eighth Annual Report of the Pleasant Island Mission.* American Board of Commissioners for Foreign Missions.

Dobell, Graham. 2007. "China and Taiwan in the South Pacific: Diplomatic Chess versus Pacific Political Rugby." *CSCSD Occasional Paper Number 1.* https://chl-old .anu.edu.au/publications/csds/cscsd_op1_4_chapter_1.pdf.

Doherty, Ben. 2015. "Almost 200 Refugees on Nauru Arrested as Police Crack Down on Peaceful Protests." *Guardian*, March 5. https://www.theguardian.com/world/2015 /mar/04/up-to-70-refugees-nauru-arrested-police-crack-down-peaceful-protests.

———. 2016. "Nauru Refugee Left with Horrific Head Wound in Attack Dismissed by Police." *Guardian*, March 10. https://www.theguardian.com/world/2016/mar/10 /nauru-refugee-left-with-horrific-head-wound-after-attack-dismissed-by-police.

Douglas, Mary. 1966. *Purity and Danger: An Analysis of Concepts of Pollution.* London: Routledge.

Duffield, Mark. 2001. *Global Governance and the New Wars: The Merging of Development and Security.* London: Zed Books.

Dzenovska, Dace. 2018. *School of Europeanness: Tolerance and Other Lessons in Political Liberalism in Latvia.* Ithaca, NY: Cornell University Press.

Elbourne, Elizabeth. 2016. "Violence, Moral Imperialism and Colonial Borderlands, 1770s–1820s: Some Contradictions of Humanitarianism." *Journal of Colonialism and Colonial History* 17(1).

Ellis, Albert. 1936. *Adventuring in Coral Seas.* Sydney: Angus and Robertson.

———. 1946. *Mid-Pacific Outposts.* Auckland: Brown and Steward.

Emsley, John. 2000. *The Shocking History of Phosphorus: A Biography of the Devil's Element.* London: Macmillan.

Erel, Umut, Karim Murji and Zaki Nahaboo. 2016. "Understanding the Contemporary Race–Migration Nexus." *Ethnic and Racial Studies* 39(8): 1339–1360.

Expert Panel on Asylum Seekers. 2012. *Report of the Expert Panel on Asylum Seekers.* Australian Government Commissioned Report. http://apo.org.au/research /report-expert-panel-asylum-seekers.

Fabricius, Wilhelm. 1895. *Nauru 1888–1900: An Account in German and English Based on Official Records of the Colonial Section of the German Foreign Office Held by the Deutsches Zentralarchiv in Potsdam.* Translated and edited by D. Clark and S. Firth. Canberra: Australian National University.

Farrell, Paul, Nick Evershed, and Helen Davidson. 2016. "The Nauru Files: Cache of 2,000 Leaked Reports Reveal Scale of Abuse of Children in Australian Offshore Detention." *Guardian*, August 10. https://www.theguardian.com/australia-news /2016/aug/10/the-nauru-files-2000-leaked-reports-reveal-scale-of-abuse-of -children-in-australian-offshore-detention.

Fassin, Didier. 2010. "Inequality of Lives, Hierarchies of Humanity: Moral Commitments and Ethical Dilemmas of Humanitarianism." In *In the Name of Humanity: The Government of Threat and Care*, edited by Ilana Feldman and Miriam Ticktin, 238–255. Durham, NC: Duke University Press.

Fassin, Didier, and Estelle d'Halluin. 2005. "The Truth from the Body: Medical Certificates as Ultimate Evidence for Asylum Seekers." *American Anthropologist* 107(4): 597–608.

Fassin, Didier, and Richard Rechtman. 2009. *The Empire of Trauma: An Inquiry into the Condition of Victimhood.* Princeton: Princeton University Press.

Fearne, John. 1798. *Maritime Chronicles.* Canberra: National Archives of Australia.

Feary, Alexander. 2011. "Restoring the Soils of Nauru: Plants as Tools for Ecological Recovery." Master's thesis, Victoria University of Wellington.

Feeley, Malcolm M., and Van Swearingen. 2004. "The Prison Conditions Cases and the Bureaucratization of American Corrections: Influences, Impacts and Implications." *Pace Law School Review* 24: 433–475.

Ferguson, James. 2006. *Global Shadows: Africa in the Neoliberal World Order.* Durham, NC: Duke University Press.

Fiddian-Qasmiyeh, Elena. 2014. *The Ideal Refugees: Gender, Islam, and the Sahrawi Politics of Survival.* Syracuse: Syracuse University Press.

Filer, Colin, and Martha Macintyre. 2006. "Grass Roots and Deep Holes: Community Responses to Mining in Melanesia." *Contemporary Pacific* 18(2): 215–231.

Firth, Simon. 1973. "German Firms in the Western Pacific Islands, 1857–1914." *Journal of Pacific History* 8: 11–15.

Fiske, Lucy. 2016. *Human Rights, Refugee Protest and Immigration Detention.* Basingstoke: Palgrave Macmillan.

Fletcher, Jay. 2014. "Nauru Refugees Protest 'Cambodia Solution.'" *Green Left Weekly,* October 10. https://www.greenleft.org.au/content/nauru-refugees-protest-â%C2%80%C2%98cambodia-solutionâ%C2%80%C2%99.

Flynn, Michael, and Cecilia Cannon. 2009. "The Privatization of Immigration Detention: Towards a Global View." Geneva: Global Detention Project Working Paper.

Follis, Karolina S. 2012. *Building Fortress Europe: The Polish-Ukrainian Frontier.* Pittsburgh: University of Pennsylvania Press.

Fortun, Kim. 2001. *Advocacy after Bhopal: Environmentalism, Disaster, New Global Orders.* Chicago: University of Chicago Press.

Fox, Liam, and Sam Bolitho. 2015. "Hundreds of Nauru Refugees Protest against 'Slave-Like Living Conditions.'" ABC News, March 23. http://www.abc.net.au/news/2015-03-02/nauru-refugees-protest-against-slave-like-conditions/6275236.

Freidberg, Suzanne. 2003. "Cleaning Up Down South: Supermarkets, Ethical Trade and African Horticulture." *Social and Cultural Geography* 4(1): 27–43.

Gale, Stephen J., 2016. "The Mined-Out Phosphate Lands of Nauru, Equatorial Western Pacific." *Australian Journal of Earth Sciences* 63(3): 333–341.

Garrett, Jemima. 1996. *Island Exiles.* Sydney: ABC Books.

Gatrell, Peter. 2011. *Free World? The Campaign to Save the World's Refugees: 1956–1963.* Cambridge: Cambridge University Press.

——. 2013. *The Making of the Modern Refugee.* Oxford: Oxford University Press.

Gill, Nick. 2009. "Governmental Mobility: The Power Effects of the Movement of Detained Asylum Seekers around Britain's Detention Estate." *Political Geography* 28: 186–196.

——. 2013. "Mobility versus Liberty? The Punitive Uses of Movement within and outside Carceral Environments." In *Carceral Spaces: Mobility and Agency in Imprisonment and Migrant Detention,* edited by Dominique Moran, Nick Gill, and Deirdre Conlon, 19–36. London: Routledge.

Gilmore, Ruth Wilson. 2007. *Golden Gulag: Prisons, Surplus, Crisis, and Opposition in Globalizing California.* Berkeley: University of California Press.

Ginsburg, Faye D., Lila Abu-Lughod, and Brian Larkin, eds. 2002. *Media Worlds: Anthropology on New Terrain.* Berkeley: University of California Press.

Gleeson, Madeline. 2016. *Offshore: Behind the Wire on Manus and Nauru.* Sydney: University of New South Wales Press.

Golub, Alex. 2014. *Leviathans at the Gold Mine: Creating Indigenous and Corporate Actors in Papua New Guinea.* Durham, NC: Duke University Press.

Gómez-Barris, Macarena. 2017. *The Extractive Zone: Social Ecologies and Decolonial Perspectives.* Durham: Duke University Press.

Goodey, Dee. 2014. *Snapshots and Snippets: Old Nauru and the Phosphate Industry*. Published by the author.

Gordillo, Gastón. 2014. *Rubble: The Afterlife of Destruction*. Durham, NC: Duke University Press.

Grassley, Chuck. 2016. Letter to Jen Johnson and John Kerry. https://www.grassley .senate.gov/sites/default/files/judiciary/upload/2016-11-22%20CEG,%20Good -latte%20to%20State,%20DHS%20-%20Refugee%20Negotiations%20with%20 Australia.pdf.

Gray, Harriet, and Anja K. Franck. 2019. "Refugees as/at Risk: The Gendered and Racialized Underpinnings of Securitization in British Media Narratives." *Security Dialogue* 50(3): 275–291.

Green, Jim. 2017. "Radioactive Waste and Australia's Aboriginal People." *Angelaki* 22(3): 33–50.

Green, Michael, Andre Dao, Angelica Neville, Dana Affleck, and Sienna Merope. 2017. *They Cannot Take the Sky: Stories from Detention*. Crows Nest: Allen and Unwin.

Griffiths, Melanie. 2012. "'Vile Liars and Truth Distorters': Truth, Trust and the Asylum System." *Anthropology Today* 28(5): 8–12.

——. 2014. "Out of Time: The Temporal Uncertainties of Refused Asylum Seekers and Immigration Detainees." *Journal of Ethnic and Migration Studies* 40(12): 1991–2009.

Grüneisl, Katharina. 2020. "Second-Hand Shoe Circulations in Tunis: Processes of Valuation and the Production of Urban Space." *Articulo* 21.

Gutiérrez Rodríguez, Encarnación. 2018. "The Coloniality of Migration and the 'Refugee Crisis': On the Asylum-Migration Nexus, the Transatlantic White European Settler Colonialism-Migration and Racial Capitalism." *Refuge* 34(1): 16–28.

Hacking, Ian. 1985. "Making Up People." In *Reconstructing Individualism*, edited by T. L. Heller, M. Sosna, and D. E. Wellbery, 161–171. Stanford, CA: Stanford University Press.

Hage, Ghassan. 2000. *White Nation: Fantasies of White Supremacy in a Multicultural Society*. New York: Routledge.

——. 2002. "Multiculturalism and White Paranoia in Australia." *Journal of International Migration and Integration* 3: 417–437.

Hambruch, Paul. 1915. *Nauru. Ergebnisse der Südsee-Expedition 1908–1910*. Hamburg: Friederichsen.

Hannigan, William P. 2002. "Primary Health Care Policy Review Project: Diocese of Tarawa and Nauru." *Environmental Health* 2(1): 77–80.

Hanson-Young, Sarah. 2014. "Children at Risk: Leaked Report Details Shocking Mental Health Disaster on Nauru." Green Party Media Release, May 30. http://sarah -hanson-young.greensmps.org.au/articles/children-risk-leaked-report-details -shocking-mental-health-disaster-nauru.

Harper, Ian, Tobias Kelly, and Akshay Khanna, eds. 2015. *The Clinic and the Court: Law, Medicine and Anthropology*. Cambridge: Cambridge University Press.

Harrell-Bond, Barbara. 1986. *Imposing Aid: Emergency Assistance to Refugees*. Oxford: Oxford University Press.

Hasselberg, Ines. 2016. *Enduring Uncertainty: Deportation, Punishment and Everyday Life*. New York: Berghahn Books.

Heartfield, James. 2011. *The Aborigines' Protection Society: Humanitarian Imperialism in Australia, New Zealand, Fiji, Canada, South Africa, and the Congo, 1837–1909*. New York: Columbia University Press.

Hedrick, Kyli, Gregory Armstrong, Guy Coffey, and Rohan Borschmann. 2019. "Self-Harm in the Australian Asylum Seeker Population: A National Records-Based Study." *SSM—Population Health* 8: 1–9.

Heffernan, Shayne. 2016. "Malcolm Turnbull Looks Like an Idiot as Trump Takes Action." Live Trading News, January 24. http://www.livetradingnews.com/malcolm-turnbull-looks-like-idiot-trump-takes-action-27921.html#.WNBVZULthUS.

Hezel, Francis X. 2000. *First Taint of Civilization: A History of the Caroline and Marshall Islands in Pre-Colonial Days, 1521–1885*. Honolulu: University of Hawai'i Press.

Hiemstra, Nancy. 2019. *Detain and Deport: The Chaotic U.S. Immigration Enforcement Regime*. Athens: University of Georgia Press.

Higgins, Claire. 2017. *Asylum by Boat: Origins of Australia's Refugee Policy*. Sydney: University of New South Wales Press.

Hinton, Diana Davids. 2008. "Creating Company Culture: Oil Company Camps in the Southwest, 1920–1960." *Southwestern Historical Quarterly* 111(4): vii–387.

Hoang, Khanh. 2016. "What Will Happen to Baby Asha?" *The Conversation*, February 16. http://theconversation.com/what-will-happen-to-baby-asha-54735.

Hoang, Khanh, and Madeline Gleeson. 2016. "Nauru Abuse Reports Warrant Urgent Action to Protect Children in Offshore Detention." *The Conversation*, August 10. http://theconversation.com/nauru-abuse-reports-warrant-urgent-action-to-protect-children-in-offshore-detention-63756.

Holmes, Seth. 2013. *Fresh Fruit, Broken Bodies: Migrant Farmworkers in the United States*. Berkeley: University of California Press.

Howard, Neil. 2017. *Child Trafficking, Youth Labour Mobility and the Politics of Protection*. Houndsmill: Palgrave Macmillan.

Howe, Joanna, and Ankur Singh. 2020. "Covid-19 and Undocumented Workers in the Australian Horticulture Industry." Report published by the United Workers Union, University of Adelaide Law Research Paper No. 2020-137.

Howe, K. R. 2000. *Nature, Culture, and History: The "Knowing" of Oceania*. Honolulu: University of Hawai'i Press.

Hughes, Helen. 2004. "From Riches to Rags What Are Nauru's Options and How Can Australia Help?" *Centre for Independent Studies: Issue Analysis* 50.

Human Rights Watch and Amnesty International. 2016. "Australia: Appalling Abuse, Neglect of Refugees on Nauru." Human Rights Watch, August 2. https://www.hrw.org/news/2016/08/02/australia-appalling-abuse-neglect-refugees-nauru.

Hutter, Michael and David Stark. 2015. *Moments of Valuation: Exploring Sites of Dissonance*. Oxford: Oxford University Press.

Isaacs, David. 2016. "Are Healthcare Professionals Working in Australia's Immigration Detention Centres Condoning Torture?" *Journal of Medical Ethics* 42(7): 413–415.

Isaacs, Mark. 2014. *The Undesirables: Inside Nauru*. Richmond: Hardie Grant Books.

Itsimaera, Alf. 1992. "History and Growth of Nauru Police Force." Republic of Nauru Publication.

IWP-Nauru and Alice Leney, 2004. "The Way Ahead: An Assessment of Waste Problems for the Buada Community, and Strategies toward Community Waste Reduction in Nauru." *IWP-Pacific Technical Report (International Waters Project)* No. 9. Samoa: Secretariat of the Pacific Regional Environment Programme.

JAC. 2014. *Nauru Site Visit Report*. 16–19 February. https://assets.documentcloud.org/documents/1175048/hmhsc-jac-site-visit-report-final-1.txt.

Jacka, Jerry K. 2018. "Environmental Impacts of Resource Extraction in the Mineral Age." *Annual Review of Anthropology* 47: 61–77.

Jalbert, Kirk, Anna Willow, David Casgrande, and Stephanie Paladino. 2017. "Introduction: Confronting Extraction Taking Action." In *ExtrACTION: Impacts, Engagements, and Alternative Futures*, edited by Kirk Jalbert, Anna Willow, David Casgrande, and Stephanie Paladino, 1–13. Routledge: New York.

Jeffries, Damon. 2016. "Final Hours: Obama Moves to Grant Asylum to 1,800 'High Threat' Muslims DENIED by Australia. *Conservative Daily Post*, December 1. https://conservativedailypost.com/final-hours-obama-moves-grant-asylum -1800-high-threat-muslims-denied-australia/.

Johnson, Heather. 2011. "Click to Donate: Visual Images, Constructing Victims and Imagining the Female Refugee." *Third World Quarterly* 32(6): 1015–1037.

Jupp, James. 2002. *From White Australia to Woomera: The Story of Australian Immigration*. Cambridge: Cambridge University Press.

Kampmark, Binoy. 2016. "Nauru, Refugees and Australia's 'Torture Complex.'" *Global Research*, October 19. http://www.globalresearch.ca/nauru-refugees-and-the-torture -complex/5551781.

Karlsen, Elibritt. 2016. "Australia's Offshore Processing of Asylum Seekers in Nauru and PNG: A Quick Guide to Statistics and Resources." Parliamentary Library Research Publications Monthly Statistical Bulletin, December 19. http://www .aph.gov.au/About_Parliament/Parliamentary_Departments/Parliamentary _Library/pubs/rp/rp1617/Quick_Guides/Offshore.

Keane, Webb. 2003. "Semiotics and the Social Analysis of Material Things." *Language and Communication* 23: 409–425.

Kelly, Paul. 2014. *Triumph and Demise: The Broken Promise of a Labor Generation*. Melbourne: Melbourne University Press.

Kelly, Tobias. 2012. "Sympathy and Suspicion: Torture, Asylum and Humanity in the UK. Malinowski Memorial Lecture." *Journal of the Royal Anthropological Institute* 18(4): 253–268.

Kenny, Chris. 2015. "Nauru: Sifting Truth from Spin." *The Australian*, October 26. http://www.theaustralian.com.au/news/inquirer/nauru-sifting-truth-from-spin /story-e6frg6z6-1227581753809.

——. 2016. "Limbo Is Nauru's Real Torture for Asylum Seekers." *The Australian*, August 13. http://www.theaustralian.com.au/opinion/columnists/chris-kenny/limbo-is-naurus -real-torture-for-asylumseekers/news-story/343a631a27e9709b76c440c2ca378507.

Khambalia, Amina, Philayrath Phongsavan, Ben J. Smith, Kieren Keke, Li Dan, Andrew Fitzhardinge, and Adrian E. Bauman. 2011. "Prevalence and Risk Factors of Diabetes and Impaired Fasting Glucose in Nauru." *BMC Public Health* 11(719): 1–10.

Kirsch, Stuart. 2014. *Mining Capitalism: The Relationship between Corporations and Their Critics*. Berkeley: University of California Press.

Kneebone, Susan. 2014. "The Bali Process and Global Refugee Policy in the Asia–Pacific Region." *Journal of Refugee Studies* 27(4): 596–618.

Kolbert, Elizabeth. 2021. "The Deep Sea Is Filled with Treasure, but It Comes at a Price." *New Yorker*, June 21.

Koptyoff, Igor. 1986. "The Cultural Biography of Things: Commoditization as Process." In *The Social Life of Things: Commodities in Cultural Perspective*, edited by Arjun Appadurai, 64–91. Cambridge: Cambridge University Press.

Kuchinskaya, Olga. 2014. *The Politics of Invisibility: Public Knowledge about Radiation Health Effects after Chernobyl*. Cambridge, MA: MIT Press.

Kun, Ruben, Whitlam Togomae, and Roland Kund. 2004. *Nauru National Integrity Systems: Country Study Report*. Blackburn South: Transparency International Australia.

Lau, Estelle T. 2007. *Paper Families: Identity, Immigration Administration, and Chinese Exclusion*. Durham, NC: Duke University Press.

Lauder, Simon. 2016. "Nauru Government Denies Refugee Children Are Abused in Schools." ABC News, March 9. http://www.abc.net.au/news/2016-03-09/nauru -govt-denies-abuse-of-refugee-school-children/7234772.

Lentin, Alana, and Gavan Titley. 2011. *The Crises of Multiculturalism: Racism in a Neoliberal Age*. London: Zed Books.

Lerner, Steve. 2010. *Sacrifice Zones: The Front Lines of Toxic Chemical Exposure in the United States*. Cambridge, MA: MIT Press.

Levin, Lisa A., Diva J. Amon, and Hannah Lily. 2020. "Challenges to the Sustainability of Deep-Seabed Mining." *Nature Sustainability* 3: 784–794.

Libesman, Terri, and Linda Briskman. 2018. "Indigenous Australians: Continuity of Colonialism in Law and Social Work." In *Social Work in the Shadow of the Law*, edited by Simon Rice, Andrew Day, and Linda Briskman, 256–276. Leichhardt: Federation Press.

Limbert, Mandana. 2010. *In the Time of Oil: Piety, Memory, and Social Life in an Omani Town*. Stanford, CA: Stanford University Press.

Lindberg, Annika. 2020. "In the Best Interest of Whom? Professional Humanitarians and Selfie Samaritans in the Danish Asylum Industry." In *Asylum For Sale: Profit and Protest in the Migration Industry*, edited by Siobhán McGuirk and Adrienne Pine, 219–230. Oakland: PM Press.

Lipman, Jana K. 2009. *Guantanamo: A Working-Class History between Empire and Revolution*. Berkeley: University of California Press.

Loescher, Gil, and John A. Scanlan. 1986. *Calculated Kindness: Refugees and America's Half-Open Door 1945-present*. New York: Free Press.

Loop. 2016. "Nauru Government Critical of 'Four Corners—Forgotten Children' TV program." *Loop News*, October 18. http://www.loopnauru.com/content/nauru-government-critical-'four-corners-forgotten-children'-tv-progam#.WAVWj00 VebQ.facebook.

Loyd, Jenna M., Emily Mitchell-Eaton, and Alison Mountz. 2016. "The Militarization of Islands and Migration: Tracing Human Mobility through US Bases in the Caribbean and the Pacific." *Political Geography* 53: 65–75.

Loyd, Jenna M., Matt Mitchelson, and Andrew Burridge, eds. 2013. *Beyond Walls and Cages: Prisons, Borders, and Global Crisis*. Athens: Georgia University Press.

Lusher, Dean, and Haslam, Nick, eds. 2007. *Yearning to Breathe Free: Seeking Asylum in Australia*. Annadale: Federation Press.

Macintyre, Martha, and Simon Foale. 2002. *Politicised Ecology: Local Responses to Mining in Papua New Guinea*. Working Paper No. 33. Canberra: Resource Management in Asia-Pacific Program Seminar Series, Australian National University.

Mackinnon, Rea Hearn. 2014. "Comparative RSD Systems—Nauru." Paper presented at the International Association of Refugee Law Judges Conference, Tunis.

——. 2015. "Refugee Processing on Nauru." Paper presented at the Kaldor Centre Annual Conference, Sydney, November 20.

Maclean, Ken. 2008. "Sovereignty after the Entrepreneurial Turn: Mosaics of Control, Commodified Spaces, and Regulated Violence in Contemporary Burma." In *Taking Southeast Asia to Market: Commodities, Nature, and People in a Neoliberal Age*, edited by Nancy Peluso and Joe Nevins, 140–157. Ithaca, NY: Cornell University Press.

Maclellan, Nick. 2013. "What Has Australia Done to Nauru?" *Overland* 212 (Spring). https://overland.org.au/previous-issues/issue-212/feature-nic-maclellan/.

MacSporran, Peter. H. 1995. "Land Ownership and Control in Nauru." *Murdoch University Journal of Law* 2(2).

Mahmud, Tayyab. 2010. "Colonial Cartographies, Postcolonial Borders, and Enduring Failures of International Law: The Unending Wars along the Afghanistan Pakistan Frontier." *Brooklyn Journal of International Law* 36(1): 1–74.

Malkki, Liisa H. 1995. "Refugees and Exile: From 'Refugee Studies' to the National Order of Things." *Annual Review of Anthropology* 24: 495–523.

——. 1996. "Speechless Emissaries: Refugees, Humanitarianism, and Dehistoriciza-tion." *Cultural Anthropology* 11(3): 377–404.

Mann, Surender, and Gerry Ritchie. 1994. "Changes in the Forms of Cadmium with Time in Some West Australian Soils." *Australian Journal of Soil Research* 32(2): 241–250.

Mares, Sarah, and Louise Newman. 2007. *Acting from the Heart: Australian Advocates for Asylum Seekers Tell Their Stories.* Sydney: Finch Publishing.

Marlowe, Jay. 2018. *Belonging and Transnational Refugee Settlement: Unsettling the Everyday and the Extraordinary.* London: Routledge.

Marlowe, Jay, and Carole Adamson. 2011. "Teaching Trauma: Critically Engaging a Troublesome Term." *Social Work Education* 30(6): 623–634.

Marr, David, and Marion Wilkinson. 2003. *Dark Victory.* Crows Nest: Allen and Unwin.

Mathiesen, Karl. 2014. "Refugees Living on Nauru Say They Want to Return to Detention to Flee Violence." *Guardian* Australia, December 31. https://www.theguardian .com/australia-news/2014/dec/31/refugees-living-on-nauru-say-they-want-to -return-to-detention-to-flee-violence.

Mau, Faith. 2012. "Nauru Again Assists Australia with Asylum Seeker Issue." *Mwinen Ko Nauru Community Newspaper,* August, 29th ed.

Maude, Honor. 1971. *The String Figures of Nauru Island.* Adelaide: Libraries Board of South Australia.

Maurer, Bill. 1998. "Cyberspatial Sovereignties: Offshore Finance, Digital Cash, and the Limits of Liberalism." *Indiana Journal of Global Legal Studies* 5(2): 493–519.

McKenna, Sheila. A., David J. Butler, and Amanda Wheatley. 2014. *Rapid Biodiversity Assessment of Republic of Nauru.* Apia, Samoa: Secretariat of the Pacific Regional Environment Programme.

McKittrick, Katherine. 2013. "Plantation Futures." *Small Axe* 17(3): 1–15.

McLennan, Amy K. 2017. "Local Food, Imported Food, and the Failures of Community Gardening Initiatives in Nauru." In *Postcolonialism, Indigeneity and Struggles for Food Sovereignty: Alternative food networks in subaltern spaces,* edited by Marisa Wilson, 127–145. London: Routledge.

——. 2020. "The Rise of Nutritionism and the Decline of Nutritional Health in Nauru." *Food, Culture and Society* 23(2): 249–266.

McLennan, Amy K., and Stanley Ulijaszek. 2014. "Obesity Emergence in the Pacific Islands: Why Understanding Colonial History and Social Change Is Important." *Public Health Nutrition* 18(8): 1499–1505.

Meade, Amanda. 2016. "Only 'Respectful and Objective' Media Outlets Are Welcome, Says Nauru." *Guardian,* June 21. https://www.theguardian.com/world/2016/jun /22/only-respectful-and-objective-media-outlets-are-welcome-says-nauru.

Metcalfe, Susan. 2010. *The Pacific Solution.* Melbourne: Australian Scholarly Publishing.

Mezzadra, Sandro, and Brett Neilson. 2013. *Border as Method, Or, the Multiplication of Labor.* Durham, NC: Duke University Press.

——. 2017. "On the Multiple Frontiers of Extraction: Excavating Contemporary Capitalism." *Cultural Studies* 31(2-3): 185–204.

Miller, Greg, and Philip Rucker. 2017. "'This Was the Worst Call by Far': Trump Badgered, Bragged and Abruptly Ended Phone Call with Australian Leader." *Washington Post,* February 2. https://www.washingtonpost.com/world/national-security/no-gday-mate -on-call-with-australian-pm-trump-badgers-and-brags/2017/02/01/88a3bfb0-e8bf -11e6-80c2-30e57e57e05d_story.html?tid=sm_tw&utm_term=.72d4a1387719.

Miller, Kathryn A., Kirsten F. Thompson, Paul Johnston, and David Santillo. 2018. "An Overview of Seabed Mining Including the Current State of Development, Environmental Impacts, and Knowledge Gaps." *Frontiers in Marine Science* 4. https://www.frontiersin.org/articles/10.3389/fmars.2017.00418/full.

Missbach, Anje. 2015. *Troubled Transit: Asylum Seekers Stuck in Indonesia*. Singapore: ISEAS Publishing.

Mitchell, Timothy. 2002. *Rule of Experts: Egypt, Techno-politics, Modernity*. Berkeley: University of California Press.

——. 2011. *Carbon Democracy: Political Power in the Age of Oil*. London: Verso.

Mitropoulos, Angela. 2015. "Archipelago of Risk: Uncertainty, Borders and Migration Detention Systems." *New Formations* 84: 163–83.

Moran, Dominique. 2015. *Carceral Geography: Spaces and Practices of Incarceration*. Farnham: Ashgate.

Moran, Dominique, Nick Gill, and Deirdre Conlon, eds. 2013. *Carceral Spaces: Mobility and Agency in Imprisonment and Migrant Detention*. London: Routledge

Morris, Julia. 2016. "In the Market of Morality: International Human Rights Standards and the Immigration Detention 'Improvement' Complex." In *Intimate Economies of Immigration Detention*, edited by Deirdre Conlon and Nancy Hiemstra, 51–69. London: Routledge.

——. 2017. "Power, Capital and Immigration Detention Rights: Making Networked Markets in Global Detention Governance at UNHCR." *Global Networks* 17: 400–422.

——. 2019. "Refugee Extractivism: Law and Mining a Human Commodity in the Republic of Nauru." *Saint Louis University Law Journal Special Issue* 64(1): 59–90.

——. 2020. "Coping and Confinement on the Border: The Affective Politics of Music Workshops in British Immigration Detention." *Ethnomusicology Forum* 29(1): 107–125.

——. 2021a. "The Value of Refugees: UNHCR and the Growth of the Global Refugee Industry." *Journal of Refugee Studies* 34(3): 2676–2698.

——. 2021b. "Colonial Afterlives of Infrastructure: From Phosphate to Refugee Processing in the Republic of Nauru." *Mobilities* 16(5): 688–706.

——. 2022. "Strange Bedfellows? NGOs and Offshore Detention." In *Forced Displacement and NGOs in Asia Pacific*, edited by Gul Inanc and Themba Lewis, 165–180. London: Routledge.

Morrison, Robert John, and Harley I. Manner. 2005. "Pre-mining Patterns of Soils on Nauru, Central Pacific." *Pacific Science* 59(4): 523–540.

Moss, Frederick J. 1889. *Through Atolls and Islands in the Great South Sea*. London: Sampson, Low, Marston, Searle, and Rivington.

Murphy, Michelle. 2006. *Sick Building Syndrome and the Problem of Uncertainty: Environmental Politics, Technoscience, and Women Workers*. Durham, NC: Duke University Press.

Murray Li, Tania. 2008. "Contested Commodifications: Struggles over Nature in a National Park." In *Taking Southeast Asia to Market: Commodities, Nature, and People in a Neoliberal Age*, edited by Nancy Peluso and Joe Nevins, 124–139. Ithaca, NY: Cornell University Press.

——. 2014. "What Is Land? Assembling a Resource for Global Investment." *Transactions of the Institute of British Geographers* 39(4): 589–602.

Nader, Laura. 1972. "Up the Anthropologist: Perspectives Gained from Studying Up." In *Reinventing Anthropology*, edited by Dell Hymes, 284–311. New York: Pantheon Books.

Nash, June. 1993. *We Eat the Mines and the Mines Eat Us: Dependency and Exploitation in Bolivian Tin Mines*. New York: Columbia University Press.

Nauru Philatelic Bureau. 1983. *Kaleidoscope of Nauru*. Republic of Nauru: Philatelic Bureau.

Needham, Andrew. 2014. *Power Lines: Phoenix and the Making of the Modern Southwest*. Princeton, NJ: Princeton University Press.

Nettelbeck, Amanda, and Lyndall Ryan. 2017. "Salutary Lessons: Native Police and the 'Civilising' Role of Legalised Violence in Colonial Australia." *Journal of Imperial and Commonwealth History* 46(1): 47–68.

Nevins, Joseph. 2010. *Operation Gatekeeper and Beyond: The War on "Illegals" and the Remaking of the U.S.—Mexico Boundary*. London: Routledge.

Oakes, Laurie. 2017. "Laurie Oakes: Malcolm Turnbull Doesn't Realise He's Been Trumped." *Daily Telegraph*, January 27. http://www.dailytelegraph.com.au/news /opinion/laurie-oakes-malcolm-turnbull-doesnt-realise-hes-been-trumped /news-story/81252daa3da54d6116aa0b0505f8c43f.

Obeyesekere, Gananath. 1992. *The Apotheosis of Captain Cook: European Mythmaking in the Pacific*. Princeton: Princeton University Press.

O'Connell Davidson, Julia. 2015. *Modern Slavery: The Margins of Freedom*. Houndsmill: Palgrave Macmillan.

Olien, Roger, and Diana Davids Hinton. 1982. *Oil Booms: Social Change in Five Texas Towns*. Omaha: University of Nebraska Press.

O'Neill, Margot. 2008. *Blind Conscience*. Sydney: University of New South Wales.

Ong, Aihwa. 1999. *Flexible Citizenship: The Cultural Logics of Transnationality*. Durham, NC: Duke University Press.

——. 2003. *Buddha Is Hiding: Refugees, Citizenship, the New America*. Berkeley: University of California Press.

Oshinski, David M. 1996. *"Worse Than Slavery": Parchman Farm and the Ordeal of Jim Crow Justice*. New York: Free Press Paperbacks.

Palafox, Neal A., Seiji Yamada, Alan C. Ou, Jill S. Minami, David B. Johnson, and Alan R. Katz. 2004. "Cancer in Micronesia." *Pacific Health Dialogue* 11(2): 78–83.

Palan, Ronen. 2006. *The Offshore World: Sovereign Markets, Virtual Places, and Nomad Millionaires*. Ithaca, NY: Cornell University Press.

Peatling, Stephanie, and Gareth Hutchens. 2015. "Australia Ready to Take More Refugees from Syria, Tony Abbott Says." *Sydney Morning Herald*, September 6. http:// www.smh.com.au/federal-politics/political-news/australia-ready-to-take-more -refugees-from-syria-tony-abbott-says-20150906-gjg6ud.html.

Perera, Suvendrini. 2009. *Australia and the Insular Imagination: Beaches, Borders, Boats, and Bodies*. New York: Palgrave Macmillan.

Perera, Suvendrini, and Joseph Pugliese. 2018. "Sexual Violence and the Border: Colonial Genealogies of US and Australian Immigration Detention Regimes." *Social and Legal Studies* 30(1): 66–79.

Petrou, Kirstie, and John Connell. 2018. "'We Don't Feel Free at All': Temporary ni-Vanuatu Workers in the Riverina, Australia." *Rural Society* 27(1): 66–79.

——. 2019. "Overcoming Precarity? Social Media, Agency and ni-Vanuatu Seasonal Workers in Australia." *Journal of Australian Political Economy* 84: 116–146.

Petryna, Adriana. 2002. *Life Exposed: Biological Citizens after Chernobyl*. Princeton, NJ: Princeton University Press.

Pezzullo, Phaedra C. 2007. *Toxic Tourism: Rhetorics of Pollution, Travel, and Environmental Justice*. Tuscaloosa: University of Alabama Press.

Phillips, Janet, and Harriet Spinks. 2013. "Boat Arrivals in Australia since 1976." Commonwealth of Australia Parliamentary Library. http://www.aph.gov.au/about _parliament/parliamentary_departments/parliamentary_library/pubs/bn/2012 -2013/boatarrivals#_ftnref15.

Picozza, Fiorenza. 2021. *The Coloniality of Asylum: Mobility, Autonomy and Solidarity in the Wake of Europe's Refugee Crisis*. Lanham: Rowman & Littlefield.

Pittaway, Eileen. 2002. "A Brief History of Refugee Policy in Australia." Perth: University of Western Australia, Centre for Refugee Research. http://motspluriels.arts .uwa.edu.au/MP2102edito1_1.html.

Pittaway, Eileen, Linda Bartolomei, and Richard Hugman. 2010. "'Stop Stealing Our Stories': The Ethics of Research with Vulnerable Groups." *Journal of Human Rights Practice* 2(2): 229–251.

Pittman, George Alfred. 1959. *Nauru, the Phosphate Island*. London: Longman.

Pollock, Nancy. 2014. "Nauru Phosphate History and the Resource Curse Narrative." *Journal de la Société des Océanistes* 138–189(1–2): 107–120.

Porteous, J. D. 1970. "The Nature of the Company Town." *Transactions of the Institute of British Geographers* 51: 127–142.

Power, Michael. 1994. *The Audit Explosion*. London: Demos.

——. 2007. *Organized Uncertainty: Designing a World of Risk Management*. Oxford: Oxford University Press.

Powles, Michael. 2011. "Dr Ludwig Keke Recalls Hammer deRoburt." Radio New Zealand, August 5.

Pupavac, Vanessa. 2008. "Refugee Advocacy, Traumatic Representations and Political Disenchantment." *Government and Opposition* 43(2): 270–292.

Raguparan, Menaka. 2017. "'If I'm Gonna Hack Capitalism': Racialized and Indigenous Canadian Sex Workers' Experiences within the Neo-Liberal Market Economy." *Women's Studies International Forum* 60: 69–76.

Rajaram, Prem Kumar. 2002. "Humanitarianism and Representations of the Refugee." *Journal of Refugee Studies* 15(3): 247–264.

——. 2018. "Refugees as Surplus Population: Race, Migration and Capitalist Value Regimes." *New Political Economy* 23(5): 627–639.

Ramsay, Georgina. 2019. "Humanitarian Exploits: Ordinary Displacement and the Political Economy of the Global Refugee Regime." *Critique of Anthropology* 40(1): 3–27.

Ratuva, Steve. 2011. "The Gap between Global Thinking and Local Living: Dilemmas of Constitutional Reform in Nauru." *Journal of Polynesian Society* 120(3): 241–268.

Refugee Action Committee. 2017. "Refugee Stories." Refugee Action Campaign. https:// refugeeaction.org/information/refugee-stories/.

Republic of Nauru (RON). 2001. "Special Edition: The President's Address to the Nation." *Naoero Bulletin* 17(1). Nauru Media Bureau, September 7.

——. 2012a. "New Home Owners Awarded Housing Loan from the Nauru Government's Housing Scheme." *Republic of Nauru Bulletin* 72(21), October 30.

——. 2012b. "Civil Servants and Private Sector Learn Innovative New Business Ideas." *Republic of Nauru Bulletin* 73(22), November 13.

——. 2013. *Nauru National Assessment Report for the Third International Conference on Small Island Developing States* (SIDS). Republic of Nauru.

——. 2015a. "Experienced Legal Mind Appointed to Nauru Supreme Court." Republic of Nauru Government Information Office, Media Release. http://www.naurugov .nr/government-information-office/media-release/experienced-legal-mind -appointed-to-nauru-supreme-court.aspx.

——. 2015b. "Nauru Engages New Settlement Agency." *Republic of Nauru Bulletin* 1(119), January 20.

——. 2015c. "New Settlement Services Provider Offers Integration and Awareness Programs for Refugees." *Republic of Nauru Bulletin* 2(120), February 17.

——. 2016a. "Nauru Demonstrations Will Not Alter Australia's Position." Republic of Nauru Government Information Office, Media Release. http://www.naurugov.nr /government-information-office/media-release/nauru-demonstrations-will-not -alter-australia's-position.aspx.

——. 2016b. "Nauru Bank a Big Hit." Republic of Nauru Government Information Office, Media Release. http://www.naurugov.nr/government-information-office/media-release/nauru-bank-a-big-hit.aspx.

——. 2016c. "'We Won't Cop it Anymore'–Nauru Police." February 2. http://www.naurunews.com/#!We-wont-cop-it-anymore-Nauru-Police/cjds/56b938030cf2dc1600ea69e6.

——. 2019. *Convention on Biological Diversity: Sixth National Report of Nauru*. Republic of Nauru. https://www.cbd.int/doc/nr/nr-06/nr-nr-06-en.pdf.

Robertson, Morgan 2007. "Discovering Price in All the Wrong Places: The Work of Commodity Definition and Price under Neoliberal Environmental Policy." *Antipode* 39: 500–526.

Ross, Michael L. 2015. "What Have We Learned about the Resource Curse?" *Annual Review of Political Science* 18: 239–259.

Round, Sally. 2016. "Pacific Nations Call for Help at UN Refugee Summit." Radio New Zealand, September 20. http://www.radionz.co.nz/international/pacific-news/313795/pacific-nations-call-for-help-at-un-refugee-summit.

RPC Community Newsletter. 2014. October–November. Nauru Regional Processing Centre.

Sala, Miguel Tinker. 2009. *The Enduring Legacy: Oil, Culture, and Society in Venezuela*. Durham, NC: Duke University Press.

Sassen, Saskia. 2014. *Expulsions: Brutality and Complexity in the Global Economy*. Cambridge: Harvard University Press.

Sawyer, Suzana, 2004. *Crude Chronicles: Indigenous Politics, Multinational Oil, and Neoliberalism in Ecuador*. Durham, NC: Duke University Press.

Schept, Judah. 2020. *Coal, Cages, Crisis: The Rise of the Prison Economy in Central Appalachia*. New York: New York University Press.

Scott, James C. 1998. *Seeing Like a State: How Certain Schemes to Improve the Human Condition Have Failed*. New Haven, CT: Yale University Press.

Shacknove, Andrew E. 1985. "Who Is a Refugee?" *Ethics* 95(2): 274–284.

Shapiro, Nicholas. 2015. "Attuning to the Chemosphere: Domestic Formaldehyde, Bodily Reasoning, and the Chemical Sublime." *Cultural Anthropology* 30(3): 368–93.

Sharma, Nandita. 2020. *Home Rule: National Sovereignty and the Separation of Natives and Migrants*. Durham, NC: Duke University Press.

Sharp, Lesley A. 2000. "The Commodification of the Body and Its Parts." *Annual Review of Anthropology* 29: 287–328.

Sheller, Mimi. 2003. *Consuming the Caribbean: From Arawaks to Zombies*. London: Routledge.

Shigematsu, Setsu, and Keith L. Camacho, eds. 2010. *Militarized Currents. Toward a Decolonized Future in Asia and the Pacific*. Minneapolis: University of Minnesota Press.

Shipton, Parker. 1989. *Bitter Money: Cultural Economy and Some African Meanings of Forbidden Commodities*. American Ethnological Society Monograph Series, 1. Washington, DC: American Anthropological Association.

Simpson, T. Beckford. 1843. *Nautical Surveys*. Canberra: National Archives.

Smith, Neil. 2007. "Nature as Accumulation Strategy." *Socialist Register* (43): 19–41.

Smith, Derek, and Peter Leggat. 2005. "The Historical Development of Occupational Health in Australia Part 2: 1970–2000." *Journal of University of Occupation & Environmental Health* 27(2): 137–50.

Solah, Benjamin. 2015. "Refugees on Nauru Demand Freedom." *RedFlag: A Voice of Resistance*, March 10. https://redflag.org.au/article/refugees-nauru-demand-freedom.

Speers, David. 2017. "Donald Trumps Australia's Interests." *Switzer*, January 27. http://www.switzer.com.au/the-experts/david-speers/donald-trumps-australias-interests/.

Stoler, Ann Laura. 1995. *Race and the Education of Desire: Foucault's History of Sexuality and the Colonial Order of Things*. Durham, NC: Duke University Press.

——. 2002. *Carnal Knowledge and Imperial Power: Race and the Intimate in Colonial Rule*. Berkeley: University of California Press.

——. 2008. "Imperial Debris: Reflections on Ruins and Ruination." *Cultural Anthropology* 23(2): 191–219.

Story, Brett. 2019. *Prison Land: Mapping Carceral Power across Neoliberal America*. Minneapolis: University of Minnesota Press.

Strathern, Marilyn, ed. 2000. *Audit Cultures: Anthropological Studies in Accountability*. Abingdon: Routledge.

Stratton, Jon, and Ien Ang. 1994. "Multicultural Imagined Communities: Cultural Difference and National Identity in Australia and the USA." *Continuum: The Australian Journal of Media and Culture* 8(2): 124–158.

Strom, Megan, and Emily Alcock. 2017. "Floods, Waves, and Surges: The Representation of Latin@ Immigrant Children in the United States Mainstream Media." *Critical Discourse Studies* 14(4): 1–18.

Sukarieh, Mayssoun, and Stuart Tannock. 2019. "Subcontracting Academia: Alienation, Exploitation and Disillusionment in the UK Overseas Syrian Refugee Research Industry." *Antipode* 51(2): 664–680.

Sundram, Suresh, and Samantha Loi. 2012. "Long Waits for Refugee Status Lead to New Mental Health Syndrome." *The Conversation*, May 23.

Taussig, Michael. 1980. *The Devil and Commodity Fetishism in South America*. Chapel Hill: University of North Carolina Press.

Taylor, R., and K. Thoma. 1985. "Mortality Patterns in the Modernized Pacific Island Nation of Nauru." *American Journal of Public Health* 75(2): 149–155.

Teaiwa, Katerina Martina. 2015. *Consuming Ocean Island: Stories of People and Phosphate from Banaba*. Bloomington: Indiana University Press.

Teaiwa, Teresia K. 1994. "bikinis and other s/pacific n/oceans." *Contemporary Pacific* 6(1): 87–109.

Teaiwa, Teresia, Sandra Tarte, Nic Maclellan, and Maureen Penjueli. 2002. *Turning the Tide: Towards a Pacific Solution to Conditional Aid*. Sydney: Greenpeace.

Thoma, Godfrey, and Dantes Tstitsi. 2009. Status Report for Aiwo. Local report.

Thu Win Tin, Si, George Iro, Eva Gadabu, and Ruth Colagiuri. 2015. "Counting the Cost of Diabetes in the Solomon Islands and Nauru." *PLoS One* 10(12): 1–13.

Ticktin, Miriam. 2006. "Where Ethics and Politics Meet: The Violence of Humanitarianism in France." *American Ethnologist* 33(1): 33–49.

——. 2011. *Causalities of Care: Immigration and the Politics of Humanitarianism in France*. Berkeley: University of California Press.

Tofighian, Omid. 2020. "Introducing Manus Prison Theory: Knowing Border Violence." *Globalizations* 17(7): 1138–1156.

Tornero, Victoria, and Georg Hanke. 2016. "Chemical Contaminants Entering the Marine Environment from Sea-based Sources: A Review with a Focus on European Seas." *Marine Pollution Bulletin* 112(1–2): 17–38.

Tsing, Anna Lowenhaupt. 2005. *Friction: An Ethnography of Global Connection*. Princeton, NJ: Princeton University Press.

——. 2009. "Supply Chains and the Human Condition." *Rethinking Marxism* 21(2): 148–176.

United Nations. 1965. *Report on the Visiting Mission to the Trust Territories of Nauru and New Guinea*. UN Trusteeship Council, 32nd session.

United Nations High Commissioner for Refugees (UNHCR). 2017. Population Statistics Database. http://popstats.unhcr.org/en/overview.

Verma, Sanmati. 2019. "'We Feed You': The Real Cost of Undocumented Labour in Australia." *Overland*, March 22. https://overland.org.au/2019/03/we-feed-you-the -real-cost-of-undocumented-labour-in-australia/.

Vitalis, Robert. 2007. *America's Kingdom: Mythmaking on the Saudi Oil Frontier*. Stanford, CA: Stanford University Press.

Viviani, Nancy. 1970. *Nauru: Phosphate and Political Progress*. Canberra: Australian National University Press.

Vohra, Shyla. 2014. "Establishment of a New National Refugee Determination System: Threats and Opportunities; the Case of Nauru." Paper presented at the Access to Asylum: Current Challenges and Future Directions Conference, Monash University Prato Centre, Prato, Italy, May 29.

Voyles, Traci Brynne. 2015. *Wastelanding: Legacies of Uranium Mining in Navajo Country*. Minneapolis: University of Minnesota Press.

Vrachnas, John, Mirko Bagaric, Athula Pathinayake, and Penny Dimoploulos. 2012. *Migration and Refugee Law: Principles and Practice in Australia*. Cambridge: Cambridge University Press.

Waqa, Baron. 2015a. "Nauru Mocked by Media Bullies." *Daily Telegraph*, August 2. http://www.dailytelegraph.com.au/news/opinion/nauru-mocked-by-media -bullies/news-story/db2a66f9a7b44e7764bdc6f8b2103024.

——. 2015b. 47th Independence Day Speech. *Mwinen Ko Nauru Community Newspaper*. January, 51st ed.

——. 2016a. "Media Mudslingers Distort the Image of Nauru." *Australian Opinion*, August 22. http://www.theaustralian.com.au/opinion/media-mudslingers-distort -the-image-of-nauru/news-story/e6330a8de43691a2b0fbd882ffee8a91.

——. 2016b. "President Concerned That Refugees Told to Quit Work." *Media and Public Information*, May 4. http://www.nauru-news.com/single-post/2016/05/04/President -concerned-that-refugees-told-to-quit-work.

Watts, Michael. 2001. "Petro-Violence: Community, Extraction, and Political Ecology of a Mythic Commodity." In *Violent Environments*, edited by Nancy Lee Peluso and Michael Watts, 189–212. Ithaca, NY: Cornell University Press.

——. 2004. "Oil as Money: The Devil's Excrement and the Spectacle of Black Gold." In *Reading Economic Geography*, edited by Trevor J. Barnes, Jamie Peck, Eric Sheppard, and Adam Tickell, 205–219. Malden, MA: Blackwell.

——. 2015. "Securing Oil: Frontiers, Risk, and Spaces of Accumulated Insecurity." In *Subterranean Estates: Life Worlds of Oil and Gas*, edited by Hannah Appel, Arthur Mason, and Michael Watts, 211–236. Ithaca, NY: Cornell University Press.

Weeramantry, Christopher. 1992. *Nauru: Environmental Damage Under International Trusteeship*. Oxford: Oxford University Press.

Wenzel, Jennifer. 2014. "Petro-Magic-Realism Revisited: Unimagining and Reimagining the Niger Delta." In *Oil Culture*, edited by Ross Barrett and Daniel Worden, 211–225. Minneapolis: University of Minnesota Press.

Weskalnys, Gisa. 2014. "Anticipating Oil: The Temporal Politics of a Disaster Yet to Come." *Sociological Review* 62(S1): 211–235.

West, Paige. 2012. *From Modern Production to Imagined Primitive: The Social World of Coffee from Papua New Guinea*. Durham, NC: Duke University Press.

——. 2016. *Dispossession and the Environment: Rhetoric and Inequality in Papua New Guinea*. New York: Columbia University Press.

Williams, Maslyn. 1971. *Three Islands*. Melbourne: British Phosphate Commissioners.

Williams, Maslyn, and Macdonald, Barrie. 1985. *The Phosphateers: A History of the British Phosphate Commissioners and the Christmas Island Phosphate Commissioners*. Melbourne: Melbourne University Press.

Xiang, Biao. 2006. *Global "Body Shopping": An Indian Labor System in the Information Technology Industry*. Princeton, NJ: Princeton University Press.

Young, Allan. 1995. *The Harmony of Illusions: Inventing Post-Traumatic Stress Disorder*. Princeton, NJ: Princeton University Press.

Zaloom, Caitlin. 2004. "The Productive Life of Risk." *Cultural Anthropology* 19(3): 365–391.

——. 2006. *Out of the Pits: Traders and Technology from Chicago to London*. Chicago: Chicago University Press.

Zion, Deborah. 2019. "Dual Loyalty, Medical Ethics, and Health Care in Offshore Asylum-Seeker Detention." In *The Health of Refugees: Public Health Perspectives from Crisis to Settlement*, edited by Pascale Allotey and Daniel Reidpath, 260–272. Oxford: Oxford University Press.

Index

Note: Page numbers in *italics* indicate figures in the book.